Serverless Development on AWS

Building Enterprise-Scale Serverless Solutions

Sheen Brisals and Luke Hedger

Foreword by Jeff Barr

Beijing · Boston · Farnham · Sebastopol · Tokyo

Serverless Development on AWS

by Sheen Brisals and Luke Hedger

Published by O'Reilly Media, Inc., 1005 Gravenstein Highway North, Sebastopol, CA 95472.

O'Reilly books may be purchased for educational, business, or sales promotional use. Online editions are also available for most titles (*http://oreilly.com*). For more information, contact our corporate/institutional sales department: 800-998-9938 or *corporate@oreilly.com*.

Acquisitions Editor: Megan Laddusaw
Development Editor: Sara Hunter
Production Editor: Gregory Hyman
Copyeditor: Rachel Head
Proofreader: Kim Cofer

Indexer: BIM Creatives, LLC
Interior Designer: David Futato
Cover Designer: Karen Montgomery
Illustrator: Kate Dullea

February 2024:   First Edition

Revision History for the First Edition

2023-01-23:   First Release

See *http://oreilly.com/catalog/errata.csp?isbn=9781098141936* for release details.

978-1-098-14193-6

[LSI]

To my late parents, Mr. V. Brisals and Mrs. Lalitha Joylent. Their struggles and sacrifices in life made me what I am today. —Sheen Brisals

For Alice and Lois. —Luke Hedger

Table of Contents

Foreword

From interactive programming on minicomputers and mainframes in junior high school and high school, to taking a bit of a step back to a batch-oriented, card-powered mainframe in college, while actually earning money first selling and then later writing code for the first generation of personal computers, I have seen many forms of computers and computing come and go. While the programming models for each of these systems differed, they invariably had one thing in common—there was a fixed amount of compute power, memory, and storage. My job, as a developer, was to write code that made the best use of all three of these then-precious resources, trimming features, compressing data, and so forth.

With the emergence of cloud computing in 2006 with the launch of Amazon Elastic Compute Cloud (EC2), this model began to change. Developers could pick and choose the instance size and type that was the best match for their code, make changes later, and add or remove instances quickly in response to changing workloads. This was a big step forward, and one that paved the way for the introduction of serverless computing in 2014 with the launch of AWS Lambda.

In the decade since the launch of Lambda, developers have used it to build applications that are more flexible, scalable, and cost-effective than ever before. While the word "revolutionary" is used far too often in our industry, I believe that it applies here. Freed from the constraints and able to focus on applications instead of on servers, developers can devote more of their time to building applications that will meet the needs of their customers.

If you want to participate in this ongoing revolution, you have come to the right place! The book that you are holding in your hands will teach you what you need to know about serverless computing so that you can put it to work in your environment.

In this book, Sheen and Luke show you how to reap all of the benefits that serverless computing promises. In the succeeding chapters you will learn about how to prepare your organization for serverless, build powerful serverless architectures, understand

and manage security, make use of serverless design patterns, understand serverless costs and economics, and much more.

While the chapters certainly build on each other and are best read fully and in order, you can also start by sampling the ones that are of personal and immediate interest to you. Either way, I am confident that you will quickly learn something new that you can put to use on your current serverless project.

The eleven chapters that make up this book contain a great mix of theoretical background and practical advice, knowledge that Sheen and Luke have gained through years of experience designing, building, and running serverless applications at global scale. You are now in a position to learn from this experience and to get a running start on your serverless journey.

— Jeff Barr
VP & Chief Evangelist, Amazon Web Services
Seattle, Washington
January 2024

Preface

Helsinki. It was a warm spring morning in 2019, and I (Sheen) was in the city to speak at ServerlessDays. A couple of engineers I met there during the break sought my advice on taking the serverless story to the public sector department they were working in. They were looking for inspirational serverless adoption stories to bring to their team. Almost a year later, an engineer at AWS Community Day in Stockholm asked an innocent but important question: *What is this "serverless," and is it good for my company?*

Several similar conversations on different occasions led me to a realization: engineers who are new to serverless need a basic understanding of the technology, clarity on the applicability of serverless to enterprise workloads, and guidance on how to design, develop, and operate serverless applications. Above all, they need to know how to take the serverless story to their CTOs and stakeholders with a clear plan, get buy-in, and make the investment profitable and valuable for the organization.

Though I had been writing articles about serverless on different topics, bringing everything together as a serverless development lifecycle was not in my mind then. Then one day, during the COVID-19 lockdown, a publisher approached me to discuss the possibility of developing a specific concept I had written about into a book. While I wasn't confident enough to expand that concept into a whole book, that was the spark that led me to explore the opportunity of bringing the end-to-end serverless development spectrum into focus in one place for the benefit of all the eager engineers I interacted with.

A few days later, I arranged a call with my friend Danilo Poccia, Chief Evangelist at AWS. Danilo is the author of *AWS Lambda in Action: Event-Driven Serverless Applications* (Manning), and a good resource on industry trends and needs. Our brief chat left me with some interesting ideas and the confidence to explore further.

With a draft idea in mind, I pitched it to a few engineers to assess the need for such a book, and all the feedback was encouragingly positive. By that time, I had known Luke for a few months. During my conversations with him, I secretly admired the depth of his serverless knowledge and the freshness in his thinking. Luke had previously led a serverless team at Cancer Research UK, a charitable organization, and had firsthand experience of the cost benefits of serverless. One afternoon, we sat down for a chat, and I explained in detail the outline of the book. Luke's instant reaction was: *I wish I'd had such a book on my desk when I started my serverless journey!*

This book is the result of that initial conversation: a comprehensive collection of our combined experiences, ideas, thoughts, lessons, and better practices designed to introduce you to serverless and show you a path to structure your development and operate your applications in a secure and sustainable way.

Thank you for your interest. Let's start our journey together!

Who We Wrote This Book For

Serverless as a technology continues to mature and evolve along with its industry adoption. Due to its unique benefits, it attracts a wide spectrum of technology audiences. When Luke and I were discussing the tone and depth of the content, we wanted it to appeal to developers who are new to serverless, engineers who are familiar with and progressing on their journey with serverless, and architects and CTOs who make some of the core decisions and influence the adoption of serverless in their organizations.

By no means is this book a one-stop solution to all your serverless queries and worries. It is a collection of options and ideas that you can draw upon to prepare your serverless meal according to your and your organization's dietary requirements. Along with serverless technology, the popularity of several development frameworks, runtimes, build and infrastructure tools, etc., is also on the rise. Consequently, there are as many approaches to implementing your application as there are frameworks and runtimes out there. As suggested by the widespread phrase in the software industry, *the code you write today is legacy tomorrow*, it is hard to maintain the code you have written today in this fast-evolving technology space. This is not a book that delves deep into hands-on implementation examples. Its aim is to teach you the underlying concepts that you can rely on in the future, regardless of your circumstances; to teach you to fish, as it were, rather than feeding you just once.

The book starts with a discussion of the evolution of serverless technology and the preparations necessary for successful adoption. It then introduces you to the core security principles of serverless, leading you through event-driven architecture and implementation patterns. Understanding the core principles guides you through the development cycle and operating your serverless applications in the cloud. The cost of serverless is a key part of its adoption, and we have a chapter dedicated to making you aware of the main cost factors. In addition, modern application development requires thinking about our environmental ecosystem and the world we live in. Sustainability is an essential and core part of cloud operation, and you will learn several patterns and best practices to build and operate serverless applications in a sustainable way. The book closes with a look at how you can make your serverless journey rewarding and refreshing for decades into the future.

Conventions Used in This Book

The following typographical conventions are used in this book:

Italic
> Indicates new terms, URLs, email addresses, filenames, and file extensions.

`Constant width`
> Used for program listings, as well as within paragraphs to refer to program elements such as variable or function names, databases, data types, environment variables, statements, and keywords.

`Constant width italic`
> Shows text that should be replaced with user-supplied values or by values determined by context.

This element signifies a tip or suggestion.

This element signifies a general note.

This element indicates a warning or caution.

Supplemental Material

Three online-exclusive appendices to this book are available to readers for download:

- Appendix A: "PostNL's Serverless Journey" (*https://oreil.ly/riwzp*)
- Appendix B: "Taco Bell's Serverless Journey" (*https://oreil.ly/R325t*)
- Appendix C: "Templates and Worksheets" (*https://oreil.ly/Nw9fs*)

O'Reilly Online Learning

 For more than 40 years, *O'Reilly Media* has provided technology and business training, knowledge, and insight to help companies succeed.

Our unique network of experts and innovators share their knowledge and expertise through books, articles, and our online learning platform. O'Reilly's online learning platform gives you on-demand access to live training courses, in-depth learning paths, interactive coding environments, and a vast collection of text and video from O'Reilly and 200+ other publishers. For more information, visit *https://oreilly.com*.

How to Contact Us

Please address comments and questions concerning this book to the publisher:

O'Reilly Media, Inc.
1005 Gravenstein Highway North
Sebastopol, CA 95472
800-889-8969 (in the United States or Canada)
707-827-7019 (international or local)
707-829-0104 (fax)
support@oreilly.com
https://www.oreilly.com/about/contact.html

We have a web page for this book, where we list errata, examples, and any additional information. You can access this page at *https://oreil.ly/serverless-dev-on-aws*.

For news and information about our books and courses, visit *https://oreilly.com*.

Find us on LinkedIn: *https://linkedin.com/company/oreilly-media*

Follow us on Twitter: *https://twitter.com/oreillymedia*

Watch us on YouTube: *https://youtube.com/oreillymedia*

Acknowledgments

First of all, our deepest thanks to you, the readers of the book. Our inspiration to write this book originated from the many people like you we've interacted with. Your stories from the trenches motivated us to share our collective experiences with everyone.

We would like to thank our acquisition editors at O'Reilly, Jennifer Pollock and Megan Laddusaw, for helping us with the initial proposal and successfully guiding us in shaping the structure of the book. Thanks also to Cassandra Furtado and Chelsea Foster from the O'Reilly contracts and accounting teams, respectively.

We wouldn't have reached this point without our amazing development editor, Sara Hunter. Thank you, Sara, for being patient and supportive, and guiding us with positivity and encouragement. We always wondered the secret behind your quick and thorough reviews.

We also thank the amazing production team at O'Reilly: Kristen Brown, Gregory Hyman, and Rachel Head. Content editing is only complete once Rachel has edited it! Working with you and observing many things about content writing has been our privilege. Thank you, Rachel, for making this book readable and understandable to everyone!

Thanks also to our O'Reilly marketing team, Suzanne Huston and Gabriella Train, and everyone at O'Reilly for giving us this opportunity we'd never dreamed of.

As authors, we were fortunate to work with some of the powerhouses of the tech industry as our technical reviewers. Our sincere thanks to Jeff Barr, Luca Mezzalira, and Mike Roberts. Jeff Barr is an inspiration to many, and his support for this book has been invaluable. As one of our technical reviewers, Jeff's thoughtful feedback helped us shape the content, and he kindly agreed to write the foreword for the book. Thank you, Jeff!

Throughout the book, we have industry leaders and subject matter experts sharing the most relevant and thoughtful insights on serverless for every reader to benefit from. Our special thanks to the book's chapter experts, Danilo Poccia, David Anderson, Matt Lewis, Nicole Yip, Jeremy Daly, Sara Gerion, Sarah Hamilton, Yan Cui, Ben Ellerby, Adrian Cockroft, and Farrah Campbell.

The unique serverless case studies in the book cover a wide spectrum of the industry, from a global hospitality giant to a highly regarded postal and logistics company. Sharing experiences and learning from each other is the core of a vibrant tech community. As part of the AWS and serverless communities, we are fortunate to have several leading organizations and technology thought leaders helping others to prosper. We are indebted to and thankful for the contributions of Luc van Donkersgoed, Robbie Kohler, and Vadim Parizher.

On several occasions while writing this book, we reached out to our well-wishers in the industry, shared our ideas, and sought their advice and direction. We offer our gratitude and thanks to everyone who participated in this process.

We are thankful to our colleagues at work who constantly course-corrected our serverless journeys and to everyone who gave us opportunities and encouraged, trusted, and molded us along the way. This work wouldn't be possible without what we learned from you.

To our families:

- Sheen would like to thank his wife and sons.
- Luke would like to thank Alice and Lois.

Finally, when we started this work, the world was going through the worst pandemic of our time—COVID-19. While our journey progressed, many didn't. We take a pause to remember those dark days and salute those who kept our hopes alive and got us this far. We are better together.

CHAPTER 1

Introduction to Serverless on AWS

The secret of getting ahead is getting started.
—Mark Twain

Welcome to serverless! You are stepping into the vibrant ecosystem of a modern, exciting computing technology that has radically changed how we think of software, challenged preconceptions about how we build applications, and enabled cloud development to be more accessible for everyone. It's an incredible technology that many people love, and we're looking forward to teaching you all about it.

The software industry is constantly evolving, and the pace of evolution in software engineering is faster than in just about any other discipline. The speed of change disrupts many organizations and their IT departments. However, for those who are optimistic, change brings opportunities. When enterprises accept change and adjust their processes, they lead the way. In contrast, those who resist change get trampled by competition and consumer demands.

We're always looking for ways to improve our lives. Human needs and technology go hand in hand. Our evolving day-to-day requirements demand ever-better technology, which in turn inspires innovation. When we realize the power of these innovations, we upgrade our needs, and the cycle continues. The industry has been advancing in this way for decades, not in giant leaps all the time but in small increments, as one improvement triggers the next.

To fully value serverless and the capabilities it offers, it is beneficial to understand its history. To stay focused on our subject without traveling back in time to the origins of bits and bytes, we'll start with the cloud and how it became a force to reckon with.

Sit back, relax, and get ready to journey through the exciting world of serverless!

The Road to Serverless

During the early 2000s, I (Sheen) was involved in building distributed applications that mainly communicated via service buses and web services—a typical service-oriented architecture (SOA). It was during this time that I first came across the term "the cloud," which was making a few headlines in the tech industry. A few years later, I received instructions from upper management to study this new technology and report on certain key features. The early cloud offering that I was asked to explore was none other than Amazon Web Services.

My quest to get closer to the cloud started there, but it took me another few years to fully appreciate and understand the ground-shifting effect it was having in the industry. Like the butterfly effect, it was fascinating to consider how past events had brought us to the present.

 The butterfly effect is a term used to refer to the concept that a small change in the state of a complex system can have nonlinear impacts on the state of that system at a later point. The most common example cited is that of a butterfly flapping its wings somewhere in the world acting as a trigger to cause a typhoon elsewhere.

From Mainframe Computing to the Modern Cloud

During the mid-1900s, mainframe computers became popular due to their vast computing power. Though massive, clunky, highly expensive, and laborious to maintain, they were the only resources available to run complex business and scientific tasks. Only a lucky few organizations and educational institutions could afford them, and they ran jobs in batch mode to make the best use of the costly systems. The concept of time-sharing was introduced to schedule and share the compute resources to run programs for multiple teams (see Figure 1-1). This distribution of the costs and resources made computing more affordable to different groups, in a way similar to the on-demand resource usage and pay-per-use computing models of the modern cloud.

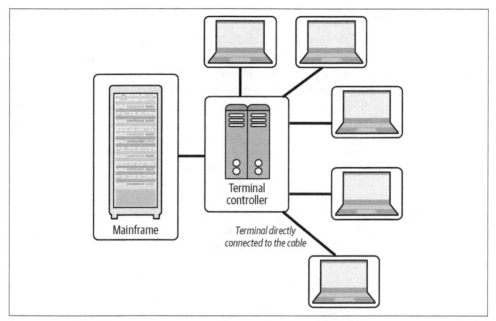

Figure 1-1. Mainframe computer time-sharing (source: adapted from an image in Guide to Operating Systems by Greg Tomsho [Cengage])

The emergence of networking

Early mainframes were independent and could not communicate with one another. The idea of an *Intergalactic Computer Network* (*https://oreil.ly/Zrs-q*) or *Galactic Network* to interconnect remote computers and share data was introduced by computer scientist J.C.R. Licklider, fondly known as Lick, in the early 1960s. The Advanced Research Projects Agency (ARPA) of the United States Department of Defense pioneered the work, which was realized in the Advanced Research Projects Agency Network (ARPANET) (*https://oreil.ly/ejbz1*). This was one of the early network developments that used the TCP/IP protocol, one of the main building blocks of the internet. This progress in networking was a huge step forward.

The beginning of virtualization

The 1970s saw another core technology of the modern cloud taking shape. In 1972, the release of the *Virtual Machine Operating System* by IBM allowed it to host multiple operating environments within a single mainframe. Building on the early time-sharing and networking concepts, virtualization filled in the other main piece of the cloud puzzle. The speed of technology iterations of the 1990s brought those ideas to realization and took us closer to the modern cloud. Virtual private networks (VPNs) and virtual machines (VMs) soon became commodities.

The term *cloud computing* originated in the mid to late 1990s. Some attribute it to computer giant Compaq Corporation, which mentioned it in an internal report (*https://oreil.ly/pVVni*) in 1996. Others credit Professor Ramnath Chellappa and his lecture at INFORMS 1997 on an "emerging paradigm for computing." Regardless, with the speed at which technology was evolving, the computer industry was already on a trajectory for massive innovation and growth.

The first glimpse of Amazon Web Services

As virtualization technology matured, many organizations built capabilities to automatically or programmatically provision VMs for their employees and to run business applications for their customers. An ecommerce company that made good use of these capabilities to support its operations was Amazon.com.

During early 2000, engineers at Amazon were exploring how their infrastructure could efficiently scale up to meet the increasing customer demand. As part of that process, they decoupled common infrastructure from applications and abstracted it as a service so that multiple teams could use it. This was the start of the concept known today as *infrastructure as a service* (IaaS). In the summer of 2006, the company launched Amazon Elastic Compute Cloud (EC2) to offer virtual machines as a service in the cloud for everyone. That marked the humble beginning of today's mammoth Amazon Web Services, popularly known as AWS!

Cloud deployment models

As cloud services gained momentum thanks to the efforts of companies like Amazon, Microsoft, Google, Alibaba, IBM, and others, they began to address the needs of different business segments. Different access models and usage patterns started to emerge (see Figure 1-2).

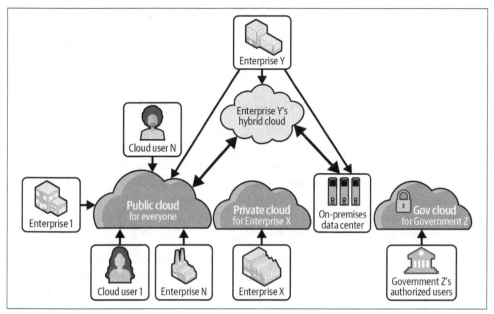

Figure 1-2. Figurative comparison of different cloud environments

These are the main variants today:

Public cloud
> The cloud service that the majority of us access for work and personal use is the *public cloud,* where the services are accessed over the public internet. Though cloud providers use shared resources in their data centers, each user's activities are isolated with strict security boundaries. This is commonly known as a multitenant environment.

Private cloud
> In general, *a private cloud* is a corporate cloud where a single organization has access to the infrastructure and the services hosted there. It is a single-tenant environment. A variant of the private cloud is the *government cloud* (for example, AWS GovCloud), where the infrastructure and services are specifically for a particular government and its organizations. This is a highly secure and controlled environment operated by the respective country's citizens.

Hybrid cloud
> A *hybrid cloud* uses both public and private cloud or on-premises infrastructure and services. Maintaining these environments requires clear boundaries on security and data sharing.

Enterprises that prefer running their workloads and consuming services from multiple public cloud providers operate in what is called a *multicloud* environment. We will discuss this further in the next chapter.

The Influence of Running Everything as a Service

The idea of offering something "as a service" is not new or specific to software. Public libraries are a great example of providing information and knowledge as a service: we borrow, read, and return books. Leasing physical computers for business is another example, which eliminates spending capital on purchasing and maintaining resources. Instead, we consume them as a service for an affordable price. This also allows us the flexibility to use the service only when needed—virtualization changes it from a physical commodity to a virtual one.

In technology, one opportunity leads to several opportunities, and one idea leads to many. From bare VMs, the possibilities spread to network infrastructure, databases, applications, artificial intelligence (AI), and even simple single-purpose functions. Within a short span, the idea of *something as a service* advanced to a point where we can now offer almost anything and *everything as a service*!

Infrastructure as a service (IaaS)

IaaS is one of the fundamental cloud services, along with platform as a service (PaaS), software as a service (SaaS), and function as a service (FaaS). It represents the bare bones of a cloud platform—the network, compute, and storage resources, commonly housed in a data center. A high-level understanding of IaaS is beneficial as it forms the basis for serverless.

Figure 1-3 shows a bird's-eye view of AWS's data center layout at a given geographic area, known as a *Region*. To offer a resilient and highly available service, AWS has built redundancy in every Region via groups of data centers known as *Availability Zones* (AZs). The core IaaS offerings from AWS include Amazon EC2 and Amazon Virtual Private Cloud (VPC).

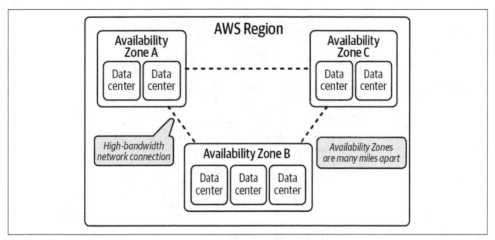

Figure 1-3. An AWS Region with its Availability Zones

Platform as a service (PaaS)

PaaS is a service abstraction layer on top of IaaS to offer an application development environment in the cloud. It provides the platform and tools needed to develop, run, and manage applications without provisioning the infrastructure, hardware, and necessary software, thereby reducing complexity and increasing development velocity. AWS Elastic Beanstalk is a popular PaaS available today.

Software as a Service (SaaS)

SaaS is probably the most used and covers many of the applications we use daily, for tasks such as checking email, sharing and storing photos, streaming movies, and connecting with friends and family via conferencing services.

Besides the cloud providers, numerous independent software vendors (ISVs) utilize the cloud (IaaS and PaaS offerings) to bring their SaaS solutions to millions of users. This is a rapidly expanding market, thanks to the low costs and easy adoption of cloud and serverless computing. Figure 1-4 shows how these three layers of cloud infrastructure fit together.

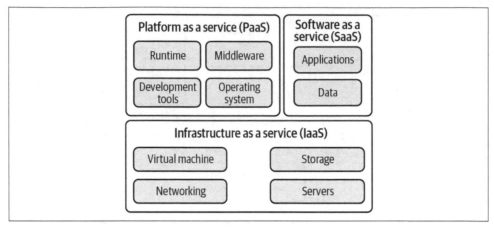

Figure 1-4. The different layers of cloud infrastructure

Database as a service (DBaaS)

DBaaS is a type of SaaS that covers various data storage options and operations. Along with the traditional SQL relational database management systems (RDBMSs), several other types of data stores are now available as managed services, including NoSQL, object storage, time series, graph, and search databases.

Amazon DynamoDB is one of the most popular NoSQL databases available as a service (see Figure 1-5). A DynamoDB table can store billions of item records and still provide CRUD (Create, Read, Update, and Delete) operations with single-digit or low-double-digit millisecond latency. You will see the use of DynamoDB in many serverless examples throughout this book.

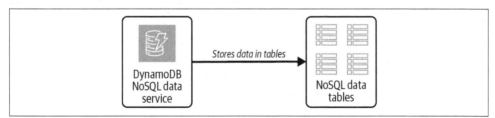

Figure 1-5. Pictorial representation of Amazon DynamoDB and its data tables

Amazon Simple Storage Service (S3) is an object storage service capable of handling billions of objects and petabytes of data (see Figure 1-6). Similar to the concept of tables in RDBMSs and DynamoDB, S3 stores the data in *buckets,* with each bucket having its own specific characteristics.

The emergence of services such as DynamoDB and S3 are just a few examples of how storage needs have changed over time to cater to unstructured data and how the cloud enables enterprises to move away from the limited vertical scaling and mundane operation of traditional RDBMSs to focus on building cloud-scale solutions that bring value to the business.

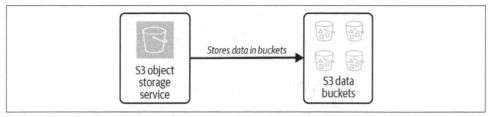

Figure 1-6. Pictorial representation of Amazon S3 and its data buckets

Function as a service (FaaS)

In simple terms, FaaS is a type of cloud computing service that lets you run your function code without having to provision any hardware yourself. FaaS provided a core piece of the cloud computing puzzle by bringing in the much-needed compute as a service, and it soon became the catalyst for the widespread adoption of serverless. AWS Lambda is the most used FaaS implementation available today (see Figure 1-7).

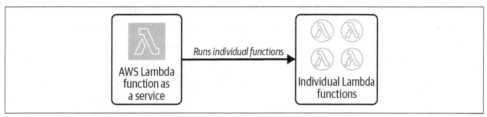

Figure 1-7. Pictorial representation of AWS Lambda service and functions

Managed Versus Fully Managed Services

Before exploring the characteristics of serverless in detail, it is essential to understand what is meant by the terms *managed services* and *fully managed services*. As a developer, you often consume APIs from different vendors to fulfill business tasks and abide by the API contracts. You do not get access to the implementation or the operation of the service, because the service provider manages them. In this case, you are consuming a managed service.

The distinction between managed and fully managed services is often blurred. Certain managed services require you to create and maintain the necessary infrastructure before consuming them. For example, Amazon Relational Database Service (RDS) is a managed service for RDBMSs such as MySQL, SQL Server, Oracle, and so on. However, its standard setup requires you to create a virtual network boundary, known as a virtual private cloud (VPC), with security groups, instance types, clusters, etc., before consuming the service. In contrast, DynamoDB is a NoSQL database service that you can set up and consume almost instantly. This is one way of distinguishing a managed service from a fully managed one. Fully managed services are sometimes referred to as *serverless services*.

Now that you have some background on the origins and evolution of the cloud and understand the simplicity of fully managed services, it's time to take a closer look at serverless and see the amazing potential it has for you.

The Characteristics of Serverless Technology

Serverless is a technological concept that utilizes fully managed cloud services to carry out undifferentiated heavy lifting by abstracting away the infrastructure intricacies and server maintenance tasks.

John Chapin and Mike Roberts, the authors of *Programming AWS Lambda* (O'Reilly), distill this in simple terms:

> Enterprises building and supporting serverless applications are not looking after that hardware or those processes associated with the applications. They are outsourcing this responsibility to someone else, i.e., cloud service providers such as AWS.

As Roberts notes in his article "Serverless Architectures" (*https://oreil.ly/m22jj*), the first uses of the term serverless seem to have occurred around 2012, sometimes in the context of service providers taking on the responsibility of managing servers, data stores, and other infrastructure resources (which in turn allowed developers to shift their focus toward tasks and process flows), and sometimes in the context of continuous integration and source control systems being hosted as a service rather than on a company's on-premises servers. The term began to gain popularity following the launch of AWS Lambda in 2014 and Amazon API Gateway in 2015, with a focus on incorporating external services into the products built by development teams. Its use picked up steam as companies started to use serverless services to build new business capabilities, and it's been trending ever since.

 During the early days, especially after the release of AWS Lambda (the FaaS offering from AWS), many people used the terms serverless and FaaS interchangeably, as if both represented the same concept. Today, FaaS is regarded as one of the many service types that form part of the serverless ecosystem.

Definitions of serverless often reflect the primary characteristics of a serverless application. Along with the definitions, these characteristics have been refined and redefined as serverless has evolved and gained wider industry adoption. Let's take a look at some of the most important ones.

Pay-per-Use

Pay-per-use is the main characteristic that everyone associates with serverless. It mainly originated from the early days of serverless, when it was equated with FaaS: you pay for each function invocation. That interpretation is valid for ephemeral services such as AWS Lambda; however, if your application handles data, you may have a business requirement to store the data for a longer period and for it to be accessible during that time. Fully managed services such as Amazon DynamoDB and Amazon S3 are examples of services used for long-term data storage. In such cases, there is a cost associated with the volume of data your applications store every month, often measured in gibibytes (GiB). Remember, this is still pay-per-use based on your data volume, and you are not charged for an entire disk drive or storage array.

Figure 1-8 shows a simple serverless application where a Lambda function operates on the data stored in a DynamoDB table. While you pay for the Lambda function based on the number of invocations and memory consumption, for DynamoDB, in addition to the pay-per-use cost involved with its API invocations for reading and writing data, you also pay for the space consumed for storing the data. In Chapter 9, you will see all the cost elements related to AWS Lambda and DynamoDB in detail.

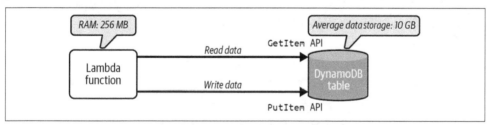

Figure 1-8. A simple serverless application, illustrating pay-per-use and data storage cost elements

Autoscaling and Scale to Zero

One of the primary characteristics of a fully managed service is the ability to scale up and down based on demand, without manual intervention. The term *scale to zero* is unique to serverless. Take, for example, a Lambda function. AWS Lambda manages the infrastructure provisioning to run the function. When the function ends and is no longer in use, after a certain period of inactivity the service reclaims the resources used to run it, scaling the number of execution environments back to zero.

> ## AWS Lambda Execution Environments
>
> When a Lambda function is invoked, the AWS Lambda service runs the function code inside an execution environment. The execution environment is run on a hardware-virtualized virtual machine (MicroVM) known as Firecracker. The execution environment provides a secure and isolated runtime environment for function execution. It consists of the function code, any extensions, temporary local filesystem space, and language runtime.
>
> One execution environment is associated with one Lambda function and never shared across functions.

Conversely, when there is a high volume of requests for a Lambda function, AWS automatically scales up by provisioning the infrastructure to run as many concurrent instances of the execution environment as needed to meet the demand. This is often referred to as *infinite scaling*, though the total capacity is actually dependent on your account's concurrency limit.

 With AWS Lambda, you can opt to keep a certain number of function containers "warm" in a ready state by setting a function's *provisioned concurrency* value.

Both scaling behaviors make serverless ideal for many types of applications.

> ## Lambda Function Timeout
>
> At the time of writing, a Lambda function can run for a maximum execution time of 15 minutes. This is commonly referred to as the *timeout period*. While developing a Lambda function, you can set the timeout to any value up to 15 minutes. You set this value based on how long the function requires to complete the execution of its logic, and expect it to finish before its timeout. If the function is still executing when it reaches its set timeout, the AWS Lambda service terminates it.

High Availability

A *highly available* (HA) application avoids a single point of failure by adding redundancy. For a commercial application, the service level agreement (SLA) states the availability in terms of a percentage. In serverless, as we employ fully managed services, AWS takes care of the redundancy and data replication by distributing the compute and storage resources across multiple AZs, thus avoiding a single point of failure. Hence, adopting serverless provides high availability out of the box as standard.

Cold Start

Cold start is commonly associated with FaaS. For example, as you saw earlier, when an AWS Lambda function is idle for a period of time its execution environment is shut down. If the function gets invoked again after being idle for a while, AWS provisions a new execution environment to run it. The latency in this initial setup is usually called the *cold start* time. Once the function execution is completed, the Lambda service retains the execution environment for a nondeterministic period. If the function is invoked again during this period, it does not incur the cold start latency. However, if there are additional simultaneous invocations, the Lambda service provisions a new execution environment for each concurrent invocation, resulting in a cold start.

Many factors contribute to this initial latency: the size of the function's deployment package, the runtime environment of the programming language, the memory (RAM) allocated to the function, the number of preconfigurations (such as static data initializations), etc. As an engineer working in serverless, it is essential to understand cold start as it influences your architectural, developmental, and operational decisions (see Figure 1-9).

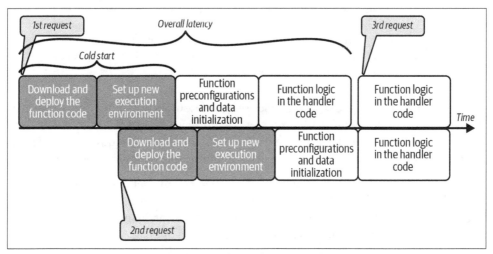

Figure 1-9. Function invocation latency for cold starts and warm executions—requests 1 and 2 incur a cold start, whereas a warm container handles request 3

The Unique Benefits of Serverless

Along with the core characteristics of serverless that you saw in the previous section, understanding some of its unique benefits is essential to optimize the development process and enable teams to improve their velocity in delivering business outcomes. In this section, we'll take a look at some of the key features serverless supports.

Individuality and Granularity of Resources

"One size fits all" does not apply to serverless. The ability to configure and operate serverless services at an individual level allows you to look at your serverless application not just as a whole but at the level of each resource, working with its specific characteristics. Unlike with traditional container applications, you no longer need to set a common set of operational characteristics at the container level.

Say your application has several Lambda functions. Some functions handle user requests from your website, while others perform batch jobs on the backend. You may provide more memory for the user-facing functions to enable them to respond quickly, and opt for a longer timeout for the backend batch job functions where performance is not critical. With Amazon Simple Queue Service (SQS) queues, for example, you configure how quickly you want to process the messages as they come into the queue, or you can decide whether to delay when a message becomes available for processing.

 Amazon SQS is a fully managed and highly scalable message queuing service used to send, receive, and store messages. It is one of AWS's core services and helps build loosely coupled microservices. Each SQS queue has several attributes; you can adjust these values to configure the queue as needed.

When you build an application that uses several resources—Lambda functions, SQS queues, DynamoDB tables, S3 buckets, etc.—you have the flexibility to adjust each resource's behavior as dictated by the business and operational requirements. This is depicted in Figure 1-10, which shows part of an order processing microservice.

The ability to operate at a granular level brings many benefits, as you will see throughout this book. Understanding the individuality of resources and developing a granular mindset while building serverless applications helps you design secure, cost-effective, and sustainable solutions that are easy to operate.

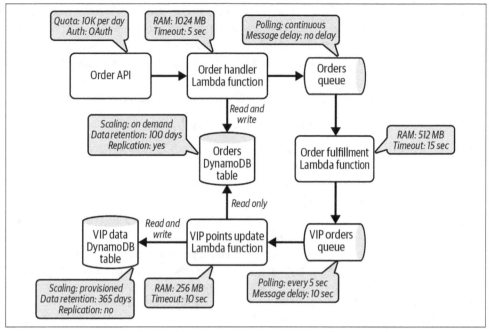

Figure 1-10. A section of an order processing microservice, illustrating how each server-less resource has different configurations

Ability to Optimize Services for Cost, Performance, and Sustainability

Cost and performance optimization techniques are common in software development. When you optimize to reduce cost, you target reducing the processing power, memory consumption, and storage allocation. With a traditional application, you exercise these changes at a high level, impacting all parts of the application. You cannot select a particular function or database table to apply the changes to. In such situations, if not adequately balanced, the changes you make could lead to performance degradations or higher costs elsewhere. Serverless offers a better optimization model.

Serverless enables deeper optimization

A serverless application is composed of several managed services, and it may contain multiple resources from the same managed service. For example, in Figure 1-10, you saw three Lambda functions from the AWS Lambda service. You are not forced to optimize all the functions in the same way. Instead, depending on your requirements, you can optimize one function for performance and another for cost, or give one function a longer timeout than the others. You can also allow for different concurrent execution needs.

Based on their characteristics, you can exhibit the same principle with other resources, such as queues, tables, APIs, etc. Imagine you have several microservices, each containing several serverless resources. For each microservice, you can optimize each individual resource at a granular level. This is optimization at its deepest and finest level in action!

Optimizing for Sustainability

In addition to the traditional cost and performance optimization strategies, there is now a need to consider sustainability as well. Chapter 10 explains this in detail, presenting several patterns for developing and operating your applications in a sustainable AWS cloud environment.

Optimizing for sustainability may have an impact on cost and performance. As a general principle, when you optimize to reduce cost, you are likely to consume fewer compute resources, resulting in lower power consumption, thus promoting sustainability. However, optimizing for higher performance often results in consuming more energy and may not align with sustainability goals. In such situations, you'll need to make trade-offs: identify the expected performance level, and optimize up to it and not beyond.

Storage optimization

Modern cloud applications ingest huge volumes of data—operational data, metrics, logs, etc. Teams that own the data might want to optimize their storage (to minimize cost and, in some cases, improve performance) by isolating and keeping only business-critical data.

Managed data services provide built-in features to remove or transition unneeded data. For example, Amazon S3 supports per-bucket data retention policies to either delete data or transition it to a different storage class, and DynamoDB allows you to configure the Time to Live (TTL) value on every item in a table. The storage optimization options are not confined to the mainstream data stores; you can specify the message retention period for each SQS queue, Kinesis stream, API cache, etc.

 DynamoDB manages the TTL configuration of the table items efficiently, regardless of how many items are in a table and how many of those items have a TTL timestamp set. However, in some cases, it can take up to 48 hours for an item to be deleted from the table. Consequently, this may not be an ideal solution if you require guaranteed item removal at the exact TTL time.

AWS Identity and Access Management (IAM)

AWS IAM is a service that controls the authentication and authorization of access to AWS services and resources. It helps define who can access which services and resources, under which conditions. Access to a service or resource can be granted to an identity, such as a user, or a resource, such as a Lambda function. The object that holds the details of the permissions is known as a policy and is stored as a JSON document, as shown in Example 1-1.

Example 1-1. IAM policy to allow read actions on DynamoDB Orders table

```
{
  "Version": "2012-10-17",
  "Statement": [
    {
      "Effect": "Allow",
      "Action": [
        "dynamodb:BatchGet*",
        "dynamodb:Get*",
        "dynamodb:Query"
      ],
      "Resource": "arn:aws:dynamodb:eu-west-1:12890:table/Orders"
    }
  ]
}
```

Support for Deeper Security and Data Privacy Measures

You now understand how the individuality and granularity of services in serverless enable you to fine-tune every part of an application for varying demands. The same characteristics allow you to apply protective measures at a deeper level as necessary across the ecosystem.

Permissions at a function level

Figure 1-11 shows a simple serverless application that allows you to store orders and query the status of a given order via the POST /orders and GET /orders/{id}/ status endpoints, respectively, which are handled by the corresponding Lambda functions. The function that queries the Orders table to find the status performs a read operation. Since this function does not change the data in the table, it requires just the dynamodb:Query privilege. This idea of providing the minimum permissions required to complete a task is known as the *principle of least privilege*.

The principle of least privilege is a security best practice that grants only the permissions required to perform a task. As shown in Example 1-1, you define this as an IAM policy by limiting the permitted actions on specific resources. It is one of the most fundamental security principles in AWS and should be part of the security thinking of every engineer. You will learn more about this topic in Chapter 4.

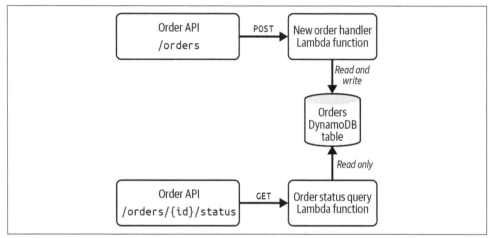

Figure 1-11. Serverless application showing two functions with different access privileges to the same data table

Granular permissions at the record level

The IAM policy in Example 1-1 showed how you configure access to read (query) data from the Orders table. Table 1-1 contains sample data of a few orders, where an order is split into three parts for better access and privacy: SOURCE, STATUS, and ADJUSTED.

Table 1-1. Sample Orders table with multiple item types

PK	SK	Status	Tracking	Total	Items
SOURCE	100-255-8730	Processing	44tesYuwLo	299.99	{ … }
STATUS	100-255-8730	Processing	44tesYuwLo		
SOURCE	100-735-6729	Delivered	G6txNMo26d	185.79	{ … }
ADJUSTED	100-735-6729	Delivered	G6txNMo26d	175.98	{ … }
STATUS	100-735-6729	Delivered	G6txNMo26d		

Per the principle of least privilege, the Lambda function that queries the status of an order should only be allowed to access that order's STATUS record. Table 1-2 highlights the records that should be accessible to the function.

Table 1-2. STATUS records accessible to the status query function

PK	SK	Status	Tracking	Total	Items
SOURCE	100-255-8730	Processing	44tesYuwLo	299.99	{...}
STATUS	100-255-8730	Processing	44tesYuwLo		
SOURCE	100-735-6729	Delivered	G6txNMo26d	185.79	{...}
ADJUSTED	100-735-6729	Delivered	G6txNMo26d	175.98	{...}
STATUS	100-735-6729	Delivered	G6txNMo26d		

To achieve this, you can use an IAM policy with a dynamodb:LeadingKeys condition and the policy details listed in Example 1-2.

Example 1-2. Policy to restrict read access to a specific type of item

```
{
  "Version": "2012-10-17",
  "Statement": [
    {
      "Sid": "AllowOrderStatus",
      "Effect": "Allow",
      "Action": [
        "dynamodb:GetItem",
        "dynamodb:Query"
      ],
      "Resource": [
        "arn:aws:dynamodb:…:table/Orders"
      ],
      "Condition": {
        "ForAllValues:StringEquals": {
          "dynamodb:LeadingKeys": [
            "STATUS"
          ]
        }
      }
    }
  ]
}
```

The conditional policy shown here works at a record level. DynamoDB also supports attribute-level conditions to fetch the values from only the permitted attributes of a record, for applications that require even more granular access control.

Policies like this one are common in AWS and applicable to several common services you will use to build your applications. Awareness and understanding of where and when to use them will immensely benefit you as a serverless engineer.

Incremental and Iterative Development

Iterative development empowers teams to develop and deliver products in small increments but in quick succession. As Eric Ries says in his book *The Startup Way* (Penguin), you start simple and scale fast. Your product constantly evolves with new features that benefit your customers and add business value.

Event-driven architecture (EDA), which we'll explore in detail in Chapter 3, is at the heart of serverless development. In serverless, you compose your applications with loosely coupled services that interact via events, messages, and APIs. EDA principles enable you to build modular and extensible serverless applications.[1] When you avoid hard dependencies between your services, it becomes easier to extend your applications by adding new services that do not disrupt the functioning of the existing ones.

Multiskilled, Diverse Engineering Teams

Adopting new technology brings changes as well as challenges in an organization. When teams move to a new language, database, SaaS platform, browser technology, or cloud provider, changes in that area often require changes in others. For example, adopting a new programming language may call for modifications to the development, build, and deployment processes. Similarly, moving your applications to the cloud can create demand for many new processes and skills.

Influence of DevOps culture

The DevOps approach removes the barriers between development and operations, making it faster to develop new products and easier to maintain them. Adopting a DevOps model takes a software engineer who otherwise focuses on developing applications into performing operational tasks. You no longer work in a siloed software development cycle but are involved in its many phases, such as continuous integration and delivery (CI/CD), monitoring and observability, commissioning the cloud infrastructure, and securing applications, among other things.

---

1 A module is an independent and self-contained unit of software.

Adopting a serverless model takes you many steps further. Though it frees you from managing servers, you are now programming the business logic, composing your application using managed services, knitting them together with infrastructure as code (IaC), and operating them in the cloud. Just knowing how to write software is not enough. You have to protect your application from malicious users, make it available 24/7 to customers worldwide, and observe its operational characteristics to improve it continually. Becoming a successful serverless engineer thus requires developing a whole new set of skills, and cultivating a DevOps mindset (see Figure 1-12).

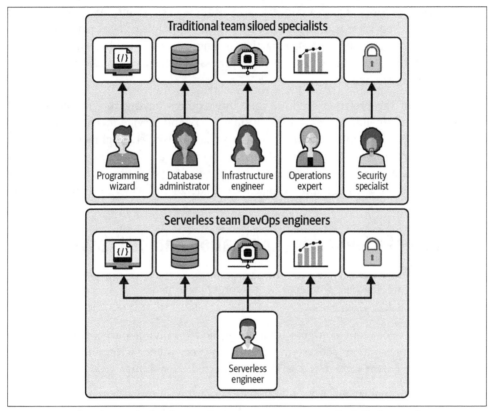

Figure 1-12. Traditional siloed specialist engineers versus multiskilled serverless engineers

Your evolution as a serverless engineer

Consider the simple serverless application shown in Figure 1-8, where a Lambda function reads and writes to a DynamoDB table. Imagine that you are proficient in TypeScript and have chosen Node.js as your Lambda runtime environment. As you implement the function, it becomes your responsibility to code the interactions with DynamoDB. To be efficient, you learn NoSQL concepts, identify the partition key (PK) and sort key (SK) attributes as well as appropriate data access patterns to write your queries, etc. In addition, there may be data replication, TTL, caching, and other requirements. Security is also a concern, so you then learn about AWS IAM, how to create roles and policies, and, most importantly, the principle of least privilege. From being a programmer proficient in a particular language, your engineering role takes a 360-degree turn. As you evolve into a serverless engineer, you pick up many new skills and responsibilities.

As you saw in the previous section, your job requires having the ability to build the deployment pipeline for your application, understand service metrics, and proactively act on production incidents. You're now a multiskilled engineer—and when most engineers in a team are multiskilled, it becomes a diverse engineering team capable of efficient end-to-end serverless delivery. For organizations where upskilling of engineers is required, Chapter 2 discusses in detail the ways to grow serverless talents.

The Parts of a Serverless Application and Its Ecosystem

> An ecosystem is a geographic area where plants, animals, and other organisms, as well as weather and landscape, work together to form a bubble of life.
>
> —NationalGeographic.org

In nature, an ecosystem contains both living and nonliving parts, also known as *factors*. Every factor in an ecosystem depends on every other factor, either directly or indirectly. The Earth's surface is a series of connected ecosystems.

The ecosystem analogy here is intentional. Serverless is too often imagined as an architecture diagram or a blueprint, but it is much more than FaaS and a simple framework. It has both technical and nontechnical elements associated with it. Serverless is a technology ecosystem!

As you learned earlier in this chapter, managed services form the bulk of a serverless application. However, they alone cannot bring an application alive—many other factors are involved. Figure 1-13 depicts some of the core elements that make up the serverless ecosystem.

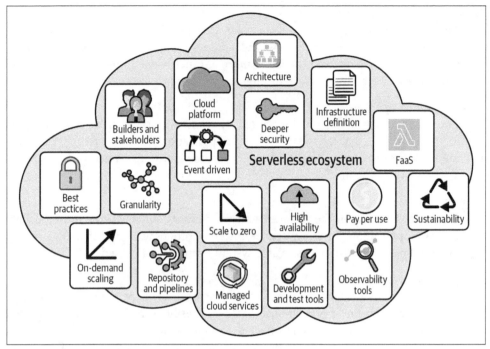

Figure 1-13. Parts of the serverless technology ecosystem

They include:

The cloud platform
: This is the enabler of the serverless ecosystem—AWS in our case. The cloud hosting environment provides the required compute, storage, and network resources.

Managed cloud services
: Managed services are the basic building blocks of serverless. You compose your applications by consuming services for computation, event transportation, messaging, data storage, and various other activities.

Architecture
: This is the blueprint that depicts the purpose and behavior of your serverless application. Defining and agreeing on an architecture is one of the most important activities in serverless development.

Infrastructure definition
: Infrastructure definition—also known as infrastructure as code (IaC) and expressed as a descriptive script—is like the circuit diagram of your application. It weaves everything together with the appropriate characteristics, dependencies, permissions, and access controls. IaC, when actioned on the cloud, holds the power to bring your serverless application alive or tear it down.

Development and test tools

The runtime environment of your FaaS dictates the programming language, libraries, plug-ins, testing frameworks, and several other developer aids. These tools may vary from one ecosystem to another, depending on the product domain and the preferences of the engineering teams.

Repository and pipelines

The repository is a versioned store for all your artifacts, and the pipelines perform the actions that take your serverless application from a developer environment all the way to its target customers, passing through various checkpoints along the way. The infrastructure definition plays a pivotal role in this process.

Observability tools

Observability tools and techniques act as a mirror to reflect the operational state of your application, offering deeper insights into how it performs against its intended purpose. A non-observable system cannot be sustained.

Best practices

To safeguard your serverless application against security threats and scaling demands and ensure it is both observable and resilient in the face of unexpected disruptions, you need well-architected principles and best practices acting as guardrails. The AWS Well-Architected Framework is an essential best practices guide; we'll look at it later in this chapter.

Builders and stakeholders

The people who come up with the requirements for an application and the ones who design, build, and operate it in the cloud are also part of the ecosystem. In addition to all the tools and techniques, the role of humans in a serverless ecosystem is vital—they're the ones responsible for making the right decisions and performing the necessary actions, similar to the role we all play in our environmental ecosystem!

Why Is AWS a Great Platform for Serverless?

As mentioned earlier in this chapter, although the term serverless first appeared in the industry in around 2012, it gained traction after the release of AWS Lambda in 2014. While the large numbers of people who jumped on the Lambda bandwagon elevated serverless to new heights, AWS already had a couple of fully managed serverless services serving customers at this point. Amazon SQS was released almost 10 years before AWS Lambda. Amazon S3, the much-loved and widely used object store in the cloud, was launched in 2006, way before the cloud reached the corners of the IT industry.

This early leap into the cloud with a futuristic vision, offering container services and fully managed serverless services, enabled Amazon to roll out new products faster than any other provider. Recognizing the potential, many early adopters swiftly realized their business ideas and launched their applications on AWS. Even though the cloud market is growing rapidly, AWS remains the top cloud services provider globally.

The Popularity of Serverless Services from AWS

Working closely with customers and monitoring industry trends has allowed AWS to quickly iterate ideas and launch several important serverless services in areas such as APIs, functions, data stores, data streaming, AI, machine learning, event transportation, workflow and orchestration, and more.

What's in a Name?

When you look at the AWS service names, you'll notice a mix of "Amazon" and "AWS" prefixes—for example, Amazon DynamoDB and AWS Step Functions. This confuses everyone, including employees at Amazon. Apparently, it's not a random selection but a way to differentiate services based on their fundamental characteristics.

The most popular and relevant theory suggests that services with the *Amazon* prefix work on their own (standalone services), whereas the ones with the *AWS* prefix support other services (utility services) and are not intended to be used on their own. AWS Lambda, for example, is triggered by other services. However, as services evolve over time with new capabilities, you may find exceptions where this distinction no longer holds true.

AWS is a comprehensive cloud platform offering over 200 services to build and operate both serverless and non-serverless workloads. Table 1-3 lists some of the most commonly used managed serverless services. You will see many of these services featured in our discussions throughout this book.

Table 1-3. Popular serverless services from AWS

Category	Service
Analytics	Amazon Kinesis, Amazon Athena, AWS Glue, Amazon QuickSight
App building	AWS Amplify
API building	Amazon API Gateway, AWS AppSync
Application integration	Amazon EventBridge, AWS Step Functions, Amazon Simple Notification Service (SNS), Amazon Simple Queue Service (SQS), Amazon API Gateway, AWS AppSync
Compute	AWS Lambda
Content delivery	Amazon CloudFront
Database	Amazon DynamoDB, Amazon Aurora Serverless

Category	Service
Developer tools	AWS CloudFormation, AWS Cloud Development Kit (CDK), AWS Serverless Application Model (SAM), AWS CodeBuild, AWS CodeCommit, AWS CodeDeploy, AWS CodePipeline
Emails	Amazon Simple Email Service (SES)
Event-driven architecture	Amazon EventBridge, Amazon Simple Notification Service (SNS), Amazon Simple Queue Service (SQS), AWS Lambda
Governance	AWS Well-Architected Tool, AWS Trusted Advisor, AWS Systems Manager, AWS Organizations
High volume event streaming	Amazon Kinesis Data Streams, Amazon Kinesis Data Firehose
Identity, authentication, and security	AWS Identity and Access Management (IAM), Amazon Cognito, AWS Secrets Manager, AWS WAF, Amazon Macie
Machine learning	Amazon SageMaker, Amazon Translate, Amazon Comprehend, Amazon DevOps Guru
Networking	Amazon Route 53
Object store	Amazon Simple Storage Service (S3)
Observability	Amazon CloudWatch, AWS X-Ray, AWS CloudTrail
Orchestration	AWS Step Functions
Security	AWS Identity and Access Management (IAM), Amazon Cognito, AWS Secrets Manager, AWS Systems Manager Parameter Store

The AWS Well-Architected Framework

The AWS Well-Architected Framework is a collection of architectural best practices for designing, building, and operating secure, scalable, highly available, resilient, and cost-effective applications in the cloud. It consists of six pillars covering fundamental areas of a modern cloud system:

Operational Excellence (https://oreil.ly/YDnvJ)
> The Operational Excellence pillar provides design principles and best practices to devise organizational objectives to identify, prepare, operate, observe, and improve operating workloads in the cloud. Failure anticipation and mitigation plans, evolving applications in small but frequent increments, and continuous evaluation and improvements of the operational procedures are some of the core principles of this pillar.

Security (https://oreil.ly/Cxkyr)
> The Security pillar focuses on identity and access management, protecting applications at all layers, ensuring data privacy and control as well as traceability and auditing of all actions, and preparing for and responding to security events. It instills security thinking at all stages of development and is the responsibility of everyone involved.

Reliability (https://oreil.ly/nnGlq)
> An application deployed and operated in the cloud should be able to scale and function consistently as demand changes. The principles and practices of the

Reliability pillar include designing applications to work with service quotas and limits, preventing and mitigating failures, and identifying and recovering from failures, among other guidance.

Performance Efficiency (https://oreil.ly/5IQkW)
The Performance Efficiency pillar is about the approach of selecting and the use of the right technology and resources to build and operate an efficient system. Monitoring and data metrics play an important role here in constantly reviewing and making trade-offs to maintain efficiency at all times.

Cost Optimization (https://oreil.ly/3S17n)
The Cost Optimization pillar guides organizations to operate business applications in the cloud in a way that delivers value and keeps costs low. The best practices focus on financial management, creating cloud cost awareness, using cost-effective resources and technologies such as serverless, and continuously analyzing and optimizing based on business demand.

Sustainability (https://oreil.ly/ns1a9)
The Sustainability pillar is the latest addition to the AWS Well-Architected Framework. It focuses on contributing to a sustainable environment by reducing energy consumption; architecting and operating applications that reduce the use of compute power, storage space, and network round trips; use of on-demand resources such as serverless services; and optimizing to the required level and not over.

AWS Technical Support Plans

Depending on the scale of your cloud operation and the company's size, Amazon offers four technical support plans (*https://oreil.ly/tFve2*) to suit your needs:

Developer
This is the entry-level support model, suitable for experimentation, building prototypes, or testing simple applications at the start of your serverless journey.

Business
As you move from the experimentation stage toward production deployments and operating business applications serving customers, this is the recommended support level. As well as other support features, it adds response time guarantees for production systems that are impaired or go down (<4 hours and <1 hour, respectively).

Enterprise on-ramp
The main difference between this one and the Enterprise plan is the response time guarantee when business-critical applications go down (<30 minutes, versus

<15 minutes with the higher-level plan). The lower-level plans do not offer this guarantee.

Enterprise

If you're part of a big organization with several teams developing and operating high-profile, mission-critical workloads, the Enterprise support plan will give you the most immediate care. In the event of an incident with your mission-critical applications, you get support within 15 minutes. This plan also comes with several additional benefits, including:

- A dedicated Technical Account Manager (TAM) who acts as the first point of contact between your organization and AWS
- Regular (typically monthly) meeting cadence with your TAM
- Advice from AWS experts, such as solution architects specializing in your business domain, when building an application
- Evaluation of your existing systems and recommendations based on AWS Well-Architected Framework best practices
- Training and workshops to improve your internal AWS skills and development best practices
- News about new product launches and feature releases
- Opportunities to beta-test new products before they become generally available
- Invitations to immersion days and face-to-face meetings with AWS product teams related to the technologies you work with

The number one guiding principle at Amazon is *customer obsession*: "Leaders start with the customer and work backwards. They work vigorously to earn and keep customer trust. Although leaders pay attention to competitors, they obsess over customers."

AWS Developer Community Support

The AWS developer community is an incredibly active and supportive technical forum. There are several avenues you can pursue to become part of this community, and doing so is highly recommended, both for your growth as a serverless engineer and to ensure the successful adoption of serverless within your enterprise. They include:

Engage with AWS Developer Advocates (DAs).

AWS's DAs connect the developer community with the different product teams at AWS. You can follow serverless developments on social media. You will find the serverless specialist DAs helping the community by answering questions and contributing technical content via blogs, live streams and videos, GitHub code shares, conferences, meetups, etc.

Reach out to AWS Heroes and Community Builders.
The AWS Heroes program (*https://oreil.ly/k3Phm*) recognizes AWS experts whose contributions make a real impact in the tech community. Outside AWS, these experts share their knowledge and serverless adoption stories from the trenches.

At the time of writing this book, Sheen Brisals has been recognized as an AWS Serverless Hero.

The AWS Community Builders program (*https://oreil.ly/6FAoW*) is a worldwide initiative to bring together AWS enthusiasts and rising experts who are passionate about sharing knowledge and connecting with AWS product teams and DAs, Heroes, and industry experts. Identifying the builders who contribute to the serverless space and learning from their experiences will deepen your knowledge.

At the time of writing this book, Luke Hedger has been recognized as an AWS Community Builder.

Join an AWS Cloud Club.
There's a thriving student-led community, with AWS Cloud Clubs (*https://oreil.ly/tsxmC*) in multiple regions worldwide. Students can join their local club to network, learn about AWS, and build their careers. Cloud Club Captains organize events to learn together, connect with other clubs, and earn AWS credits and certification vouchers, among other opportunities.

Sign up with AWS Startup or AWS Educate.
AWS has popular programs to help bring your ideas to realization. AWS Activate (*https://oreil.ly/VuoVo*) is for anyone with great ideas and ambitions or start-ups less than 10 years old. AWS offers the necessary tools, resources, credits, and advice to boost success at every stage of the journey.

AWS Educate (*https://oreil.ly/aWMEg*) is a learning resource for students and professionals. It offers AWS credits that can be used for courses and projects, access to free training, and networking opportunities.

Attend AWS conferences.
An essential part of an enterprise's serverless adoption journey is continuously evaluating its development processes, domains, team organization, engineering culture, best practices, etc. Conferences and collaborative events are the perfect platforms to find solutions for your concerns, validate your ideas, and identify actions to correct before it is too late.

The type and scale of conferences vary. For example, AWS re:Invent is an annual week-long conference that brings tens of thousands of tech and business enthusiasts together with hundreds of sessions spread over five days, whereas AWS Summits and AWS Community Summits are local events—mostly one-day—conducted around the world to bring the community and technology experts closer. Most of the content gets shared online as well. AWS Events and Webinars (*https://oreil.ly/Yl3k9*) is a good place to identify events that might suit your purposes.

Summary

As you start your serverless journey, either as an independent learner or as part of an enterprise team, it is valuable to have an understanding of how the cloud evolved and how it facilitated the development of serverless technology. This chapter provided that foundation, and outlined the significant potential of serverless and the benefits it can provide to an organization.

Every technology requires a solid platform to thrive and a passionate community to support it. While by no means the only option out there, Amazon Web Services (AWS) is a fantastic platform with numerous service offerings and dedicated developer support programs. As highlighted in this chapter, to be successful in your serverless adoption, it is paramount that you share your experiences and learn from proven industry experts.

In the next chapter, we will look at serverless adoption in an enterprise. We will examine some of the fundamental things an organization needs to evaluate and do to onboard serverless and make it a successful venture for its engineers, users, and business.

Interview with an Industry Expert

Danilo Poccia, Chief Evangelist (EMEA), Amazon Web Services

Danilo works with start-ups and companies of all sizes to support their innovation. In his role as Chief Evangelist (EMEA) at Amazon Web Services, he leverages his experience to help people bring their ideas to life, focusing on serverless architectures and event-driven programming and the technical and business impact of machine learning and edge computing. He is the author of *AWS Lambda in Action: Event-Driven Serverless Applications* (Manning) and speaks at conferences worldwide.

Q: Why does the software industry need serverless technology?

When you build an application, it can become complex to deploy, test, or add a new feature sooner or later without breaking the existing functionalities. In the last 20 years, complexity has become a science that has found similarities across many different fields, such as mathematics, physics, and social sciences. Complexity theory finds that when there are strong dependencies between components, even simple components, you might experience the emergence of "complex" and difficult-to-predict behaviors. For example, the behavior of an ant is simple, but together, ants can discover food hidden in remote locations and bring it back to their nest. The emergence of unexpected behaviors applies very well to software development.

When you have a large codebase, it requires a lot of effort to reduce side effects so that you don't break something else when you add a new feature. In my experience, monolithic applications with a large codebase only work when there is a small core team of developers that have worked for years on the same application and have accumulated a large amount of experience in the business domain. Microservices help, but you still need business domain knowledge to find where to split the application. That's what domain-driven design (DDD) calls the "bounded context." And that's why microservices are more successful if they are implemented as a migration from an existing application than when you're starting from scratch. If the boundaries are well chosen and defined, you limit the internal dependencies to reduce the overall code complexity and the emergence of unexpected issues.

But still, each microservice brings its nonfunctional requirements in terms of security, reliability, scalability, observability, performance, and so on. Serverless architecture helps implement these nonfunctional requirements in a much easier way. It can reduce the overall code size by using services to implement functionalities that are not unique to your implementation. It lets you focus on the features you want to build and not managing the infrastructure required to run the application. In this way, moving from idea to production is much faster, and the advantage of serverless technologies is not only for the technical teams but also for the business teams that are able to deliver more and faster to their customers.

Q: As the author of the first book on AWS Lambda, what has changed in serverless since your early experience?

When I wrote the book in 2016, there was very little tooling around AWS Lambda. In some examples of my book, I call Lambda functions directly from the browser using the AWS SDK for JavaScript. In a way, I don't dislike that. It makes you focus more on the business functions you need to implement. Also, even if many customers were interested in AWS Lambda at the time, there were very few examples of serverless workloads in production.

The idea for the book started from a workshop I created where I wanted to show how to make building an application easier. For example, I start with data. Is data structured? Put it in a fully managed database like Amazon DynamoDB. Is it unstructured data? Put it in an Amazon S3 bucket. Where is your business logic? Split it into small functions and run them on AWS Lambda. Can those functions run on a client or in a web browser? Put them there, and don't run that code in the backend. Maybe the result is what we now call "serviceful" architecture.

Today, we have many tools that support building serverless event-driven applications to manage events (like Amazon EventBridge) or to coordinate the execution of your business logic (like AWS Step Functions). With better tooling, customers are now building more advanced applications. It's not just about serverless functions like in 2016. Today, you need to consider how to use the tools together to build applications faster and have less code to maintain.

Q: In your role as a technology evangelist, you work with several teams. How does serverless as a technology enable teams of different sizes to innovate and build solutions faster?

Small teams work better. Serverless empowers small teams to do more because it lets them remove the parts that can be implemented off the shelf by an existing service. It naturally leads them to adopt a microservice architecture and use distributed systems. It can be hard at first if they don't have any experience in these fields, but it's rewarding when they learn and see the results.

If you need to make a big change in the way you build applications, for example, adopting serverless or microservices, put yourself in a place where you can make mistakes. It's by making mistakes that we learn. As you move to production, collecting metrics on code complexity in your deployment pipeline helps keep the codebase under control. To move that a step further, I find the idea of a "fitness function" (as described in the book *Building Evolutionary Architectures* by Rebecca Parsons, Neal Ford, and Patrick Kua [O'Reilly]) extremely interesting, especially if you define "guardrails" about what the fitness of your application should be.

Automation helps at any scale but is incredibly effective for small teams. The AWS Well-Architected Framework also provides a way to measure the quality of your implementation and provides a Serverless Lens with specific guidance.

Q: As the leading cloud platform for developing serverless applications, what measures does AWS take to think ahead and bring new services to its consumers?

I started at AWS more than 10 years ago. Things were different at the time. Just starting an EC2 instance in a couple of minutes was considered impressive. But even if some time has passed, at AWS, we always use the same approach to build new services and features: we listen to our customers. Our roadmap is 90 to 95% based on what our customers tell us. For the rest, we try to add new ideas from the experience we have accumulated over the years in Amazon and AWS.

We want to build tools that can help solve customers' problems, not theoretical issues. We build them in a way so that customers can choose which tools to use. We want to iterate quickly on new ideas and get as much feedback as possible when we do it.

Q: What advice would you give to the readers starting their personal or organizational serverless adoption journey?

Learn the mental model. Don't focus on the implementation details. Understand the pros and cons of using microservices and distributed architectures. Time becomes important because there is latency and concurrency to be considered. Design your systems for asynchronous communication and eventual consistency.

Faults are a natural part of any architecture. Think of your strategy to recover and manage faults. Can you record and repeat what your application is doing? Can events help you do that? Also, two core requirements that are more important now than before are observability and sustainability. They are more related than one might think at first.

Offload the parts that are not unique to your application to services and SaaS offerings that can implement those functionalities for you. Focus on what you want to build. It's there where you can make a difference.

CHAPTER 2

Enterprise Readiness for Serverless

I do not believe you can do today's job with yesterday's methods and be in business tomorrow.
   —Nelson Jackson

When a renowned coach takes charge at a sports club, they bring their team of assistants and support staff—mainly due to the comfort of working with a known team and their mutual understanding—and the club prepares to adapt to the changes needed to make the transition successful. A similar phenomenon can be observed with new technology adoption in an organization. New technologies bring changes, sometimes minor and at other times considerable. Adopting modern technologies such as the cloud and serverless can require significant changes to teams, tools, processes, and even people's thinking.

Before hiring a new coach, the club usually conducts an extensive assessment process to evaluate their past achievements, understand their attitudes and what they will bring to the club, and ensure the club's future vision aligns with the coach's. It's a lengthy exercise, but a crucial one. When an organization plans to adopt serverless, it should be prepared to undergo a similar process to map out the organization's business ambitions with the capabilities of serverless. A *readiness evaluation* is thus critical to identify the best strategy before starting on the serverless journey.

This chapter begins by walking you through how to create a serverless mindset and assessing your migration needs. We'll go through some common migration patterns to help you identify the best-fit strategy for your domain and workloads. We'll also look at topics like getting stakeholder buy-in and growing a successful serverless team. Just as every successful sports club puts significant effort into the development of new talent, for serverless adoption to succeed a vital part of the journey is nurturing talented serverless engineers within your organization.

Preparing for "Thinking in Serverless"

Your confidence in any new technology will grow over time as you use it, just as daily tasks in life become more manageable with experience. Serverless adoption is similar—you'll become increasingly fluent as you continue to work on it. To provide the optimal conditions for success, however, organizations that are newly adopting serverless require clarity in their understanding and guidance with their strategy.

This book aims to guide you through the essentials—organizational standards, architectural constructs, developmental practices, operational principles, and other fundamentals—so that you, your team, and your organization are well equipped as you embark on your serverless adoption journey.

Creating a Serverless Mindset

Humans constantly *think*, both consciously and subconsciously. But *thinking* as a process to solve a particular problem or outline the growth strategy for your company is not easy. When we are *forced* to think and produce an outcome, we rely naturally on our experience to find ideas and draw parallels to apply. When facing a problem with methodology or technology, we tend to follow a similar approach. Hence, switching from legacy practices to modern ones takes time and requires training and orientation. With cloud technology as its base and using the latest developmental practices, serverless requires you to transform your thinking to higher levels.

What are the mental changes you and your organization need to go through? This section describes how you can transform your thinking and cultivate a serverless mindset.

Aligning your thought process to serverless

As you saw in Chapter 1, the first thought transformation you should focus on is to view serverless technology as an ecosystem, and recognize that you need both technical and nontechnical factors to work together to succeed. Keeping this ecosystem view in mind and understanding serverless's characteristics and unique benefits is crucial to developing a serverless mindset (see Figure 2-1).

Many elements in the serverless ecosystem, such as the source code repository and deployment pipelines, will likely already be familiar to you. But while many of the basic concepts remain the same, the tools and deployment targets will differ—for example, your deployment target will now be the cloud, and the operating environment will change.

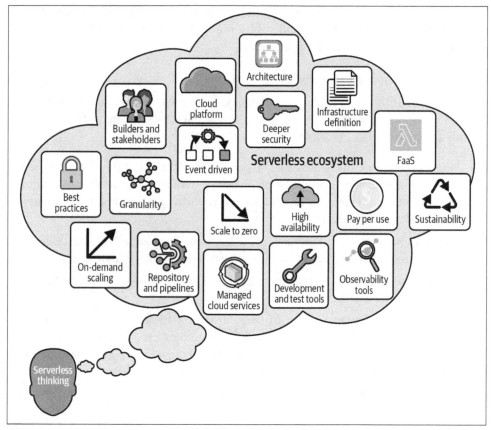

Figure 2-1. The importance of keeping the serverless ecosystem view as a whole

The essentials of serverless thinking

The ability to operate at a granular level in serverless can be challenging to understand if you have been working with containerized or monolithic applications. Here are some essential areas to focus on to equip your mind to think about the new ways of working with serverless:

- Developing knowledge of the serverless technology ecosystem and its parts
- Gaining a practical understanding of the characteristics of serverless
- Determining how to map the benefits of serverless to your business requirements
- Recognizing that observability principles are as important as business logic
- Creating cost awareness while architecting and building your serverless application
- Trusting AWS as your cloud provider and using managed services

Alongside the serverless-specific areas, your experience with Agile development practices, microservices, and DevOps principles will be highly beneficial. You will see all these points discussed throughout this book.

Habits to offboard from a legacy mindset

As well onboarding the essentials mentioned in the previous section, removing some of the traditional thoughts and habits you might have been clinging to for years is equally important. Here are some tips:

- Move away from the legacy siloed development rituals followed in waterfall models. For example, lengthy testing phases by dedicated QA teams or infrequent production deployment by designated teams won't suit an agile team iteratively building serverless solutions.

- Disperse "superstar" teams and encourage equal participation and delegation. The idea is to equip and develop all engineers to share the responsibility.

- As there are no servers to manage, accept that you don't need to SSH into virtual machines to troubleshoot.

- The roles and responsibilities of team members need not be fixed and permanent. As serverless favors multiskilled engineers (see "Multiskilled, Diverse Engineering Teams" on page 20), you may not find a dedicated database administrator, infrastructure, or network engineer in every serverless team.

- The flow of architecture and design proposals is not one-way between architects and engineering teams. With the cloud and serverless, it's a collaboration between architects, tech leads, and engineers.

These are just a few of the changes you will commonly notice in serverless teams, but remember, these practices vary between organizations and teams.

Technology alone cannot be the sole contributor to your success. Without the right *people* (engineering, product, and business stakeholder teams) and the necessary *processes* (analysis, design principles, best practices, etc.), serverless adoption is not guaranteed to yield the expected long-term success. The following section takes you through what you need to realize this goal and explains how all three of these elements are vital for successful serverless adoption.

First Principles for Successful Serverless Adoption

Developing, deploying, and invoking a Lambda function is easy, as demonstrated in many conference sessions, learning portals, and YouTube videos. Once you have experienced the process once, repeating it to write more Lambda functions is straightforward. Does that mean you can simply declare that serverless is easy and instruct your teams to go forth and go serverless? Many enterprise teams make mistakes here.

While implementing and running a Lambda function may be easy, remember, as you learned in Chapter 1, that FaaS is just one part of the serverless ecosystem. Success of operating a simple function cannot be used as the yardstick to measure your organization's ability to adopt serverless—building and operating production-ready enterprise-scale serverless applications involves far more than creating a few Lambda functions! Enterprises with multiple teams and many engineers need to develop the endurance for a marathon, not a quick-burst hundred-meter sprint.

Serverless is not a silver bullet

As discussed earlier, developing a serverless mindset is critical for successful serverless adoption. You need to prepare yourself psychologically. The technical and product teams should have a clear understanding of the reasons why serverless requires a change of scenery. In an organization riddled with years of technical neglect, team misalignment, Stone Age thinking, and stubborn engineering minds that resist change, serverless adoption is a tough act to pull off. There is considerable preparation work required to bring such an organization into a state conducive to serverless adoption and growth.

You'll hear the term *serverless-first* a lot in the industry. However, there is much to consider when determining whether serverless is the best-fit technology choice to build and operate business applications to deliver value faster. It requires strategic thinking, not a compulsion to jump in headfirst and build *everything* serverless.

When enterprises force their way into developing applications using serverless technology and scale quickly without the necessary scaffolding, they often end up creating a tangled web of distributed monolith known as a *ball of serverless mud* (BoSM), as shown in Figure 2-2, rather than a smaller, self-contained, modular, and extendable architecture. As an engineer, architect, technology advisor, or CTO, your responsibility is to prevent such calamities from unfolding in front of your eyes. Instead of leaping straight to serverless-first thinking, your focus should start with an understanding of a few other first principles.

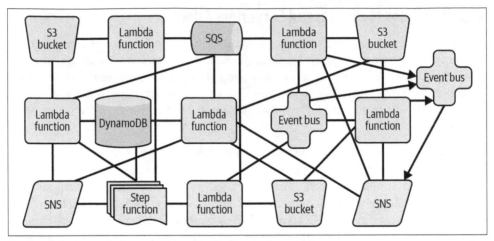

Figure 2-2. A tangled event-driven ball of serverless mud

 First principles thinking is a thought process that can help you get to the fundamentals of a problem. Rather than focusing on the problem as a whole, you break it into parts to identify the basic elements and causes. Understanding the basics often makes it simpler to find innovative solutions to the business problems your enterprise is trying to solve. In this space, serverless is just a technology enabler.

The first principles that you will need to understand before adopting a serverless-first mindset include domains, teams, APIs, microservices, and events. Let's take a look at how you might approach each of these elements to see how they lay the foundation for success in an organization on the verge of adopting serverless. Then we'll come back to the idea of serverless-first.

Domain-first

Domain-first thinking is heavily influenced by the principles discussed by Eric Evans in his book *Domain-Driven Design: Tackling Complexity in the Heart of Software* (Addison-Wesley Professional). For enterprise-scale serverless adoption, domain-first thinking is a necessary precursor to serverless-first thinking. Understanding the problem you are trying to solve is crucial. In start-ups or small-scale businesses, the business domain or problem may be clear and concise. However, this isn't always the case in larger enterprises. While most enterprises operate in one domain—retail, hospitality, insurance, gaming, toys, etc.—bigger ones often have multiple domain areas. For example, Microsoft sells laptop computers and cloud computing services, and Amazon runs a retail business and Amazon Web Services.

Going deep into domain-driven design is beyond the scope of this book. A good resource with practical examples is *Learning Domain-Driven Design: Aligning Software Architecture and Business Strategy* by Vlad Khononov (O'Reilly).

As you distill things further and break your business domains into subdomains, you identify the *bounded contexts* (see Figure 2-3 for an example). A bounded context is a boundary within a domain where a particular domain model applies. It reveals distinct characteristics and interacts with other bounded contexts via well-defined communication mechanisms such as APIs.

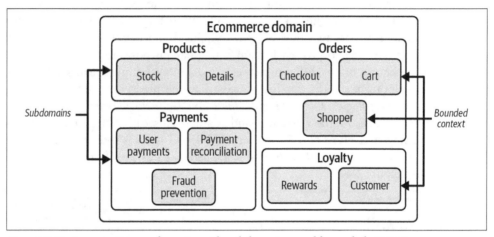

Figure 2-3. An ecommerce domain with subdomains and bounded contexts

Answering the following questions becomes easier when you get to this level:

- Who is responsible for protecting the domain boundary and implementing the domain logic?
- How will you safeguard the domain boundary to control the information flow into and out of that domain?
- Within a guarded boundary, which technology is apt to implement the business logic?

Once you've mapped out your subdomains and their boundaries, you need people who are well versed in each subdomain and speak the common business (ubiquitous) language used by the domain experts and business stakeholders. These people/teams must be aligned to focus on one thing and work together with a single purpose. This, then, is the starting point for thinking about the team structure.

The *two-pizza team* rule at Amazon stipulates that a team should be small enough to be fed by two pizzas. According to founder Jeff Bezos, smaller teams collaborate better because there are fewer communication links between the members. This in turn allows them to move faster with development and releases. This approach requires removing silos and giving teams end-to-end visibility of their products—that is, an ownership culture.

Team-first

Amazon's two-pizza team concept is often brought up in discussions about modern software development teams. But while it's become common to measure the size of a team based on their appetite for pizza, people often forget that these teams are intentionally kept small because the business domains they are part of are also broken down to a granular level to give each team a singular purpose, focus, and identity. Such teams are known under different names: product development teams, engineering teams, development squads, product squads, feature squads, service teams, etc. In their book *Team Topologies: Organizing Business and Technology Teams for Fast Flow* (IT Revolution Press), Mathew Skelton and Manual Pais call them *stream-aligned teams*. According to Skelton and Pais, a stream-aligned team is a team aligned to a single, valuable stream (flow) of work that is aligned to a business domain, as shown on the right in Figure 2-4.

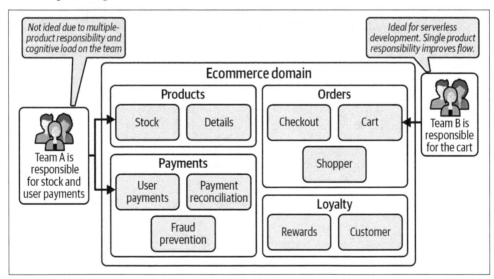

Figure 2-4. Team ownership of multiple bounded contexts versus a single bounded context

Enabling Teams

Team Topologies (https://teamtopologies.com) introduces new thinking around effective team structures for enterprise software delivery. It discusses four team types: stream-aligned, enabling, platform, and complicated subsystem teams.

A key observation is that not all engineering teams in an enterprise are responsible for building products and services that express domain logic. *Enabling teams* act as enablers for those stream-aligned teams so they can perform efficiently. Their focus might be on the platform, DevOps practices, tooling, developer experience, security measures, auditing, and observability principles, among other things. These teams may have different names in different organizations, but their general responsibilities remain the same.

A common misconception in the industry is that serverless technology does not require some of the roles and responsibilities an enabling team fulfills. This is not entirely true, even though serverless eliminates most platform and infrastructure heavy lifting. Your organization requires engineers with the expertise to set up guardrails and processes, such as security principles, well-architected service audit processes, etc. Unlike the siloed team structure, the key difference here is that enabling teams don't carry out the work on behalf of the stream-aligned teams; instead, they empower others to perform better with a reduced cognitive load and work efficiently to increase velocity and flow.

In addition to establishing different types of teams with distinct responsibilities, many organizations adopting cloud and serverless form a working group commonly known as the cloud center of excellence (CCoE), described in more detail in Chapter 11.

API-first

In Chapter 1, you saw that multiskilled, diverse engineering teams are better for serverless development. When such a team owns and operates its single-purpose product, it becomes the guardian responsible for protecting its contextual boundary by employing adequate technical and communication measures. *API-first* is a thought process and mechanism for implementing these measures.

Once you have identified and marked the boundaries of each subdomain, it becomes easier to answer the following questions:

- How can you protect the boundary?
- Who can get access to interact with the system?
- How can you grant access to external systems?
- What information can be transacted across the border?

To effectively accomplish these tasks, you must consider published interfaces to your application—that is, application programming interfaces (APIs). An API acts as an agreed contract for exchanging data without knowing the implementation details.

An *API-first* approach is about identifying, implementing, and publishing the interfaces to the system you are building. The API becomes a first-class citizen and plays a significant role in the tactical design and evolution of the application. Figure 2-5 illustrates a customer microservice with its API to perform defined actions. It promotes loose coupling and interoperability between multiple services within and outside the product domain.

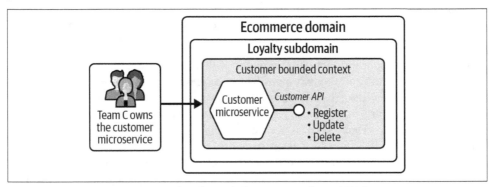

Figure 2-5. A microservice inside a bounded context with its API for interaction

 API governance and discoverability are the two most common issues enterprises face when several teams own and operate APIs. API portals often help discover and consume APIs in a *self-service* model. However, if you are just starting out with your API-first strategy and initial APIs, don't get overburdened with these different processes, as they can be worked on in parallel as you create more APIs and gain experience.

Microservices-first

With a marked boundary (bounded context) and well-defined (micro) interfaces (API), it becomes easier to own and manage the implementation of the business logic. In this context, microservices offer a suitable development pattern to realize the domain logic. Each microservice has a purpose and identity. In most designs, you will find a microservice related to a bounded context as a one-to-one mapping, but that isn't the only option. You saw in Chapter 1 that granularity is one of the unique characteristics of serverless. Utilizing the power of granularity, you can break down the problem domain within a bounded context into several smaller microservices, as shown in the card payments bounded context in Figure 2-6.

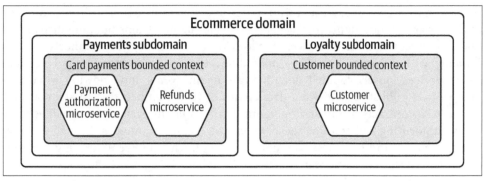

Figure 2-6. Mapping one microservice to a bounded context, versus multiple microservices

A microservice should be owned and operated by one team. Never have two teams share ownership of one microservice. This clear responsibility and business alignment reduces the cognitive load on engineers, thereby increasing development velocity and flow. Chapter 3 discusses designing microservices in detail.

Event driven–first

Asynchronous communication and *event-driven architecture* are terms you will often hear in serverless and throughout this book. These terms sometimes trouble traditional engineering minds that are accustomed to developing monolithic applications using legacy practices and on-premises technologies. Even if the event-driven concept is new to your teams, it is essential that they begin to understand its significance. Asynchronicity, eventual consistency, and event-driven communication are the driving forces behind the managed services that power serverless. To highlight their significance in serverless and modern cloud computing, Dr. Werner Vogels, CTO of Amazon.com, declared in his keynote at AWS's annual re:Invent conference in 2022 that "The world is asynchronous." The core of Dr. Werner's message was to demonstrate how event-driven architecture with serverless technology enables businesses to innovate at scale.

 An *event*, in general, is something that has already happened. A *domain event* is about something that has happened within your business domain. Event-driven architecture (EDA) is an architectural concept that uses events to communicate between decoupled microservices asynchronously. In EDA, there are systems that produce events (producers), systems that consume events (consumers), applications that transport events (event buses, messaging systems, etc.), and systems that react to events. Among several other benefits, EDA is key to the scaling and resiliency of applications.

Approaching serverless adoption with a clear understanding of event-driven concepts and their application in practice is core to stream-aligned teams building distributed and loosely coupled microservices. *Event-driven thinking* elegantly connects *domain thinking* with *serverless thinking*—upholding contractual boundaries and keeping microservices loosely coupled. Identifying domain events and knowing what data goes out (is published) and what data comes in (is subscribed to) are as important as the API contracts. Familiarizing yourself with domain events and activities such as EventStorming is therefore crucial when your organization goes through a digital transformation and serverless adoption. You will learn why EventStorming is essential in serverless development in Chapter 3.

Figure 2-7 shows a simple event-driven architecture where two applications consume an "order placed" event published by an ordering app to update the inventory and ship the order, respectively.

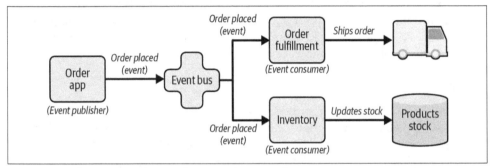

Figure 2-7. Illustration of a simple event-driven architecture

Chapters 3 and 5 discuss event-driven concepts alongside serverless architectures and implementation patterns, respectively.

Serverless-first

When an organization gets ready to adopt serverless, it has already decided on a *cloud-first* strategy utilizing the public cloud (e.g., AWS) to host, develop, and operate its business applications, over on-premises and self-managed legacy systems. *Serverless-first* is a way of thinking that views serverless as the best-fit technology choice to build and operate business applications to deliver value faster.

While discussing how organizations can transform with a clear purpose and increase velocity with modern technologies, in the book *The Value Flywheel Effect: Power the Future and Accelerate Your Organization to the Modern Cloud* (IT Revolution Press), David Anderson sums it up nicely:

> It's about doing the simplest thing to deliver value by removing the unnecessary baggage. Today serverless-first is the perfect strategy to achieve this; it's a quiet revolution

happening right in front of us. A serverless-first mindset enables teams to focus on business outcomes and business impact, not keeping the lights on.

It's about driving value for your business in this modern, fast-paced, and highly competitive world. Organizations are constantly iterating and finding ways to reach customers and bring value to the business quicker than before. As an engineer, architect, or CTO, you are part of the fast-spinning value flywheel. Hence, you must learn to leave the heavy engineering to the managed cloud service providers, such as AWS, and evolve your business solutions on top with a pragmatic and practical mindset. *Serverless-first* as a principle and strategy becomes part of that value-generation process.

Though not an exhaustive list,[1] adopting the principles described in the previous sections will help you broaden your serverless mindset with the essentials crucial for your journey. Building your serverless technology ecosystem without a strong business foundation, team alignment, and clearly defined purpose will eventually lead to ambiguity and unsustainable applications that hamper progress.

Not all enterprises start serverless adoption with exclusively green-field product development. Many have a mix of legacy systems, newer applications, and upcoming future requirements. So, how do you make sure serverless is the best-fit technology choice? The following section takes you through an evaluation process to understand its suitability in your business domain.

Assessing Workloads for Serverless Suitability

A common use case that became popular during the early days of serverless was image processing with Amazon S3 and Lambda functions. It showed how easy it was to upload a file and execute code in the cloud without manual intervention. Countless trivial serverless use cases and how-to articles soon flooded the tech media. While such simple examples give firsthand reports on the possibilities of serverless, enterprises have bigger challenges to overcome (both functional and nonfunctional). These include:

- The complexity of business logic tucked inside legacy monoliths
- Engineering teams spread across multiple departments
- The volume of users flocking to the website to consume the services
- Unpredictability of visitor traffic during certain times, days of the week, and special occasions
- Making sure the services are available around the clock and globally

---

1 Depending on your business domain and priorities, you may also consider principles such as *DevOps-first*, *security-first*, *DevX-first*, *observability-first*, etc.

- Releasing new features and fixes without impacting users
- Securing customers' personal information and confidential business data
- Protecting the business from malicious users, bots, and malware

This list is already long, but the suitability assessment should consider all aspects of the application, not just the implementation part. While a serverless enthusiast might assure you that it's suited to every workload, there are some fundamental questions you should ask. For example:

- Will this application perform *efficiently* on serverless?
- Will it be *cost-effective*?
- Can I trust the serverless expert to be objective?

Efficient and *cost-effective* are tricky to explain in a cloud and serverless context. In distributed computing, being efficient doesn't always relate to speed. *Sufficiently* is an equivalent term that you can use to evaluate suitability in many cases. Similarly, cost-effectiveness does not always mean being cheaper than your on-premises or cloud-hosted container applications in like-for-like comparisons.

> When you assess the suitability of serverless technology with *serverless-first* thinking, you consider serverless as your first technology choice. This does not mean you overrule other technologies with a *serverless-must* mindset.

Understanding the performance measures of distributed serverless applications

Unlike in legacy systems, where performance is mostly measured by the speed of an operation as one big unit, in modern serverless applications, there isn't a simple yardstick to measure performance. This is because there are different parts to an application that can be independently measured for efficiency, and each part can be unique in its criteria. In some cases, you look at each part in isolation and measure the latency; in others, you group a few or all of them to measure the end-to-end performance or the completion of a business process. Here are some examples of possible performance measures for different use cases:

End-to-end efficiency
An API that fetches the price of a given product and returns it to the frontend to display on the website should be highly performant end-to-end, as you don't want a frustrated customer leaving your site for a competitor's. This action crosses several layers in the architecture and chains multiple applications (possibly including external third-party applications) in the flow. Here, the end-to-end latency becomes the measure of efficiency.

Part efficiency

A customer who submits their order as the final step of a checkout flow only cares about receiving a quick acknowledgment to confirm everything is fine. The API that accepts the order details should efficiently serve the customer with a low latency. The actual processing of the order, which is hidden from the customer, still needs to be performant, but not necessarily as efficient as that API. Here, the efficiency is relative to each part.

Deliberate efficiency and inefficiency

In an event-driven architecture, you may deliberately configure one processing pipeline to be faster than another. For example, an image processing website might handle images uploaded by a premium account holder faster than an anonymous customer. Here, you work with serverless resources capable of providing the same efficiency level, but you deliberately downgrade one according to your business policy.

Expected efficiency

When the end-to-end latency is not time-bound, different parts of the solution can have different expected efficiency. For example, there are situations where a microservice expects to receive a domain event as quickly as possible from the producer. However, processing of the event data may take longer or be deferred to later.

Contractual efficiency

This measure is appropriate for use cases where there is time criticality in the flow of information from the start to delivery to a consuming application and the data may become obsolete or non-processable beyond a certain period, defined by SLAs and contract agreements. With ticket booking systems, for example, there is a session validity period; the overall success depends on the customer's actions during the session, but contractual efficiency is required of the application supporting those actions within a session.

 A legacy system that chains multiple applications in a synchronous end-to-end call cannot be considered "efficient" in modern computing if using low latency as the only measure of efficiency. The ability to scale with demand, 24/7 availability, resilience during disruptions, and operating in a secure environment all count toward being performant and efficient.

While assessing your business use cases and applications, you may identify some that are not a perfect match for serverless. These include:

Compute-heavy, complex applications

A compute-heavy engineering application that performs structural analysis and has high memory demands running on a High-Performance Computing (HPC) EC2 instance is one such example. AWS offers HPC-optimized instances as one of the high-end instance types, and you cannot match their power and performance with the resources available to a Lambda function. A serverless application can pick up the results of the computation and continue with the flow, but that core compute part won't be efficient with serverless.

Long-running applications

Certain data processing batch jobs at banks and insurance companies, complex biomedical research tasks, etc., can take a very long time to complete, stretching beyond the timeout limit of a Lambda function. Unless you rearchitect to split a batch into manageable chunks of extract, transform, load (ETL) tasks, you cannot achieve the required efficiency with serverless.

Low-level computing tasks

Highly complex low-level programs require access to the underlying operating system, processors, and networking that are not suitable to operate as Lambda functions.

Applications that must consistently provide ultrafast response times

If you have a highly critical use case where the application is expected to respond within, say, 10 ms for almost 100% of the invocations, regardless of the frequency of invocations, you may find it challenging to meet this expectation with serverless.

Durable connection to ports using proprietary protocols

Legacy integrations that require maintaining connections to ports using nonstandard protocols are not ideal for serverless. Here, you can consider a hybrid architecture that uses container apps for such integrations and serverless to handle the downstream processing.

Assessing for cost-effectiveness

As you saw in the previous chapter, the common understanding around cost in serverless is based on the cost of computing and the volume of data you store. Sounds simple, right? But take another look at the resources shown in Figure 1-10, in "Individuality and Granularity of Resources" on page 14. With different configurations, each of those Lambda functions and DynamoDB tables will vary in cost. In addition, each service sends logs and metrics to Amazon CloudWatch (a service for collecting logs and metrics for monitoring and observability), and the use of CloudWatch adds to the cost. The Lambda functions use services, such as AWS Secrets Manager, to store and read credentials that also contribute to overall spending. Though you are not expected to unpick the costs of every service and its associations with others at a granular level, some overall awareness and understanding are valuable. Chapter 9 discusses in detail the cost of serverless operation, but here are some examples of assessments of various use cases and how they influence the cost:

Compute-intensive data processing
> The back-office computing operation of a big corporation continuously runs highly complex, long-running data manipulation jobs. Several processes run in parallel as the data gets fed in from branch offices worldwide. Each process takes around 10 minutes to complete and handles, on average, 7 GB of data.
>
> *Assessment*: This is a clean use case for Lambda functions, with the resource requirements within its limits. However, with several long-running Lambda functions with high consumption of RAM constantly being invoked, the cost of computing could become a concern here.
>
> *Verdict*: Consider rearchitecting to achieve cost-effectiveness with serverless. For example, splitting each batch into smaller batches requires functions with lower memory needs and shorter execution times.

Ingestion and processing of data from thousands of IoT devices
> An environmental agency measures the air quality of cities worldwide, receiving data feeds from hundreds of thousands of devices multiple times per day. Data is cleansed and analyzed as the feeds come in before storing the consolidated and essential details in a big data platform. A team of dedicated engineers currently looks after the infrastructure and data storage needs.
>
> *Assessment*: This is a cost-effective use case to migrate to serverless. In addition to the powerful and low-cost data streaming services available for ingestion, processing, and storage, there is a potential to reduce the engineering hours spent on managing the current infrastructure.
>
> *Verdict*: Potential cost savings with serverless in different areas. For example, Amazon Kinesis offers a high-volume event ingestion service and with the combination of S3, Lambda, and other fully managed services, you can implement a resilient and highly scalable architecture.

High volume of CloudWatch metrics calls
> A popular online retail platform has its backend applications running as several microservices. The frontend and backend applications send a high volume of logs and metrics to a third-party monitoring tool for observability and business insights. Several dashboards and metric queries are performed by teams that look after the business in multiple countries.
>
> *Assessment*: Migrating the backend microservices to serverless would bring scalability and availability benefits. In terms of collecting and reporting on logs and metrics, CloudWatch has options that can be utilized to send data to third-party

monitoring tools. However, the volume and the length of logs stored in Cloud-Watch must be assessed for cost, and the high number of CloudWatch metrics API calls can result in costly operation.

Verdict: Find the optimal log retention period to lower the cost. Rearchitect to send (stream) metrics to the third-party tool to minimize the metric query API calls and reduce costs.

 All managed services within the serverless technology ecosystem offer automated ways to remove unwanted data and transition static data to low-cost storage. Unlike legacy applications that go through routine cleanup operations that are costly, risky, and often disruptive, serverless offers efficient and smooth operations with no side effects. Such measures also aid you in operating sustainably as you consume fewer cloud resources.

As you can imagine, it would be impossible to cover all the different flavors of real-world use cases here to analyze performance and cost efficiency measures. Your use cases will differ from the ones we've discussed, and from those you see elsewhere. When you are looking for someone to guide you at a crossroads, reach out to AWS teams and the serverless developer community for direction.

Once you understand the appropriate efficiency measures for your applications and use cases and have determined that serverless is a good fit, you'll face one of the main challenges of serverless adoption: convincing the people you work with about its merits. Some people will be on a different wavelength than you are with new technologies and ways to utilize them for business gains. In enterprises, getting the message across to all the relevant teams can take considerable time and perseverance. Business stakeholders are a vital group to work with, and the next section focuses on bringing them into the serverless ecosystem.

How Do You Bring Serverless Awareness to Business Stakeholders?

Convincing product teams and business stakeholders of the necessity of a new technology is a tough ask. Though they may not directly influence the choice of technology, they're responsible for the final approval in many enterprises. Surprisingly or otherwise, in such situations, the main reason these stakeholders reject new technology is often fear of change—and the two main fear factors center around business disruption and cost of operation.

Business disruption does not always mean service unavailability or downtime. Stakeholders may fear technology change because of the risk of poorer quality of service, customer revolt, performance degradations, reduced business insights, changes to developer velocity that affect outcome and flow, and more. Moreover, many enterprises still operate in siloed team structures where business stakeholders are not always kept updated on upcoming technology changes and often only learn about changes when things go badly, or through hearsay from peers and canteen gossip, which is unhealthy for any organization.

Serverless adoption adds extra mystery for your stakeholders, because it's not always well understood. If engineers find a serverless mindset is hard to attain, you can imagine the difficulty for others. Hence, it's essential to keep the stakeholders in the loop and start the conversations with them as early as possible.

Speak a common language, and avoid serverless language

Does serverless have a language? Well, it depends on how you talk about it! At least during the early days of selling serverless to stakeholders, try not to use specific service names such as Lambda, DynamoDB, and S3 or possibly unfamiliar phrases like managed services, FaaS, SaaS, etc. You should not expect everyone to know what these are. Instead, use universal terms like cloud, programs, functions, databases, tables, and files, and understandable flows such as "a function is called or executed when the user enters data," "data is stored in a table," "a notification is sent when a customer account is created," etc.

 While working on solution designs, include high-level context and flow diagrams with basic notations for everyone to understand the problem domain. Keep the cloud and serverless service icons and technical drawings aimed at engineers in a detailed design section.

Invite stakeholders to team showcases

If your teams conduct regular sprint reviews or showcases to demonstrate their work that includes serverless experimentation or PoCs, these are ideal opportunities to invite business stakeholders. Even if these showcases are tech-heavy, they can still provide clues about the utility of serverless to observers from outside the teams. Phrases like "Serverless works great in this case," "We were able to develop this quickly," "This prototype can be easily extended further with serverless services," etc., are the kinds of signals that can trigger curiosity and further conversations with non-engineering colleagues.

If that's not feasible in your organization due to the team structure or culture, arrange special product demo meetings with the relevant stakeholder teams. This is a practical approach as it brings everyone together and is suited to a question-and-answer format that can encourage nontechnical people to get involved in the conversation.

When engineering teams interact closely with stakeholders, they should remember to speak the common language mentioned earlier. They can also use simple logical model diagrams, like the one in Figure 2-8, to make sure everyone understands the context, explain the approach, and highlight the benefits to the business.

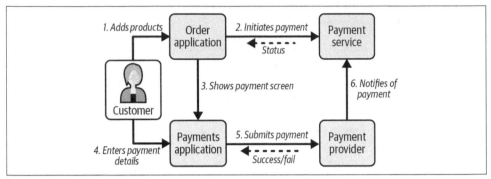

Figure 2-8. A simple logical flow diagram showing the interactions between a user, order application, and payments system

Map technology reasons to business gains

As an engineer, you likely get disgruntled when a business stakeholder rejects or overlooks your proposal to improve certain technical aspects of the system. While you are good at diving deep into the technicalities of your recommendations, perhaps you could be better at correlating them with the business gains for your nontechnical colleagues to digest. The following are a few examples of how to translate technical improvements into recognizable business gains:

1. *Technical reason for using queues*: Serverless offers many benefits by allowing you to use managed services in your implementation. Amazon Simple Queue Service (SQS) is a highly scalable and hugely popular message queue service. It is one of the core services used in event-driven architectures, capable of ingesting hundreds of thousands of messages. It allows downstream services such as a Lambda function to process messages either one at a time or in batches, enabling frontend applications to receive a high volume of requests.

   Stakeholder translation: The serverless queue service allows us to serve more customers. It easily handles fluctuating customer demand and always provides a fast response.

2. *Technical reason for using automated data deletion*: DynamoDB is a high-performing NoSQL database. One of its features is TTL, to set an expiry time. By enabling TTL on a table and adding a timestamp in epoch format to an item, you can ensure that DynamoDB will automatically remove that item from the table once the expiry time is reached. This allows you to optimize storage requirements and ensure that old items are removed or that sensitive data is deleted soon after processing to comply with regulatory requirements.

Stakeholder translation: Automatically deleting data after keeping it for the length of time required by the business reduces the amount of data stored and, thereby, the storage cost.

 Engineering teams' interaction with business stakeholders is not a one-time affair but an ongoing collaboration. Following on from the initial icebreaker meeting on serverless, invite them to witness the progress of every iteration. The goal should be to provide as much visibility into the new technology as possible and demonstrate how it accelerates business.

Highlight the serverless cost benefits

As you saw in Chapter 1, *pay-per-use* is a fundamental driver behind serverless adoption, and it sparks a lot of interest. It is beneficial to highlight the possible cloud spending economies that can be achieved by using serverless during stakeholder interactions. To make the message stick, staying at a high level and not delving into more minor details is essential. For example, if you're discussing the execution of a few Lambda functions to perform some business logic, stay at the level of the number of invocations per month and the expected overall cost; don't split it into invocation costs, compute costs, etc.

An important aspect of serverless is the reduction in the amount of time spent on managing the infrastructure. This unique advantage should be brought up during conversations with stakeholders and explained in an understandable manner. Though applications built with serverless technology still require operational activities, serverless frees engineers from infrastructure and platform heavy lifting, thus saving considerable engineering time.

Discuss the convenience of serverless as a technology

Though lower cloud costs is a key driver for serverless, you must illustrate its other benefits to the business stakeholders as well. Solutions built for the modern consumer world have many demands. For example:

- Applications are expected to be highly secure and withstand brutal cyberattacks.
- Companies are pressured to comply with regulatory policies to protect personally identifiable information (PII) and other sensitive data.
- Customer demands constantly fluctuate; keeping them engaged and serving them faster is crucial.

As technology evolves, it pulls the entire industry along with it, moving faster with each iteration. Organizations often get caught in this flywheel with little time to react. As a result:

- Businesses are looking for the *easiest* way to run their workloads.
- Stakeholders are looking for the *fastest* way to release a feature.
- Engineers are looking for the *safest* way to handle data.
- Customers are looking for the *simplest* way to purchase a product.

The COVID-19 pandemic of 2020 shook every corner of our world. While many businesses went through hardship, some thrived even during those dark days as they quickly adapted to the world's changing needs, making course corrections on a practically daily basis. For many of them, it was the convenience and flexibility of serverless that made the difference. According to a BBC survey, new company registrations in the UK actually increased during the COVID-19 lockdown period, as shown in Figure 2-9.

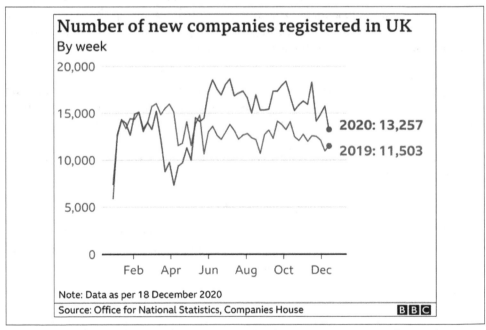

Figure 2-9. Statistics showing the increase in new business registrations during the COVID-19 lockdown period

Working from home, engineers were able to capitalize on the capabilities of cloud and serverless to launch new products and services and rapidly deliver them to consumers' living rooms. Serverless technology enables anyone to build and operate global-scale applications from anywhere. Along with its cost benefits, you must bring the *convenience* of delivering solutions faster using serverless technology to the attention of business stakeholders.

Talk about serverless success stories

Identify serverless adoption success stories from the industry and invite people from those organizations to share their experiences with stakeholders. This information is relevant to both engineering and business teams, but ensure the content is balanced and suitable for both audiences. To make these collaborations efficient, create a clear agenda and share it with the teams in advance. Though not always possible, hearing serverless success stories from organizations that operate in a similar business domain as yours can help stakeholders relate and understand the applicability of serverless quickly. Refer to the serverless case studies included in Appendixes A and B as a guide to preparing your agenda and discussion points.

Here are a few points you might want to cover in your success stories:

- Business pain points or constraints with the legacy technology
- Motivation behind moving to serverless
- Business and technology teams' buy-in on serverless
- Development approach, including team structures and communication
- Benefits since migrating to serverless
- Lessons learned and things to be aware of

You might also want to identify and invite serverless experts—independent consultants, AWS solution architects, and serverless training providers—to share their experiences.

The Role of Organizational Culture

Organizational culture, which can be expressed in various ways—corporate principles, mottos, enterprise themes, business ethics, company values, etc.—plays a vital role in successful adoption of serverless. Enterprises often strive for a culture that favors innovation, bravery, and curiosity. Though not always successful, the aim is to instill a culture that encourages experimentation and removes the fear of failure from its employees. Jeff Lawson narrates this beautifully in his book *Ask Your Developer: How to Harness the Power of Software Developers and Win in the 21st Century* (Harper Business). Experimentation is the prerequisite to innovation, and every big idea starts small. Thinking, trialing, succeeding, and adopting serverless in your organization requires such an environment and culture.

The two camps of serverless adoption

In engineering teams, it is common to find two camps of people: those with a practical mindset versus a purist mindset. Purists often look for perfection in everything, invest in processes before practice (establishing development and coding guidelines before acquiring an in-depth knowledge and understanding of the technology, or outlining detailed operational procedures before gaining hands-on experience), are reluctant to take risks, and tend to follow a safer path. On the other hand, those with a practical mindset experiment in small steps, look for a workable solution first rather than perfection, and improve incrementally and iteratively. Faced with the rapid evolutionary pace of technology, those with a practical mindset tend to be able to adapt and move faster than perfectionists, who often get bogged down in lengthy processes and left behind.

The organizational culture plays a vital part in the attitude and approach of these teams. Lack of encouragement for experimentation can be a factor, but it can also be due to engineers with a legacy mindset who are unwilling to change. If your organization operates in a consumer domain, the competition is stiff, and customer needs change frequently. With the exception of those who work in a research and development (R&D) environment predicting and devising the future of technology, everyone else is constantly climbing the technology curve after it has evolved. Hence, it is paramount to create the mindset that will enable you to be part of the fast adoption camp, as shown in Figure 2-10.

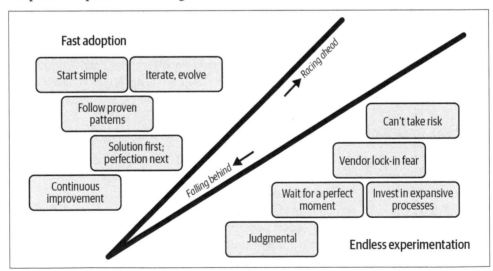

Figure 2-10. The two ways of approaching serverless: fast adoption versus endless experimentation

The magic quadrant for serverless adoption

Amazon founder Jeff Bezos once said, "Speed matters in business." Speed is also important when it comes to successful serverless adoption, as the previous section showed. If you draw a four-quadrant chart with success and speed of adoption on the two axes, as shown in Figure 2-11, which quadrant would you like your organization to be in?

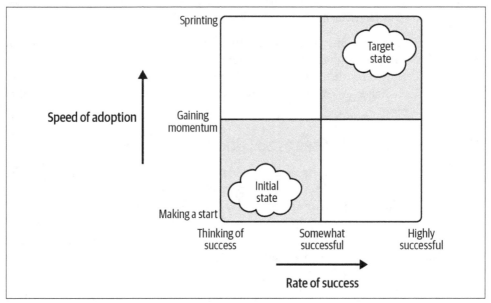

Figure 2-11. The serverless adoption magic quadrant

As you start your serverless adoption journey, you are at the initial state shown in the bottom-left quadrant. Your aim is to reach the target state quadrant at the top right. For this, you need speed and a high success rate.

When it comes to technology adoption, speed is relative—it's not about attaining a certain velocity (like a car traveling east at 100 mph), but about experimenting with the technology sooner rather than being slow to try it out. The faster you identify, evaluate, and adopt suitable modern technologies, the faster you'll understand how to accelerate your business. Start with some of the best practices highlighted in Figure 2-10, and make sure you thoroughly understand the first principles of serverless adoption explained earlier in this chapter. You don't want to go so fast that you spin out of control!

There can be many hazards and speed bumps on the road to serverless adoption. One of them, as mentioned in Figure 2-10, is the fear of vendor lock-in. We'll look at that next.

Vendor Lock-in Demystified

Vendor lock-in is a hotly debated topic in cloud adoption, and serverless in particular. It creates fear among technology decision-makers, curbs progress, and creates confusion. Although in the modern cloud era people often associate the term *vendor* with a cloud provider and *lock-in* with a cloud platform, the concept is not new, and certainly not specific to cloud or serverless—these are generic terms that are also applicable to non–cloud technology providers and products.

Vendor lock-in is a condition an organization gets into by becoming dependent on the specific vendor of a given product or platform they use. This typically happens because switching to a different product or platform from another vendor would incur technical challenges, resulting in high porting or migration costs and potential service disruption.

Why Is Vendor Lock-in Seen as So Critical?

The choice of any technology, product, or platform results in some form of lock-in, be it a programming language, RDBMS, payroll application, customer relationship management system, enterprise resource planning software, or cloud platform. And although it can be challenging and time-consuming, at some point every enterprise moves from one technology, product, or platform to another, whether for reasons of cost, feature richness, ease of use, better SLAs, the needs of the company's product teams, or to gain a competitive advantage.

When it comes to the cloud and consuming managed services, cost is a critical differentiator. With serverless, you consume several cloud services to compose your application, each with its own pricing structure. If the cost of a critical service you consume is higher with your current provider than with others, you might decide to switch to its equivalent in another provider. However, your options will likely be limited, as it will disrupt the functioning of your application. Many enterprises face such decisions. Often, it makes more sense to consider all the advantages the current platform yields rather than comparing individual services.

Is It Possible to Avoid Getting Locked In?

Well, maybe. Selecting a cloud provider to grow your business is a conscious business decision. While it may be possible to avoid lock-in in some parts of your serverless operation (e.g., by implementing function logic in a cloud-agnostic way), whether the extra effort yields sufficient benefit is something to be evaluated.

Here are some ways you might consider to reduce the dangers of lock-in:

Open API standards

In software, conformance to API standards allows you to consume solutions from different vendors who conform to the same standard. Unlike with electrical equipment, pure plug-and-play compatibility is rare in software, and you'll probably need to make some changes to your code. However, following standards reduces the complexities.

Open source software

You might be wondering if using open source software can get you out of lock-in. Unfortunately, it's unlikely. Open source software may not have a cloud provider's name associated with it, but product lock-in is still an issue. In an enterprise, switching from one open source product to another is not as simple as it sounds in marketing speak. One can argue that the impact may be low compared to changing cloud platforms, but it is a business disruption, nevertheless.

 To operate open source software for the needs of a globally distributed modern consumer base, you require scalability, availability, security, and resiliency. You will likely run it on a cloud platform to achieve all these goals. Even if you use containers and bare metal, switching from one platform to another does involve effort and disruption.

Software patterns

Architectural patterns (such as hexagonal architecture, discussed in Chapter 3) can help you architect and build your solution in a way that provides encapsulation around the data assets, for example. Though the details of how the pattern is realized are specific to a given platform or provider, you can usually implement the same pattern as it was initially intended on another platform. If your team follows the solution design process, you will likely incorporate the design patterns that fit the purpose. As Mike Roberts, author of *Programming AWS Lambda* (O'Reilly), opines, if 90% of your Lambda function code is unaware of running in a Lambda function, then only 10% of it will need to be recoded if you move to a different cloud provider's compute host environment.

Patterns won't eliminate the lock-in but will speed up your implementation efforts on the target platform by acting as a blueprint to replicate the solution quickly.

Should You Be Worried About Vendor Lock-in in Serverless?

Managed services from cloud providers take care of the undifferentiated heavy lifting, to let you focus on building business solutions. Though many of these services align regarding their purpose on each cloud platform, they do not follow common standards to enable you to move seamlessly from one provider to another. Due to the nature of cloud services, switching between providers can be confusing, costly, and time-consuming.

Should this cause you concern with regard to your plans to adopt serverless in your organization? Provided that you're aware of the matter, have a clear understanding of the pros and cons of your selected cloud platform and provider, and carefully choose the services you build your applications with, it's not really a concern but a business or corporate decision.

In making this decision, you'll likely have to weigh different priorities, such as:

- Business growth
- Gaining and maintaining a competitive edge
- Development velocity (releasing features faster)
- Satisfying your customers with their ever-changing demands
- Bringing value to the business

You can either make trade-offs among these priorities or spend X amount of extra time, engineering effort, and cost trying to find the perfect solution. Along the way, you'll probably reinvent many wheels with the unrealistic long-term goal of achieving *technical purity*, not business velocity.

Gregor Hohpe, an enterprise architecture strategist and author of *Cloud Strategy— A Decision-Based Approach to Successful Cloud Migration*, highlights the *mental lock-in* in certain situations that affects people's thinking based on their experience or situations they are familiar with. The most important thing is to not get into a state where the vendor lock-in causes a mental lock-down that curbs your progress and stops you moving forward by delivering value and business growth.

Consider the Cloud Provider (AWS) as Your Partner, Not a Vendor

The change of mindset that's necessary when you work with serverless goes beyond technology. Often, the way you work with the cloud and third-party application providers also requires adjustment. After all, everyone—yourself, your team, the organization, and third parties—should work together to bring value to the business. Your cloud provider, who runs your serverless workloads, is also part of the equation.

The term *vendor* refers to someone who sells or trades. It originated as a description of the street vendors who sell various consumer goods and then evolved to cover business establishments and enterprises that sell industrial products, retail goods, and software applications. When you buy a license to install and use a database application, you take care of most of its day-to-day operation yourself. You contact the vendor only when you encounter an issue with the product.

The situation is different in the cloud, where you consume multiple services—both infrastructure-heavy container applications and fully managed serverless services—to compose your business applications. Consequently, you form a working relationship with your cloud provider to identify the most efficient and cost-effective services for your business and the optimal operational configurations. Furthermore, when your team prepares for special events such as new product launches, movie trailer releases, or festive sale events such as Black Friday, you seek your cloud provider's expertise and work with their infrastructure event management (IEM) team to get your organization through the occasion smoothly.

There should be mutual trust between your organization as a cloud service consumer and your cloud service provider. This partnership is more warm and cordial than your typical impersonal third-party vendor relationship.

Strategies for Migrating Legacy Applications to Serverless

Perhaps surprisingly, the questions companies ask when they're thinking about adopting serverless are often not related to technology, but strategy. Back in 2010, when the cloud was gaining attention (and serverless wasn't even a word!), Gartner published its 5 Rs model (*https://oreil.ly/Ilryo*) as a framework for developing a strategy for migrating to the cloud: Rehost, Refactor, Revise, Rebuild, or Replace. Later, Stephen Orban, author of *Ahead in the Cloud: Best Practices of Navigating the Future of Enterprise IT* (CreateSpace), created the 6 Rs strategy: Rehost, Replatform, Repurchase, Refactor, Retire, and Retain. While these strategies focus on cloud migration as a whole, they are relevant to serverless adoption as well.

Every technology migration has challenges. Compared to a start-up, with a simple domain, a smaller customer base, and fewer employees, enterprises have many strategic angles to contemplate before deciding on a serverless migration strategy. These include:

- The experience and relevant skills of their engineering teams (i.e., whether they will be able to successfully execute the migration tasks)
- Making the business stakeholders understand the technology, the necessity of migration, and its business impact
- A clear assessment of the impact on customers worldwide or in specific areas where the business operates
- Presenting the case to the executive team and the board of directors
- Possibly, assuring the shareholders of their investment's benefits and monetary value

For an organization serving customers 24×7, unsurprisingly, customer impact is usually the first question raised about migration. In our competitive business world, a minor blip in one's trading can lead to significant gains for someone else.

Downtime and Disruption

Every technology migration raises two common concerns: service downtime and disruption. Service downtime is when an entire application or parts of it become unavailable to its end users. It may be planned or unplanned. Depending on how the system is architected and built, disruption during downtime can be severe, minimal, or nonexistent.

Whereas with scheduled downtime there are usually defined steps (a playbook) to keep the system operational, unexpected disruption requires problem investigation and mitigation. Depending on the nature of the root cause, the disruption can be minor or devastating.

With cloud and modern architectural patterns, consumers expect 100% uptime of services. Even a few milliseconds of downtime in a competitive consumer market could be extremely costly. Hence, serverless migration tasks should be well-thought-out and carefully coordinated activities.

Convincing your business and stakeholders about the benefits of serverless is only part of the process, as soon after you will be asked questions like the following:

- What do we do with the acres of tech spread across our organization?
- How do we decide which applications are suitable for the serverless stack?
- How quickly can we move everything over to serverless?

The standard answer to all such questions in the software industry is, *it depends*! And while the appropriate strategy does depend on your domain, the state of existing applications, their complexity, etc., you must be able to offer the proper guidance. In the following sections, we'll take a look at the three most common serverless migration approaches:

- Lift-and-shift
- All-at-once service rewrite
- Phased migration

Lift-and-Shift

Lift-and-shift as a migration strategy is synonymous with rehosting—lifting the application from its current platform and hosting it in the cloud. Though lift-and-shift was once the most common cloud migration strategy, its popularity is steadily declining. As you have observed already in this book, serverless has unique characteristics. To reap the real benefits of serverless, you must build applications that utilize the strengths of managed services and employ modern development practices. A lift-and-shift approach does not do this, and hence it's considered the least favored approach for serverless.

That said, there are some situations where specific workloads can be lifted and shifted with some scaffolding and care, often as a stopgap solution or short-term plan. AWS Fargate and AWS App Runner are two services that can provide stopgap solutions to shift a legacy application onto a container service first before fronting it with an AWS API Gateway endpoint and migrating the backend to AWS Lambda.

Suitability

Applications migrated to serverless with a lift-and-shift approach primarily originate from two domains:

- A self-managed on-premises setup
- A cloud-hosted container stack

Here are some examples of applications where lifting and shifting to serverless with minimal effort may be suitable:

- Applications developed with the most recent technologies and following modern development practices
- Modular applications written in a language supported by the AWS Lambda runtime
- Self-contained microservices that do not bring a deeper dependency chain and keep the deployment artifact size within reasonable limits
- Containerized applications suitable to package as a container image and run as Lambda functions
- Batch jobs with resource requirements that are within the limits of Lambda

Migration considerations

Here are some important characteristics to consider before continuing with a lift-and-shift migration:

Timeouts

As a FaaS, Lambda has a timeout limit (15 minutes at the time of writing). If re-creating REST APIs on Amazon API Gateway, it has a timeout of 29 seconds.

Memory limits

A Lambda function can be allocated a maximum of 10 GB RAM (at the time of writing).

Payload size constraints

The data payload sizes of cloud services differ. It's not just about the API request and response payload; events and messages pushed to queues also have size constraints to comply with.

Code package and container image size limits

At the time of writing, the maximum deployment package size is 50 MB for a *.zip* archive and 250 MB for unzipped files, and the size limit for container image deployment packages is 10 GB.

Concurrency limits

Lambda has a default concurrent execution limit per account (you can request AWS to raise it with a valid use case). Knowledge of the limits of managed services is important before migrating to avoid throttling and failures.

Monoliths and big balls of mud

Lifting and shifting a monolithic application with tangled communications and hard dependencies and running it as-is in serverless may not be ideal. It may end up as a ball of serverless mud, as shown in Figure 2-2—a dampener for serverless adoption.

All-at-Once Service Rewrite

Applications developed with a serverless-native approach benefit from using the full potential of managed services. For example, if your legacy application stores binary large objects (BLOBs) in its relational database, you will find Amazon S3 is the better storage option as the application is migrated to serverless.

Rewriting the business logic confined inside your legacy application enables you to untangle the hard dependencies and rearchitect it as event-driven and loosely coupled microservices to support future scaling and business growth. Migrating legacy monolithic applications to microservices requires a good understanding of the business domain and microservices principles and patterns. Sam Newman's book

Monolith to Microservices (O'Reilly) is a great resource on this topic and covers several migration patterns.

Workload suitability

An all-at-once service rewrite is a useful migration strategy for just about any workload, with the exception of a few outliers mentioned in "Assessing Workloads for Serverless Suitability" on page 47. Apart from those special cases, serverless technology is well suited for most applications in this modern world.

Here are a few use cases as a guide, but bear in mind that this is not an exhaustive list:

High-volume event ingestion and processing
There are a range of workloads that ingest, store, process, and distribute events in high volume. For example, website clickstream events reveal user behavior and offer opportunities for personalization. When you multiply hundreds of events generated per customer visit by thousands or millions of customers concurrently browsing the website, you get the potential scale of this operation.

The number of visitors to the website can vary dramatically depending on the time of the day, day of the week, season of the year, special occasions, weather patterns, and global and local economic and political events. A simple architecture is enough for scaling, availability, and near-real-time processing.

Scheduling and activating a large number of tasks
Organizations often have several business functions that run on a schedule: expired session data cleanup, policy renewal reminders, special occasion greetings, etc. Some are deliberately scheduled to happen at a particular time of day, such as batch jobs set to run when energy consumption is low, or low-priority tasks scheduled for when fewer users are using the services. You can use serverless services to schedule millions of one-time and recurring tasks, eliminating mundane and inefficient custom logic.

Highly scalable backend applications
A variety of backend applications power both small- and large-scale web applications. As you saw in the event-streaming example, the scale of operation of these applications varies. The volume of users, the unpredictability of visitor patterns, and the ease of extending the services are some of the basic concerns of enterprises that operate in ecommerce, insurance, finance, gaming, multimedia, and other domains. Once they've successfully migrated to serverless, organizations will see a reduction in their total cost of ownership (TCO) and, critically, will have a technology platform that allows them to innovate faster.

Big data and data lakes
Successful organizations collect and use data in the right way. The more useful the data, the better. Organizations that battle with legacy tech stacks constrained

by the vertically scalable nature of databases can benefit immensely from server-less. AWS offers a variety of data stores as managed services to operate with unimaginable volumes of data—there's a data store for every type of data in AWS. With the services offered for data lakes and lake formation, running analyses and building insights, archiving and deleting data, etc., teams can focus on extracting value from the data to make data-driven business decisions.

 Data-driven is a strategy where business decisions are made based on evidence found in the data. Data-driven organizations collect and analyze data to find insights that enable them to make informed decisions, rather than making hasty decisions without any solid basis. To make decisions based on data, companies require the technical capabilities to ingest, process, store, analyze, interpret, and report on vital clues and patterns that emerge from the data landscape—hence the necessity for big data platforms and related services.

Migration risks

Here are some of the risk factors to understand before opting for an all-at-once migration:

Misunderstanding of serverless technology
While discussing the structure of this book, we spent a considerable amount of time on the content of the first two chapters. We deliberately decided to start from the basics to provide a solid foundation rather than diving straight into technical details. A mistake often repeated during serverless adoption is jumping in headfirst without a clear understanding of serverless technology or whether it's actually a good fit for your business. Familiarity with the characteristics of serverless (described in Chapter 1) and how to assess your workloads for suitability is crucial.

Inadequate or poor planning
Trying to make a quick start on serverless without a thorough understanding and deep thinking is like building on sand. You won't be able to extend your solution to add services and features on the initial foundation. It's important to take the time to lay the groundwork for successful serverless adoption, taking into account the first principles and other factors outlined in this chapter.

Time and cost
Rearchitecting and rewriting legacy applications using serverless technologies will pose challenges and can become time-consuming and costly. When facing situations beyond your team's capabilities, seek help from AWS and serverless experts sooner rather than later, as lost engineering time is expensive.

If you are up against moving a mountain of a task, pause, have a rethink, and see if the phased migration approach explained in the following section suits you better.

Legacy influence

As you move to serverless development, you will inevitably carry your past experience with you—but it's important not to make the same mistakes or fall into the same trenches. Rewriting legacy systems demands fresh thinking and the mindset change explained earlier. Let everything be new, including your thinking.

Phased Migration

For organizations with many subdomains and applications that use different technologies spread across many teams, an all-at-once service rewrite is impractical. A phased migration with an incremental approach will suit them better, as it gives them more control and provides greater visibility of the progress. The duration of each phase will depend on the domain complexity, criticality, availability of engineering expertise, and business priorities.

If your enterprise is entirely new to serverless, start in a noncritical business area as your first phase. For example, suppose the head office runs several nightly data consolidation jobs to generate downloadable daily reports for internal teams. This is a non-customer-facing and non-business-critical area with relatively low impact. It's a perfect use case to launch your serverless adoption. Once you have successfully completed your first serverless migration, you can showcase your success to build further momentum for subsequent use cases.

Once you have grown your team of serverless engineers and gained experience with successful product migrations, you may plan for parallel migration phases depending on business priorities and technical fluency, but make sure you don't end up in a situation where you chase two rabbits and catch none!

Organizational suitability

As with an all-at-once service rewrite, a phased migration is suitable for almost any workload. However, certain organizational principles are essential for this approach to succeed:

Clear vision

Migrating applications to serverless in phases is like making strategic moves on a chessboard. It requires a high-level business vision with clarity and purpose. Business stakeholders, engineering leads, and architects should collaborate to plan each phase and the dependencies between the phases.

Long-term growth plan

For a success-oriented organization, serverless adoption is not a mere cost-saving measure but a growth strategy. Migrating suitable applications to serverless is like the cherry on top of a cloud cake! Enterprises that successfully start with serverless witness increased development velocity and product release cycles. Serverless acts as a catalyst for those with a clear growth strategy for the future.

Focus on continuous improvement

Modern development teams follow a rigorous incremental and iterative product delivery cycle. As explained in Chapter 1, as a technology, serverless is ideal for such a development practice. Unlike with the legacy waterfall model and its maintenance phase, modern agile teams engage in continuous refactoring and improvement. This is a required trait for serverless as the technology is evolving so fast. Teams with the right attitude can benefit from a phased migration as they constantly improve, feeding from one phase to the next. (In Chapter 11, you will learn about the measures you can take to keep up with the evolution of serverless.)

Migration considerations

In addition to the risk factors described for an all-at-once service rewrite strategy, here are some things to watch out for with a phased migration:

Dependencies between the phases

As you migrate from on-premises to serverless, you will inevitably find yourself with a mix of cloud and legacy stacks to manage. Managing the dependencies between them can cause technical issues. Having APIs to communicate between the applications in different stacks reduces the complexity, but you cannot expect these to be available in all cases.

Getting stranded due to unforeseen complexities

Unexpected technical challenges are common in software engineering, and serverless migration is no exception. A delay in the completion of one phase can cause delays in other dependent phases. This may cause tension between the teams and can lead to blaming the technology itself.

Service disruptions and unhappy customers

With a phased migration strategy, unpleasant situations can arise due to the incompatibility of services on different stacks (API protocols, data formats, programming languages, synchronous versus asynchronous operations, etc.). The service limits on the two sides may also differ, and it is essential to find common ground for services to mitigate service disruptions impacting customers.

Comparing Migration Strategies

Take a look at Figures 2-12 and 2-13, which compare the three strategies based on time to completion and level of risk.

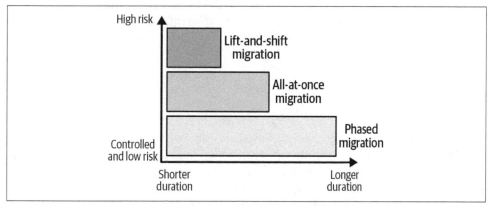

Figure 2-12. Serverless migration strategies based on time to completion

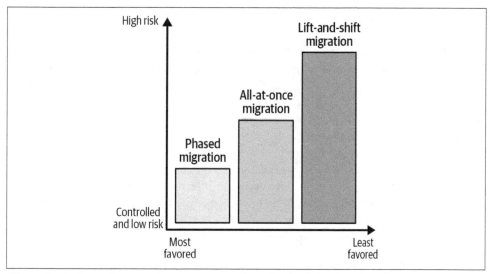

Figure 2-13. Serverless migration strategies based on risk level and preference

Once you have gained knowledge of the technology, identified the appropriate workloads to migrate, and charted a transition strategy, there's one more important area to focus on. This is perhaps the most crucial factor of the ecosystem: the engineers. Their attitudes and skills will be a defining factor in the success of your organization's serverless journey. We will complete this chapter by looking at ways to develop your knowledge base.

In some business scenarios it may be appropriate to apply a mix of strategies. Whether you take an all-at-once or phased migration approach, you may decide to retain some complex and core logic in its existing form but change the code around it to fit within the new environment. For example, suppose you are rewriting legacy logic as Lambda functions using TypeScript. However, there is a critical piece of logic originally written in C# that you prefer not to rewrite. You can use the .NET runtime for AWS Lambda with minimal changes to the event handling part of the function.

Growing Serverless Talent

The renowned author Robin Sharma once said "the swiftest way to grow a company is to grow its people." People are the most valuable commodity in every organization, and it's important to nurture and care for this asset. Along with technological advancements, engineers' growth is attributed to their soft skills, happiness, self-esteem, attitude, and belonging, among other things. Improvements, however, don't happen overnight but are made over time with adequate support.

Growing Versus Building

Why do we talk about "growing" serverless talent? Growing is organic, whereas building is a matter of assembling and joining components. To build something, you source the parts and raw materials, employ labor, and make a blueprint or equivalent. Enterprises often apply the *fast-track build* principle to quickly make a product by hiring specialist consultants, doing a bit of team scaffolding, and setting it to work. Though this approach may produce the intended outcome, it doesn't necessarily grow the skills of the engineering staff or promote a culture of togetherness and belonging. Driven by business pressure and a need for fast outcomes, leaders disregard the distribution of knowledge from the consultants to internal engineers. This is a mistake teams make time and time again. A failure to grow the internal serverless knowledge base can be devastating for an organization in the long run, resulting in a lack of commitment and ownership of applications (or services and features).

Growing talent takes time and effort, though. If a fast-track build approach generates the expected product outcome, why endure the hardship? The answer is in the philosophy mentioned earlier: *the swiftest way to grow a company is to grow its people!* When there is no people growth, there is no team growth. When there is no team growth, there is no organizational growth. Needless to say, in such organizations there won't be any serverless growth either.

So, how can you grow serverless engineers and teams in your organization? Organic growth takes time. Do you have the patience and energy to embark on a growth mission?

The Demoralizing Fast-Track Build Formula

The fast-track development mantra is common in the software industry. This approach comprises the following phases:

Hiring consultants

> In the initial phase, talent acquisition teams in an organization reach out to industry experts and enter into fixed-term contracts to utilize their expertise, agreeing to pay a premium price.

Assembling a team

> Forming a team in this context is mainly a matter of assembling a collection of individuals capable of performing the tasks required to develop the desired solution. Depending on the engineers' specialist skills, they take possession of different parts of the serverless ecosystem (architecture, tooling, testing, operations, etc.), reflecting a siloed setup within the team itself.

Developing the product(s)

> The serverless development, in this setup, is based on the experiences the individual engineers bring in. Usually, the most aptly skilled engineer will take the lead and replicate their experience. The team's main goal is to build the product quickly, not to lay the groundwork for future projects in the organization.

Delivering the product(s)

> Deploying the products in the production environment to the satisfaction of the business stakeholders marks the completion of the work. Management will start reducing the team size at this stage to reduce costs. In the majority of cases, the operational aspects of the product will become the responsibility of internal teams.

Dispersing the team

> Retaining consultants once they've served their core purpose is costly, so they rapidly get offboarded from the team and organization. This may happen as soon as their contracted term ends or more gradually, depending on the agreement. Once the experts are all gone, the internal engineers, who never received proper training or knowledge transfer, become the *maintenance team* for the product. These engineers are often the most demoralized people in an organization.

With the fast-track template now in place, enterprise teams get sucked into a spinning flywheel as a shortcut to success. The organization's formula becomes:

> Repeat [Hire, Assemble, Develop, Deliver, Disperse]

> The adverse by-product of this fast-track development flywheel is disgruntled, demotivated, demoralized, and growth-deprived engineers. With no people growth, there is no team growth. With no team growth, there is no organizational growth. This is not an environment for serverless growth either.

Essential Ingredients for Growing a Serverless Team

As you saw in Chapter 1, builders and stakeholders are one of the essential components of the serverless technology ecosystem. Builders (i.e., engineers) are the people who architect, build, and operate serverless applications. When we talk about growing an engineer in a serverless ecosystem, we can draw parallels with how a plant grows in our environmental ecosystem. Taking inspiration from nature, here are some of the essentials for growing a successful team of serverless engineers:

- A fertile field (a conducive environment)
- Healthy seeds (passionate pilot engineers)
- A gardener (a serverless enabler to guide the team)
- Water, sunlight, and nutrients (training and a knowledge base)

Let's take a closer look at each of these key ingredients.

Conducive team environment

A healthy serverless ecosystem needs a favorable enterprise environment with a culture that fosters growth in the fertile surroundings. As you saw earlier in this chapter, adopting serverless requires adequate space for experimentation and innovation.

As shown in Figure 2-14, the characteristics of a fertile environment include:

- Freedom to take risks to build self-belief among the engineers
- Encouragement to experiment with ideas to foster product inventions
- Teams' involvement in technical and operational decision making to build trust and promote motivation
- Autonomy to self-govern, removing bureaucracy and allowing increased team velocity

- Nurturing an ownership culture to create a sense of belonging that encourages responsibility
- Sufficient learning opportunities to keep engineers in the know about advances in technology

Figure 2-14. Characteristics of a growth-promoting enterprise environment

You cannot readily source these traits from outside; they must be initiated by the leadership teams and radiated down to everyone in the organization.

Passionate pilot engineers

If your organization is starting fresh on serverless, you will unlikely have serverless specialists in-house. In such situations, it is beneficial to identify the best engineers with a forward-thinking mind and set them up as the torchbearers for serverless adoption. They will assume the role of pilot engineers and act as catalysts to spearhead the serverless revolution, inspiring others and laying the foundation for success.

In addition to solid software engineering skills, including architecture and security, pilot engineers should possess a positive attitude and willingness to take on challenges and identify pathways to success (see Figure 2-15). They'll work closely with the business stakeholders and product teams, guided by the serverless enabler (see the next section), to map your organization's serverless journey.

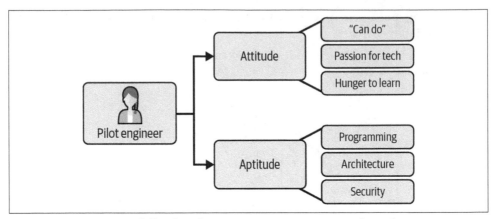

Figure 2-15. Necessary skills of a pilot engineer to promote serverless adoption

A serverless enabler to guide the team

With a fertile field and healthy seeds, the ground is ready for serverless growth. The role of a "gardener" to cultivate that ground during serverless adoption's early stages is vital. Your engineers need a strong guide to help them navigate the uncharted territory of serverless in your organization. This *serverless enabler* could be a senior or lead engineer, an architect, an engineering manager, or even the CTO, depending on the structure of your organization. It's not the title that matters here; as Gregor Hohpe states in his book *The Software Architect Elevator* (O'Reilly), what you're looking for is someone who can comfortably "ride the elevator" between the ivory tower (of business stakeholders and enterprise architects) and the IT engine room (of engineers).

Serverless adoption in an organization is a journey. As illustrated in Figure 2-16, you need a committed, tech-driven, passionate, and business-friendly navigator who can show you technical direction to enable the growth of engineers in technology.

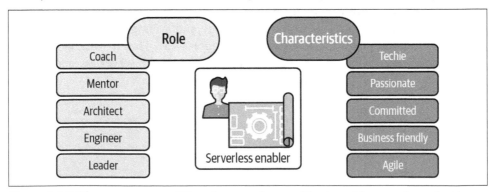

Figure 2-16. The necessary qualities of a serverless enabler to guide serverless adoption

Training and a knowledge base

Along with water and sunlight, nutrition is essential for every living entity in an eco-system. Similarly, the engineers who are part of an organization's serverless ecosystem need a constant supply of knowledge to upskill and keep up with the evolving technology landscape. New services, features, tools, frameworks, patterns, and capabilities are announced almost daily, and keeping pace with the speed of change can be challenging for a new team of serverless engineers. Hence, the necessary measures must be identified and implemented to swiftly assess and address these needs from the early days of serverless adoption. Coaching, training, workshops, and other learning methods must be considered and encouraged (see Figure 2-17).

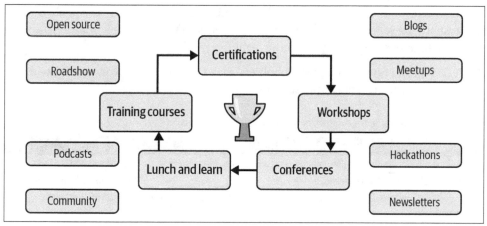

Figure 2-17. Different avenues to enrich serverless knowledge

Depending on the level of experience in your teams, you can employ two strategies for upskilling:

- Make the strengths of the engineers stronger. This means perfecting their skills and advancing them to a higher level to maximize their potential for increased performance.

- Identify and improve on the engineers' weaker skills. This means learning new skills to make them efficient in their daily tasks and enable them to experiment with new ideas for innovation.

Make sure to record your learnings and processes along the way, so they can be replicated in the future and used to help onboard future team members. See Chapter 11 for more on the importance of establishing a serverless guild/center of excellence.

Celebrating the growth of your team

Cultivating a growth-promoting enterprise environment for serverless is not a solo effort. It involves several teams—engineering, products, people partners, recruitment, etc.—working toward a unified goal. As teams of engineers grow, differences in opinion, complacency, and conflicts can arise. The role of a serverless enabler as a gardener becomes essential to nip such disputes in the bud by acting as a listener and mediator and finding quick resolutions to steady the serverless ship.

As your serverless team or teams begin to showcase their early achievements and little victories, ensure these are well communicated within the organization, especially to business stakeholders. In "How Do You Bring Serverless Awareness to Business Stakeholders?" on page 52 you saw how engineering teams can help stakeholders understand serverless technology and its benefits. It's vital to celebrate technology victories together—especially when the technology is serverless!

Table 2-1 shows how business stakeholders' views of serverless evolve along with the engineering achievements of the serverless team.

Table 2-1. Mapping team outcomes to stakeholder opinions

Engineering outcome	Stakeholder view
Proof of concept (PoC) finished and demonstrated faster and cheaper than before.	Beginning to trust the team.
Minimum viable product (MVP) completed and delivered.	The confidence in the team grows.
First serverless application deployed to production to serve customers. Lower operational and maintenance costs.	The team earns respect.

As serverless engineers and teams grow, you will have internal experts on the many factors of the serverless ecosystem. This is incredibly enriching for the organization. Depending on the engineers' backgrounds and interests, they may become proficient in more than one skill—a sign of a true serverless engineer in a multidisciplinary serverless team.

The Structure of a Multidisciplinary Serverless Team

We've covered a lot of ground since the mention of "multiskilled, diverse engineering teams" in Chapter 1 as one of the benefits serverless brings to an organization. We also discussed how the granularity of managed services aids in developing software iteratively in small increments. "First Principles for Successful Serverless Adoption" on page 39 highlighted the need for business, organizational, and technology thinking to have long-term sustainable teams.

A multidisciplinary serverless team consists of people who:

- Form a small group that can be fed with two pizzas
- Understand their business domain and interact with stakeholders
- Are responsible for their software products
- Are quality-conscious and automate their tests
- Can define and implement their deployment pipelines
- Understand security and employ threat prevention measures
- Implement good observability and engage in proactive monitoring
- Take part in architectural discussions and implement solution designs
- Are not afraid to deploy to production on a Friday afternoon

Based on these qualities (and our experience), we can sketch out the composition of a typical serverless team, as shown in Figure 2-18. Of course, this is not the only possible team composition; the makeup of a successful serverless team may vary depending on the business domain, organizational structure, and skills and experience of the engineers.

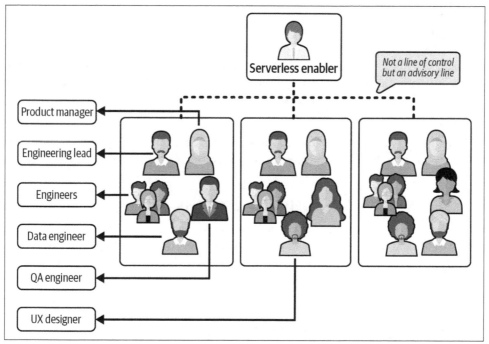

Figure 2-18. Serverless teams with different roles working with a serverless enabler

Let's break down the different roles in this figure:

Product manager or product owner

The product manager or product owner is the person who connects the engineers with the product teams and business stakeholders. They work closely with the engineering lead to set team goals and outcomes.

Engineering lead

The engineering lead is the technology counterpart of the product manager, responsible for the engineering efforts of the team. They set the technology direction, help the engineers grow their skills, introduce engineering practices and principles, and ensure best practices are adhered to.

Engineers

There is generally a mix of engineers with varied levels of experience, from senior to junior, responsible for the engineering activities in the team. These engineers possess most of the traits listed earlier in this section.

Data engineer(s)

As many teams produce and own their data, they will need engineers with the necessary skills to provide guidance on data management, governance, models, algorithms, etc.

QA engineer(s)

There are often one or two quality assurance specialists who work closely with other engineers to define and execute the testing strategy. It is essential for the team's growth that these engineers be involved in all the team's activities, such as design discussions, ideation sessions, etc.

UX designer (optional)

Teams responsible for web apps, user interactions, etc., usually include designers specialized in the user experience domain, for better collaboration and outcomes.

Serverless Engineers

The term *serverless engineer* is common today in tech media and on industry job boards. It refers to an engineer who works with serverless technology—but what are the characteristics hidden behind the term? How different is a serverless engineer from a software engineer? We can define the role as follows:

> A serverless engineer is a software engineer who is innovative and capable of building efficient, secure, cost-effective, functional, and event-driven solutions iteratively using managed services and operating them on the cloud.

In addition, a serverless engineer is expected to grow with a deeper understanding of cloud and serverless technologies, analytical and architectural skills, and an operational and ownership attitude.

Responsibilities of a serverless engineer

Everyone has responsibilities based on their role in the ecosystem they are part of. With no silos, smaller, stream-aligned teams promote communication and sharing of knowledge and tasks between engineers. Everyone in the team becomes aware of all the disciplines of a serverless team mentioned in the previous section. For software engineers whose primary focus is developing applications, this means they will become fluent with many of the activities that are part of the end-to-end cycle of a product increment.

In Chapter 1, while discussing how serverless technology enables the growth of diverse engineering teams, you saw the need for a DevOps mindset and related traits to help engineers evolve into serverless engineers. Serverless engineers are part of a team that contributes to business growth by employing serverless technologies and modern development practices—it's not the title that counts, but the role and responsibilities. We'll talk more about these responsibilities in later chapters, as we explore the development and operational aspects of serverless applications.

Frequently asked questions about serverless teams

Here are some common questions people ask about serverless teams, and some analysis about the accuracy of the underlying conceptions and misconceptions:

Is a serverless team a backend team?
> This is not always true. In a commercial product development organization, you'll see teams that focus on domain logic implementation as microservices, teams that own the end-to-end flow of user-facing features, teams that focus mainly on the user experience and aesthetics, and teams that handle data processing and utility services. All these teams could use serverless technology in part or in full.

Is a full-stack team ideal for serverless development?
> A stream-aligned engineering team that owns a feature or a product is responsible for its end-to-end flow, including both frontend and backend functionality. Such a team functions with engineers capable of working on any part of the application stack and avoids the frontend and backend silos. Serverless thrives in environments where knowledge is shared and there is a greater collaboration.

Is serverless technology only for developing microservices?
> Modern applications have several parts, and many of these parts can benefit from serverless. The backend microservices that implement business logic, the Backend for Frontend (BFF) layers that use GraphQL federation, and the frontend user experience implementations that require server-side rendering, data processing pipelines, etc., can all use serverless technologies.

Summary

This chapter explored the many facets of an enterprise, assessing them from a serverless adoption point of view. As authors, our aim is to equip you with all the information you'll need as you bring serverless technology to your organization, to enable effective collaboration between your technical and business colleagues during critical decision-making processes and ensure your engineers have the right attitude and skills and the necessary support to capitalize on the benefits of serverless. We hope these first two chapters have helped get you into the serverless mindset, with a clear vision of the tasks involved in adopting serverless in your organization.

In the next couple of chapters, we'll start to get closer to the technical aspects of serverless adoption by exploring the underlying architectural concepts, microservices principles, and design patterns before delving into the serverless development cycle and processes.

Your serverless journey is well and truly underway!

Interview with an Industry Expert

David Anderson, Architect, G-P Globalization Partners

David is a technical leader who enjoys writing and speaking about the leading edge of technology. After starting out as a software engineer in leading telecom companies (including Three, Nokia, and Ericsson), David moved to Liberty Mutual in 2007, where he continued to drive technology change and cloud adoption. As a practicing architect with G-P, he continues to empower and enable peers with a focus on serverless-first, well-architected principles, and engineering excellence, all to enable digital transformation, AI, improved time to value, and high-performing teams. His book *The Value Flywheel Effect*, published by IT Revolution in fall 2022, continues to inspire modernization journeys. David is based in Belfast, writes on The Serverless Edge (*https://oreil.ly/wIehw*), is the lead organizer for ServerlessDays Belfast (*https://oreil.ly/NqCTp*), and is a member of the Wardley Mapping community. You can find him on X (formerly Twitter) at @davidand393 (*https://oreil.ly/je9WK*) and @david-anderson-belfast (*https://oreil.ly/sc9GF*) on LinkedIn.

Q: What is a serverless mindset, and why is it essential to serverless adoption?

For me, the serverless mindset is a set of tenets or principles that must be true for the technical and executive leadership and the engineers. I see many companies building on legacy cloud (i.e., treating the cloud like a data center), but they have yet to experience the transformational change the cloud should bring. It's important they ask the question of why a company would spend 25–50% of their technology budget building an infrastructure platform that (in most cases) is not needed and will, in the long term, slow delivery.

"The technology strategy is the business strategy." We speak the same language and can relate technology efforts to the top line.

"Offload as much as possible to external cloud providers." You think differently about architecture, but that's okay.

"Embrace the fallback." Start with serverless and fall back when you need to. Don't be dogmatic—containers are not evil, but make sure engineers don't fall back because "we don't know serverless."

"Code is a liability; the system is the asset you are creating." You don't need to build everything. Spend time on the big picture of what you are building, and don't code your way out of trouble. Step back and look at the overall design. Create logical components over actual classes.

Finally, "be brave about your approach." What seems like a complicated feature could be a solved problem by a managed service; don't be afraid to use it. No one will think less of an engineer who can deliver a six-month project in two weeks.

The serverless mindset embraces evolutionary architecture and uses cloud providers to create business value quickly. Get features in the hands of users and adapt based on feedback. Don't be pressured into using a vendor recommendation—think for yourself and use vendor services as building blocks. Don't get locked into a framework.

By the way, you will notice I didn't mention functions. If you think serverless is functions, you need to broaden your thinking. Serverless is "access to capability when needed"—but we still don't have a good name for it.

Q: You played a pivotal role in Liberty Mutual's adoption of serverless. The term *serverless-first* became a mantra from those days. What does it mean to an organization thinking of adopting serverless?

Following the principle of "building blocks, not frameworks," it's essential that technology leaders understand that their outcomes drive the company forward. Technology is not a cost center; it's an engine for business growth. There was a phase when companies would say, "We are not an X company; we are a technology company that sells X." Liberty Mutual is an insurance company with a deep understanding of technology—this happens when you make a long-term bet on "technology as a differentiator." Policyholders don't care how cool the event logger for the web app is or that the backend is Lambda; they just need help quickly. The journey at Liberty Mutual was awesome, and there are a lot of nice articles if you google "Liberty Mutual serverless."

Specifically, for an organization-wide adoption of serverless, there are several key areas:

Infrastructure

There is a significant evolution required for the infrastructure teams. We are not building a wrapper around the cloud, and the infrastructure team is not the conduit for everything external—this is not sustainable. Don't wrap application engineers in cotton wool; clear guardrails will enable them to move quickly. Serverless allows application teams to do some infrastructure as code, and the infrastructure teams focus on management and governance of the cloud. The cloud provider is now one of your platform teams (you have several).

Security

Security [experts] must think in a very purist way about the cloud. The traditional approach of building a wall around the data center does not work for the cloud. The principle of least privilege is critical, and the application engineers now become the front line of security. We need to train our engineers in security (teach them the threat model) and partner with them. Serverless may be a challenge for some of the existing security tools, so we need to think differently.

IT and product leadership

Courage is required, as serverless is a paradigm shift. The technology and techniques that IT leaders used when they were engineers (or executing projects) have often changed dramatically. Some leaders will say, "When I was an engineer, we did this." That is correct sometimes; other times, it is the opposite of what needs to happen in a serverless environment. IT leaders must learn about the serverless mindset and trust their technology leaders. It's difficult for busy executives and managers to carve out time to learn about new technology, but it is critical for success.

Engineering capability

We must ensure the engineers and architects are comfortable with the new technology and techniques, maybe through cloud certification, workshops and labs, or even external speakers and internal conferences. Regardless, bring your engineers on the journey and invest in them. You won't hire a new cohort of serverless engineers; bring your engineers today through the journey, and they won't let you down.

One of the critical blockers against serverless is "we can't get buy-in." Pitching a "let's rebuild everything in this new tech" effort is challenging. It's better to focus on key problem areas and show the value of serverless through results: "We built this solution in 50% of the time," "We've reduced running costs by 80%," or "We can now scale to meet our demand, and our costs are lower." Start with showing the results and demonstrate that a serverless mindset was the technique that made it possible—show, don't tell.

Finally, it's critical to value tech leadership. The cloud is changing quickly, so you need technical leaders who are switched on and will spot new developments early. Technical leaders will drive engineering excellence (EE). For me, EE is the cornerstone of a serverless organization. I define it as three things: autonomy for teams (build it, own it, run it), mastery (the engineers apply good practices consistently across the organization), and purpose (business KPIs drive tech efforts, and the teams know exactly why they are building). Yes, this is borrowed from Dan Pink's *Drive*, but don't be afraid to reuse!

Q: Could you share some of the measures you have employed to promote the growth of serverless skills in an organization?

When teams take more responsibility, we must ensure they are executing well. Looking through the lens of the three engineering excellence areas, we can measure high performance through:

Mastery
> The critical measure here uses the Well-Architected Framework (from AWS, but it equally applies to the version from Google or Azure). I like to use a process called SCORP (Security, Cost, Operational Excellence, Reliability, Performance—it's detailed in my book) that enables teams to gather metrics for these five pillars and publish them in a single dashboard (a wiki page or whiteboard). This is updated and reviewed every sprint. *Well-architected* becomes front of mind, not just an audit-type activity.
>
> Speed of delivery is also essential, so we look at the four key DORA metrics (*https://oreil.ly/tGInu*). I dislike being too formal about these, but deployment frequency is a great leading indicator.

Autonomy
> I'm a huge fan of Team Topologies, and there are many measures for fast flow around team metrics. What is the team type, team size, work prioritization, and effectiveness of process? There is a sociotechnical element to the serverless organization. You have to get the technology environment and system design right. You also have to get the team dynamics right to ensure the people can interact with the technology effectively.

Purpose
> This is the easiest one, but the one that is often most ignored. Does the team own a business KPI? (It could also be two teams contributing to the same KPI.) The best measure is to ask an engineer about the business KPI—is the team aware of what it is and how they are changing it?

There are some antipatterns or smells that I often look out for:

- The team's purpose is "looking after technology X"—"We are the Kafka team."
- The stack is not ephemeral. If we deleted that stack now, could you recover it quickly?
- You're locked into a process, and a QA/infrastructure/security team is slowing down delivery.
- What is the Time to Try?

Time to Try is a great metric. Let's imagine a new cloud service announcement at noon on a Monday. How long will it take for an engineer in a regular team to access the service (in a compliant manner) with a view to using it in production? Many traditional organizations will give estimates from weeks to months (we need to make security updates, add to our internal portal, write some Terraform, train our platform team, etc.). My expectation would be 24 hours, for a security review and an update to the cloud policies to add the service to the allow list.

Q: Your book The Value Flywheel Effect has a chapter dedicated to discussing the "environment for success." In your opinion, what should the environment be for an enterprise adopting serverless?

There are four phases in the book *The Value Flywheel Effect*: Clarity of Purpose (ensures the goal is clear), Challenge (creating an environment for success), Next Best Action (applying a serverless-first approach for rapid execution), and Long-Term Value (using the Well-Architected Framework for sustainable change). My coauthors (Mark McCann and Michael O'Reilly) and I have observed this pattern in many companies. When it's in effect, change happens rapidly and repeatedly.

The second phase addresses "the environment for success." The primary method is the ability to challenge. I have found that Wardley Mapping is an excellent technique to open up Challenge (and by Challenge, I mean the environment to ask questions and respectfully critique strategy).

What we describe here is the opposite of the HIPPO (Highest Paid Person's Opinion) effect. Technical leaders should always have the environment to dig into how and what we are doing to solve a problem. The Amazon leadership principle "Have backbone; disagree and commit" captures this well.

In short, we are talking about psychological safety in the organization. Do engineers (at all levels of the organization) have the confidence and are comfortable in their ability to perform? You don't want "beaten down engineers." If your engineers do not exceed your expectations, you need to look at their environment.

Q: You are active in the AWS and serverless communities, organizing meetups and conferences and sharing technical content via blogs and videos. How do tech communities help engineers and organizations begin their serverless journey?

Everyone needs the time and space to explore new ideas. I always enjoyed the old joke about training: "*CFO:* What happens if we train them and they leave? *CEO:* What happens if we don't, and they stay?"

What I always try to do is two things. First, help people with the time to learn by curating good content and making it easy to discover new things. Second, help people with the space to learn via events like Lean Coffee, Open Space, or tech talks/conferences.

I do this in my own time at TheServerlessEdge.com, a blog and podcast where the team share content. I also founded ServerlessDays Belfast, a community event to give engineers a platform to share their tech talks. (And please look out for a ServerlessDays near you!)

I firmly believe that engineers listen to other engineers. Creating a sense of community or tapping into an existing one will change perspectives, accelerate learning, and build confidence. We are trying to encourage humility—true mastery is simply the willingness to learn.

A final saying that has stayed with me for many years is, "Show me the person who knows it all, and I'll show you the fool." Serverless is constantly evolving, so don't lock into a particular set of practices—technology is evolving faster than any single organization, so keep up.

CHAPTER 3

Software Architecture for Building Serverless Microservices

Man: "I just don't think it's that simple. Nothing is."
Woman: "Everything is when you break it down!"
—From the movie *Mamma Mia! Here We Go Again*

The word *architecture* has different interpretations depending on the context. As you read this book on serverless development, naturally, you relate it to the *software* context, or the *serverless* context, to be precise. If you detach the context, you are likely to relate architecture to buildings—this is where the term originated, from the days of our hunter-gatherer ancestors as they built structures for their shelter and safety.

When you appreciate something as good architecture, you likely admire its aesthetics or appeal. However, architecture has three main parts: art, structure, and technique to hold everything together. This is true in any context, including software and serverless.

There is a difference, however. You can stand in front of and admire the appearance of a Mayan temple or the Taj Mahal, but you don't get to *see* the architecture of your flight booking system. Software architecture has an invisible appeal. The art of software architecture—represented by its component elements (databases, processes, queues, functions, etc.) and the relationships between them—resides with the team that built it.

The elements and their relationships vary based on the context of the software. You may not see all the software elements and relationships of a legacy system you worked on in the past in a serverless application. Moreover, these elements and their interrelationships evolve, even in the same context. Your role as an engineer or architect is to understand, apply, and update as necessary to sustain the architecture for as long as possible.

Many legacy multitier applications portrayed architecture as a vast web of complex interconnections of diverse shapes spread across stacks of layers. But software architecture need not be complex—serverless architecture is not measured by its breadth or complexity, but by its fitness for purpose!

A critical difference between the architecture of a building and a serverless application is the possibility for change. Once completed, it is almost impossible to change the architecture of a building. We acknowledge this with older structures recognized as architectural successes, saying they have "stood the test of time"—they're unchanged but still attractive. In contrast, serverless architecture can evolve, and we can apply the changes without impacting the existing solution. Over time, it may cease to resemble the initial architecture completely.

Advances in serverless technology, user demands, business strategies, and architectural patterns can influence your architecture. While architecting, you must consider your design's ability to incorporate technical improvements, new features, etc. This chapter is about equipping you with modern approaches to design solutions that you can iterate and evolve. It delves deep into event-driven architecture and the essentials of designing serverless applications, and discusses domain-driven design and how to apply it to building microservices. Microservices introduce you to a new way of breaking down a problem domain and building extendable services.

Popular Architectural Patterns

Architectural patterns are *repeatable styles* of architecture. As an engineer, you might be familiar with design patterns in software development. Architectural patterns, on the other hand, work at a higher level. (We'll talk more about design patterns in serverless development in Chapter 5.)

These repeatable styles are common in buildings and software. Looking at past and present buildings, you'll notice different styles influenced by era, culture, geography, religion, available building materials and technologies, etc. A simple illustration is the Egyptian pyramids: there isn't just one pyramid, but hundreds following a similar architectural style.

Similarly, several factors influence the architectural style you choose for your application. These patterns often change as technology evolves, but a few survive the test of time and technological advancement, usually because they are fundamental to several other architectural patterns. One such pattern is the client/server architecture discussed later in this chapter. However, we'll start with the most popular architectural pattern in serverless: the event-driven architecture.

Event-Driven Architecture

The event-driven architecture is arguably the most common pattern you will use in serverless. The previous chapter briefly introduced this pattern while discussing the first principles for serverless adoption:

> Event-driven architecture (EDA) is an architectural concept that uses events to communicate between decoupled microservices asynchronously. In EDA, there are systems that produce events (producers), systems that consume events (consumers), applications that transport events (event buses, messaging systems, etc.), and systems that react to events.

The following are the four main elements of EDA, as illustrated in Figure 3-1:

- Events (also, in some cases, known as messages)
- Event producers (also known as event sources, publishers, or senders)
- Event consumers (also known as event targets, subscribers, or receivers)
- Event carriers (also known as event routers, buses, channels, or mediators)

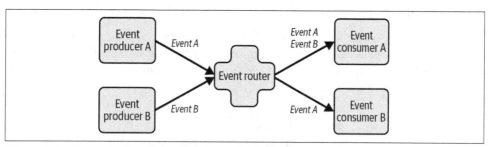

Figure 3-1. The basic elements of an event-driven architecture

Events

As discussed in Chapter 2, an event is something that has already happened. For example, *a customer has paid for their order* is an event. In the context of an application, an event carries information about what happened, and most importantly, it cannot change—that is, it's immutable. For example, an event about a customer's payment for an order will contain the customer's identification, order number, payment type, amount, and other related details, as shown in Example 3-1.

Example 3-1. An event containing the details of a customer's payment for an order

```
{
  "metadata": {
    "version": "1.0",
    "created_at": "2023-12-30T09:12:27Z",
    "trace_id": "skdj834sd3-j3ns-cmass23",
```

```
    "domain": "ecommerce",
    "subdomain": "orders",
    "service": "service-payments",
    "category": "domain_event",
    "type": "data",
    "name": "payment_received"
  },
  "data": {
    "customer_id": "730e-4dfb-9166",
    "order_number": "123-987-456",
    "payment_reference": "cc-visa-9076-cv3s5s",
    "payment_type": "creditcard",
    "amount": 35.99,
    "currency": "GBP",
    "paid_at": "2023-12-30T09:12:27Z"
  }
}
```

You will learn more about the structure, categories, and types of events in "Domain Events, Event Categories, and Types" on page 142.

Event producers

Event producers are applications that create and publish events, as shown in Figure 3-2. Various applications can produce events, including web applications, microservices, database systems, IoT devices, etc. Some applications produce a high volume of events (for example, tracking users' activities on a website).

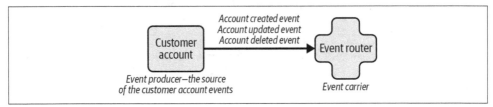

Figure 3-2. A customer account application emits multiple events as an event producer

Event producers are usually agnostic to the consumers of their events. An event should carry details about the occasion that triggered the producer system to emit the event. The event producer should not make assumptions about who or what might consume it, or tailor its contents based on such an assumption. This behavior keeps microservices decoupled, which is one of the benefits of event-driven architecture.

Event consumers

Applications that subscribe to one or more events, as shown in Figure 3-3, are known as event consumers. Depending on the event data, consumers may know the identity of the event producer, but this is not always the case. Consumers receive events in near real time, and depending on their logic they may handle them either immediately or after some delay.

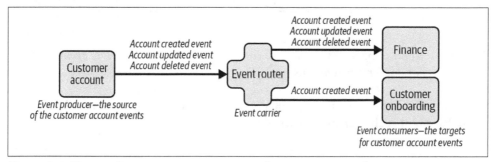

Figure 3-3. Two applications consuming events from an event producer

 Though event-driven architecture portrays event publishers and consumers as two separate applications, it is common for an application to act as both a publisher and a consumer of events.

Event carriers

An event carrier is a service that accepts events from producers and securely delivers them to the subscribers. Terms like event router, event bus, event channel, event mediator, event broker, event bridge, event hub, and so on are often used interchangeably to represent the same service, although there can be slight variations between these components.

As shown in Figure 3-4, some of the basic capabilities of event carriers include:

- Support for event producers to publish events
- Support for event filtering to identify and channel events
- Support for transforming events where needed
- Support for routing the filtered events to one or more event consumers
- Support for successfully delivering events to the target consumers

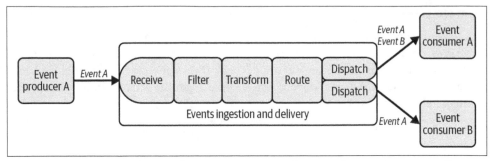

Figure 3-4. Main components of an event carrier application that receives events from producers and delivers them to consumers

Besides the basic features, services such as Amazon EventBridge, discussed in greater detail later in this chapter, provide capabilities to:

- Store events
- Replay events for a certain time window
- Register the schema of the events
- Retry event delivery to a consumer in case of failure
- Collect the events that failed to be delivered to a consumer
- Encrypt events
- Invoke HTTP endpoints to deliver events

How relevant is event-driven architecture to serverless?

Based on what you've learned so far, it should be clear that EDA is core to serverless. In addition to using EDA in building your serverless applications, most of the managed cloud services from AWS are also event-driven.

When we discussed the event driven–first mindset in Chapter 2, we mentioned that asynchronicity and event-driven communication are core characteristics of the serverless technology ecosystem. Within this ecosystem, it's common to find both simple event-driven architecture constructs like the one shown in Figure 3-5 and distributed architectures that span across multiple applications, as shown in Figure 3-6.

 In an event-driven architecture with multiple event producers and consumers, there is a possibility that consumers may receive duplicate events. It is the responsibility of the consumer to implement the required measures to identify and eliminate the consequences of event duplication. You will learn more about this later in the chapter.

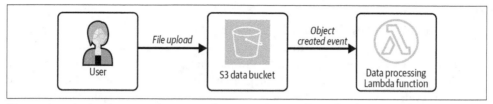

Figure 3-5. A simple event-driven application where a file upload to an S3 bucket creates an event and invokes a Lambda function

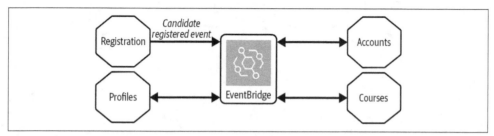

Figure 3-6. A distributed application where decoupled microservices coordinate via Amazon EventBridge, acting as their event router

Client/Server Architecture

The client/server architectural pattern has existed for many decades. As shown in the simple example in Figure 3-7, it has two distinct components, the client and server, which communicate via an established protocol. Let's take a closer look at these three elements:

Server

A server provides a service or shares a resource for others to consume. Traditionally, a server is a computer system that hosts data files, databases, HTML pages, etc. These types of servers are still in common use today, but now there are also servers hosting software programs that implement business logic to offer as a service to clients.

Client

A client consumes the resources or services of a server. For example, when you open your email client on your laptop, tablet, or mobile phone, it communicates with the server to fetch your emails. You can think of a client as a lightweight computing device that fetches the data from one or more servers.

Communication

Communication establishes the relationship between a client and one or more servers; without it, the architecture does not function and is inactive. Computer networks and protocols are the backbone of this communication. In a client/server architecture, the client primarily initiates the communication with the server. For example, when you open your inbox, your email client sends a request to the email server to establish communication.

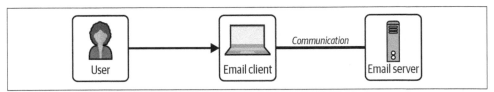

Figure 3-7. A simple client/server architecture

 Though there is no direct reference to a server in serverless architecture, the concept of a server as the provider of resources and services for clients to consume is common terminology.

Two-tier client/server architecture

The client/server architecture shown previously is the simplest form, a two-tier client/server pattern. Here, you have a server as the information provider and a client as the consumer. Before the browser-based technologies transformed the user interface, two-tier architectures provided a graphical user interface (GUI) on local computers to read and enter data. Over time, these client applications began to perform more functionality, enriching their ability to input, validate, and translate data. This came to be known as the presentation tier, as shown in Figure 3-8.

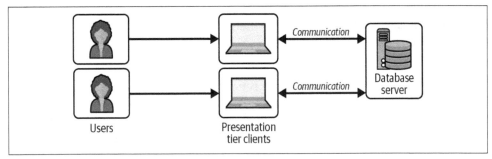

Figure 3-8. A two-tier client/server architecture where clients communicate with a remote database server

Three-tier client/server architecture

In a two-tier architecture, the client is responsible for both the presentation layer and the application layer (the application interface and the logical operations). Some of the business logic is shared with the data tier, meaning that a change in logic affects both tiers.

The motivation of the three-tier client/server architecture is to separate the business logic as much as possible from the presentation and data tiers and abstract in a middle tier, known as the application tier, as shown in Figure 3-9. You may also see this referred to as the business logic or service tier.

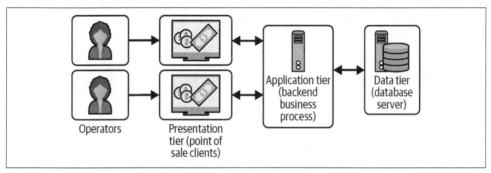

Figure 3-9. A three-tier client/server point of sale (POS) system

Introducing this middle tier brought a few important changes to the architecture:

- It prevented the presentation tier from directly manipulating the data in the data tier.
- It reduced the processing power needed at the presentation tier, enabling the use of thin clients instead of rich clients.
- It allowed different types of clients, such as desktop and web applications, to access the same application tier.

One technology evolution that fueled the popularity of the application tier during the 1990s was interfaces. An *interface*, in this context, is a communication protocol that the presentation tier uses to connect remotely with one or more applications in the middle tier. The introduction of interfaces allowed engineers to package business logic into software modules or components, with each component publishing its interface definition using technologies such as the Common Object Request Broker Architecture (CORBA), Component Object Model (COM), Distributed COM (DCOM), Enterprise Java Beans (EJB), etc.

How relevant is client/server architecture to serverless?

Though technology has gone through many iterations since the client/server pattern was first introduced, if you are coming from a client/server application development background and are adopting serverless you will notice many resemblances bridging the old with the new, as highlighted in the following list:

Distribution of applications
> The primary pattern you'll notice in client/server architecture is separating applications to run in different computing environments. Distributed computing has existed in this pattern for many decades.
>
> The principle of breaking an application and operating as distributed services is a core concept you will find in serverless architectures.

Interfaces to communicate with software components
> Interfaces are integral to everything you do in modern software architecture. You learned about *API-first* thinking in the preceding chapter as one of the fundamentals for adopting serverless. The interpretation and protocols may vary with regard to how serverless APIs function, but the principle is the same.

Modular systems and components
> Engineers have been building applications split into modules, subsystems, components, libraries, etc., since well before the introduction of microservices. Two crucial differences were:
>
> - Legacy software modules did not always map to business domains.
> - Hard dependencies between modules and tight coupling were common in legacy applications.
>
> Though many of the modules and subsystems of the past were built as monoliths, the concept of modularization of applications is very relevant in a serverless architecture.

Your client/server architecture knowledge will help you quickly adapt to serverless, with the necessary changes to your mindset. Moreover, if you are migrating legacy client/server applications to serverless, this chapter will help you reflect on what you know and what you need to know.

Layered Versus Tiered Architecture

The layered architecture pattern has a close resemblance to the tiered client/server patterns discussed in the previous section. Though the terms are often used interchangeably, there is an important difference: the layered architecture pattern focuses on the *logical* separation of components that perform different functions, whereas tiered architecture focuses on their *physical* separation. Figure 3-9 shows the physical separation of the presentation, data, and application tiers in a simple system. But as an architect, when you design a client/server architecture, you don't start with the physical separation of tiers. Rather, you conceptualize and identify the *layers* of the system and their interactions.

As the complexity of systems increased over the years, separation of concerns and grouping of related business and processing logic became recommended practices. These groupings then evolved to become layers of the application. Figure 3-10 shows a tax application where the logic for rule computation and data access has been split into separate layers.

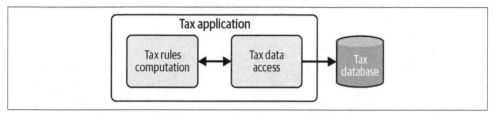

Figure 3-10. A tax system with its application tier split into two layers

Layered architecture

Figure 3-8 depicts a simple two-tier client/server application with a physical separation of the presentation and data tiers. In Figure 3-11, you see the same shown as a layered architecture.

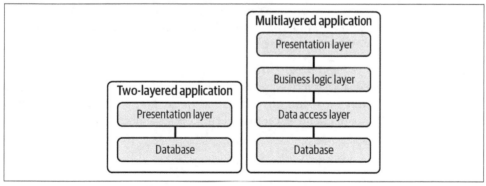

Figure 3-11. A two-layered versus a multilayered application architecture

Typically, with this pattern each layer depends on the layer beneath it. The popularity of layered architecture rose with object-oriented programming, as it helped break down functionality into several thin layers. The benefits of layered architecture include:

- Separation of concerns and grouping of functionality that changes together
- Code reuse and ease of testing of individual layers

The downside of this approach is that without careful consideration it can lead to *lasagne architecture*, an antipattern of layered architecture where you have too many layers.

Tiered architecture

As you saw earlier, the advantages of tiered architecture include the physical separation of the parts of a system that perform different functions, modularity, and clear interfaces. The combination of tiers and layers, as illustrated in the example architecture in Figure 3-12, adds flexibility, as it promotes the modularity of applications and their distribution.

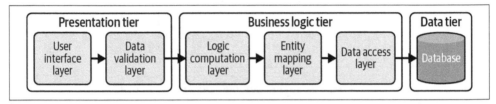

Figure 3-12. A three-tier architecture with multiple layers

How relevant are layered and tiered architectures to serverless?

These patterns evolved to provide options to build scalable applications with redundancy, to make them resilient. Though terms such as *modules* and *distribution* sound similar, how you architect and operate serverless applications differs; hence, you may not find a perfect alignment, but you will still find your knowledge transferable to serverless. Here are some commonalities:

Applications are deployed and run on physical tiers
> As you've learned, in serverless, you do not think of machines, computers, or servers, nor do you provision or manage hardware. Due to this, the separation of a *physical tier,* as in client/server architecture, has a modified representation in serverless.
>
> Figure 3-13 is a high-level cloud architecture version of the three-tier client/server architecture shown in Figure 3-9.

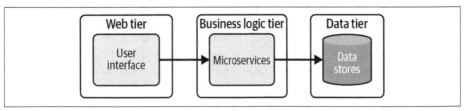

Figure 3-13. A simple representation of the cloud version of a three-tier client/server architecture

Though Figure 3-13 shows the separation of tiers, it does not show the mode of separation in a cloud environment, as each tier's application components and services could exist in any of the following deployment scenarios:

- Applications in all three tiers are deployed and operated by a single AWS account in one Region.

- Applications in each tier are deployed and operated in one AWS account but in different Regions.

- Applications in each tier are deployed and operated in individual AWS accounts in different Regions.

- Each application in each tier is deployed and operated in a separate AWS account and Region.

Though the capability to distribute your application in a cloud architecture may seem difficult to comprehend, it brings an array of benefits in terms of security, resilience, scalability, and flexibility.

Logical separation of application layers

The logical separation of applications and services as layers is still relevant in serverless, but with a difference. Unlike the stacked layers in a layered architecture, in serverless you can think of the architectural separation of distributed parts of an application.

Figure 3-14 shows an ecommerce application as three layers. Each of these layers can be divided into multiple sublayers as necessary. In serverless, visualizing your application as a distribution of logical layers and physical components is more important than thinking about physical tiers.

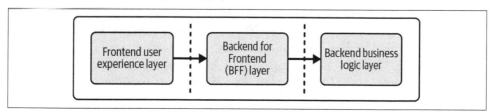

Figure 3-14. High-level architectural view of the layers of an ecommerce application

Hexagonal Architecture

Dr. Alistair Cockburn proposed hexagonal architecture (*https://oreil.ly/-iAcn*) as a pattern to ease component dependency issues between the architectural layers. Hard dependencies between layered components restrict flexibility to change. Hexagonal architecture promotes loose coupling between service components and consumers, allowing applications to be driven by users, programs, automated tests, or batch scripts, developed and tested in isolation from runtime devices and databases.

As shown in Figure 3-15, hexagonal architecture achieves its objective by using two important elements: ports and adapters. Hence, it's sometimes also known as the ports and adapters pattern.

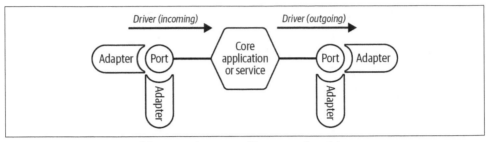

Figure 3-15. Depiction of the core elements of hexagonal architecture

Let's take a closer look at the different items in this figure:

Core application or service
> This is the domain application or a microservice with the business logic implementation. It has the domain model and entities at its core, as shown in Figure 3-16.

Ports
> These are interfaces that the core application defines. Outside systems (drivers) interact with the application via ports. Ports are also the gateway for the core application to interact with outside (driven) systems. You can think of ports as APIs, database protocols, topics, etc.

Adapters
> These are specific implementations for interacting via the ports. They are not part of the application but belong to the outer adapter layer, as illustrated in Figure 3-16. Their implementation is specific to the drivers or target systems on the driven side. Examples of adapters include HTTP adapters, REST API adapters, NoSQL adapters, event bus adapters, legacy customer relationship management (CRM) adapters, etc.

> Per Wikipedia (*https://oreil.ly/cjp4K*), "The term 'hexagonal' comes from the graphical conventions that show the application component like a hexagonal cell. The purpose was not to suggest that there would be six borders or ports but to leave enough space to represent the different interfaces needed between the component and the external world."

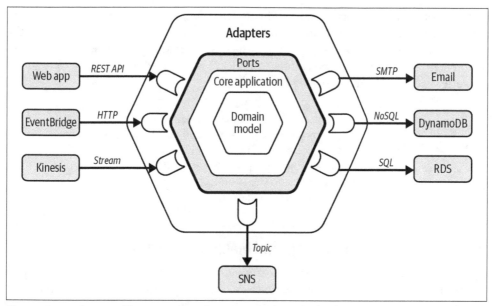

Figure 3-16. A typical hexagonal architecture with several adapters interacting via ports

How suitable is hexagonal architecture for serverless?

The main motivation of hexagonal architecture is to decouple core business components from the technology-specific service consumers and providers. While achieving its goal, it inadvertently brings more complexities, especially when you're looking for development efficiency by using managed cloud services.

The concept of ports as interfaces to your core application or microservices is applicable in many contexts, including serverless. The purpose is to make your services decoupled and relevant in serverless development.

The need for an adapter or a layer acting as an adapter is situation-specific. When you compose microservices using serverless technology, you leverage the benefits of managed cloud services, meaning you are not always looking to build adapters. However, there can be situations where you use an adapter to resolve technology incompatibilities between what you are building with serverless and the decades-old legacy system you will be integrating.

A common theme for hexagonal architecture is using adapters for testing purposes. Though this may sound appealing, you need to assess the value you gain versus the extra effort involved, especially when you have smaller single-purpose microservices with clear communication interfaces. You'll learn about testing strategies to apply in serverless development in Chapter 7.

 Hexagonal architecture has its place when you have a heavy core domain shared by several applications and teams across the organization that use different technologies. For most smaller teams that own and operate single-purpose services within a bounded context, assess the need and the overhead before employing full-scale implementation of ports and adapters.

Onion, Clean, and MACH Architectures

There are many architectural patterns in the industry, and it is beyond the scope of this book to analyze each from a serverless development point of view. However, for completeness, here are a few you're likely to come across:

Onion architecture

The onion architecture was originally conceived by Jeffrey Palermo (*https://oreil.ly/3G8Kt*). It is yet another software design pattern influenced by the popularity of object-oriented programming and based on the *inversion of control* principle. Like an onion, it has a core and several outer layers, which interact with each other and the core.

The core of the onion architecture represents the core domain and its business model. The layers represent different responsibilities, with the outer layers depending on the inner layers, whereas the inner layers need not be aware of the outer layers. This architecture supports the creation of core business logic central to many applications.

Clean architecture

The clean architecture was introduced by Robert C. Martin (*https://oreil.ly/V3koE*), fondly referred to as Uncle Bob. Like the onion architecture, it uses the concept of circles, with the inner circle representing the core entities and business logic. The motivation is to separate concerns and build your application layers independently of frameworks, user interfaces, databases, and external systems. The data passed between the layers follows a standard structure, with outer layers not influencing the data formats used in the inner layers.

MACH architecture

MACH (*https://machalliance.org*) is an architectural pattern that motivates enterprises to compose modular business applications and integrate with third-party solutions with agility and velocity. It promotes pluggable, scalable, replaceable, and independently deployable software components to achieve its goal. The name is an acronym for:

Microservices

Microservices are small, independent pieces of business functionality that communicate via well-defined APIs and events. You will learn more about microservices in the next section.

API-first

As you learned in the previous chapter, the API-first approach is about identifying and implementing interfaces to the system you are building. The API becomes a first-class citizen and plays a significant role in the tactical design of the application.

Cloud native

By taking full advantage of the cloud and shifting the heavy lifting to the cloud provider, you can build applications for modern consumer demands using Agile and DevOps principles. Adopting serverless takes this a step further, as you use managed cloud services to compose and operate your products in the cloud.

Headless

API-first services enable you to decouple the frontend, or the user experience layer, from the backend microservices. This is an entirely different architectural approach to the two-tier client/server architecture pattern you saw earlier.

Characteristics of a Microservice

The previous chapter gave a brief introduction to microservices, and you've seen the term in several places so far in this chapter—but what exactly are microservices?

In his book *Building Microservices*, 2nd Edition (O'Reilly), Sam Newman provides this simple definition that serves as a good starting point: "Microservices are independently releasable services that are modeled around a business domain." Figure 3-17 shows a microservice you saw in Chapter 2. We will use it here to study the main characteristics of microservices.

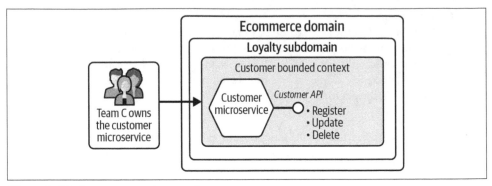

Figure 3-17. A customer microservice

In sum, a microservice:

- Is independently deployable
- Represents part of a business domain
- Has a single purpose
- Has a well-defined communication boundary
- Is loosely coupled
- Is observable at a granular level
- Is owned by a single team

This is not a definitive list, and you may argue that some elements are missing, such as microservices being modular and extendable (to which we might reply that loose coupling already incorporates those aspects). However, it serves our purpose here, which is not to analyze them with a theoretical lens but simply to provide a practical introduction to working with microservices and serverless. That said, let's dig a bit more deeply into the implications of each of the characteristics mentioned in the preceding list.

Independently Deployable

You should be able to deploy every microservice without impacting other microservices or needing them to be deployed along with it, as shown in Figure 3-18.

Independently deployable microservices, each owned and operated by a single team, allow engineers to work in parallel, avoiding dependencies and merge conflicts and enabling team velocity and flow.

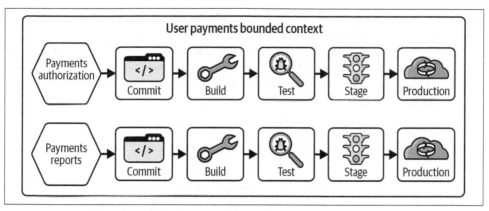

Figure 3-18. Independent deployment pipelines of microservices inside a bounded context

Represents Part of a Business Domain

The implementation of a microservice represents some business logic. The use of the words *part* and *some* here is intentional. You don't always represent the entire business logic inside a bounded context with a single microservice. One or more serverless microservices can share the business logic, as shown in Figure 3-19; together, they accomplish the business logic of the bounded context.

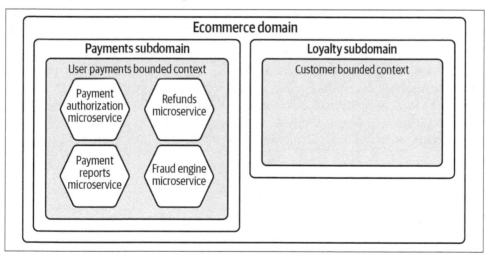

Figure 3-19. One or more microservices may share the implementation of the business logic of a bounded context

When a need arises for adding new business logic or a new feature, depending on the nature of the change, you can isolate the logic in a new microservice. Changes to microservices should not violate the existing interfaces and provide backward and forward compatibility. For example, in Figure 3-19, if the business wants to support payments via a secure web payment link emailed to customers, you can implement this as a new microservice.

The Single-Responsibility Principle

The single-responsibility principle (SRP) is another concept developed by software engineer and author Robert C. Martin (*https://oreil.ly/DFY8v*). According to Martin, "each software module should have one and only one reason to change."

In object-oriented (OO) programming, for example, this means that a class should have only one job. You can also apply the SRP at the method level, so each method in a class is responsible for doing one thing (such as finding a customer with the given account number). Likewise, each instance of a class—an object—represents the data and its operations of a single entity.

Single Purpose

Domain-driven design guides you to split each business domain into subdomains and bounded contexts. Each bounded context has its own boundary, business logic, and model, and distinct characteristics. The implementation of the business logic might involve microservices, web applications, etc.

As described in the previous section, and per the single-responsibility principle, each microservice is responsible for a single piece of business logic, and that's its sole purpose. A microservice's purpose, responsibility, and identity should be clearly defined. Figure 3-20 depicts this with a microservice that acts as a mediator between an external system and internal microservices.

 The term *anti-corruption layer* (ACL) comes from *Domain-Driven Design* by Eric Evans (Addison-Wesley Professional). It is a layer implemented between different systems to translate the requests between them to ensure the domain model of a system is not affected (corrupted) by its dependency on another system.

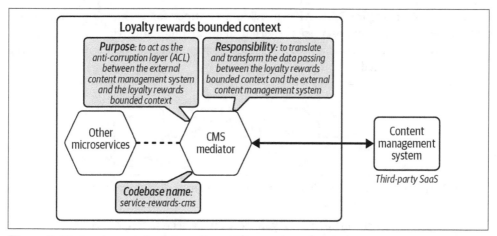

Figure 3-20. A microservice interacting with an external system

The identity of a microservice is the name used to identify it, which should be consistent in all designs and implementations. Usually, the name of a service reminds everyone of its purpose and responsibility. Though it sounds simple, teams often have lengthy debates about microservice names!

> Some teams assign nicknames to important microservices they own. One of this book's authors was once part of a team that named a microservice *PUPPy*. It stood for *Product Update Post-Processor*, and the *y* represented the upside-down Lambda notation λ. Though the codebase used a longer service name, PUPPy stuck with everyone, including the business stakeholders.

Well-Defined Communication Boundary

The concepts of bounded contexts, separation of concerns, and having a single responsibility and purpose are design patterns that enable you to build applications that are independent, modular, and extendable. Yet, microservices typically must coordinate with applications both inside and outside their bounded context. Establishing a clear communication channel thus becomes necessary to keep them loosely coupled and allow internal changes without impacting external interactions.

As illustrated in Figure 3-21, APIs provide a contract for exchanging information without exposing a microservice's internal details. Interacting via events, as in an event-driven architecture, is a widely adopted communication mechanism and keeps the services decoupled.

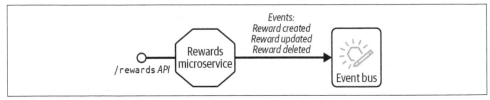

Figure 3-21. A microservice with a defined API that emits domain events

 Not all microservices you develop in serverless offer APIs. A microservice can rely on event-driven communication to trigger its functionality. For example, a report generation microservice may work on a schedule or rely on the arrival of certain events to trigger the reporting process and need no API.

Loosely Coupled

Loose coupling allows a microservice to be independently deployable without impacting other microservices. As loose coupling avoids hard dependencies between services, each one knows little or nothing about the others.

Microservices communicate via well-defined APIs and events. When a microservice exposes an API, it publishes a data schema and contract that service consumers must comply with, promoting the goals of independence and loose coupling. Similarly, communicating using events promotes asynchronous invocation between services and is vital to keep the services decoupled.

Observable at a Granular Level

The operational benefits of microservices are as important as their independent deployability. Though you might consider a microservice as a closed box from the outside except for its defined communication channels, you must be able to observe its operational status at all times—in other words, the box should be made of glass.

Unlike the obfuscated operational view of a monolith, a serverless microservice, due to its use of cloud resources, can provide a deeper and more granular view of its operation. Chapter 8 contains tips on implementing the best observability principles for your serverless applications.

The Significance of Domain-Driven Design in Serverless

Back in 1995, Amazon's retail system was a single monolithic application called Obidos. A few years later, Amazon published the Distributed Computing Manifesto (*https://oreil.ly/H9n2Z*). It enabled it to break Obidos up and build a three-tier architecture by separating the presentation (client), business logic (service), and data layers. This approach was called *service-based* architecture. Microservices, as a term and an implementation pattern, came to exist a few years after the publication of Eric Evans's revolutionary book *Domain-Driven Design* in 2003. Viewing an organization as a set of interconnected business domains with subdomains, core domains, bounded contexts, and domain models inspired object-oriented developers used to working with monolithic applications to think in terms of modules. While DDD promoted modularity, VM and containerization technologies enabled the deployment and operation of these independent components as microservices.

All the early references on microservices focused on packaging components as independent mini-monoliths adhering to the characteristics of microservices. As the popularity of the cloud and containers grew, deploying and operating microservices on containers became the norm, and this continues to be the case across many organizations.

The evolution of serverless as a parallel technology ecosystem to containers gathered momentum a few years after microservices rose to popularity. The early serverless adoptions focused on utility tasks, image processing, data conversions, scheduled batch jobs, etc., partly because the cold-start latency concerns of Lambda functions in the early days meant many teams were reluctant to use serverless for critical customer-facing business functionality.

Another reason for the slow influence of DDD on serverless was that for many engineers who'd started their careers with cloud and web development, learning and applying a design concept that was two decades old wasn't their priority (Evans's seminal book on DDD was published 20 years ago and uses unified modeling language models and object-oriented code examples).

Often, when engineers start experimenting with serverless to build their proofs of concept, their priority is to prove serverless is well suited for building and releasing applications quickly (as the marketing of serverless created the impression that it would enable engineers to get things done quickly and deployed to production in no time). Such quick-fix efforts brought success in most cases. This early experimentation success encouraged teams to enhance and extend the solutions in an ad hoc and unstructured manner. As you can imagine, this style of application development is susceptible to distasteful experiences and failures. Many of these efforts ultimately yielded tangled event-driven applications and balls of serverless mud like the one shown back in Figure 2-2.

Enterprises adopting serverless cannot be naïve and take risks with such an unstructured approach. Simple PoCs to evaluate certain services for a given purpose are fine, but beyond that, solutions must be executed with upfront thinking and adequate planning. The principles of domain-driven design act as a guide to steer enterprise teams on the right path, enabling them to avoid the mistakes mentioned previously and successfully adopt serverless. DDD is the forerunner for serverless adoption at your enterprise.

Owned by a Single Team

Ownership is an essential aspect of microservices. As discussed in "Microservices-first" on page 44, a single team should have ownership of each microservice. A microservice should never become the responsibility of two teams. Single ownership improves flow, increases velocity, and reduces the cognitive load on engineers.

If your organization has structured its teams based on the breakdown of business domains, it becomes easier to assign the ownership of a bounded context and its microservices to a stream-aligned team.

Microservice Communication Strategies

At least some of your serverless microservices will communicate with other services and external systems. As mentioned earlier, not every microservice offers an API or publishes events, so the communication strategies vary. The main differentiator is whether the communication is asynchronous or synchronous. The coupling level between services decreases as you move from a synchronous (request/response) to an asynchronous (event-based) communication pattern.

Synchronous Communication

Synchronous (request/response-based) communication over HTTP is the most common form of interaction used by microservices. Figure 3-22 shows an example where a microservice acting as a client (*checkout*) requests the service of another microservice or application (here, *payments*), invokes its API, and waits for a response.

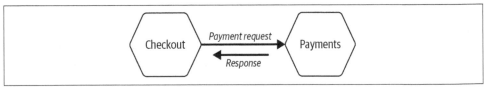

Figure 3-22. Synchronous communication between microservices

Depending on the nature of the functionality offered by the API and the network round-trip time, the response could be instantaneous (within a few milliseconds), fast (within a few seconds), or slower. The client is blocked from proceeding further while waiting for a response, which creates a coupling between the two services. Suppose the payments API takes a long time to respond, or the service is unavailable; this will directly impact the checkout service, causing complications in the application.

The three main implementation patterns of synchronous communication are:

- Simple request/response
- Request with an acknowledgment response
- Request with an acknowledgment and client polling

Simple request/response

Extending the example shown in Figure 3-22, Figure 3-23 depicts a realistic use of the synchronous request/response pattern. It shows a chained synchronous call involving four parties. The web application that initiates the call is unaware of the call chain between the checkout and payments services and the third-party payment provider. If any of those parties experiences operational issues or outages, it directly impacts the web application serving its users. To increase availability and resiliency in such situations, you should consider reducing the number of synchronous hops between the microservices.

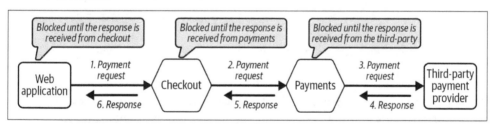

Figure 3-23. A microservices communication architecture showing a synchronous request/response pattern

An architectural challenge in this example is the risk of service timeouts. For instance, Amazon API Gateway has a maximum timeout of 29 seconds for REST APIs. From a user experience (UX) point of view, it is not ideal to keep a user waiting for this long. From an operations perspective, unexpected high latency or performance degradations in downstream services can result in the connection from the web application being abruptly terminated. In Chapter 5, you will learn about a circuit breaker pattern to handle such situations.

When a Lambda function initiates a synchronous API call and waits for the API provider to respond, it sits idle, and the waiting time gets added to its overall execution time. The cost calculation for a Lambda function takes into account both the execution time and the memory (RAM) allocation.

Request with an acknowledgment response

A variation of the simple request/response pattern that introduces an element of asynchronicity is *request with an acknowledgment response*. With this pattern, when a client invokes a service and the service's API receives the request, rather than immediately fulfilling the request it responds with an acknowledgment (HTTP status code 202 Accepted). The handling of the request then happens asynchronously, and the client does not wait for it to be completed. This decouples the service from the caller. Whether or not the service processes the request immediately depends on the business logic. Figure 3-24 shows this scenario.

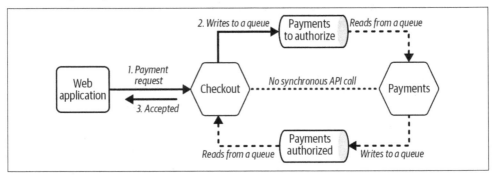

Figure 3-24. A synchronous call pattern where the response is an acknowledgment of acceptance

Authorization of the payment for an online purchase, for example, can take anywhere from a few seconds to minutes depending on the type of payment, bank, verification, user authentication process, etc. To avoid this unpredictable and long delay degrading the user experience, the checkout service receives the payment request, writes the details to a queue for the payments service to process, and sends an acknowledgment that the request has been accepted to the web application. The example in Figure 3-24 uses message queues for communication between the checkout and payments services; later, you'll see the use of other patterns for this purpose.

This example illustrates one of several use cases that benefit from this communication pattern. Others include:

Submitting bulk data processing tasks
   Many businesses request that the funds for a purchase be transferred from the buyer's account to the merchant's when the order is shipped. This process is

called *settlement* or *capture*. They do this in batches throughout the day, so the finance application will call the payments service at certain times during the day with batches of perhaps thousands of payment references. The finance application need not keep the network connection open while waiting for the processing of each batch to be completed.

Generating large volumes of discount codes for distribution
A business that offers unique discount codes for redemption may require hundreds of thousands of such codes. A microservice that provides this service will receive the request, send an acknowledgment, and disconnect from the requestor. The request to generate the codes and eventually dispatch them to the recipient will be handled asynchronously.

Processing uploaded images and videos
An image processing facility receives links to images and videos throughout the day. However, downloading and storing the content happens at night, when the energy consumption is low in that particular AWS Region. The API customers use to submit the links accepts the details with an acknowledgment reference. A scheduler then invokes the content downloader service at the desired time.

An important thing to notice with these example use cases is that there is no communication back to the requestor upon successful completion of the request—the initial acknowledgment is just to confirm the validity of the request (i.e., that it conforms to the API contract). The following section describes a pattern that enables a service to determine the final status of the submitted request.

Request with an acknowledgment and client polling

In the example in Figure 3-24, when the checkout service writes a request it has received from the web application to the "payments to authorize" queue, it sends an acknowledgment to the web application and disconnects. Later, it receives a corresponding payment authorized message in the "payments authorized" queue. However, as the web application that submitted the request is now disconnected from the checkout service, how does it know if the request succeeded? One way of making this information available to the web application is by providing an additional communication mechanism so that it can *query* the checkout service for the status of its payment request. This method of querying or pulling the status details from a service provider is known as *polling*.

Figure 3-25 illustrates this scenario. The checkout service provides a special API endpoint called /status to query the status. Depending on when the web application makes its first status query, the payment authorization might not have been completed. So, it repeats the call at certain intervals until the final status is known; hence the term polling.

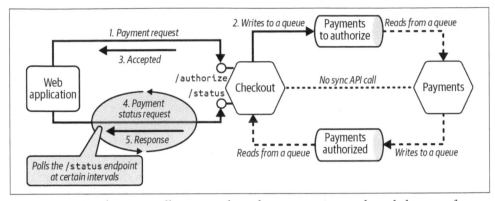

Figure 3-25. Synchronous call pattern where the response is an acknowledgment of acceptance, but the client polls for the status of the original request

Though polling works in most cases, it has some disadvantages:

- Clients need to invoke a different endpoint to know the status.
- Clients need to implement the logic to call the status endpoint repeatedly at an interval.
- Clients may need to make several network round trips to determine the status.
- Clients need to keep track of the number of calls or duration before giving up in case of no final status from the service.
- To cope with the service provider being down, clients need to implement exponential backoff and retry logic.
- Additional API calls add to the cost of the provider service.
- Additional API calls add to the call quota of the clients.

The following section discusses an improvement over polling-based communication with an asynchronous *push* notification.

Synchronous request/response with an asynchronous webhook notification

Another option for adding asynchronicity to the synchronous request/response pattern is by using a webhook, as shown in Figure 3-26. This approach facilitates push notifications. Instead of the web application polling for the status, it provides an endpoint (webhook) for the checkout service to call when the payment is authorized. Similarly, the payments service provides a webhook for the third-party payment provider to call. With this pattern, the service provider is *pushing* the information out to the clients by invoking the webhook endpoint. It is an efficient way of communicating and reduces the load on the service provider.

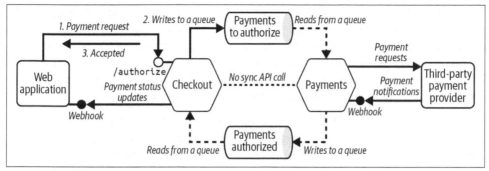

Figure 3-26. Synchronous call pattern with an asynchronous notification to the client via a webhook

 A webhook is a form of user-defined HTTP callback. To receive notifications, the client registers an endpoint URL with the service provider to call back with the information. The client then reacts to the incoming information to trigger further processing. Webhooks are an efficient way of communicating compared to polling.

Asynchronous Event-Driven Communication

As you saw in the previous section, with synchronous communication between a service provider and consumer there is a connection, or a form of coupling, as the client needs to understand the API contract, protocol, and URL. When a client establishes a connection with the service provider and makes an API call, the service provider serves the request and responds as part of the same connection.

In asynchronous communication, the services are decoupled with no durable connection established between them. As you learned earlier in the chapter, *events* carry the information from producers to consuming services and trigger some action. We'll talk more about EDA and asynchronous communication in "Event-Driven Architecture for Microservices Development" on page 135.

Breaking Down a Problem to Identify Its Parts

In Chapter 2, you learned about the common migration strategies enterprises choose when adopting serverless. Inside every organization, you will find legacy monolith systems of varying sizes, shapes, and complexities. Many of these systems grew organically from simple applications as various business features were bolted on, numerous customizations scaffolded, and countless bug fixes hacked in, with the evolution of their architectures bringing in a mix of technologies.

But the problem isn't always existing monoliths. Organizations constantly embark on new product development projects to meet modern customer needs and stay ahead of the competition. They look for technologies that will help them quickly deliver the products to bring value to their business. The problems modern organizations tackle vary in breadth, width, and volume. They span from user-facing web front-end and browser technologies to process-heavy complex business logic at the back. Applications must be available to everyone worldwide and capable of working with mountains of data to extract incredibly fine-grained insights.

When presented with an existing legacy monolith or a yet-to-be-built, mightily ambitious new initiative, a common problem faced by engineers and teams is knowing where and how to make a start—and, once you have made a start, how you can keep progressing in the right direction.

Domain-driven design and the first principles discussed in the previous chapter provide guidance and help you bring some form of order and structure to the process of transitioning to serverless. Event-driven architecture, EventStorming (an activity we'll talk about later in this chapter), and several implementation patterns can help you along the way. One of the strengths of serverless, as you'll hear often in this book, is the ability to think, build, and operate services at a granular or fine-grained level. Among other things, it helps organizations:

- Get clarity on the different parts of an application
- Plan and develop solutions incrementally and iteratively
- Gain operational visibility and control at deeper levels
- Implement separation of concerns and isolation levels, to have a resilient and highly available system

There are countless other benefits, depending on your business domain and application. To get you started, let's dive into an approach you can use for envisioning and structuring your application or parts of your applications as pieces—*set pieces*, to be more specific.

Using a Set Piece Analogy to Identify the Parts

Vision and *focus* are two important aspects of everyone's lives. You have a vision of what you want to achieve in your personal and professional life. Your employer has visions too—growth vision, product vision, technology vision, etc. Your initial vision of what you want to accomplish acts as a guide as you navigate toward it. You may have an overarching high-level vision that's divided into smaller "subvisions." When you picked up this book, your vision might have been to understand a structured approach to serverless development and successfully guide your team and organization to adopt it.

Focus, on the other hand, is the instrument that enables you to achieve your vision. It's the harder of the two. Focus makes you apply your mental and physical effort as you edge toward achieving your vision. As shown in Figure 3-27, when you focus, you typically define or mark a small part of your overall vision and accomplish it before focusing on the next area. So, with vision, you visualize the whole, or the big picture (the forest); with focus, you concentrate on smaller portions, parts, or pieces (the trees). For example, your current focus is on completing this section of the chapter and understanding how to break down a problem domain, but this is just one step in the path to achieving your vision.

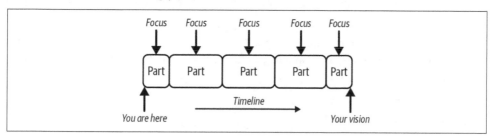

Figure 3-27. Your vision as a whole and how you focus on achieving parts of that vision over a period of time

 Though Figure 3-27 shows the parts as a sequence of focus items, in reality, they need not be completed in that order.

In *Lean Software Development* (Addison-Wesley Professional), Mary and Tom Poppendieck introduce the following statement: *think big; act small; fail fast; learn rapidly.* It adds a great deal of meaning to some of the thought processes and development concepts echoed in this book.

Vision and Focus—A Cosmos Analogy to Break Down a Complex Problem

When you look at the vastness of a clear night sky, you get a glimpse of our cosmos—a visualization of the great universe. As you gaze, you don't see much other than the bright sandy and orange dots across the canvas. It's like a complex problem domain that you are trying to understand or a monolith puzzle you are trying to solve. No matter how hard you stare at it, you see the same things, with the possible exception of a few shooting stars, depending on the season and where you are on Earth.

Consider each of those bright spots as different parts of the cosmos. You now focus on a big orange dot. With the right equipment, you zoom in. Soon, you realize you are looking at a galaxy hundreds of light-years away. What you have just focused on as one of the many parts of the cosmos has become a blurry object—a subvision.

You are not giving up. You repeat, focusing in on the galaxy only to find more bright spots—a sun! Each sun reveals its star pattern: the planets and their moons.

If you were in a faraway galaxy, this iteration of vision and focus might continue until, at some point, you encountered the Earth, its land, seas, and cloud formations—and finally, somewhere on the planet, you would find yourself (and us)!

Clearly, this is an oversimplification. However, it teaches us how a vision of impossibilities can be turned into a focus on possibilities. As you adopt serverless and build applications, develop the discipline to carefully analyze the task at hand and break it into manageable pieces to focus your work on.

What is a set piece?

When a production company decides to make a motion picture or movie, its vision is to create a financially successful product based on a given topic, story, or concept. However, the filming process does not start with the opening scene and continue in a linear fashion until the end. Instead, the production team identifies the set pieces, breaking it down into scenes or sequences of scenes that may be completed in any order. The term *set piece* is also common in theater, where it refers to a realistic piece of stage scenery built to stand independently as part of a stage set, and in music, to refer to individual parts of a composition that are written, rehearsed, recorded, and then edited together.

A similar concept is applied in team sports, model building, and more. Here are some of the general characteristics of a set piece:

- A set piece is part of a whole thing (the vision).
- When a person or a team works on a set piece, the *focus* is on the piece.
- Every set piece goes through adequate planning.
- Rehearsal, practicing, or testing is essential for a successful set piece.
- Different groups of people can work on different set pieces.
- All the pieces are brought together to make the whole.

Applying set piece thinking in serverless development

One of the challenges enterprise teams face in building modern cloud and serverless applications is the varying depth and breadth of skills engineers possess. Not everyone has been through a domain-driven design phase in their career; many have never studied or worked with object-oriented programming, unified modeling language (UML), or many analysis and design principles or processes that would equip them in the right way to think about and break down a given problem domain. One of the advantages of the first principles of serverless adoption that you learned about in the previous chapter is that they encourage engineers to own a part of the domain and focus inside their specific bounded context boundary. The set piece analogy and mode of thinking becomes easier to apply when serverless teams migrate, refactor, or design and build new solutions within their ownership boundary. Let's consider an example use case. The following is the problem statement for a customer reward system:

> Your business is looking for a way to offer several types of digital and physical rewards to its online retail customers. Stakeholders create and upload files with the reward details to their content management system (CMS). The CMS can propagate content changes to its consumers. The rewards uploaded to the CMS need to be configured in the backend system to keep track of their usage and apply the required business logic for issuing and redemption. There is a third-party CRM system that acts as a rewards ledger and receives all updates on the rewards.

This is a simple business use case common in the industry. You can identify certain details based on the problem statement:

- The business domain is *online retail* or *ecommerce*.
- The subdomain could be *customer*.
- The bounded context could be *customer rewards*.

Your task is to analyze and design the solution with a set piece mindset, bearing in mind the characteristics mentioned in the previous section.

Customer rewards system vision. Figure 3-28 shows the initial vision of this requirement as a logical representation. It covers all the main elements given in the problem statement.

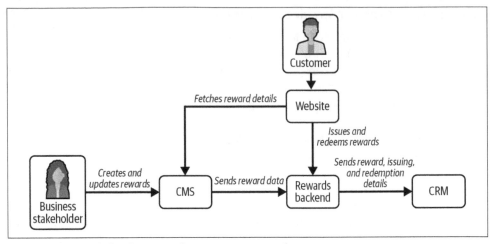

Figure 3-28. High-level vision of a customer rewards system

With monolithic thinking, you might be tempted to develop the entire thing as a single microservice. You normally see this approach in non-serverless tech stacks, where you think of traditional or textbook-style microservices and operate them in containers.

Figure 3-29 shows some prompts that give clues as to how you might divide your vision into focusable parts.

Based on the details available in Figure 3-29, you can start to capture some additional information that will assist you in identifying the set pieces:

- Reward content is created in advance. A reward's lifetime is controlled by its validity period. This indicates that the reward upload and configuration processes are asynchronous.

- The CMS sends notifications of content creation and changes. The rewards system needs a way of receiving these notifications. This is an ideal candidate for the callback communication pattern with a webhook that you saw earlier.

- The content from the CMS (as supplied by the stakeholders) requires some cleansing and translation before mapping it into the rewards model at the backend. This functionality resembles the anti-corruption layer of DDD.

- Implementing the business logic to assist the frontend serving customers requires a way to consume the services offered by the rewards backend. This is a user-facing synchronous operation with a request/response communication pattern and is a candidate for a microservice.

- The interaction between the rewards backend and the external CRM system involves transforming data to fit each one's model. This indicates a need for an ACL between the rewards backend and the CRM system.

- How about the availability of the third-party CRM platform? Do you know its SLA, usage quota limits, etc.? Consider separating these concerns related to CRM away from the main rewards backend.

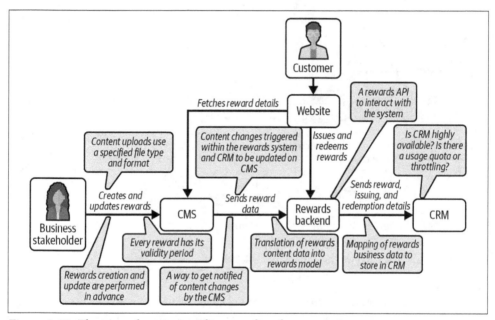

Figure 3-29. The rewards system with some of its characteristics

Identification of the set pieces. With the ideas you've gathered, you're ready to identify the actionable parts. Figure 3-30 shows the result, with each of the *potential* set pieces marked with a boundary for easy recognition and focus.

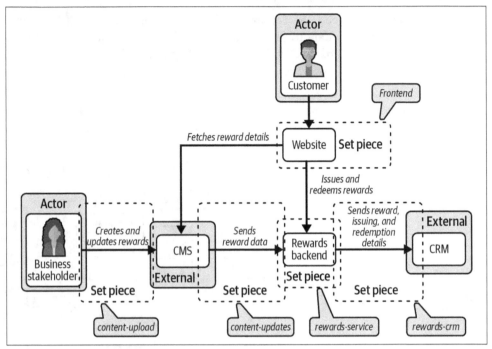

Figure 3-30. The rewards system with its set pieces

Let's take a look at each of these possible set pieces:

content-upload
> This is currently an *independent* manual activity between the content creators and the CMS. If you think of a future extension to this work, you can consider building an uploader service, but for the discussion here, we won't be talking much about it.

Frontend
> The frontend covers the web part of the feature where customers interact with the system to find and redeem rewards. As it is bigger than it sounds, we won't be delving into its details. We consider the frontend as a consumer of the rewards service.

content-updates

From the problem statement and the details gleaned earlier, we know that the three main functions of this set piece are:

- Implementing a callback webhook to enable notifications of content changes
- Translating the rewards data between the CMS and the backend
- Updating the CMS of any rewards data changes to keep the models in sync

When you think of the implementation pattern for this set piece, you will find it fits perfectly as a microservice.

rewards-service

This is where most of the business logic lives. It provides the rewards service to several consumers, including the frontend. As it handles issuing and redeeming rewards, it is likely to coordinate with other services and systems, both synchronously and asynchronously. For brevity, we will not explore its full responsibilities.

From an architecture and implementation point of view, the *rewards-service* set piece also fits well as a microservice.

rewards-crm

This set piece resembles the *content-updates* one, as both interact with external applications. In addition to its basic requirements of data transformation and updating both the CRM system and the backend, it must consider operational constraints such as the CRM system's SLA, downtime, usage quotas, etc. It then becomes the responsibility of the *rewards-crm* set piece to implement the necessary measures so that none of the other pieces of the system get impacted.

Another possibility, though not part of the problem statement, is that there could be a future need to listen for updates from the CRM system. In that event, the architecture should be extendable to accommodate it.

As you might have guessed, this is also a good candidate for a serverless microservice.

You've now made good progress in breaking down your vision (i.e., the problem domain) and identifying the parts with a set pieces mindset. If we redraw Figure 3-30 based on the preceding discussion, it will resemble Figure 3-31.

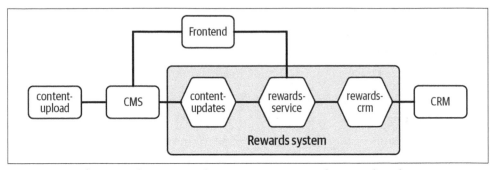

Figure 3-31. The rewards system with its microservices and external applications

Figure 3-31 is simple, clean, and straightforward to understand. However, it does not reveal an important characteristic. Intentionally, the diagram shows the connecting lines without any arrows—we'll discuss the reason for this in the next section.

Bringing the set pieces together. You might be thinking: breaking a monolith or the problem domain into many parts, focusing on each part as a set piece, and developing them independently is all good, but how do they come together to work in harmony as one system? To find the answer, you need to go back to where we started with set pieces as a concept in movies, theater, and music. A movie, for example, goes through an editing process, and background music or dialog is added to make the transitions between set pieces and other scenes understandable.

In serverless, you also have powerful ways to make the set pieces work together. They are:

- APIs, for synchronous request/response communication
- Events, as in the publish/subscribe model in event-driven architecture for asynchronous communication
- Messages, for more direct and decoupled communication between a producer and a consumer

You can use these primary concepts as appropriate to add meaning to the lines connecting the shapes in Figure 3-31, as the annotations in Figure 3-32 show. Remember, in addition, there are several architectural and implementation patterns (such as choreography and orchestration) that you will use as a blueprint to coordinate and orchestrate the services to perform the business functionality. In Chapter 5, you will learn about several patterns that are common in serverless development.

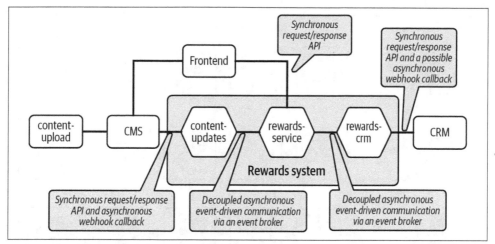

Figure 3-32. The potential communication techniques between the microservices, service consumers, and external applications

The individuality of set pieces.   Earlier we mentioned that one of the main benefits of thinking and working in set pieces is that it allows you to focus on one part of the overall vision and do the necessary planning, storyboarding, and rehearsals or testing before marking it as ready. If more than one piece is in the making, then different engineers or teams can work in parallel and in isolation, as there is no overlap.

With the implementation techniques and communication strategies between these pieces identified and agreed upon, you can reap the same benefits if you take these characteristics forward and apply them in serverless development:

- You can assign one or more engineers from the team that owns the rewards system to work on a set piece.

- You can focus on the planning (architecture and design) of each piece in isolation.

- Development and testing for each microservice can be carried out in an individual pipeline, with no or minimal conflicts with other development streams (as depicted in Figure 3-33).

- With few or no dependencies between these pieces, each service can be released soon after it progresses from the testing stage to a ready state.

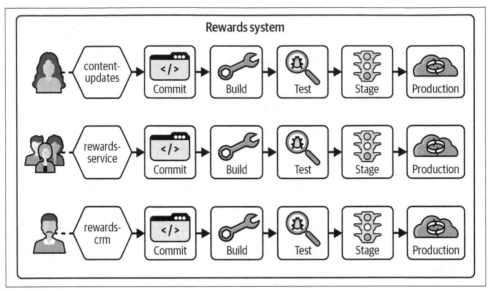

Figure 3-33. A pictorial representation of the individuality of microservices' CI/CD pipelines

Completing the vision of the rewards system. Though you design, build, and deploy most of your set pieces in isolation, they all need to come together, communicate, and coordinate to function as one rewards system (see Figure 3-34). Internally in each microservice, you will use services such as AWS Lambda, Amazon API Gateway, SQS, and DynamoDB, and several others, depending on the needs of the services. You will employ Amazon EventBridge to coordinate between the microservices and decouple them with event-driven capability.

The rewards system example used here to demonstrate how to break down a problem using analogies such as whole and parts, vision and focus, and set pieces was deliberately kept simple. In the real world you will face much more complex systems, but you should always approach the complexity with the view that any problem can be broken down into simple, manageable pieces that you can then focus on to successful completion.

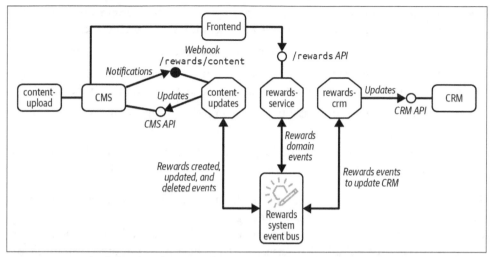

Figure 3-34. A high-level architectural representation of the rewards system

If you follow DDD, break your business domains into subdomains, core domains, and bounded contexts, and apply an event-driven approach, you'll no longer have to face the giant architectural blueprints of the past complex network of monolithic applications that span the entire organization. Instead, you'll be able to work with architectural constructs that stay within smaller boundaries owned and operated by smaller teams.

Techniques to identify set pieces. This section has introduced several new concepts that will help prepare you to tackle domain complexities. Here is some common thinking you can apply to help you break down a problem and identify its parts:

- Using DDD, break your business domain into subdomains and identify the bounded contexts.

- Identify synchronous interactions that require request/response API contracts.

- Isolate business logic that can be performed asynchronously.

- Look for external interactions (for example, with legacy systems, third-party platforms, SaaS applications, data feeds to your corporate data lake, etc.) and assess the need for dedicated microservices to handle them as an ACL implementation.

- Group administrative activities that are specific to the system boundary (API client creation, credential rotation, API usage quota monitoring, etc.).

- Dispatch push notifications from your application to its service consumers.

- Identify common resources and static data, such as size measurements, currency conversions, and country codes, that are accessed by different microservices.

- Think about your observability needs: log streaming, analysis, and filtering activities.

- Determine fraud prevention and intelligence activities that should be part of your business logic (inspecting data, monitoring user activities, etc.).

This is by no means a complete list, but it should help trigger ideas and allow you to identify points for further discussion among your team members with regard to validating your model and splitting the complexity into manageable pieces. Remember, as mentioned earlier, not all microservices need to host API endpoints or publish and subscribe to custom domain events. For example:

- You may have a microservice to perform nightly batch jobs or data cleansing activities that runs on a schedule.

- You may have a microservice that is responsible for sourcing and persisting all the events in your application. It may not have any API but can act as a catch-all for the domain events.

- You may have a microservice that provides APIs to serve its consumers with static data, utility computations, or service status checks. It may log all its functioning for observability, but not emit any events.

Incorporating a new set piece.   When you follow an agile and iterative development process, it is a necessity that you accommodate new features as you progress incrementally from your early minimum viable product (MVP) vision toward your maximum value product (another MVP!) vision. A challenge teams often face and debate for a long time is how to incorporate a new feature into the application—is it preferable to make changes to the existing services, or make changes to extend the application? It can be difficult to decide without knowing the details. However, where possible, your priority should be to look at ways of extending the application, such as by adding a new part or set piece.

Consider this new requirement for the rewards system:

> After receiving customer feedback, your business now wants to offer to email the reward codes to the users of the rewards system.

Assuming that millions of customers use the rewards system worldwide, you need a robust emailing service to support the business's ambition and growth. Amazon

Simple Email Service (SES) is a fully managed email service provider ideal for your use case. However, there are some important factors you need to consider:

- Amazon SES has strict policies regarding send quotas per second, per day, etc. Your architecture should be capable of utilizing the service in accordance with the account quota limits.

- Your business may want to use different email templates based on the season, reward type, value, country, language, etc., meaning you need to associate the right template with every email request to send to SES.

- Dispatching emails to customers happens in near real time.

- Sending emails to customers is more of a utility task or helper activity that is not part of the core business logic.

- If this is the first evolution of the rewards system, the business may have future ambitions to send other forms of emails, such as for account registration, monthly reports, etc.

Considering these points, it will be beneficial to consider adding a new set piece (and microservice) to the current rewards system, as shown in Figure 3-35.

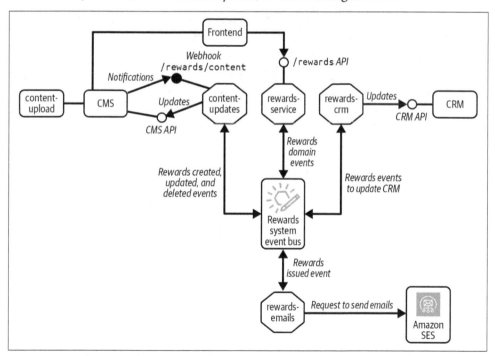

Figure 3-35. The rewards system, with the addition of a service to send emails to customers

Now suppose you've developed and rolled out the emailing feature worldwide in a phased manner, and it has become popular with customers. After a while, you begin to hear the following from stakeholders:

> Some customers have raised concerns via the support center about missing emails or not receiving emails with the reward codes. To assess the validity of such claims and help customers, we need end-to-end visibility of the emailing process.

To support this new business requirement, the *rewards-emails* service needs to keep a log of when an email was sent to a customer and what happened at the receiving end. Luckily, SES can help here by providing feedback on the delivery of each email, including whether the email was opened, the link was clicked, the email was bounced, and more. Collecting these crucial insights will help the business to understand and validate each claim.

Though this late requirement seems like it might be a good fit as a set piece, a better strategy in this case would be to incorporate it into the existing dedicated *rewards-emails* service, as shown in Figure 3-36, for the following reasons:

- The *rewards-emails* service already holds the record of all the emails it has dispatched, and it's beneficial to have visibility and traceability in one place.

- With SES, the sender (*rewards-emails*) can attach custom tags to the outgoing requests to SES. SES will then associate the custom tags with the feedback events, making it easier to correlate them with individual requests.

- Receiving email feedback from SES involves handling streams of events and processing them for business insights. With this approach, *rewards-emails* can act as the point of contact for SES and the gateway to everything related to emails for the rewards system.

 When you're building a service for sending emails via Amazon SES, depending on the scale of the organization and the business domains, there may be more than one business area sending different types of emails to customers. In such cases, you may benefit from having a dedicated team owning the emailing service with an architecture and implementation to support the needs of multiple teams.

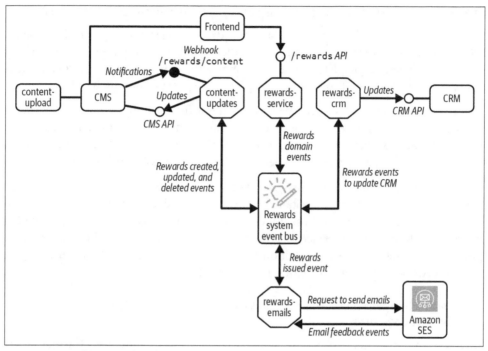

Figure 3-36. The rewards system, with the option to receive and handle email feedback events from SES

Building Microservices to Serverless's Strengths

How big a microservice should be is arguably the most debated topic in microservices forums. This is because you cannot quantify a microservice based on the number of lines of code or the size of its deployment package. While these are good measures to stop you from losing control and building monoliths, one size does not fit all when it comes to microservices. And when you're building microservices in a serverless technology ecosystem, they have many more characteristics to consider on top of what a standard microservice has. Here are a few points to keep in mind.

The size of a serverless microservice is not measured by the number of Lambda functions

One of the primary differentiators (and mindset changes that you need to make) when building serverless microservices is that you're not *programming* everything using a particular language to create your microservice. Instead, you are *composing* it using managed services. Programming is part of the process, but not all of it.

If you're new to serverless, it can be hard to digest that writing Lambda functions is not necessarily the primary development task in building a serverless application. If you think back to Chapter 1, where we looked at the serverless technology ecosystem and how the role of a serverless engineer requires diverse skills, this is why.

There are several use cases where a serverless microservice may not even need a Lambda function. It may contain business logic orchestration using AWS Step Functions, and its integration capability with other AWS services may be provided via AWS SDK and native service integrations. In some cases, unless there is a specific purpose, you may not need a function to handle an API request. You can integrate Amazon API Gateway directly with services other than AWS Lambda.

The infrastructure definition of your serverless microservice is as important as the business logic code

In traditional microservice development, you are likely to code your business logic and bundle it to deploy to an application server or a cloud-hosted container. A siloed team responsible for managing the container clusters and the server infrastructure will take care of operating your microservices. As you'll have gathered from the discussions in the book, the approach is different in serverless development. You select your tool to represent the infrastructure definition at the point at which you start developing, similar to choosing your compiler in a traditional programming environment. You and your team decide to use AWS Cloud Development Kit (CDK), AWS CloudFormation, AWS Serverless Application Model (SAM), or other frameworks before you even begin your development work.

Say you've decided to use a Node.js runtime for your Lambda functions and will develop using TypeScript. On top of this, you are using CDK to model and define the serverless infrastructure of your application. In this setup, you are programming your business logic and infrastructure in TypeScript. You use the same syntax to compose your API Gateway endpoint that integrates with a Lambda function that contains the business logic of the service you offer via the API. This is an example of how serverless development comprises business and infrastructure logic.

The more granularity, the deeper the observability

As you have seen, granularity and fine-grained control are some of the strengths of serverless. Unlike with traditional microservices running in containers, you have much control over each resource in a serverless microservice. Each managed resource may provide several operational metrics, and you can pick and choose the essential ones. For example, you may be keeping a watch on the latency of an API endpoint or the memory consumption of a Lambda function. In contrast, for an SQS queue, you are interested in the volume of messages it handles.

When a managed service provides you with a granular level of visibility, you benefit from the deeper observability targets for your microservice. The operational benefits you gain from serverless yield improvements in business visibility, service quality, and end-user satisfaction.

In the previous section, you learned how to split your problem and build smaller microservices. That approach lets you focus on each piece of your solution and gauge its functioning, setting up observability targets and measures for each service. For example, a customer-facing microservice's monitoring needs differ from those of a report-generating utility service. Always remember that observing the activities in a pond is way more manageable than in an ocean!

Event-Driven Architecture for Microservices Development

We've covered a lot of ground with regard to architecting serverless applications, including:

- The many components of the serverless technology ecosystem
- The unique characteristics of serverless technology
- The importance of thinking about domains, boundaries, smaller teams, APIs, and event-driven architecture (that is, the *first principles*)
- Common approaches for migrating legacy applications to serverless
- The important concepts of domain-driven design and how they are relevant to building microservices
- Microservices, their characteristics, and how to architect and build them to serverless's strengths
- Some common software architectures and the relevance of event-driven architecture in serverless development

That's a long list of great information that you have been exposed to. If you are new to modern architectural patterns, the encouraging news is that you have done all the hard work and are ready to move forward. In the remainder of this chapter, we'll fill in some of the remaining but crucial details about event-driven architecture that will become part of your daily serverless development process.

Event-Driven Computing and Reactive Services

You'll often hear the terms *event-driven architecture* and *event-driven computing* used interchangeably, but are they the same? Consider the following definitions:

- Event-driven architecture is an architectural paradigm that uses events to communicate asynchronously between decoupled microservices.

- Event-driven computing is the implementation or realization of event-driven architecture and the behavior of systems that work asynchronously.

In other words, event-driven architecture is a high-level thought process used in designing applications and microservices that promotes asynchrony and eliminates hard dependencies to make them loosely coupled or decoupled. Event-driven computing then turns those design ambitions into implementation artifacts, making the concepts a reality.

You saw the four main parties in event-driven architecture—events, event carriers, event producers, and event consumers—earlier in this chapter. The key member of the event-driven ecosystem is the event carrier, also known as an event router, bus, mediator, broker, etc. Though these terms have subtle differences in their meaning, for your overall understanding, you can consider all of them to be services that ingest events from applications and deliver them to one or more applications.

Is My Microservice a Reactive Service?

By definition, a reactive service is loosely coupled, resilient, and scalable. Importantly, it responds to events promptly, according to its purpose and operational responsibilities. When we say a microservice is reactive, we're talking about its behavior at an architectural level. Consider the example shown in Figure 3-37, where the customer account microservice of a media company emits an event when a customer subscribes to a particular channel, and the media enablement microservice *reacts* to channel subscription events. At this level, beyond loose coupling, it does not reveal much about its characteristics as a reactive service; we don't know how scalable or resilient it is.

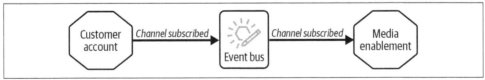

Figure 3-37. Depiction of simple event-driven and reactive microservices

Suppose you now look at the internal design and implementation of the media enablement microservice, as shown in Figure 3-38. Here, you will notice the different cloud services that it uses to fulfill its task asynchronously using event-driven computing implementation constructs.

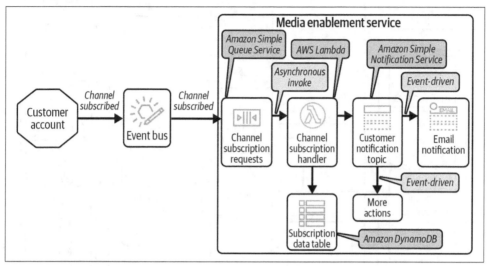

Figure 3-38. A detailed view of the internals of a simple event-driven microservice

If you inspect the AWS services that compose the media enablement microservice, you'll find that each has scalability, high availability, and resiliency built into it. Individually and collectively, as microservices, they are reactive services.

Event-driven computing and reactive services are core to serverless. They complement serverless technology in that they enable on-demand computing, scale to zero, and pay per use, among other things. As you are not running services and consuming cloud resources when they're not needed, this reduces energy consumption and aids with cloud sustainability measures (we'll talk about patterns and best practices for sustainability in serverless development in Chapter 10).

An Introduction to Amazon EventBridge

Amazon EventBridge (*https://oreil.ly/qC3wO*) is a fully managed serverless event bus that allows you to send events from multiple event producers, apply event filtering to detect events, perform data transformation where needed, and route events to one or more target applications or services (see Figure 3-39). It's one of the core fully managed and serverless services from AWS that plays a pivotal role in architecting and building event-driven applications. As an architect or a developer, familiarity with the features and capabilities of EventBridge is crucial. If you are already familiar with EventBridge and its capabilities, you may skip this section.

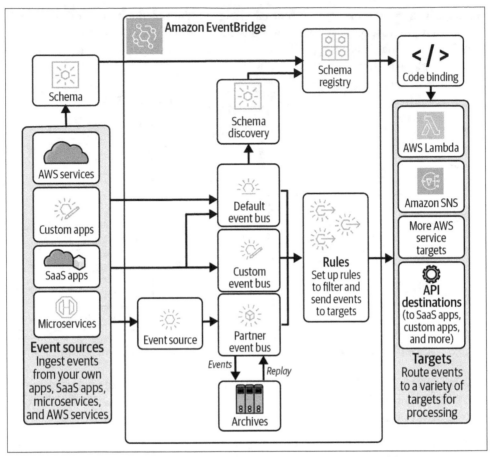

Figure 3-39. The components of Amazon EventBridge (source: adapted from an image on the Amazon EventBridge web page [https://oreil.ly/mW-Ku])

The technical ecosystem of EventBridge can be divided into two main categories. The first comprises its primary functionality, such as:

- The interface for ingesting events from various sources (applications and services)
- The interface for delivering events to configured target applications or services (consumers)
- Support for multiple custom event buses as event transportation channels
- The ability to configure rules to identify events and route them to one or more targets

The second consists of features that are auxiliary (but still important), including:

- Support for archiving and replaying events
- The event schema registry
- EventBridge Scheduler for scheduling tasks on a one-time or recurring basis
- EventBridge Pipes for one-to-one event transport needs

Let's take a look at some of these items, to give you an idea of how to get started with EventBridge.

Event buses in Amazon EventBridge

Every event sent to EventBridge is associated with an event bus. If you consider EventBridge as the overall event router ecosystem, then event buses are individual channels of event flow. Event producers choose which bus to send the events to, and you configure event routing on each bus.

The EventBridge service in every AWS account has a *default event bus*. AWS uses the default bus for all events from several of its services.

You can also create one or more *custom event buses* for your needs. In addition, to receive events from AWS EventBridge partners, you can configure a partner event source and send events to a *partner event bus*.

Event routing rules

The rules you create in EventBridge are the logic behind the filtering and routing of events that you associate with an event bus. These rules are effectively part of your application logic, and are designed, documented, deployed, and tested as such. A rule comprises three parts: the event filter pattern, event data transformation, and the target(s).

To filter an event in and send it to a target, you configure an event pattern as your filter condition. The sample pattern in Example 3-2 will match events like the one in Example 3-1 based on the `domain`, `service`, `type`, and `payment_type` attribute values.

Example 3-2. An example event filter pattern

```
{
  "detail": {
    "metadata": {
      "domain": [
        "ecommerce"
      ],
      "service": [
        "service-payments"
```

```
    ],
    "type": [
      "payment_received"
    ]
  },
  "data": {
    "payment_type": [
      "creditcard"
    ]
  }
}
}
```

As part of each rule, you can perform simple data transformations. At the time of writing, for each rule you can add up to five targets to send matching events to.

An important fact to keep in mind is that EventBridge guarantees *at least once delivery* of events to targets. This means a target may receive an event more than once (i.e., it may receive duplicate events). You will learn how to handle this situation later in the chapter.

Event archiving and replay

In EventBridge, you can store events in one or more archives. The events you archive depend on the event filter pattern. For example, you could create an archive to store all the events that match the pattern shown in Example 3-2.

You can create multiple archives to cater to your needs. Then, based on your business requirements, you can identify the events within your bounded context that need archiving and send them to the appropriate archives using different filter conditions. Unless there is a specific requirement to archive all the events, keep your archives as lean as possible as a best practice. Figure 3-40 shows a comparison of the different approaches for a better understanding.

To replay events from an archive, you specify the archive name and the time window. EventBridge reads the events from the archive and puts them onto the same event bus that originally emitted them. To differentiate a replayed event from the original event, EventBridge adds a replay-name attribute.

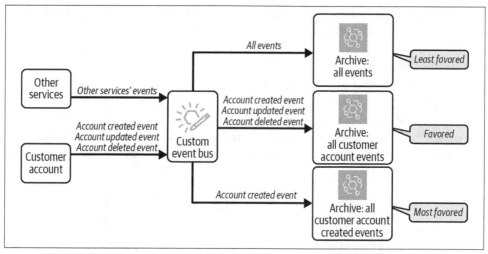

Figure 3-40. Different event archiving approaches, from least to most favored

Event schema registry

Every event has a structure, defined by a *schema*. EventBridge provides the schema for all the AWS service events, and it can infer the schemas of any other events sent to an event bus. In addition, you can create or upload custom schemas for your events.

Schema registries are holding places or containers for schemas. As well as the default registries for built-in schemas, discovered schemas, and all schemas, you can create your own registries to provide groupings for your schemas.

 EventBridge provides code bindings for schemas, which you can use to validate an event against its schema. This is useful to protect against introducing any breaking changes that might affect the downstream event consumers.

EventBridge Scheduler

EventBridge Scheduler is a way to configure tasks to be invoked asynchronously, on a schedule, from a central location. It is fully managed and serverless, which allows scheduling of millions of tasks either for one-time invocation or repeatedly. The schedules you configure are part of your architecture.

The EventBridge Scheduler can invoke more than 270 AWS services; it has a built-in retry mechanism and a flexible invocation time window.

EventBridge Pipes

Earlier, we discussed using EventBridge routing rules to filter events and send them to multiple targets. EventBridge Pipes, on the other hand, builds a one-to-one integration *pipeline* between an event publisher and a subscriber. Within a pipe, you have the option to perform event filtering, data transformation, and data enrichment (see Figure 3-41). This is quite a powerful feature, and it reduces the need for writing custom code in many use cases.

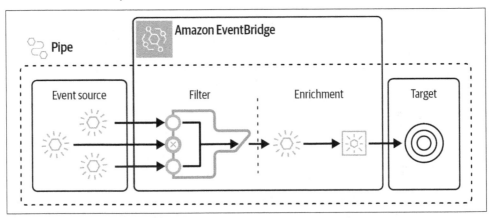

Figure 3-41. A representation of EventBridge Pipes integration between an event source and its target (source: adapted from an image on the Amazon EventBridge Pipes web page [https://oreil.ly/ciXEj])

Domain Events, Event Categories, and Types

As mentioned earlier in this chapter, in its simple and pure form, an event is something that has already happened. In the context of EventBridge, it's a notification about that thing happening—a data capsule containing information about the event that has occurred. The place where the event happened could be your backend microservice, a web application serving customers, a third-party system you interact with, or a legacy on-premises system in your enterprise.

An event is single-purpose and carries details about one thing. Event producers are the applications that *publish* information about the thing that happened. Event consumers are the applications that show interest by *subscribing* to certain events.

How do you represent an event?

Defining the structure of an event is not as easy a task as it may sound, due to differing standards and usage patterns. The difficulty and disagreements mainly center around deciding on a particular standard so that your events are portable across different applications, event carriers, and cloud platforms.

Events are represented as JSON objects. The structure of the events used in this book follows the pattern used by Amazon EventBridge. Example 3-3 shows all the possible fields or attributes in an EventBridge event.

Example 3-3. A sample EventBridge event

```
{
  "version": "0",
  "id": "6a7e8feb-b491-4cf7-a9f1-bf3703467718",
  "detail-type": "Order submission",
  "source": "service-checkout",
  "account": "111122223333",
  "time": "2023-12-22T18:43:48Z",
  "region": "eu-west-1",
  "resources": [
    "arn:service-identifier"
  ],
  "detail": {
  }
}
```

When you send an event from your application to EventBridge, it must contain the following mandatory fields:

detail-type
> A string value that describes the type of the event

source
> A string value that identifies the source of the event

detail
> A JSON object that contains the information about the event

The detail field carries the actual event data payload. You can think of this field as user-specific, whereas the other fields are AWS-specific.

As the detail field takes a JSON object as its value, it is up to you to add the necessary data as the event payload. However, it is highly recommended that you devise a common, high-level structure that every team in your organization can follow.

If you refer back to Example 3-1, you will notice that it follows a pattern—it splits the event payload into metadata and data sections, as shown here:

```
{
  "detail": {
```

```
        "metadata": {
        },
        "data": {
        }
      }
    }
```

You can use the `metadata` section to include all the common data items, as illustrated in Example 3-4. In the majority of cases, one or more of these fields and their values will become the filter criteria when setting up routing rules.

Example 3-4. Event metadata section carrying the domain and service details

```
{
  "metadata": {
    "domain": "ecommerce",
    "subdomain": "orders",
    "service": "payments",
    "category": "domain_event",
    "type": "data",
    "name": "payment_received"
  }
}
```

This is a simple representation where the `metadata` section contains the basic information about the origin of the event and its type. You can adapt and tailor its contents for use in your team and organization. Example 3-5 shows an extended use of the `metadata` field, carrying both domain-specific and critical operational details.

Example 3-5. Event metadata section carrying domain and operational details

```
{
  "metadata": {
    "version": "2.0",
    "trace_id": "skdj834sd3-j3ns-cmass23",
    "created_at": "2023-12-12T11:24:38Z",
    "domain": {
      "name": "ecommerce",
      "subdomain": "orders",
      "service": "payments",
      "category": "domain_event",
      "type": "data",
      "event": "payment_received"
    },
    "TTL": 1730419200
  }
}
```

Adding a TTL value, as in this example, is a way of propagating the data retention policy to the potential consumers.

The data section contains the event instance details. This might be information about a specific customer order, for instance, as shown in Example 3-6.

Example 3-6. Event data specific to the customer order

```
{
  "data": {
    "customer_id": "730e-4dfb-9166",
    "order_number": "123-987-456",
    "payment_reference": "cc-visa-9076-cv3s5s",
    "payment_type": "creditcard",
    "amount": 35.99,
    "currency": "GBP",
    "paid_at": "2023-12-30T09:12:27Z"
  }
}
```

The data section can be simple and compact, as in this example, or contain nested structures, depending on the information it carries.

It is beneficial to adhere to a standard structure for defining events across your organization or at a business domain level. This promotes uniformity and will make it easier to interpret events produced and consumed by applications across different domains. While teams may introduce certain variations and adaptations, it's a good idea to have a common base structure.

Event categories in serverless development

Categorization of events has always been a discussion point among software engineers. From a business point of view, domain events are the most important events. However, those who look after a distributed system will likely say operational events carry equal importance. In serverless development, it will be advantageous to understand the different categories of events you will encounter and use them where they fit. These include:

- Domain events
- Operational events
- AWS events
- Internal events

- Local events
- Transformed events
- Custom events

Differentiating event categories from event types. The event categories mentioned in the previous section are a logical way of separating events based on their origin, boundary, and ownership. This is one way of classifying events, but it may vary across teams and organizations.

The terms *event category* and *event type* are often used interchangeably, and there is no written specification explaining how to differentiate them. The type of an event reflects its purpose and is explicitly associated with the event. Though events are primarily envelopes of data, and each set of data represents something that happened in the system, if you shift your mindset from being a purist to a practical thinker you will soon find ways to add more meaning to your events. For example, you can add a field within the `metadata` section to indicate the event type.

The following are some common event types in event-driven architecture:

Command
> An instruction from the publisher directing the subscriber to perform an action. This type of event is useful in cases where the publisher has no direct control over another service, application, or third-party system.

Data
> A publish-and-forget style informational event. A data event is simply a carrier of some data.

Query
> An informational request from the event publisher. Similar to the request type, but the publisher is asking for data, not a service.

Request
> A request for downstream consumers to fulfill. For example, if service A is handling an order, it might require service B to send some data to another system so that it can eventually set a flag or data item. Service A raises a request event and updates its system when it receives a response event (described next) from service B.

Response
> An event emitted by a consumer in reply to a request event.

Status
> An informational event (similar to the data type) carrying information about the status of some activity. For example, customer update action failed, third-party system down, etc.

Task

> This type of event is used to coordinate multiple tasks as part of a higher-level task handled by the primary publisher. It is useful when you have workflows that span multiple microservices.

With that differentiation in mind, let's take a look at some of the categories listed earlier.

Domain events. A domain event represents a significant business occurrence reported by an application that implements the business logic of a domain. According to Martin Fowler (*https://oreil.ly/UuSjN*), it's an event that "captures the memory of something interesting which affects the domain." In an enterprise, domain events flow between systems that are part of different domains. They connect the dots to depict a user's journey across the different systems or data flows across the enterprise.

Example 3-7 is a typical example of a domain event emitted when a payment is successfully received for an order. It states its domain along with the necessary details about the payment.

Example 3-7. A domain event providing information about the receipt of a credit card payment

```
{
  "detail": {
    "metadata": {
      "version": "1.0",
      "created_at": "2023-12-30T09:12:27Z",
      "trace_id": "skdj834sd3-j3ns-cmass23",
      "domain": "ecommerce",
      "subdomain": "orders",
      "service": "payments",
      "category": "domain_event",
      "type": "data",
      "name": "payment_received"
    },
    "data": {
      "customer_id": "730e-4dfb-9166",
      "order_number": "123-987-456",
      "payment_reference": "cc-visa-9076-cv3s5s",
      "payment_type": "creditcard",
      "amount": 35.99,
      "currency": "GBP",
      "paid_at": "2023-12-30T09:12:27Z"
    }
  }
}
```

A main differentiator for a domain event is its representation of business data that is valid across the organization. Domain events are often classified as business confidential and rarely shared with external systems.

 Use past tense to name domain events: for example, `pay ment_received`, `order_submitted`, etc. In an organization with multiple domains, subdomains, teams, microservices, and so on, you can adopt a fully qualified name pattern for naming events: `com.<your-org>.<domain>.<bounded-context>.<micro service>@<event-name>`. For example, `com.myorg.ecom.orders .payments@PaymentReceived`.

Operational events.   Events that convey the operational health of an application, the latency of an API endpoint, the deployment status of a microservice, and so on are examples of operational events. You can argue that operational events are also domain events as they capture something that affects the domain. If you associate the domain events with the business functioning of a system—`customer_account _created`, for example—operational events help to draw a separation between business functionality and system behavior.

Most of the operational events stay within a team's own boundary, but there may be operational events that get routed to the central operation team or platform team, depending on the organizational structure. Example 3-8 shows an example of an operational event that indicates a change in the uptime of a service.

Example 3-8. A sample operational event

```
{
  "metadata": {
    "version": "1.0",
    "created_at": "2023-12-20T02:22:27Z",
    "trace_id": "skdj834sd3-j3ns-cmass23",
    "domain": "holiday-travel",
    "subdomain": "flight-booking",
    "service": "service-status-checker",
    "category": "operational_event",
    "type": "status",
    "status": "down"
},
  "data": {
    "system": "anytime-payment-provider",
    "current_status": "down",
    "previous_status": "up",
    "status_count": "2",
    "checked_at": "2023-12-20T02:15:00Z"
  }
}
```

AWS events. AWS events are events owned and produced by AWS services. We are mentioning them here as a type of event in order to create awareness of them as distinct from the domain and operational events your applications emit. The AWS cloud platform generates hundreds of events during the development and operation of serverless applications. You may not handle many, but they drive the asynchronous operation of the managed services. Example 3-9 shows an example of an S3 event for uploading a new file, *discount_codes.csv,* to the bucket `festival-promotions`.

Example 3-9. A sample Amazon S3 event

```
{
  "Records": [
    {
      "eventVersion": "2.0",
      "eventSource": "aws:s3",
      "awsRegion": "eu-west-1",
      "eventTime": "2023-12-01T00:00:00.000Z",
      "eventName": "ObjectCreated:Put",
      "userIdentity": {
        "principalId": "EXAMPLE"
      },
      "requestParameters": {
        "sourceIPAddress": "127.0.0.1"
      },
      "responseElements": {
        "x-amz-request-id": "EXAMPLE123456789",
        "x-amz-id-2": "EXAMPLE123/5678abcdefghi/mnopqrsEFGH"
      },
      "s3": {
        "s3SchemaVersion": "1.0",
        "configurationId": "testConfigRule",
      "bucket": {
        "name": "festival-promotions",
        "ownerIdentity": {
          "principalId": "EXAMPLE"
        },
        "arn": "arn:aws:s3:::festival-promotions"
      },
      "object": {
        "key": "discount_codes.csv",
        "size": 1024,
        "eTag": "0123456789a6789abcdef",
        "sequencer": "0A1B2C3D4E5F678901"
      }
    }
  ]
}
```

The term *custom event* is a generic name given to any event that your applications emit. The domain and operational events you saw earlier are examples of custom events. When your application emits a custom event, it typically sends the event to one of the custom event buses you manage. When you work with AWS cloud services, this is a way of differentiating your events from the AWS events.

Internal events. Similar to operational events, internal events are local within your bounded context; they are vital for driving the loosely coupled microservices inside the boundary but are never shared outside it. Unlike domain events, internal events may not contain information that is meaningful for services outside of their bounded contexts. Internal events are also commonly referred to as *local events*, as they are local within the application boundary. Example 3-10 shows an example of an internal event emitted by a service that sends updated reward details to a CRM system, informing it about a server error and setting the status to "retry".

Example 3-10. A sample internal event

```
{
  "detail": {
    "metadata": {
      "version": "1.0",
      "created_at": "2023-12-30T09:12:27Z",
      "trace_id": "skdj834sd3-j3ns-cmass23",
      "domain": "rewards",
      "service": "third-party-CRM",
      "category": "internal_event",
      "type": "status",
      "status": "retry"
    },
    "data": {
      "customer_id": "730e-4dfb-9166",
      "reward_code": "DXT876LSA536MBS",
      "order_numer": "123-987-456",
      "info": {
        "activity": "reward_update",
        "code": 500,
        "cause": "Internal Server Error"
      }
    }
  }
}
```

Transformed events. In Amazon EventBridge, you can modify source events before sending them to one or more targets. These *transformed* events get formed at runtime and do not comply with the original schema representation—in other words, the events that go to the targets may not have all the original details included in the source events. Keep in mind that the event transformation logic is part of your architecture and design logic and should be treated as such.

There are several use cases for transformed events, as you will understand when you start building distributed microservices. For example:

- The source event contains sensitive data you want to remove before sending it to a target. Here, you are limiting the exposure of sensitive data in downstream systems.

- The target application requires just the event's data part and is not interested in the metadata. Here, you are following the policy of sharing just the required data.

- The source event acts as a prompt to initiate some action in the target application. In this scenario, you create a new event with values from the source or an event with static data for the target. Here, you are performing data hiding.

Differentiating Events and Messages

The terms *message* and *event* are often used interchangeably in serverless. However, their original intent and the purpose they serve are different. A message is information for a specific receiver or target application. It may contain details about something that happened in the past, activities to be performed in the future, or a command to instruct the receiver to carry out a specific activity. An example is a Lambda function that adds the details of an order as a message to an SQS queue for the order shipping application to process. Handling a message by a consumer usually involves acknowledging receipt of the message and, in most cases, deleting the message soon after processing it.

An event is a kind of message, but as we've seen, it exclusively conveys information about something that has already happened. Events get published on *topics* to which consumers subscribe to register their interest in receiving those events. For example, an online gaming site could send an event upon the creation of a new member account. Applications such as accounts, payments, and others may be interested in consuming this event to initiate customer onboarding processes.

With the broader adoption of event-driven architecture in serverless, a clear separation between events and messages is not always maintained.

Event producers and event publishing best practices

Event producers are applications that create and publish events. As you develop on AWS, you publish your events to one of your custom event buses on Amazon EventBridge. Here are some best practices for event publishers to follow:

Event publishers should be agnostic of the consumers of their events.

One of the golden rules in event-driven architecture is that event producers remain agnostic of the consumers. The event producers should not make assumptions about who or what might consume their events and tailor the data. This agnosticism lets you keep applications decoupled—one of the main benefits of EDA.

 In its pure form, consumer agnosticism suggests the use of a *publish-and-forget* model. However, the reality, as you develop granular microservices in serverless, can be different. There will be situations (still within the loosely coupled services construct) where a publisher may want to know the outcome of the handling of an event by a downstream consumer so that it can update its status for recordkeeping, trigger an action, etc. The event types listed in "Differentiating event categories from event types" on page 146 can be indicators for this purpose.

Every event should carry a clear identification of its origin.

The details of the domain, service, function, etc., are important information to identify the origin of an event. Not all events need to follow a strict pattern of the hierarchy of their origin, but it benefits cross-domain consumers to set the event filters as part of consumption.

In a secured and regulated environment, teams apply event encryption measures to protect data privacy. Often, third-party systems sign the event payload, and consumers perform IP address checks to validate the event origin before consumption.

Treat domain events as data contracts that conform to event schemas.

With distributed services, event producers should conform the events to the published schema definitions, treating them as the equivalent of API contracts.

Versioning your events is essential to avoid introducing breaking changes.

Event producers should adhere to an agreed structure for uniformity across the organization.

As discussed earlier, uniformity in the event structure at the organizational, domain, or department level helps make the development process smoother in many ways.

It may be challenging to create a standard format for your events at the outset. You can evolve it as you gain experience and learn from others. Allow flexibility within the overall design to enable teams that need to accommodate information specific to them to do so.

An event should carry just the required data to denote the occurrence of the event.
Often it takes time to decide on the content of an event. If you follow the structure shown earlier, with `metadata` and `data` sections, start with the `metadata`, as you may already have clarity on most of those fields.

Begin from the context of when and where the event occurred, and build from there. It's a good practice to include a minimal set of *shareable* data that is just enough to understand the event as an entity.

Event producers should add a unique tracing identifier for each event.
Including a unique identifier that can travel with the event to its consumers improves your application's tracing capabilities and observability.

Be aware of the event payload size limit and service quota.
The maximum payload size of an event in Amazon EventBridge is 256 KB (at the time of writing). In high-volume event publishing use cases, consider the limit on how many events you can send to EventBridge per second, and have measures in place to avoid losing critical events if you exceed this limit.

When you publish events with sensitive data, you can add a metadata attribute—say, `severity`—to indicate the level of severity of the risk of this data being exposed, with values like RED, AMBER, and GREEN. You can then implement logic to prevent certain subscribers from receiving high-severity events, for example.

The gatekeeper event bus pattern described in Chapter 5 can make use of the severity classification of events to consider encryption measures when sharing events outside of its domain.

Event consumers and event consumption best practices

Event consumers are applications on the receiving end. They set up subscription policies to identify the events that are of interest to them. As you get started with Amazon EventBridge, here are a few tips and best practices for event consumers to keep in mind:

Consumer applications may receive duplicate events and should be idempotent.
In event-driven computing, in the majority of cases, the event delivery is guaranteed to be *at least once* (as opposed to *exactly once* or *at most once*). If you don't properly account for this, it can cause severe consequences. Imagine your bank account getting debited twice for a purchase you made!

Building idempotency into an application that reacts upon receipt of events is the most critical measure to implement.

Storing the event data while processing it has benefits.

Depending on the event consumer's logic, the event processing may happen in near real time or with a delay. A practice often adopted by event subscribers is to store the event data—temporarily or long-term—before acting on it. This is a form of storage-first pattern, which you will learn about in Chapter 5.

There are several benefits to this practice. Primarily, it helps to alleviate the problem of events potentially being received more than once by providing a register that can be checked for duplicates before handling an event. In addition, storing the events eases the retry burden on the consumer application; if a downstream application goes down, for example, it won't need to request that the producer resend all of the events that application needs to process.

Ordering of events is not guaranteed.

Maintaining the order of events in a distributed event-driven architecture with multiple publishers and subscribers is hard. EventBridge does not guarantee event ordering. If the order of events is crucial, you'll need to work with the event producers to add sequence numbering. If that's not possible, subscribers can implement sorting based on the event creation timestamps to put them into the correct order.

Avoid modifying events before relaying them.

There are situations where applications engage in an asynchronous chain of actions known as the event relay pattern: the service receives an event, performs an action, and emits an event for a downstream service. In such situations, the subscriber should never modify the source event and publish a modified version. It must always emit a new event with its identity as publisher and the schema it is responsible for.

Collect events that failed to reach the target consumer.

In a resilient event-driven architecture, a consumer may have all the measures it needs to process an event successfully—but what happens if the event gets lost in transit and does not arrive, or if the consumer experiences an unforeseen outage?

EventBridge retries event delivery until successful for up to 24 hours. If it fails to deliver an event to the target, it can send the failed event to a dead letter queue (DLQ) for later processing. As you saw earlier, you can also use EventBridge's archive and replay feature to reduce the risk of missing critical business events.

CloudEvents (*https://cloudevents.io*) is a specification for describing event data in a common way. It's supported by the Cloud Native Computing Foundation (CNCF). Adopting CloudEvents as the standard for defining and producing your event payloads will ensure your events remain interoperable, understandable, and predictable, particularly as usage increases across the domains in your organization.

AsyncAPI (*https://www.asyncapi.com*) is the industry standard for defining asynchronous APIs, and it can be used to describe and document message-driven APIs in a machine-readable format. Whereas the CloudEvents specification constrains the schema of your event payloads, AsyncAPI helps you to document the API for producing and consuming your events. AsyncAPI is to event-driven interfaces as OpenAPI is to RESTful APIs.

The Importance of Event Sourcing in Serverless Development

Event sourcing is a way of capturing and persisting the changes happening in a system as a sequence of events.

Figure 3-3 showed a customer account service that emits account created, account updated, and account deleted events. Traditionally, when you store and update data in a table, it records the latest state of each entity. Table 3-1 shows what this might look like for the customer account service. There's one record (row) per customer, storing the latest information for that customer.

Table 3-1. Sample rows from the Customer Account table

Customer ID	First name	Last name	Address	DOB	Status
100-255-8730	Joe	Bloke	99, Edge Lane, London	1966/04/12	ACTIVE
100-735-6729	Biz	Raj	12A, Top Street, Mumbai	1995/06/15	DELETED

While Table 3-1 provides an up-to-date representation of each customer's data, it does not reveal whether customers' addresses have changed at any point. Event sourcing helps provide a different perspective on the data by capturing and persisting the domain events as they occur. If you look at the data in Table 3-2, you'll see that it preserves the domain events related to a customer account. This data store acts as the source for the events if you ever want to reconstruct the activities of an account.

Table 3-2. Event source data store for the customer account service

PK	SK	Event ID	First name	Last name	Address	DOB	Status
100-255-8730	2023-04-05T08:47:30.718Z	Hru343t5-jvcj	Joe	Bloke	99, Edge Lane, London	1966/04/12	UPDATED
100-735-6729	2023-01-15T02:37:20.545Z	Igojk834sd3-r454	Biz	Raj	12A, Top Street, Mumbai	1995/06/15	DELETED
100-255-8730	2022-10-04T09:27:20.443Z	Jsd93ebhas-xdfgns	Joe	Bloke	34, Fine Way, Leeds	1966/04/12	UPDATED
100-255-8730	2022-06-15T18:57:43.148Z	Zxjfie294hfd-kd9e7n	Joe	Bloke	15, Nice Road, Cardiff	1966/04/12	CREATED
100-735-6729	2009-11-29T20:49:40.003Z	skdj834sd3-j3ns	Biz	Raj	12A, Top Street, Mumbai	1995/06/15	CREATED

Uses for event sourcing

Although early thoughts on event sourcing focused on the ability to re-create the current state of an entity, many modern implementations use event sourcing for additional purposes, including:

Re-creating user session activities in a distributed event-driven system
> Many applications capture user interactions in timeboxed sessions. A session usually starts at the point of a user signing into the application and stays active until they sign out, or the session expires.

> Event sourcing is valuable here to help users resume from where they left off or resolve any queries or disputes, as the system can chart each user's journey.

Enabling audit tracing in situations where you cannot fully utilize logs
> While many applications rely on accumulated, centrally stored logs to trace details of system behaviors, customer activities, financial data flows, etc., enterprises need to comply with data privacy policies that prevent them from sending sensitive data and PII to the logs. With event sourcing, as the data resides inside the guarded cloud accounts, teams can build tools to reconstruct the flows from the event store.

Performing data analysis to gain insights
> Data is a key driver behind many decisions in the modern digital business world. Event sourcing enables deeper insights and analytics at a fine-grained level. For example, the event store of a holiday booking system harvests every business event from several microservices that coordinate to help customers book their vacations. Often customers will spend time browsing through several

destinations, offers, and customizable options, among other things, before completing the booking or, in some cases, abandoning it. The events that occur during this process carry clues that can be used, for example, to identify popular (and unpopular) destinations, packages, and offers.

 Since the conception of event sourcing a couple of decades ago, due to the emergence of the cloud and managed services, there have been vast changes in the volume of data captured and the available ingestion mechanisms and storage options. The data models of many (but not all) modern applications accommodate storing the change history for a certain period alongside the actual data, as per the business requirements, to enable quickly tracing all the activities.

Architectural considerations for event sourcing

At a high level, the concept of event sourcing is simple—but its implementation requires careful planning. When distributed microservices come together to perform a business function, you face the challenge of having hundreds of events of different categories and types being produced and consumed by various services. In such a situation:

- How do you identify which events to keep in an event store?
- How do you collect all the related events in one place?
- Should you keep an event store per microservice, bounded context, application, domain, or enterprise?
- How do you handle encrypted and sensitive data?
- How long do you keep the events in an event store?

Finding and implementing the answers to these critical questions involves several teams and business stakeholders working together. Let's take a look at some of the options.

Dedicated microservice for event sourcing. Domain events flow via one or more event buses in a distributed service environment. With a dedicated microservice for event sourcing, you separate the concerns from different services and assign it to a single-purpose microservice. It manages the rules to ingest the required events, perform necessary data translations, own one or more event stores, and manage data retention and transition policies, among other tasks.

Event store per bounded context. A well-defined bounded context will benefit from having its own event store, which can be helpful for auditing purposes or for reconstructing the events that led to the current state of the application or a particular business entity. For example, in the rewards system we looked at earlier in this chapter (Figure 3-36), you might want to have an event store to keep track of rewards updates. With an extendable event-driven architecture, it's as simple as adding another set piece microservice for event sourcing, as shown in Figure 3-42.

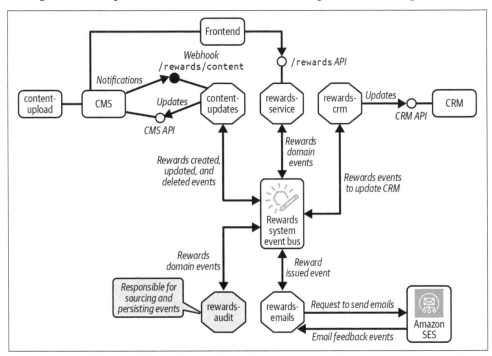

Figure 3-42. Adding a dedicated rewards-audit microservice for event sourcing to the rewards system

Application-level event store. Many applications you interact with daily coordinate with several distributed services. An ecommerce domain, for example, has many subdomains and bounded contexts, as you saw back in Figure 2-3 (in "Domain-first" on page 40). Each bounded context can successfully implement its own event sourcing capability, as discussed in the previous subsection, but it can only capture its part in the broader application context.

As shown in Figure 3-43, your journey as an ecommerce customer purchasing items touches several bounded contexts—product details, stock, cart, payments, rewards, etc. To reconstruct the entire journey, you need events from all these areas. To plot a customer's end-to-end journey, you must collate the sequence of necessary events. An application-level event store is beneficial in this use case.

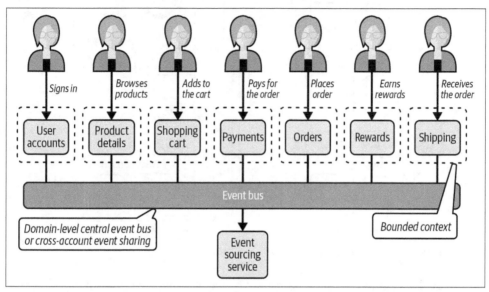

Figure 3-43. An ecommerce customer's end-to-end order journey, with the different touchpoints

Centralized event sourcing cloud account. So far, you have seen single-purpose dedicated microservice, bounded context, and application-level event sourcing scenarios. A centralized event store takes things to an even more advanced level, as shown in Figure 3-44. This is an adaptation of the centralized logging pattern, where enterprises use a consolidated central cloud account to stream all the CloudWatch logs from multiple accounts from different AWS Regions. It provides a single point of access for all their critical logs, allowing them to perform security audits, compliance checks, and business analysis.

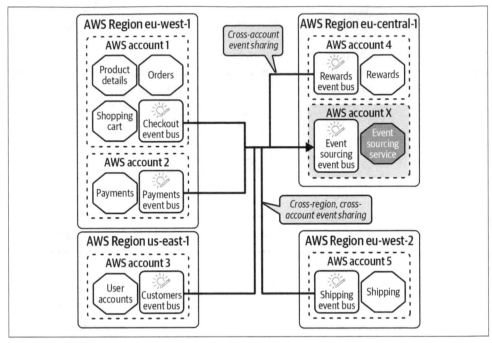

Figure 3-44. A central cloud account for event sourcing

There are, however, substantial efforts and challenges involved in setting up a central event sourcing account and related services:

- The first challenge is agreeing upon a way of sharing events. Not all organizations have a central event bus that touches every domain. EventBridge's cross-account, cross-region event sharing is an ideal option here.

- Identifying and sourcing the necessary events is the next challenge. A central repository is required in order to have visibility into the details of all the event definitions. EventBridge Schema Registry is useful, but it is per AWS account, and there is no central schema registry.

- With several event categories and types, structuring the event store and deriving the appropriate data queries and access patterns to suit the business requirements requires careful planning. You may need multiple event stores and different types of data stores—SQL, NoSQL, object, etc.—depending on the volume of events and the frequency of data access.

- Providing access to the event stores and events is a crucial element of this setup, with consideration given to data privacy, business confidentiality, regulatory compliance, and other critical measures.

Event sourcing is an important pattern and practice for teams building serverless applications. Even if your focus is primarily on delivering the core business features (to bring value), enabling features such as event sourcing is still crucial. As mentioned earlier, not every team will need the ability to reconstruct the application's state based on the events; however, all teams will benefit from being able to use the event store for auditing and tracing critical business flows.

EventStorming

One of the classic problems in software engineering is balancing what's in the requirements, and what gets implemented and delivered. Misunderstandings of business requirements and misalignments between what the business stakeholders want and what the engineering team actually builds are common in the software industry. Applying the first principles of serverless development brings clarity to what you are building, making it easier to align with the business needs. Developing iteratively and in small increments makes it easier to correct when things go wrong before it is too late and becomes expensive.

You cannot expect every serverless engineer to have participated in requirements engineering workshops and UML modeling sessions or to understand domain-driven design. Often, engineers lack a complete understanding of why they are building what they are building. EventStorming is a collaborative activity that can help alleviate this problem.

What is EventStorming?

EventStorming (*https://oreil.ly/hnuuO*) is a collaborative, non-technical workshop format that brings together business and technology people to discuss, ideate, brainstorm, and model a business process or analyze a problem domain. Its inventor, Alberto Brandolini, drew his inspiration from domain-driven design. EventStorming is a fast, inexpensive activity that brings many thoughts to the board as a way of unearthing the details of a business domain using simple language that everybody understands. The two key elements of EventStorming are *domain experts* (contributors) and *domain events* (outcomes). Domain experts are subject matter experts (SMEs) who act as catalysts and leading contributors to the workshop. They bring domain knowledge to the process, answer questions, and explain business activities to everyone (especially the technical members). Domain events are significant events that reflect business facts at specific points. These events are identified and captured throughout the course of the workshop.

The EventStorming process looks at the business process as a series of domain events, arranges the events over a timeline, and depicts a story from start to finish. From the thoughts gathered and domain events identified, you begin to recognize the actors, commands, external systems, and, importantly, pivotal events that signal the change of context from one part to the other and indicate the border of a bounded context.

A *command* is a trigger or action that emits one or more domain events. For example, the success of a *redeem reward* command produces a *reward-redeemed* domain event. You will see the domain model emerging as aggregates (clusters of domain objects) as you identify the actors, commands, and domain events. In the previous example, the *reward* is an aggregate that receives a command and generates a domain event.

A full explanation of how you conduct an EventStorming workshop is beyond the scope of this book, but several resources are available. In addition to the ones listed on the website (*https://oreil.ly/AoCnL*), Vlad Khononov's book *Learning Domain-Driven Design* (O'Reilly) has a chapter on EventStorming.

The importance of EventStorming in serverless development

EventStorming is a great way to collaborate and to learn about business requirements, identify domain events, and shape the model before considering architecture and solution design. However, depending on the scale of the domain or product, the outcome of EventStorming could be high-level.

Say your organization is transforming the IT operations of its manufacturing division. The EventStorming exercise will bring together several domain experts, business stakeholders, enterprise and solution architects, engineering leads and engineers, product managers, UX designers, QA engineers, test specialists, etc. After a few days of collaboration, you identify various business process flows, domain events, model entities, and many bounded contexts, among other things. With clarity about the entire domain, you start assigning ownership—stream-aligned teams—to the bounded contexts.

These teams then delve into each bounded context to identify web applications, microservices, APIs, events, and architectural constructs to implement. While the artifacts from the domain-level EventStorming sessions form a base, serverless teams need more granular details. Hence, it is useful in serverless development if you employ EventStorming in two stages:

Domain-level EventStorming
  According to Brandolini, this is the "Big Picture" EventStorming workshop aimed at identifying the business processes, domain events, commands, actors, aggregates, etc.

Development-level EventStorming
  This is a more small-scale activity that involves an engineering team, its business stakeholders, the product manager, and UX designers. This is similar to what Brandolini calls "Design Level EventStorming."

Here, the focus is on the bounded context and developments within it. The team identifies the internal process flows, local events, and separation of functionality and responsibilities. These become the early sketches for set-piece microservices, their interfaces, and event interactions. The outcome from the development-level EventStorming feeds into the solution design process (explained in Chapter 6) as engineers start thinking about the serverless architecture.

Let's consider an example situation for development-level EventStorming:

Context: Figure 2-3 (in "Domain-first" on page 40) shows the breakdown of an ecommerce domain. A domain-level EventStorming workshop has identified the subdomains and bounded contexts. A stream-aligned team owns the user payments bounded context.

Use case: Due to customer demand and to prevent fraud, the stakeholders want to add a new feature where customers who call the customer support center to place orders over the phone can make their payments via a secure link emailed to them rather than providing the card number over the phone.

The proposed new feature only requires part of the ecommerce team to participate in a (development-level) EventStorming session. It is a small-scale activity within a bounded context with fewer participants.

Summary

You've just completed one of the most crucial chapters of this book on serverless development. The architectural thoughts, best practices, and recommendations you've learned here are essential whether you work as an independent consultant or part of a team in a big enterprise. Irrespective of the organization's size, your ambition is to architect solutions to the strengths of serverless. Business requirements and problem domains can be complex and hard to comprehend, and it is the same in other fields and walks of life. You can observe and learn how people successfully solve non-software problems and apply those principles in your work.

Serverless architecture need not be a complex and tangled web of lines crisscrossing your entire organization. Your vision is to architect single-purpose, loosely coupled, distributed, and event-driven microservices as set pieces that are easier to conceive, develop, operate, observe, and evolve within the serverless technology ecosystem of your organization.

You will carry the learnings from these initial chapters with you as you go through the remainder of the book. You will begin to apply the architectural lessons in Chapter 5, which will teach you some core implementation patterns in serverless development. But first, the next chapter delves into one of the fundamental and critical topics in software development: security.

Interview with an Industry Expert

Matt Lewis, Chief AWS Architect, IBM UK, AWS Data Hero

Matt is an AWS Data Hero and holds multiple AWS certifications. He works as Chief AWS Architect at IBM, growing the AWS capability and ensuring customers make the best use of AWS services to achieve their outcomes and deliver business value. Previously, he was Chief Architect at a UK central government agency, where he introduced serverless technologies that successfully handle several billion requests each month. He set up and runs the AWS South Wales user group and is an organizer of ServerlessDays Cardiff.

Q: Matt, you have worked in public and private sector organizations architecting highly critical systems. Is there a fundamental shift in the technology and architectural decision-making process between these organizations?

I don't believe there is a fundamental shift in the technology and architectural decision-making process between public and private sector organizations. Instead, I see that differences in approaches are linked back to the underlying culture of an organization. This is related to aspects like their risk appetite, their cloud operating model, and the levels of autonomy individual engineering product teams have.

As these organizations move to the cloud, many of their existing processes need to adapt. As these organizations move along the maturity model, the willingness to adopt new technologies and make rapid architectural decisions increases. This is because practices such as DevSecOps and the automatic enforcement of controls through guardrails such as service control policies means that changes can be applied in a secure and controlled manner.

I believe we will see more organizations adopting serverless technologies when architecting highly critical systems. The UK's National Cyber Security Centre notes that adopting serverless components makes things easier for you as it moves more of the shared responsibility model to the cloud provider. This means you can focus on delivering business value whilst letting the cloud provider manage important capabilities such as patching, scaling, high availability, and resilience.

Q: While you were at the DVLA [Driver and Vehicle Licensing Agency], I [Sheen] delivered a talk to a group of developers and leaders on the benefits of serverless and shared some industry case studies. How much do such sessions influence technology adoption in a public sector environment?

I am a huge believer in the value of community and have found these types of sessions to be influential. I would definitely encourage people to find their local meetup group and become part of a community. The value that one person brings to an organization isn't just what they know individually, but it includes their network. Technology evolves so quickly, and with it the number of new features and services, as well as patterns and best practices. It's not possible for one person to keep up-to-date on everything. There is also the challenge that working within an organization, you can be blinkered to just the scope of what is being delivered. Therefore, reaching out and hearing from experts in the field is vital and plays a really important role.

From a public sector perspective, the digital services offered are ones that we, as citizens, interact with. We expect the same kind of user experience we get from major ecommerce sites. It makes sense to listen to experts across the private and public sectors and find out what worked and what they would do differently if starting again. This is something I am passionate about, as it results in delivering higher-quality services at a lower cost point and ultimately delivering better value to the taxpayer.

Q: As an AWS Data Hero, you have experience working with several data and storage services on AWS. With a myriad of DBaaS options available, what would be your advice to organizations migrating their legacy monolith applications that heavily depend on relational database systems handling structured data?

When looking at migrating applications to the public cloud, I would always start by mapping the applications against the "7 Rs." This is an industry approach setting out the seven most common migration strategies. The three most popular for migrating a legacy monolith application that depends on an RDBMS are re-host, re-platform, and refactor.

Re-hosting an application is typically the fastest approach to move to the cloud but results in the highest total cost of ownership. This is often the first step on a journey to allow a data center or on-premises servers to be decommissioned before the application is optimized to take advantage of cloud capabilities.

Re-platforming an application allows you to reshape it. Major opportunities include migrating to an open source or AWS cloud native database engine and adopting a managed database service such as Amazon RDS or Amazon Aurora. This way, the cloud provider is responsible for administrative tasks like server provisioning, patching, automated backups, and recovery, and you take advantage of continuous monitoring, self-healing storage, and scaling. You can use the AWS Schema Conversion Tool (SCT) and Database Migration Service (DMS) tools to help migrate the data.

Refactoring involves rearchitecting the application, often carried out in phases over time. The industry move to microservices involves breaking apart monolithic legacy applications into smaller microservices, which allows the associated data to be broken up. As Dr. Werner Vogels once wrote (*https://oreil.ly/R58YH*), "a one size fits all database doesn't fit anyone." When you break apart a monolith, you can look at NoSQL alternatives for particular data domains that may be more appropriate and offer more advantages. AWS provides a family of purpose-built databases, with many offering a serverless flavor. Amazon themselves migrated all data from their consumer business from Oracle to various AWS database services, including Amazon DynamoDB, Amazon RDS, Amazon Aurora, and Amazon Redshift.

Q: You were at AWS re:Invent 2022 when Werner mentioned the significance of asynchrony and event-driven architecture in his keynote. Why do you think these two are some of the core architectural principles in building serverless applications?

Services offered today need to adapt to changes around them. Applications built using synchronous request/response communication end up brittle and introduce tight coupling. Issues in one component such as error rate or latency can cause cascading failures, and it's difficult to introduce new functionality.

Asynchrony and event-driven architectures are core principles in building modern cloud native serverless applications. Key to this is decoupling the producer from the consumers of an event. There are many benefits this introduces for serverless applications, such as:

Scalability
Scalability is critical to handle unpredictable workloads. Loosely coupled and stateless components can be scaled individually as needed.

Flexibility
New producers and consumers can be added without any impact on other components, allowing the overall system to evolve over time.

Fault tolerance

An issue with one event consumer does not prevent other consumers from receiving and processing that event. Events can also be buffered and delivered once the consumer is back online.

Responsiveness

Event consumers can process an event as soon as they receive it. For example, using EventBridge or S3 notifications, an AWS Lambda function will be invoked asynchronously with the details of the event. There is no polling required to check if an event has taken place.

Simplicity

The concept of events being used to communicate between components creates an architecture that is simple to understand and comprehend.

Cost efficiency

With no blocking between producers and consumers of events, and no running servers constantly polling, there is typically no or little cost for components when not in use. This results in a more cost-efficient architecture.

Q: You know from working in government organizations the importance of sustainability considerations in digital. How do you balance performance, cost, and sustainability when proposing new serverless architectures?

Sustainability has rightly become much more important when designing systems, with its own pillar in the Well-Architected Framework that sets out best practices and an AWS Customer Carbon Footprint Tool that will enable you to track emissions and quantify the effect of architectural changes over time. From the outset, I would ensure that proposed architectures focus on asynchronous over synchronous communication and are event-driven rather than using polling, for all the reasons previously mentioned.

In almost all cases, there is a direct correlation between cost and sustainability. This makes sense with services where AWS manages the scaling, and you are only charged for resources used. The ability of AWS Lambda to scale to zero means you are not paying for idle compute when there is no traffic. In addition, I would always look to take advantage of new and more efficient hardware and software offerings, such as adopting ARM-based Graviton processors over x86 where supported by the workload.

The approach to handling data can also have a big impact. Architectures should use efficient file formats like Parquet, and data should be compressed to reduce its size before moving it over the network. Lifecycle management policies should be used that will automatically move data to more energy-efficient storage tiers and enforce strict data retention policies. The use of caching and edge services places data closer to the customer and reduces the amount of data that needs to be transferred over long distances. All of these approaches also improve performance.

Another consideration is around SLAs and the impact these have on performance, cost, and sustainability. Performance must be good enough, but the more stringent the nonfunctional requirements (NFRs) around performance, availability, resilience, etc., the higher the overall cost with more components running that impact sustainability. Does all data need to be backed up, or only the most critical elements? Can you support eventually consistent versus strongly consistent reads with Amazon DynamoDB?

Finally, once the application has been deployed, it is important to continuously monitor and optimize. This will allow you to tune any long-running queries, restructure data as new access patterns emerge, take advantage of provisioned capacity versus on-demand, and more accurately determine the memory allocated to functions.

CHAPTER 4

Serverless and Security

We can only see a short distance ahead, but we can see plenty there that needs to be done.
—Alan Turing

Utilizing serverless technologies means some traditional security concerns go away, such as patching operating system flaws and securing network connections. Yet, as with any technological advancement, serverless introduces new challenges while solving existing problems. Serverless security is no different. This chapter examines the security threats to a serverless application and delves into key security primitives and how they map to serverless engineering on AWS.

Unfortunately, software developers commonly only consider security once the entire application has been developed, usually in the weeks or days before going live. Even then, they tend to focus those last-minute efforts solely on securing the application's perimeter. There are two factors that contribute to this: firstly, security seems inherently complex to engineers, and secondly, engineers often feel that implementing security measures runs counter to the practice of failure-driven iteration.

While software engineering teams can utilize security tools and delegate certain tasks to these tools, security must always be a core engineering and operational concern.

Security Is a Process

As security technologist Bruce Schneier wrote in his April 2000 essay "The Process of Security" (*https://oreil.ly/TaXp2*): "Security is a process, not a product."

Schneier is referring to the fact that security vulnerabilities are inevitable in software: "Systems break, vulnerabilities are reported in the press, and still many people put their faith in the next product, or the next upgrade, or the next patch. 'This time it's secure.'"

Instead of relying on products, libraries, vendors, or services, you should optimize your security process to maximize the potential for successful prevention, detection, and remediation of vulnerabilities: "Products provide some protection, but the only way to effectively do business in an insecure world is to put processes in place that recognize the inherent insecurity in the products."

Modern software engineering teams have a long-established development process. Traditionally, this has looked something like this: design, build, test, deploy. The DevOps movement ensured the operation of software became embedded in the software development lifecycle. Security must now also be part of the entire development process.

The popular recommendation is to *shift left* on security, bringing it into the development lifecycle much earlier, and to leverage identity and access management to provide defense in depth, not just at the perimeter. Serverless engineering presents an opportunity to embed a secure-by-design approach into your daily work. As you design, build, and operate your application, always have in mind the attack vectors, potential vulnerabilities, and mitigations available to you (see Figure 4-1).

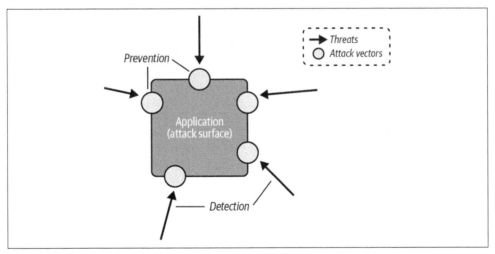

Figure 4-1. Application security involves detecting threats and applying preventative measures to attack vectors

The practice of threat modeling is increasingly becoming an essential tool to continually identify and guard against threats. It was added to the respected Thoughtworks Technology Radar (*https://oreil.ly/Pa0X2*) in 2015, with the observation that "throughout the lifetime of any software, new threats will emerge and existing ones will continue to evolve thanks to external events and ongoing changes to requirements and architecture."

As a software engineer, you must also recognize and embrace your limitations. Engineering teams will typically have limited practical experience or working knowledge of application security. Consult with security teams early in your software design and development cycles. Security teams can usually help with arranging penetration testing and security audits before you launch new applications and major features, as well as supporting vulnerability detection efforts and incident response. Always be aware of your organization's cybersecurity strategy, which should include guidance on securing cloud accounts and preserving data privacy.

Before we go any further, let's take a moment to establish an important point: security can be simple!

Security Can Be Simple

Given the stakes, ensuring the security of a software application can be a daunting task. Breaches of application perimeters and data stores are often dramatic and devastating. Besides the immediate consequences, such as data loss and the need for remediation, these incidents usually have a negative impact on trust between consumers and the business, and between the business and its technologists.

Security Challenges

Securing cloud native serverless applications can be particularly challenging for several reasons, including:

Managed services
> Throughout this book, you will see that managed services are core to serverless applications and, when applied correctly, can support clear separation of concerns, optimal performance, and effective observability. While managed services provide a solid foundation for your infrastructure, as well as several security benefits—primarily through the shared responsibility model, discussed later in this chapter—the sheer number of them available to teams building on AWS presents a problem: in order to utilize (or even evaluate) a managed service, you must first understand the available features, pricing model, and, crucially, security implications. How do IAM permissions work for this service? How is the shared responsibility model applied to this service? How will access control and encryption work?

Configurability
> An aspect all managed services share is configurability. Every AWS service has an array of options that can be tweaked to optimize throughput, latency, resiliency, and cost. The combination of services can also yield further optimizations, such as the employment of SQS queues between Lambda functions to provide batching and buffering. Indeed, one of the primary benefits of serverless that is

highlighted in this book is granularity. As you've seen, you have the ability to configure each of the managed services in your applications to a fine degree. In terms of security, this represents a vast surface area for the inadvertent introduction of flaws like excessive permissions and privilege escalation.

Emergent standards

AWS delivers new services, new features, and improvements to existing features and services at a consistently high rate. These new services and features could either be directly related to application or account security or present new attack vectors to analyze and secure. There are always new levers to pull and more things to configure. The community around AWS and, in particular, serverless also moves at a relatively fast pace, with new blog posts, video tutorials, and conference talks appearing every day. The security aspect of software engineering perhaps moves slightly slower than other elements, but there is still a steady stream of advice from cybersecurity professionals along with regular releases of vulnerability disclosures and associated research. Keeping up with all the AWS product updates and the best practices when it comes to securing your ever-evolving application can easily become one of your biggest challenges.

While cloud native serverless applications present unique security challenges, there are also plenty of inherent benefits when it comes to securing this type of software. The architecture of serverless applications introduces a unique security framework and provides the potential to work in a novel way within this framework. You have a chance to redefine your relationship to application security. Security can be simple.

Next, let's explore how to start securing your serverless application.

Getting Started

Establishing a solid foundation for your serverless security practice is pivotal. Security can, and must, be a primary concern. And it is never too late to establish this foundation.

As previously alluded to, security must be a clearly defined process. It is not a case of completing a checklist, deploying a tool, or deferring to other teams. Security should be part of the design, development, testing, and operation of every part of your system.

Working within sound security frameworks that fit well with serverless and adopting sensible engineering habits, combined with all the support and expertise of your cloud provider, will go a long way toward ensuring your applications remain secure.

When applied to serverless software, two modern security trends can provide a solid foundation for securing your application: zero trust and the principle of least privilege. The next section examines these concepts.

Once you have established a zero trust, least privilege security framework, the next step is to identify the attack surface of your applications and the security threats that they are vulnerable to. Subsequent sections examine the most common serverless threats and the threat modeling process.

Optimism Is Greater than Pessimism

The Optimism Otter says (*https://oreil.ly/3yKCb*): "People in our organisation need to move fast to meet the needs of our customers. The job of security is to help them move fast AND stay secure."

Serverless enables rapid development; security specialists should not only support this pace but also act upon it. They should enhance the safety and sustainability of the pace and, above all, not slow it down.

Software engineers should delegate to security professionals whenever there is a clear need, either through knowledge acquisition or services, such as penetration testing and vulnerability scanning.

Combining the Zero Trust Security Model with Least Privilege Permissions

There are two modern cybersecurity principles that you can leverage as the cornerstones of your serverless security strategy: zero trust architecture and the principle of least privilege.

Zero trust architecture

The basic premise of zero trust security is to assume every connection to your system is a threat. Every single interface should then be protected by a layer of authentication (who are you?) and authorization (what do you want?). This applies both to public API endpoints, or the *perimeter* in the traditional castle-and-moat model, and private, internal interfaces, such as Lambda functions or DynamoDB tables. Zero trust controls access to each distinct resource in your application, whereas a castle-and-moat model only controls access to the resources at the perimeter of your application.

Imagine a knight errant galloping up to the castle walls, presenting likely-looking credentials to the guards and persuading them of their honorable intentions before confidently entering the castle across the lowered drawbridge. If these perimeter guards form the extent of the castle's security, the knight is now free to roam the rooms, dungeons, and jewel store, collecting sensitive information for future raids or stealing valuable assets on the spot. If, however, each door or walkway had additional suspicious guards or sophisticated security controls that assumed zero trust by default, the knight would be entirely restricted and might even be deterred from infiltrating this castle at all.

Another scenario to keep in mind is a castle that cuts a single key for every heavy-duty door: should the knight gain access to one copy of this key, they'll be able to open all the doors, no matter how thick or cumbersome. With zero trust, there's a unique key for every door. Figure 4-2 shows how the castle-and-moat model compares to a zero trust architecture.

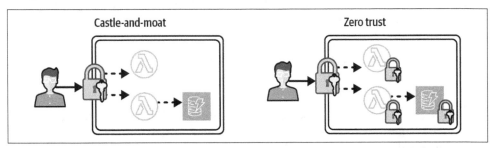

Figure 4-2. Castle-and-moat perimeter security compared to zero trust architecture

There are various applications of zero trust architecture, such as remote computing and enterprise network security. The next section briefly discusses how the zero trust model can be interpreted and applied to serverless applications.

Zero trust and serverless

Zero trust is often touted as the next big thing in network security. Buzzwords and hype aside, you will find that it is a natural fit for applying security to distributed, serverless systems. Indeed, zero trust is often the de facto methodology for securing serverless applications. Approaching application security with a zero trust mindset supports the development of good habits, such as inter-service message verification and internally accessible API security.

You cannot simply move from a castle-and-moat model to zero trust. You first need a supporting application architecture. For example, if your API, business logic, and database are running in a single containerized application, it will be very difficult to apply the granular, resource-based permissions needed to support zero trust. Serverless provides the optimum application architecture for zero trust as resources are naturally isolated across API, compute, and storage and each can have highly granular access control in place.

The principle of least privilege

Identity and access control is essential for an effective zero trust architecture. If the security perimeter must now be around every resource and asset in your system, you are going to need a highly reliable and granular authentication and authorization layer to implement this perimeter.

As your application resources interact with each other, they must be granted the minimum permissions required to complete their operations. This is an application of the principle of least privilege, introduced in Chapter 1.

Let's take a relatively simple example. Suppose you have a DynamoDB table and two Lambda functions that interact with the table (see Figure 1-11). One Lambda function needs to be able to read items from the table, and the other function should be able to write items to the table.

You might be tempted to apply blanket permissions to an access control policy and share it between the two Lambda functions, like this:

```
{
  "Version": "2012-10-17",
  "Statement": [
    {
      "Sid": "FullAccessToTable",
      "Effect": "Allow",
      "Action": [
        "dynamodb:*"
      ],
      "Resource": "arn:aws:dynamodb:eu-west-2:account-id:table/TableName"
    }
  ]
}
```

However, this would give each function more permissions than it needs, violating the principle of least privilege. Instead, a least privilege policy for the read-only Lambda function would look like this:

```
{
  "Version": "2012-10-17",
  "Statement": [
    {
      "Sid": "ReadItemsFromTable",
      "Effect": "Allow",
      "Action": [
        "dynamodb:GetItem",
        "dynamodb:Query",
        "dynamodb:Scan"
      ],
      "Resource": "arn:aws:dynamodb:eu-west-2:account-id:table/TableName"
    }
```

```
    ]
  }
```

And a least privilege policy for the write-only Lambda function would look like this:

```
{
  "Version": "2012-10-17",
  "Statement": [
    {
      "Sid": "WriteItemsToTable",
      "Effect": "Allow",
      "Action": [
        "dynamodb:PutItem",
        "dynamodb:UpdateItem"
      ],
      "Resource": "arn:aws:dynamodb:eu-west-2:account-id:table/TableName"
    }
  ]
}
```

Fortunately, the underlying permissions engine used by all AWS resources, called AWS Identity and Access Management (IAM), applies a *deny by default* stance: you must explicitly grant permissions, layering in new permissions over time as required. Let's take a closer look at the power of AWS IAM.

The Power of AWS IAM

AWS IAM is the one service you will use everywhere—but it's also often seen as one of the most complex. Therefore, it's important to understand IAM and learn how to harness its power. (You don't have to become an IAM expert, though—unless you want to, of course!)

The power of AWS IAM lies in roles and policies. *Policies* define the actions that can be taken on certain resources. For example, a policy could define the permission to put events onto a specific EventBridge event bus. *Roles* are collections of one or more policies. Roles can be attached to IAM users, but the more common pattern in a modern serverless application is to attach a role to a resource. In this way, an EventBridge rule can be granted permission to invoke a Lambda function, and that function can in turn be permitted to put items into a DynamoDB table.

IAM actions can be split into two categories: control plane actions and data plane actions. *Control plane actions*, such as PutEvents and GetItem (e.g., used by an automated deployment role) manage resources. *Data plane actions*, such as PutEvents and GetItem (e.g., used by a Lambda execution role), interact with those resources.

Let's take a look at a simple IAM policy statement and the elements it is composed of:

```
{
  "Sid": "ListObjectsInBucket", # Statement ID, optional identifier for
                                # policy statement
```

```
    "Action": "s3:ListBucket", # AWS service API action(s) that will be allowed
                              # or denied
    "Effect": "Allow", # Whether the statement should result in an allow or deny
    "Resource": "arn:aws:s3:::bucket-name", # Amazon Resource Name (ARN) of the
                                          # resource(s) covered by the statement
    "Condition": { # Conditions for when a policy is in effect
      "StringLike": { # Condition operator
        "s3:prefix": [ # Condition key
          "photos/", # Condition value
        ]
      }
    }
  }
}
```

See the AWS IAM documentation (*https://oreil.ly/wquoH*) for full details of all the elements of an IAM policy.

Lambda execution roles

A key use of IAM roles in serverless applications is Lambda function execution roles. An execution role is attached to a Lambda function and grants the function the permissions necessary to execute correctly, including access to any other AWS resources that are required. For example, if the Lambda function uses the AWS SDK to make a DynamoDB request that inserts a record in a table, the execution role must include a policy with the `dynamodb:PutItem` action for the table resource.

The execution role is *assumed* by the Lambda service when performing control plane and data plane operations. The AWS Security Token Service (STS) is used to fetch short-lived, temporary security credentials which are made available via the function's environment variables during invocation.

Each function in your application should have its own unique execution role with the minimum permissions required to perform its duty. In this way, single-purpose functions (introduced in Chapter 6) are also key to security: IAM permissions can be tightly scoped to the function and remain extremely restricted according to the limited functionality.

IAM guardrails

As you are no doubt beginning to notice, effective serverless security in the cloud is about basic security hygiene. Establishing guardrails for the use of AWS IAM is a core part of promoting a secure approach to everyday engineering activity. Here are some recommended guardrails:

Apply the principle of least privilege in policies.
> IAM policies should only include the minimum set of permissions required for the associated resource to perform the necessary control or data plane operations. As a general rule, do not use wildcards (*) in your policy statements.

Wildcards are the antithesis of least privilege, as they apply blanket permissions for actions and resources. Unless the action explicitly requires a wildcard, always be specific.

Avoid using managed IAM policies.
These are policies provided by AWS, and they're often tempting shortcuts, especially when you're just getting started or using a service for the first time. You can use these policies early in prototyping or development, but you should replace them with custom policies as soon as you understand the integration better. Because these policies are designed to be applied to generic scenarios, they are simply not restricted enough and will usually violate the principle of least privilege when applied to interactions within your application.

Prefer roles to users.
IAM users are issued with static, long-lived AWS access credentials (an access key ID and secret access key). These credentials can be used to directly access the application provider's AWS account, including all the resources and data in that account. Depending on the associated IAM roles and policies, the authenticating user may even have the ability to create or destroy resources. Given the power they grant the holder, the use and distribution of static credentials must be limited to reduce the risk of unauthorized access. Where possible, restrict IAM users to an absolute minimum (or, even better, do not have any IAM users at all).

Prefer a role per resource.
Each resource in your application, such as an EventBridge rule, a Lambda function, and an SQS queue, should have its own unique role. Permissions for those roles should be fine-grained and least-privileged.

The AWS Shared Responsibility Model

AWS uses a *shared responsibility model* to define the remit of application security consumers and the cloud provider (see Figure 4-3). The important thing here is the shift in security responsibility to AWS when using cloud services. This is increased when using fully managed serverless services, such as compute with AWS Lambda: AWS manages patching of the Lambda runtime, function execution isolation, and so on.

Serverless applications are made up of business logic, infrastructure definitions, and managed services. Ownership of these elements is split between AWS and the consumers of its public cloud services. As a serverless application engineer and AWS customer, you are responsible the for security of:

- Your function code and third-party libraries used in that code
- Configuration of the AWS resources used in your application

- The IAM roles and policies governing access control to the resources and functions in your application

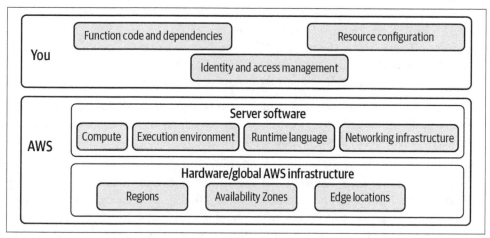

Figure 4-3. The cloud security shared responsibility model: you are responsible for security in the cloud, and AWS is responsible for security of the cloud

Think Like a Hacker

With your foundational zero trust, least privilege security strategy and a clear delineation of responsibility in place, the next step is to identify the potential attack vectors in your application and be aware of the possible threats to the security and integrity of your systems.

When you imagine the threats to your systems, you may picture bad actors who are external to your organization—*hackers*. While external threats certainly exist, they must not overshadow internal threats, which must also be guarded against. Internal threats could, of course, be deliberately malicious, but the more likely scenario is that the vulnerabilities are introduced unintentionally. The engineers of an application can often be the architects of their own security flaws and data exposures, often through weak or missing security configuration of cloud resources.

The popular depiction of a hacker performing an obvious denial of service attack on a web application or infiltrating a server firewall is still a very real possibility, but subtler attacks on the software supply chain are now just as likely. These insidious attacks involve embedding malicious code in third-party libraries and automating exploits remotely once the code is deployed in production workloads.

It is essential to adopt the mindset of a hacker and fully understand the potential threats to your serverless applications in order to properly defend against them.

Meet the OWASP Top 10

Cybersecurity is an incredibly well-researched area, with security professionals constantly assessing the ever-changing software landscape, identifying emerging risks and distributing preventative measures and advice. While as a modern serverless engineer you must accept the responsibility you have in securing the applications you build, it is absolutely crucial that you combine your own efforts with deference to professional advice and utilization of the extensive research that is publicly available.

Identifying the threats to the security of your software is one task that you should not attempt alone. There are several threat categorization frameworks available that can help here, but let's focus on the OWASP Top 10.

The Open Web Application Security Project, or OWASP for short, is a "non-profit foundation that works to improve the security of software." It does this primarily through community-led, open source projects, tools, and research. The OWASP Foundation has repeatedly published a list of the 10 most prevalent and critical security risks to web applications since 2003. The latest version, published in 2021 (*https://oreil.ly/-MSdz*), provides the most up-to-date list of security risks (at the time of writing).

While a serverless application will differ in some ways from a typical web application, Table 4-1 interprets the OWASP Top 10 through a serverless lens. Note that the list is in descending order, with the most critical application security risk, as classified by OWASP, in the first position. We've added the "serverless risk level" column as an indicator of the associated risk specific to serverless applications.

Table 4-1. Top 10 serverless application security risks

Threat category	Threat description	Mitigations	Serverless risk level
Broken access control	Access control is the gatekeeper to your application and its resources and data. Controlling access to your resources and assets allows you to restrict users of your application so that they cannot act outside of their intended permissions.	• API authentication and authorization. • Least-privilege, per-resource IAM roles.	Medium
Cryptographic failures	Weak or absent encryption of data, both in transit between components in your application and at rest in queues, buckets, and tables, is a major security risk.	• Classify data being processed, stored, or transmitted. • Identify sensitive data according to privacy laws, regulatory requirements, and business needs. • Encrypt sensitive data as a minimum. • Protect data in transit with HTTPS/TLS.	Medium

Threat category	Threat description	Mitigations	Serverless risk level
Injection	Injection of malicious code into an application via user-supplied data is a popular attack vector. Common attacks include SQL and NoSQL injection.	• Validate and sanitize external data received by all entry points to your application, e.g., API requests and inbound events.	High
Insecure design	Implementing and operating an application that was not designed with security as a primary concern is risky, as it will be susceptible to gaps in the security posture.	• Adopt a secure by design approach. • Security must be considered during business requirements gathering and solution design and formalized via threat modeling.	Medium
Security misconfiguration	Misconfigurations of encryption, access control, and computational constraints represent vulnerabilities that can be exploited by attackers. Unintended public access of S3 buckets is a very common root cause of cloud data breaches. Lambda functions with excessive timeouts can be exploited to cause a DoS attack.	• Define a paved road to secure configuration of cloud resources for engineers. • Keep application features, components, and dependencies to a minimum.	Medium
Vulnerable and outdated components	Continued use of vulnerable, unsupported, or outdated software (operating systems, web servers, databases, etc.) makes your application susceptible to attacks that exploit known vulnerabilities.	• Delegate infrastructure management and security patching to AWS by using fully managed serverless services.	Low
Identification and authentication failures	These failures can permit unauthorized usage of APIs and integrated resources, like Lambda functions, S3 buckets, or DynamoDB tables.	• Leverage an access management service to apply proper, fine-grained authentication and authorization for API gateways. • Rely on AWS IAM for inter-service communication.	Medium
Software and data integrity failures	The presence of vulnerabilities or exploits in third-party code is quickly becoming the most common risk to software applications. As application dependencies are bundled and executed with Lambda function code, they are granted the same permissions as your business logic.	• Secure your software supply chain with automated dependency upgrades and other controls. • Remove unused dependencies.	High
Security logging and monitoring failures	Attackers rely on the lack of monitoring and timely response to achieve their goals without being detected. Without logging and monitoring, breaches cannot be detected or analyzed. Logs of applications and APIs are not monitored for suspicious activity.	• Enable API Gateway execution and access logs. • Use CloudTrail monitoring to identify and report abnormal behavior.	Medium

Threat category	Threat description	Mitigations	Serverless risk level
Server-side request forgery (SSRF)	In AWS this primarily concerns a vulnerability with running web servers on EC2 instances. The most devastating example was the Capital One data breach in 2019 (*https://oreil.ly/vmgvn*).	• Serverless applications utilizing API Gateway and Lambda will not generally be susceptible to SSRF attacks. • Avoid accepting URLs in client inputs, always sanitize incoming request payloads, and never return raw HTTP responses to clients.	Low

There are two further noteworthy security risks that are relevant to serverless applications:

Denial of service
> This is a common attack where an API is constantly bombarded with bogus requests in order to disrupt the servicing of genuine requests. Public APIs will always face the possibility of DoS attacks. Your job is not always to completely prevent them, but to make them so tricky to execute that the deterrent alone becomes enough to secure the resources. Firewalls, rate limits, and resource throttle alarms (e.g., Lambda, DynamoDB) are all key measures to prevent DoS attacks.

Denial of wallet
> This kind of attack is fairly unique to serverless applications, due to the pay-per-use pricing model and high scalability of managed services. Denial of wallet attacks target the constant execution of resources to accumulate a usage bill so high it will likely cause severe financial damage to the business.

> Setting up budget alerts can help ensure you are alerted to denial of wallet attacks before they can escalate. See Chapter 9 for more details.

Now that you have an understanding of the common threats to a serverless application, next you will explore how to use the process of threat modeling to map these security risks to your applications.

Serverless Threat Modeling

Before designing a comprehensive security strategy for any serverless application, it is crucial to understand the attack vectors and model potential threats. This can be done by clearly defining the surface area of the application, the assets worth securing, and the threats, both internal and external, to the application's security.

As previously stated, security is a continuous process: there is no final state. In order to maintain the security of an application as it grows, threats must be constantly reviewed and attack vectors regularly assessed. New features are added over time, more users serviced and more data collected. Threats will change, their severity will rise and fall, and application behavior will evolve. The tools available and industry best practices will also evolve, becoming more effective and focused in reaction to these changes.

Introduction to threat modeling

By this point you should have a fairly clear understanding of your security responsibilities, a foundational security framework, and the primary threats to serverless applications. Next, you need to map the framework and threats to your application and its services.

Threat modeling is a process that can help your team to identify attack vectors, threats, and mitigations through discussion and collaboration. It can support a *shift-left* (or even *start-left*) approach to security, where security is primarily owned by the team designing, building, and operating the application and is treated as a primary concern throughout the software development lifecycle. This is also sometimes referred to as *DevSecOps*.

To ensure continuous hardening of your security posture, threat modeling should be a process that you conduct regularly, for example at task refinement sessions. Threats should initially be modeled early in the solution design process (see Chapter 6) and focused at the feature or service level.

 Threat Composer is a tool from AWS Labs that can help guide and visualize your threat modeling process.

Next you will be introduced to a framework that adds structure to the threat modeling process: STRIDE.

STRIDE

The STRIDE acronym describes six threat categories:

Spoofing
　　Pretending to be something or somebody other than who you are

Tampering
　　Changing data on disk, in memory, on the network, or elsewhere

---

Repudiation
    Claiming that you were not responsible for an action

Information disclosure
    Obtaining information that was not intended for you

Denial of service
    Destruction or excessive consumption of finite resources

Elevation of privilege
    Performing actions on protected resources that you should not be allowed to perform

STRIDE-per-element, or *STRIDE/element* for short, is a way to apply the STRIDE threat categories to elements in your application. It can help to further focus the threat modeling process.

The elements are targets of potential threats and are defined as:

- Human actors/external entities
- Processes
- Data stores
- Data flows

It is important not to get overwhelmed by the threat modeling process. Securing an application can be daunting, but remember, as outlined at the beginning of this chapter, it can also be simple, especially with serverless. Start small, work as a team, and follow the process one stage at a time. Identifying one threat for each element/threat combination in the matrix in Figure 4-4 would represent a great start.

Element	S	T	R	I	D	E
Human actor/external entity	✔		✔			
Process	✔	✔	✔	✔	✔	✔
Data store		✔	✔	✔	✔	
Data flow		✔		✔	✔	

Figure 4-4. Applying the STRIDE threat categories per element in your application

A process for threat modeling

As preparation for your threat modeling sessions, you may find it conducive to productive meetings to have the following information prepared:

- High-level architecture of the application
- Solution design documents
- Data models and schemas
- Data flow diagrams
- Domain-specific industry compliance standards

A typical threat modeling process will comprise the following steps:

1. Identify the elements in your application that could be targets for potential threats, including data assets, external actors, externally accessible entry points, and infrastructure resources.

2. Identify a list of threats for each element identified in step 1. Be sure to focus on threats and not mitigations at this stage.

3. For each threat identified in step 2, identify appropriate steps that can be taken to mitigate the threat. This could include encryption of sensitive data assets, applying access control to external actors and entry points, and ensuring each resource is granted only the minimum permissions required to perform its operations.

4. Finally, assess whether the agreed remediation adequately mitigates the threat or if there is any residual risk that should be addressed.

For a comprehensive threat modeling template, see Appendix C.

Securing the Serverless Supply Chain

Vulnerable and outdated components and supply chain–based attacks are quickly becoming a primary concern for software engineers.

According to supply chain security company Socket (*https://socket.dev*), "supply chain attacks rose a whopping 700% in the past year, with over 15,000 recorded attacks." One example they cite occurred in January 2022, when an open source software maintainer intentionally added malware to his own package (*https://oreil.ly/sGX4g*), which was being downloaded an average of 100 million times per month. A notable casualty was the official AWS SDK.

Who is responsible for protecting against these vulnerabilities and attacks? Serverless compute on AWS Lambda provides you with a clear example of the shared responsibility model presented earlier in this chapter. It is the responsibility of AWS to keep the software in the runtime and execution environment updated with the latest security patches and performance improvements, and it is the responsibility of the application engineer to secure the function code itself. This includes keeping the libraries used by the function up-to-date (*https://oreil.ly/vLinO*).

Given that it is your responsibility as a cloud application developer to secure the code you deliver to the cloud and run in your Lambda functions, what are the attack vectors and threat levels here, and how can you mitigate the related security issues?

Securing the Dependency Supply Chain

Open source software is an incredible enabler of rapid software development and delivery. As a software engineer, you can rely on the expertise and work of others in your community when composing your applications. However, this relationship is built on a fragile layer of trust. Every time you install a dependency, you are implicitly trusting the myriad contributors to that package and everything in that package's own tree of dependencies. The code of hundreds of programmers becomes a key component of your production software.

You must be aware of the risks involved in installing and executing open source software, and the steps you can take to mitigate such risks.

Think before you install

You can start securing the serverless supply chain by scrutinizing packages before installing them. This is a simple suggestion that can make a real difference to securing your application's supply chain, and to general maintenance at scale.

Use as few dependencies as necessary, and be aware of dependencies that obfuscate the data and control flow of your app, such as middleware libraries. If it is a trivial task, always try to do it yourself. It's also about trust. Do you trust the package? Do you trust the contributors?

Before you install the next package in your serverless application, adopt the following practices:

Analyze the GitHub repository.
 Review the contributors to the package. More contributors represents more scrutiny and collaboration. Check whether the repository uses verified commits. Assess the history of the package: How old is it? How many commits have been made? Analyze the repository activity to understand if the package is actively maintained and used by the community—GitHub stars provide a crude indicator of popularity, and things like the date of the most recent commit and number

of open issues and pull requests indicate usage. Also ensure the package's license adheres to any restrictions in place in your organization.

Use official package repositories.
Only obtain packages from official sources, such as NPM, PyPI, Maven, NuGet, or RubyGems, over secure (i.e., HTTPS) links. Prefer signed packages that can be verified for integrity and authenticity. For example, the JavaScript package manager NPM allows you to audit package signatures (*https://oreil.ly/r9jAb*).

Review the dependency tree.
Be aware of the package's dependencies and the entire dependency tree. Pick packages with zero runtime dependencies where available.

Try before you buy.
Try new packages on as isolated a scale as possible and delay rollout across the codebase for as long as possible, until you feel confident.

Check if you can do it yourself.
Don't reinvent the wheel for the sake of it, but one very simple way of removing opaque third-party code is to not introduce it in the first place. Examine the source code to understand if the package is doing something simple that is easily portable to a first-party utility. Logging libraries are a perfect example: you can trivially implement your own logger rather than distributing a third-party library across your codebase.

Make it easy to back out.
Development patterns like service isolation, single-responsibility Lambda functions, and limiting shared code (see Chapter 6 for more information on these patterns) make it easier to evolve your architecture and avoid pervasive antipatterns or vulnerable software taking over your codebase.

Lock to the latest.
Always use the latest version of the package, and always use an explicit version rather than a range or "latest" flag.

Uninstall any unused packages.
Always uninstall and clear unused packages from your dependencies manifest. Most modern compilers and bundlers will only include dependencies that are actually consumed by your code, but keeping your manifest clean adds extra safety and clarity.

Scan packages for vulnerabilities

You should also run continuous vulnerability scans in response to new packages, package upgrades, and reports of new vulnerabilities. Scans can be run against a code repository using tools such as Snyk (*https://snyk.io*) or GitHub's native Dependabot alerts system (*https://oreil.ly/7a9uj*).

Automate dependency upgrades

Out of all the suggestions for securing your supply chain, this is the most crucial. Even if you have a serverless application with copious packages distributed across multiple services, make sure upgrades of all dependencies are automated.

 While automating upgrades of your application's dependencies is generally a recommended practice, you should always keep in mind the "think before you install" checklist from the previous section. You should be particularly mindful of the integrity of the incoming updates, in case a bad actor has published a malicious version of a package.

Keeping package versions up-to-date ensures that you not only have access to the latest features but, crucially, to the latest security patches. Vulnerabilities can be found in earlier versions of software after many later versions have been published. Navigating an upgrade across several minor versions can be difficult enough, depending on the features of the package, the adherence to semantic versioning by the authors, and the prevalence of the package throughout your codebase—but upgrading from one major version to another is typically not trivial, given the likelihood of the next version containing breaking changes that affect your usage of the package.

Runtime updates

As well as dependency upgrades, it is highly recommended to keep up-to-date with the latest version of the AWS Lambda runtime you are using. Make sure you are subscribed to news about runtime support and upgrade as soon as possible.

 By default, AWS will automatically update the runtime of your Lambda functions with any patch versions that are released. Additionally, you have the option to control when the runtime of your functions is updated through Lambda's runtime management controls (*https://oreil.ly/Xrn0N*).

These controls are primarily useful for mitigating the rare occurrence of bugs caused by a runtime patch version that is incompatible with your function's code. But, as these patch versions will likely include security updates, you should use these controls with caution. It is usually safest to keep your functions running on the latest version of the runtime.

The same is true for any delivery pipelines you maintain, as these will likely run on virtual machines and runtimes provided by the third party. And remember, you do not need to use the same runtime version across pipelines and functions. For example, you should use the latest version of Node.js in your pipelines even before it is supported by the Lambda runtime.

Going Further with SLSA

The SLSA (*https://slsa.dev*) security framework (pronounced *salsa,* short for Supply chain Levels for Software Artifacts) is "a checklist of standards and controls to prevent tampering, improve integrity, and secure packages and infrastructure." SLSA is all about going from "safe enough" to maximum resiliency across the entire software supply chain.

If you're at a fairly high level of security maturity, you may find it useful to use this framework to measure and improve the security of your software supply chain. Follow the SLSA documentation to get started (*https://oreil.ly/5ZFPR*). The Software Component Verification Standard (SCVS) from OWASP (*https://oreil.ly/MDEFC*) is another framework for measuring supply chain security.

Lambda Code Signing

The last mile in the software supply chain is packaging and deploying your function code to the cloud. At this point, your function will usually consist of your business logic (code you have authored) and any third-party libraries listed in the function's dependencies (code someone else has authored).

Lambda provides the option to *sign your code* (*https://oreil.ly/DgIe0*) before deploying it. This enables the Lambda service to verify that a trusted source has initiated the deployment and that the code has not been altered or tampered with in any way. Lambda will run several validation checks to verify the integrity of the code, including that the package has not been modified since it was signed and that the signature itself is valid.

To sign your code, you first create one or more signing profiles. These profiles might map to the environments and accounts your application uses—for example, you may have a signing profile per AWS account. Alternatively, you could opt to have a signing profile per function for greater isolation and security. The CloudFormation resource for a signing profile looks like this, where the `PlatformID` denotes the signature format and signing algorithm that will be used by the profile:

```
{
  "Type" : "AWS::Signer::SigningProfile",
  "Properties" : {
    "PlatformId" : "AWSLambda-SHA384-ECDSA",
```

```
    }
  }
```

Once you have defined a signing profile, you can then use it to configure code signing for your functions:

```
{
  "Type" : "AWS::Lambda::CodeSigningConfig",
  "Properties" : {
    "AllowedPublishers" : [
      {
        "SigningProfileVersionArns" : [
          "arn:aws:signer:us-east-1:123456789123:/signing-profiles/my-profile"
        ]
      }
    ],
    "CodeSigningPolicies" : {
      "UntrustedArtifactOnDeployment": "Enforce"
    }
  }
}
```

Finally, assign the code signing configuration to your function:

```
{
  "Type" : "AWS::Lambda::Function",
  "Properties" : {
    "CodeSigningConfigArn" : [
      "arn:aws:lambda:us-east-1:123456789123:code-signing-config:csc-config-id",
    ]
  }
}
```

Now, when you deploy this function the Lambda service will verify the code was signed by a trusted source and has not been tampered with since being signed.

Protecting Serverless APIs

According to the OWASP Top 10 list we looked at earlier in this chapter, the number one threat to web applications is broken access control. While serverless helps to mitigate some of the threats posed by broken access control, you still have work to do in this area.

When applying the zero trust security model, you must apply access control to each isolated component as well as the perimeter of your system. For most serverless applications the security perimeter will be an API Gateway endpoint. If you are building a serverless application that exposes an API to the public internet, you must design and implement an appropriate access control mechanism for this API.

In this section, we'll explore the available authorization strategies for applying access control to serverless APIs and when to use each one. The access control options for API Gateway are summarized in Table 4-2.

 Amazon API Gateway provides two types of APIs: REST APIs and HTTP APIs. They offer different features at different costs. One of the differences is the access control options available. The compatibility for each of the access control methods we'll explore in this section is indicated in Table 4-2.

Table 4-2. Amazon API Gateway access control options

Access control strategy	Description	REST API	HTTP API
Cognito authorizers	Direct integration with the access management service Amazon Cognito and API Gateway REST APIs. Cognito client credentials are exchanged for access tokens, which are validated directly with Cognito.	Yes	No
JWT authorizers	Can be used to integrate an access management service that uses JSON Web Tokens (JWTs) for access control, such as Amazon Cognito or Okta, with API Gateway HTTP APIs.	No[a]	Yes
Lambda authorizers	Lambda functions can be used to implement custom authorization logic when using an access management service other than Cognito or to verify incoming webhook messages where user-based authentication is not available.	Yes	Yes

[a] You can still use JWTs to authorize and authenticate REST API requests, but you will need to write a custom Lambda authorizer that verifies incoming tokens.

Securing REST APIs with Amazon Cognito

There are of course many access management services and identity providers available, including Okta and Auth0. We'll focus on using Cognito to secure a REST API, as it is native to AWS and for this reason provides minimal overhead.

Amazon Cognito

Before we dive in, let's define the building blocks you will need. Cognito is often viewed as one of the most complex AWS services. It is therefore important to have a foundational understanding of Cognito's components and a clear idea of the access control architecture you are aiming for. Here are the key components for implementing access control using Cognito:

User pools
> A user pool is a user directory in Amazon Cognito. Typically you will have a single user pool in your application. This user pool can be used to manage all the users of your application, whether you have a single user or multiple users.

Application clients
> You may be building a traditional client/server web application where you maintain a frontend web application and a backend API. Or you may be operating a multitenant business-to-business platform, where tenant backend services use a client credentials grant to access your services. In this case, you can create an application client for each tenant and share the client ID and secret with the tenant backend service for machine-to-machine authentication.

Scopes
> Scopes are used to control an application client's access to specific resources in your application's API.

Application-Based Multitenancy

Multitenancy is an identity and access management architecture to support sharing the underlying resources of an application between multiple groups of users, or *tenants*. Conversely, in a single-tenant architecture each tenant is assigned to a separate instance of the application running on distinct infrastructure. Although tenants share the same infrastructure in multitenancy, their data is completely separated and never shared between tenants.

Multitenancy is a very common model that is often used in SaaS products and by cloud vendors themselves, including AWS. Multitenancy is also complementary to a zero trust architecture, where a more granular access control model is required. Consider a single consumer of your API: it is likely the consumer will have multiple services of its own consuming multiple API resources. In this scenario, a secure, zero trust approach would be to isolate usage of the API to consuming services, granting only the minimum permissions needed by that individual service to perform its requests of the API.

Application-based multitenancy is a technique that will allow your application's access control to scale, regardless of whether you start with a single user or multiple tenants. Each tenant of your application is assigned at least one *application client* and a set of scopes that determine the resources the app client can access. If you never scale beyond a single user, adopting this architecture will still serve you well. Take a look at the Cognito documentation (*https://oreil.ly/S8LB2*) for more information about implementing app client–based multitenancy.

Cognito and API Gateway

Cognito authorizers provide a fully managed access control integration with API Gateway, as illustrated in Figure 4-5. API consumers exchange their credentials (a client ID and secret) for access tokens via a Cognito endpoint. These access tokens are then included with API requests and validated via the Cognito authorizer.

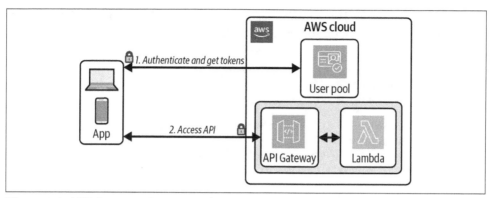

Figure 4-5. API Gateway Cognito authorizer

Additionally, an API endpoint can be assigned a scope. When authorizing a request to the endpoint, the Cognito authorizer will verify the endpoint's scope is included in the client's list of permitted scopes.

Securing HTTP APIs

If you are using an API Gateway HTTP API, rather than a REST API, you will not be able to use the native Cognito authorizer. Instead, you have a few alternative options. We'll explore examples of the most convenient two: Lambda authorizers and JWT authorizers.

 JWT authorizers can also be used to authenticate API requests with Amazon Cognito when using HTTP APIs.

JWT authorizers

If your authorization strategy simply involves a client submitting a JSON Web Token for verification, using a JWT authorizer will be a good option. When you use a JWT authorizer, the whole authorization process is managed by the API Gateway service.

 JWT is an open standard that defines a compact, self-contained way of securely transmitting information between parties as JSON objects. JWTs can be used to ensure the integrity of a message and the authentication of both the message producer and consumer.

JWTs can be cryptographically signed and encrypted, enabling verification of the integrity of the claims contained within the token while keeping those claims hidden from other parties.

You first configure the JWT authorizer and then attach it to a route. The Cloud-Formation resource will look something like this:

```
{
  "Type" : "AWS::ApiGatewayV2::Authorizer",
  "Properties" : {
    "ApiId" : "ApiGatewayId",
    "AuthorizerType" : "JWT",
    "IdentitySource" : [ "$request.header.Authorization" ],
    "JwtConfiguration" : {
      "Audience" : [ "https://my-application.com" ],
      "Issuer" : "https://cognito-idp.us-east-1.amazonaws.com/userPoolID"
    },
    "Name" : "my-authorizer"
  }
}
```

The `IdentitySource` should match the location of the JWT provided by the client in the API request; for example, the `Authorization` HTTP header. The `Jwt Configuration` should correspond to the expected values in the tokens that will be submitted by clients, where the `Audience` is the HTTP address for the recipient of the token (usually your API Gateway domain) and the `Issuer` is the HTTP address for the service responsible for issuing tokens, such as Cognito or Okta.

Lambda authorizers

Lambda functions with custom authorization logic can be attached to API Gateway HTTP API routes and invoked whenever requests are made. These functions are known as *Lambda authorizers* and can be used when you need to apply access control strategies beyond the ones the managed Cognito or JWT authorizers support. The functions' responses will either approve or deny access to the requested resources (see Figure 4-6).

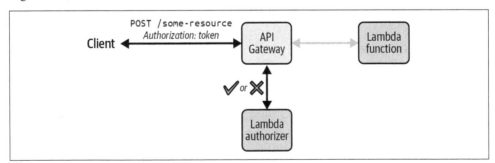

Figure 4-6. Controlling access to API Gateway resources with a Lambda authorizer

Lambda authorizers support various locations for providing authorization claims in API requests. These are known as *identity sources* and include HTTP headers and query string parameters (for example, the `Authorization` header). The identity source you use will be required in requests made to API Gateway; any requests without the required property will immediately receive a 401 Unauthorized response and the Lambda authorizer will not be invoked.

Lambda authorizer responses can also be cached. The responses will be cached according to the identity source provided by the API's clients. If a client provides the same values for the required identity sources within the configured cache period, or TTL, API Gateway uses the cached authorizer result instead of invoking the authorizer function.

> Caching the responses of your Lambda authorizers will result in quicker responses to API requests as well as a reduction in costs, as the Lambda function will be invoked significantly less frequently.

The Lambda function used to authorize requests can return an IAM policy or what is known as a *simple* response. The simple response will usually suffice, unless your use case requires an IAM policy response or more granular permissions. When using the simple response, the authorizer function must return a response matching the following format, where `isAuthorized` is a Boolean value that denotes the outcome of your authorization checks and `context` is optional and can include any additional information to pass to API access logs and Lambda functions integrated with the API resource:

```
{
  "isAuthorized": true/false,
  "context": {
    "key": "value"
  }
}
```

Validating and Verifying API Requests

There are other ways to protect your serverless API beyond the access control mechanisms we have explored so far in this section. In particular, publicly accessible APIs should always be protected against deliberate or unintentional misuse and incoming request data to those APIs should always be validated and sanitized.

API Gateway request protection

API Gateway offers two ways of protecting against denial of service and denial of wallet attacks.

First, requests from individual API clients can be throttled via API Gateway usage plans (*https://oreil.ly/agWiV*). Usage plans can be used to control access to API stages and methods and to limit the rate of requests made to those methods. By rate limiting API requests, you can prevent any of your API's clients from deliberately or inadvertently abusing your service. Usage plans can be applied to all methods in an API, or to specific methods. Clients are given a generated API key to include in every request to your API. If a client submits too many requests and is throttled as a result, they will begin to receive 429 Too Many Requests HTTP error responses.

API Gateway also integrates with AWS WAF (*https://oreil.ly/TpV8j*) to provide granular protection at the request level. With WAF, you can specify a set of rules to apply to each incoming request, such as IP address throttling.

> WAF rules are always applied before any other access control mechanisms, such as Cognito authorizers or Lambda authorizers.

API Gateway request validation

Requests to API Gateway methods can be validated (*https://oreil.ly/eFlQe*) before being processed further. Say you have a Lambda function attached to an API route that accepts the API request as an input and applies some operations to the request body. You can supply a JSON Schema definition of the expected input structure and format, and API Gateway will apply those data validation rules to the body of a request before invoking the function. If the request fails validation, the function will not be invoked and the client will receive a 400 Bad Request HTTP response.

> Implementing request validation via API Gateway can be particularly useful when using direct integrations to AWS services other than Lambda. For example, you may have an API Gateway resource that integrates directly with Amazon EventBridge, responding to API requests by putting events onto an event bus. In this architecture you will always want to validate and sanitize the request payload before forwarding it to downstream consumers.
>
> For more information about functionless integration patterns, refer to Chapter 5.

In the following example JSON model, the `message` property is required, and the request will be rejected if that field is missing from the request body:

```
{
  "$schema": "http://json-schema.org/draft-07/schema#",
  "title": "my-request-model",
  "type": "object",
  "properties": {
    "message": { "type": "string" },
    "status": { "type": "string" }
```

```
    },
    "required": ["message"]
}
```

Deeper input validation and sanitization should be performed in Lambda functions where data is transformed, stored in a database or delivered to an event bus or message queue. This can secure your application from SQL injection attacks, the #3 threat in the OWASP Top 10 (see Table 4-1).

Message Verification in Event-Driven Architectures

Most of the access control techniques we've explored generally apply to synchronous, request/response APIs. But as you learned in Chapter 3, it is highly likely that, as you and the teams or third parties you interact with are building event-driven applications, at some point you will encounter an *asynchronous* API.

Message verification is typically required at the integration points between systems—for example, of incoming messages from third-party webhooks and messages sent by your application to other systems or accounts. In a zero trust architecture message verification is also important for messaging between services in your application.

Verifying messages between consumers and producers

Typically, in order to decouple services, the producer of an event is deliberately unaware of any downstream consumers of the event. For example, you might have an organization-wide event backbone architecture where multiple producers send events to a central event broker and multiple consumers subscribe to these events, as shown in Figure 4-7.

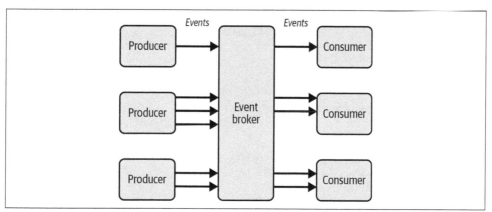

Figure 4-7. Decoupled producers and consumers in an event-driven architecture

Securing consumers of asynchronous APIs relies on the control of incoming messages. Consumers should always be in control of the subscription to an asynchronous

API, and there will already be a certain level of trust established between the event producers and the event broker—but event consumers must also guard against sender spoofing and message tampering. Verification of incoming messages is crucial in event-driven systems.

Let's assume the event broker in Figure 4-7 is an Amazon EventBridge event bus in a central account, part of your organization's core domain. The producers are services deployed to separate AWS accounts, and so are the consumers. A consumer needs to ensure each message has come from a trusted source. A producer needs to ensure messages can only be read by permitted consumers. For a truly decoupled architecture, the event broker itself might be responsible for message encryption and key management (rather than the producer), but for the purpose of keeping the example succinct we'll make this the producer's responsibility.

Encrypted and verifiable messages with JSON Web Tokens

You can use JWT as your message transport protocol. To sign and encrypt the messages you can use a technique known as *nested JWTs*, illustrated in Figure 4-8.

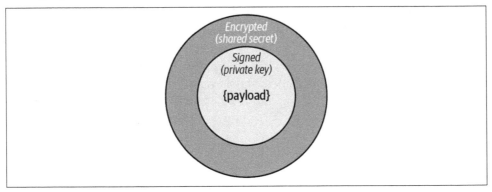

Figure 4-8. A nested JSON Web Token

The producer must first sign the message payload with the private key and then encrypt the signed message using a shared secret:

```
const payload = { data: { hello: "world" } };

const signedJWT = await new SignJWT(payload)
  .setProtectedHeader({ alg: "ES256" })
  .setIssuer("urn:example:issuer")
  .setAudience("urn:example:audience")
  .setExpirationTime("2h")
  .sign(privateKey);

const encryptedJWT = await new EncryptJWT(signedJWT)
  .setProtectedHeader({ alg: "dir", cty: "JWT", enc: "A256GCM" })
  .encrypt(sharedSecret);
```

Public/private encryption key pairs and shared secrets should be generated separately from the runtime message production and stored in AWS Key Management Service (KMS) or AWS Secrets Manager. The keys and secrets can then be fetched at runtime to sign and encrypt the message.

Upon receipt of a message, the consumer must first verify the signature using the producer's public key and then decrypt the payload using the shared secret:

```
const decryptedJWT = await DecryptJWT(encryptedJWT, sharedSecret);

const decodedJWT = await VerifyJWT(decryptedJWT, publicKey);

// if verified, original payload available at decodedJWT.payload
```

Only the producer's public key and the shared secret should be distributed to the message's consumers. The private key should never be shared.

Built-in message verification for SNS

In addition to the approach outlined in the previous section, some AWS services, such as Amazon Simple Notification Service (SNS), are now beginning to support message signatures natively (*https://oreil.ly/QqRDj*). SNS signs the messages delivered from your topic, enabling the subscribed HTTP endpoints to verify their authenticity.

Protecting Data

Data is the most valuable asset accumulated by any software application. This includes data personal to users of the application, data about third-party integrations with the application, and data about the application itself.

Cryptographic failure is the second of the OWASP Top 10 threats to web applications, after broken access control. This section examines the crucial role of data encryption in securing a serverless application and how you can encrypt your data as it moves through your system.

Data Encryption Everywhere

As you develop and operate your serverless application, you will discover both the power and the challenges that come with connecting components with events. Events allow you to decouple components and include rich data in their messages. Serverless compute is inherently stateless, which means the data a Lambda function or Step

Functions workflow needs to perform its operations must either be queried from a data store, like DynamoDB or S3, or provided in the invocation payload.

In event-driven systems, data is everywhere. This means data encryption needs to be everywhere too. Data will be stored in databases and object stores. It will be moved through message queues and event buses. Dr. Werner Vogels, the CTO and VP of Amazon, once said on stage at re:Invent, "Dance like no one is watching. Encrypt like everyone is."

What is encryption?

Encryption is a technique for restricting access to data by making it unreadable without a key. Cryptographic algorithms are used to obscure plain-text data with an encryption key. The encrypted data can only be decrypted with the same key.

Encryption is your primary tool in protecting the data in your application. It's particularly important in event-driven applications, where data constantly flows between accounts, services, functions, data stores, buses, and queues. Encryption can be divided into two categories: encryption at rest and encryption in transit. By encrypting data both in transit and at rest, you ensure that your data is protected for its entire lifecycle and end-to-end as it passes through your system and into other systems.

Most AWS managed services offer native support for encryption as well as direct integration with AWS Secrets Manager and AWS KMS. This means the process of encrypting and decrypting data and managing the associated encryption keys is largely abstracted away from you. However, encryption is not usually enabled by default, so you are responsible for enabling and configuring encryption at the resource level.

Encryption in transit

Data is in transit in a serverless application as it moves from service to service. All AWS services provide secure, encrypted HTTP endpoints via Transport Layer Security (TLS). Whenever you are interacting with the API of an AWS service, you should use the HTTPS endpoint. By default, operations you perform with the AWS SDK will use the HTTPS endpoints of all AWS services. For example, this means when your Lambda function is invoked by an API Gateway request and you make an EventBridge PutEvents call from the function, the payloads are entirely encrypted when in transit.

In addition to TLS, all AWS API requests made using the AWS SDK are protected by a request signing process, known as Signature Version 4 (*https://oreil.ly/CPmZp*). This process is designed to protect against request tampering and sender spoofing.

Encryption at rest

Encryption at rest is applied to data whenever it is stored or cached. In a serverless application, this could be data in an EventBridge event bus or archive, a message on an SQS queue, an object in an S3 bucket, or an item in a DynamoDB table.

As a general rule, whenever a managed service offers the option to encrypt data at rest you should take advantage of it. However, this is especially important when you have classified the data at rest as sensitive.

You should always limit the storage of data at rest and in transit. The more data is stored, and the longer it is stored for, the greater the attack surface area and security risk. Only store or transport data if it is absolutely necessary, and continually review your data models and event payloads to ensure redundant attributes are removed.

There are also sustainability benefits to storing less data. See Chapter 10 for more information on this topic.

AWS KMS

The key (pun intended) AWS service when it comes to encryption is AWS Key Management Service. AWS KMS is a fully managed service that supports the generation and management of the cryptographic keys that are used to protect your data. Whenever you use the native encryption controls of an AWS service like Amazon SQS or S3, as described in the previous sections, you will be using KMS to create and manage the necessary encryption keys. Whenever a service needs to encrypt or decrypt data, it will make a request to KMS to access the relevant keys. Access to keys is granted to these services via their attached IAM roles.

There are several types of KMS keys, such as HMAC keys and asymmetric keys, and these are generally grouped into two categories: *AWS managed keys* and *customer managed keys*. AWS managed keys are encryption keys that are created, managed, rotated, and used on your behalf by an AWS service that is integrated with AWS KMS. Customer managed keys are encryption keys that you create, own, and manage. For most use cases, you should choose AWS managed keys whenever available. Customer managed keys can be used in cases where you are required to audit usage of or retain additional control over the keys.

The AWS documentation has a detailed explanation of KMS concepts (*https://oreil.ly/UJ3Ae*) if you'd like to read more about this topic.

Security in Production

Making security a part of your development process is key to a holistic security strategy. But what happens when your application is ready for production and, subsequently, running in production?

Going into production can be the most daunting time when it comes to asking yourself the question: is my application secure? To help ease the process, we've created a final security checklist to run through before releasing your application to your users that also prepares you to continuously monitor your application for vulnerabilities. Remember, security is a process and something to continually iterate on, just like every other aspect of your software.

Go-Live Security Checklist for Serverless Applications

Here's a practical list of things to check before launching a serverless application. It can also form part of a security automation pipeline and your team's security guardrails:

- Commission penetration testing and security audits early in your application's development.

- Enable Block Public Access on all S3 buckets.

- Enable server-side encryption (SSE) on all S3 buckets containing valuable data.

- Enable cross-account backups or object replication on S3 buckets containing business-critical data.

- Enable encryption at rest on all SQS queues.

- Enable WAF on API Gateway REST APIs with baseline managed rules (*https://oreil.ly/xipQ8*).

- Use TLS version 1.2 or above on API Gateway APIs.

- Enable access and execution logs on API Gateway APIs.

- Remove sensitive data from Lambda function environment variables.

- Store secrets in AWS Secrets Manager.

- Encrypt Lambda function environment variables (*https://oreil.ly/I_yCx*).

- Enable Lambda function code signing.

- Enable backups on all DynamoDB tables containing business-critical data.

- Scan dependencies for vulnerabilities: resolve all critical and high security warnings, and minimize medium and low warnings.

- Set up budget alarms in CloudWatch (*https://oreil.ly/yvxaj*) to guard against denial of wallet attacks.

- Remove any IAM users where possible.

- Remove wildcards from IAM policies wherever possible to preserve least privilege.

- Generate an IAM credential report (*https://oreil.ly/fGzB9*) to identify unused roles and users that can be removed.

- Enable Security Hub reports.

- Create a CloudTrail trail to send logs to S3.

- Conduct a Well-Architected Framework review with a focus on the Security pillar and the Serverless Lens's security recommendations.

Maintaining Security in Production

In an enterprise, there are several AWS services that you can leverage to continue the process of securing your application once it is running in production.

Security monitoring with CloudTrail

AWS CloudTrail records all actions taken by IAM users, IAM roles, or an AWS service in an account. CloudTrail covers actions across the AWS console, CLI, SDK, and service APIs. This stream of events can be used to monitor your serverless application for unusual or unintended access and guard against attack #9 on the OWASP Top 10 list: security logging and monitoring failures.

 CloudTrail is a critical tool in counteracting repudiation attacks, described in "STRIDE" on page 183.

You can use Amazon CloudWatch for monitoring CloudTrail events. CloudWatch Logs metric filters can be applied to CloudTrail events to match certain terms, such as `ConsoleLogin` events. These metric filters can then be assigned to CloudWatch metrics that can be used to trigger alarms.

CloudTrail is enabled by default for your AWS account. This allows you to search CloudTrail logs via the event history in the AWS console. However, to persist logs beyond 90 days and to perform in-depth analysis and auditing of the logs you will need to configure a *trail*. A trail enables CloudTrail to deliver logs to an S3 bucket.

Once your CloudTrail logs are in S3, you can use Amazon Athena (*https://oreil.ly/ nIQFE*) to search the logs and perform in-depth analysis and correlation. For more information about Cloud Trail best practices, read Chloe Goldstein's article on the AWS blog (*https://oreil.ly/jwabT*).

Continuous security checks with Security Hub

You can use AWS Security Hub to support the security practice of your team and to aggregate security findings from other services, such as Macie, which you will discover in the next section.

Security Hub is particularly useful for identifying potential misconfigurations, such as public S3 buckets or missing encryption at rest on an SQS queue, that could otherwise be difficult to track down. Security Hub reports will rank findings by severity, providing a full description of each finding with a link to remediation information where available and an overall security score.

Vulnerability scanning with Amazon Inspector

Amazon Inspector can be used to continuously scan Lambda functions for known vulnerabilities and report findings ranked by severity. Findings can also be viewed in Security Hub to provide a central security posture dashboard.

The security benefits of Amazon Inspector come at a cost. You should understand the pricing model (*https://oreil.ly/59X3a*) before enabling Inspector.

Inspector can be used in addition to automated vulnerability scanning tools you may have running earlier in your development process, such as on the code repository itself.

Detecting Sensitive Data Leaks

As you saw in the previous section on protecting data, keeping your production data safe is critical. In particular, data that is classified as sensitive must be handled with the highest level of security.

The degree to which your application will receive, process, and store sensitive data, such as names, addresses, passwords, and credit card numbers, will depend on the purpose of the application. However, all but the simplest of applications will most likely handle some form of sensitive data.

There are four steps to managing sensitive data:

1. Understand protocols, guidance, and laws relating to data management. These could be organizational guidelines for data privacy or data protection regulations such as the Health Insurance Portability and Accountability Act (HIPAA), General Data Privacy Regulation (GDPR), Payment Card Industry Data Security Standard (PCI-DSS), and Federal Risk and Authorization Management Program (FedRAMP).

2. Identify and classify sensitive data in your system. This could be data received in API request bodies, generated by internal functions, processed in event streams, stored in a database, or sent to third parties.

3. Implement measures to mitigate improper handling and storage of sensitive data. There are often regulations preventing storing data beyond a certain period of time, logging sensitive data, or moving data between geographic regions.

4. Implement a system for detecting and remediating improper storage of sensitive data.

Mitigating sensitive data leaks

There are measures that can be applied to limit the potential of sensitive data being stored in databases, object stores, or logs, such as explicit logs and log redaction. However, it is crucial to design systems in a way that tolerates sensitive data being stored inadvertently and to react and remediate as soon as possible when this occurs.

The possibility of mishandling sensitive data exists in any system that handles such data.

It is also advisable to only store data that is absolutely necessary for the operation of your application, and only store that data for as long as it is needed. Deletion of data after a certain period of time can be automated in various AWS data stores. For example, CloudWatch log groups should be configured with a minimum retention period, DynamoDB records can be given a TTL value (*https://oreil.ly/JFSs9*), and the lifecycle of S3 objects can be controlled with expiration policies (*https://oreil.ly/endvT*).

The following sections describe some techniques to detect sensitive data leaks in application logs and object storage.

Managed sensitive data detection

Some AWS services already offer managed sensitive data detection and other services may follow in the future. Amazon SNS offers native data protection (*https://oreil.ly/vA53q*) for messages sent through SNS topics. Amazon CloudWatch offers built-in detection (*https://oreil.ly/9cw3V*) of sensitive data in application logs, for example from Lambda functions.

Amazon Macie

Amazon Macie is a fully managed data security service that uses machine learning to discover sensitive data in AWS workloads. Macie is capable of extracting and analyzing data stored in S3 buckets to detect various types of sensitive data, such as AWS credentials, PII, credit card numbers, and more.

Data can be routed from various components in your application to S3 and continually monitored for sensitive attributes by Macie. This could include events sent to EventBridge, API responses generated by Lambda functions, or messages sent to SQS queues. Macie findings events are sent to EventBridge and can be routed from there to alert you to sensitive data being stored or transmitted by your application.

Summary

The security paradox dictates that while software security should be of paramount importance to an enterprise, it is often not a primary concern for engineering teams. This disconnect is typically caused by a lack of actionable processes.

Security must, and can, be an integral part of your serverless software delivery lifecycle. You can achieve this by adopting key security strategies like zero trust architecture, the principle of least privilege, and threat modeling; following industry standards for data encryption, API protection, and supply chain security; and leveraging security tools provided by AWS, such as IAM and Security Hub.

Most importantly, remember that security can be simple, and by establishing a clear framework for securing your serverless application you can remove a lot of the usual fear and uncertainty for your engineers.

Interview with an Industry Expert

Nicole Yip, Principal Engineer

Nicole Yip has spent many years getting engineering teams up and running in AWS and helping them grow to operational maturity in Australia and the United Kingdom. Her interests in DevOps (in its many definitions), security, reliability, infrastructure, and overall system design have helped shape teams in a way that enables them to get their applications and services out to production safely and securely while maturing their understanding and processes around owning production systems (most notably a very popular global retail website).

You can find some conference talks and blog posts about her various interest areas online, but her main focus has been inspiring, challenging, and implementing growth in the teams around her in the companies she has been involved with.

Q: There is a perception in the software industry that security is hard and should be left to cybersecurity specialists. Has the cloud changed this, or should engineers still be scared of security?

In the software industry it's true that security is seen as hard and intimidating, but I would break that down to say that it's seen as "yet another requirement" and a rabbit hole, combined.

Security is seen as "hard" because it's another nonfunctional requirement to be included at every stage, from design to implementation and even to ongoing operations. Security is also hard because there is a lot to discover when you enter the world of security—it's not just the code you write, the architecture you design, or the access controls around the applications you use to meet certain standards and protocols. There are also entire categories of threats like physical security and social engineering that wouldn't come to mind when just looking at security from a software engineering point of view but can still be just as, if not more, damaging as entry points to your system.

For those in security teams, InfoSec tooling that used to be manual, cumbersome, and scheduled monthly or less frequently as a result has improved and become way more user-friendly and integrated with the software development lifecycle, making it easier for issues to be flagged before making it to production or even automatically patching vulnerable dependencies as they get reported in the community.

Software engineers are typically very curious, so I don't think they should be scared of security as a topic—it's one of those things where the more aware you are, the more you naturally make more informed decisions when choosing how to host that application, or whether to click on that link. Security is everyone's responsibility and absolutely shouldn't be "left" to security experts—each line of code written or design decision made changes the security posture of the system, so the more security-aware everyone involved in the software development lifecycle is, the less likely it is that a bad actor will be able to find enough vulnerabilities to successfully do some damage.

Where the cloud comes in is that securing parts of your system becomes the cloud provider's responsibility—security of your data centers and data at rest become a contractual agreement with the cloud provider. For small businesses that is a blessing as it is yet another thing that would need to be figured out and enforced if they had chosen to self-host and build a server room.

By using a cloud provider you are guided into configuring a more secure system by default without realizing it. The choice to start setting up an application in the cloud can already have you making decisions about security because you are presented with those decisions when configuring the services.

You can still build a system with vulnerabilities in the cloud, so stay curious; learn as much as you can about attack vectors (threat modeling helps to identify these) and the real business implications to your system when someone discovers and exploits them. It's not "if" but "when."

What does "security" mean?

The end goal is to allow your system to be used in the intended way, and all other potential abuses and access should be mitigated (limited) or not possible to begin with.

It's a risk acceptance scale—you secure a system to the point where you as a business accept the likelihood and impact of the potential attack vectors in your system. Why? Because some attack vectors you can't prevent—like insider threats from a bad actor in your development team!

Q: Serverless shifts the responsibility of infrastructure management to AWS, allowing engineers to focus on the code that is deployed to that infrastructure. Does the delegation of infrastructure management in serverless make security easier or harder?

It depends which lens you are looking from, as an infrastructure/networking engineer or as a software engineer. Overall I think serverless makes security a little easier as the environments are sandboxed, which reduces the ability to persist an entry point. But when you start introducing more complex use cases that for example introduce networking (if running in a VPC), authentication and authorization of clients (that call your APIs)… then the level of security expertise required remains the same. Instead of the responsibility maybe resting with an operations or infrastructure team who are already in the habit of thinking about network-level threats, that responsibility is then taken on by the software engineering team.

A conscious effort needs to be put in to raise the level of expectations on software engineers venturing further down the stack into serverless and infrastructure—it's not good enough to just configure the libraries you use to their recommended security levels, you now also need to consider how many permissions does the container running your code actually need to operate, how much connectivity does it need to other resources—should they be in the same network or can they be isolated on their own?

Q: You have led software teams for many years and played an active role in the cloud and DevOps community. Have you observed any shifts in the role of a software engineer as they become increasingly responsible for securing their applications when using serverless technology?

Yes, but not necessarily because software engineers become increasingly responsible for securing their applications. Software engineers typically start out in a specialty—frontend, backend, database administrator, etc.—and they learn the leading frameworks, patterns, and nonfunctional requirements (including security) for designing reliable solutions within that specialty. They then start to expand out and collect specialties and aim to become this mythical "full stack" engineer. "Full stack" used to broadly include frontend, backend, and database specialties but that can easily now include operations, networking, and infrastructure with the prevalence of cloud hosting platforms. With serverless especially this has reduced the barrier to entry to new specialties they can expand out to, including data (migration and management), machine learning, and so much more.

As I mentioned before, security is one of those nonfunctional requirements that exists in all parts of the stack, and all those specialty areas I mentioned before need to understand security and privacy with different lenses for their areas of the stack.

With serverless this enables software engineers get a foot in the door to learn networking and infrastructure with a helping hand on security and privacy built into the usage of the platform.

For example, network engineers use firewalls to block out connections from unwanted networks and on unused ports—when requesting an AWS VPC and setting up your subnets and route tables, these are all locked down by default and you specify the ports and networks that need access (although let's ignore the fact the default networking resources in new AWS accounts don't adhere to that).

The opportunities and avenues for a software engineer to grow and evolve their role will continue to expand. New technologies will emerge every few years (currently GenAI and prompt engineering) that lower the barrier for entry to other specialties (e.g., data science and creative industries) and can then add a new line into the description of what a full stack engineer could be.

Q: You have played a crucial role in the serverless and DevOps adoption at large enterprises. From your experience, how can teams and organizations foster a culture of security?

There are two things I have leveraged to foster a culture around security. First of all, by building a strong engineering team culture and keeping security topics in the day-to-day conversation to maintain security awareness.

High-performing engineering cultures tend to have transparency, fail fast, and no-blame principles at their core. In addition to building trust this also allows teams to learn collectively. No one person will be able to review an architecture and lock it down 100% with no risks to accept. Everyone has unknown unknowns, and there are just some attack vectors you can't lock down. So when something does happen, having a culture that has clear runbooks on what to do when a breach occurs and doesn't penalize someone for identifying and reporting a breach will become more security-mature much faster than a team without these principles actively being fostered.

The second is keeping security in the conversation and having enough support for slack/innovation/curiosity time. Tooling and shift-left principles highlight security concerns early on in the software development lifecycle, which generates the conversation when they are surfaced in a constructive way. Putting in requirements for threat modeling as part of the design process brings the discussion about security even further to the left. But in addition to those, what you really need is engineers who are curious, who are constantly wondering what if, and then have enough slack time to pursue those trains of thought. Regular *lunch and learn* sessions about the latest breach that was reported in the industry or a security concept can trigger those moments of "what if...?" That little prompt for an engineer to think about the thing they are working on in the moment and realize that the vulnerability that allowed that breach or that concept could also apply to the thing they are writing is what you're looking for—and then make sure they are supported if they go and try it out or play through the "what if...?" scenario. They could actually add in a mitigation before that feature gets to production!

It's those lenses on the code from a high level (threat modeling) to a low level (dependency and static analysis tools) that can supplement the secure design and implementation of a system, but it's engineers who will be able to secure the system with the business logic and constraints in mind as each line of code is being written and each part of the system is being configured. Give them the space and the knowledge to trigger their curiosity and do so!

Q: There are several standards and best practices for security on AWS, including the principle of least privilege, the shared responsibility model for cloud security, and the AWS Well-Architected Framework. For an enterprise adopting serverless, where do you think they can make a start in terms of security awareness?

The first thing to keep in mind is that security is everyone's responsibility.

I would say start at the enterprise level and go with the assumption you'll be breached tomorrow. Do you have good security foundations in place in your company? Would you know if and when you were breached, and do you know how to react and remediate?

Prevention and mitigation measures are always needed but never reduce the risk of a breach to 0%. As I've mentioned before, there are some attack vectors you cannot close and can only mitigate as best you can to bring them down to an acceptable risk level.

Some basic enterprise-level security capabilities include:

Detection
Security information and event management (SIEM) alerts that go to a responsive team

Response
Integrity assured evidence capturing system, sandboxes and isolated networks, experience in security response

Prevention
Guardrails, training, golden paths, audits, penetration tests

Zooming in from looking at the enterprise level and into platform teams, platform teams should build in security golden paths to their products that pipe everything built on that platform into their company SIEM and surface prioritized alerts to the teams. They can also support application teams by integrating security tooling into their toolchain and deployment pipelines and surfacing the results in effective ways.

Application teams should be engaged in regular security education to stay up-to-date with the latest threats out there—whether that's joining presentations breaking down the latest hack on a relevant application layer, completing company training, or being curious and learning more about security best practices from the tools in use (AWS Well-Architected Framework, GitHub Dependabot findings, static and/or dynamic analysis tools, penetration tests, etc.).

CHAPTER 5

Serverless Implementation Patterns

There are only patterns, patterns on top of patterns, patterns that affect other patterns. Patterns hidden by patterns. Patterns within patterns.

—Chuck Palahniuk

There are patterns all around you. This book follows a pattern; every chapter has a pattern. Nature is full of patterns. Chapter 3 mentioned the three elements of architecture: art, structure, and technique. You'll see patterns in each of these elements. Though patterns in physical architecture show the influence of region, climate, culture, etc., commonality still prevails in many cases. Patterns in software architecture follow a similar trend: though there are underlying commonalities, many show the influence of the business domain, programming language, operating environment, and other factors.

Irrespective of the differences, patterns aim to provide solutions to recurring and common problems related to the architecture, design, implementation, or operation of software systems. Patterns can become opinionated, especially when influenced by the abovementioned factors. Some patterns come and go quickly while others survive for much longer, although their implementations may differ over time. The circuit breaker pattern (discussed later in this chapter) is a good example; its name might not be obviously related to software, but adaptations and applications of this pattern are visible across different eras and technology stacks. Some patterns become so popular that after a while they're taken for granted. The API Gateway pattern, for example, was discussed a lot in tech media when it first appeared, but soon modern technologies and development practices made it a common, everyday implementation that no one specifically thinks about as a pattern.

In this chapter, we'll explore some of the common patterns in event-driven architecture, such as choreography, orchestration, and the strangler fig pattern (useful for migrating legacy applications to serverless). We'll also take a detailed look at the circuit breaker pattern and its implementation styles, and introduce you to newer patterns such as functionless, gatekeeper event bus, etc.

AWS Service Icons in Architectural Drawings

As you know, the diagrammatic representation of your solution architecture resonates with just about everyone. Though everything can be depicted with boxes, lines, and labels, the simplicity and visual appeal of an architecture diagram enables viewers to grasp the design quickly. Using AWS service icons in diagrams brings them closer to you as an engineer or architect, and you'll see that we've used them in many of the diagrams in this chapter and others in this book. Thus, familiarity with the icons of some of the common and popular services will be useful going forward.

As with technology, AWS evolves these icons over time. For instance, the icon of SQS you might have used a few years ago is not the version you'll see today. The best way to keep up-to-date is to check the AWS icon library (*https://oreil.ly/bqOmr*).

An Overview of Software Patterns

No conversation on software patterns can happen without reference to the venerable *Design Patterns: Elements of Reusable Object-Oriented Software* (Addison-Wesley Professional) by Erich Gamma, Richard Helm, Ralph Johnson, and John Vlissides, famously referred to as the Gang of Four (GoF). As the title suggests, this work (originally published in 1994) was mainly influenced by OO principles, but it presents several patterns that have outlived popular programming languages of the day.

Evolving from the OO-dominated '90s, web services and enterprise application integrations started to take shape. Ten years after the publication of *Design Patterns*, another classic was released: *Enterprise Integration Patterns* by Gregor Hohpe and Bobby Woolf (Addison-Wesley Professional), with its collection of 65 patterns. A decade later, Sam Newman's *Building Microservices: Designing Fine-Grained Systems* (O'Reilly) brought fresh thinking to architecting business applications. A few years after this, influenced by the popularity of microservices, *Microservices Patterns* by Chris Richardson (Manning) was released, presenting over 40 different patterns and their implementation details. Several other books on patterns are still being published with newer content.

Like the myriad types of patterns you might observe in your daily life, there are many categories of patterns in software. Here is an incomplete list:

- Software architecture patterns
- Software design patterns
- Programming patterns
- Application integration patterns
- Enterprise integration patterns
- Domain-driven design patterns

- Microservices patterns
- Messaging patterns
- Storage patterns
- Event-driven architecture patterns
- Sustainability patterns
- Cloud computing patterns

Within each of these categories, you'll find subcategories and groups based on different criteria. For example, the *Design Patterns* book divides its 23 patterns into 3 categories: creational patterns, structural patterns, and behavioral patterns.

What Is a Pattern?

In simple terms, a pattern is a proven solution to a recurring problem. A design pattern helps software designers get the software design *right* faster. An implementation pattern, on the other hand, enables a developer to build an application quickly. Most software patterns you will encounter have the following common elements, as reflected in *Design Patterns*:

- The name of the pattern
- The problem it helps solve
- The abstract solution the pattern offers
- The consequences, side effects, and trade-offs of using the pattern

Like API patterns, messaging patterns, and storage patterns, some consider serverless itself as a cloud development pattern, describing it as a way of building and operating highly scalable cloud solutions faster.

How Do Patterns Accelerate Serverless Development?

Whether you consider serverless a pattern or not, it certainly offers a new technology ecosystem for building cloud applications. As an evolution of cloud computing, serverless is influenced by several popular patterns you likely already use. As shown in Figure 5-1, these include patterns for everything from architecture to design, integration, storage, implementation, and operation. At the same time, serverless also introduces entirely new patterns.

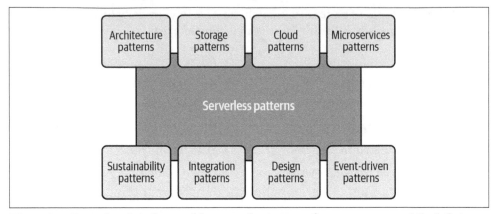

Figure 5-1. Serverless is influenced by several existing software patterns, while defining its own

Chapter 3 presented several common architectural patterns. Take, for instance, the API request/response pattern. Though this is a software pattern, without you realizing it, it is also part of your everyday serverless development. Point-to-point messaging patterns with queues and publish/subscribe patterns with topics do not have a big learning curve, because AWS services such as Amazon SQS and SNS provide you with those capabilities out of the box as standard. You then build advanced patterns and specialty use cases on top by using AWS services. Even when you use the Java language to implement your Lambda functions, you no longer handcode publish or subscribe messages using the Java Messaging Service (JMS) API. This exemplifies how serverless acts as a stepping stone to accelerate your cloud journey. The challenge, however, is knowing or deciding which service to use in a given circumstance.

> While several books discuss the full breadth of software patterns, the earliest collection of patterns specifically centered around building serverless solutions on AWS was published by Jeremy Daly (*https://oreil.ly/Scffv*), CEO of Ampt (*https://getampt.com*) and an AWS Serverless Hero, during the early days of serverless evolution in 2018. Jeremy's updated collection of patterns (*https://oreil.ly/YMcB2*) is still helping many engineers accelerate their serverless adoption.

Patterns are there, to be discovered

Though a pattern with a catchy name gets everyone's attention, as a developer you'll also come across many anonymous patterns that you'll apply repeatedly, enabling you to solve problems and develop solutions faster. You're more likely to find these patterns when you're experimenting with newer technologies than when you're working with legacy systems. As you try out different service combinations in serverless, for example, you have a good chance of identifying design constructs that will turn into new patterns. Once you have proved that a pattern fits well with a particular use case, you gain confidence and start applying it in similar situations. At this stage, your pattern may not have a name or wider visibility.

Figure 5-2 shows a simple serverless data pipeline where certain data feeds get dropped into an S3 bucket that triggers data processing and transformation activities before updating a target system. Though this simple architecture already makes use of a few patterns—event triggers, messaging, a dead letter queue, etc.—it's still just a design at this stage.

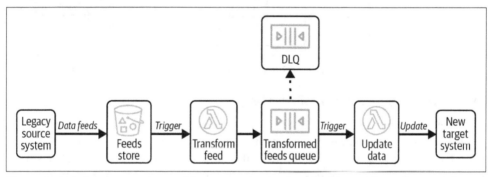

Figure 5-2. A data processing architecture to ingest data feeds, transform them, and update a target system

Say you experiment with the data processing pipeline shown here and optimize the Lambda functions and SQS queues for different types of data feeds. Soon, you hear there's a need for a similar data processing flow for different datasets. You now have the possibility of repeating the construct several times for different use cases (as shown in Figure 5-3) and across several teams. You may well be in the early discovery stages of a new pattern.

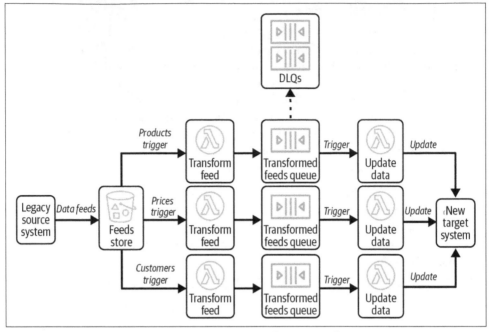

Figure 5-3. A repeatable data processing pattern that is specific to a certain use case

Serverless patterns are guides, not silver bullets

Not every pattern you come across is relevant to serverless, or can be shown with its equivalent serverless representation. Consider the patterns and examples covered in this chapter as guides to inspire you to build better serverless solutions, not as simple lift-and-shift architecture or design constructs that you can apply to every problem.

We're all amazed by snowflakes and their intricate structures. Though they look similar to the naked eye, scientists say (*https:// oreil.ly/qCroB*) that snowflakes can be sorted into about 40 categories, with an almost infinite number of possible shapes. Similarly (though to a much more modest extent!), patterns used across the software industry can have several variations and distinct implementation styles. As new technologies evolve, they bring even more possibilities. The circuit breaker pattern that we'll look at later in this chapter is one example that has several implementation flavors, from legacy to serverless.

Serverless Migration: The Strangler Fig Pattern

Strangler fig (*https://oreil.ly/cjtgB*) is the common name for a variety of tropical and subtropical plant species that begin their lives on a host tree and grow long vines that, over the years, gradually strangle (and in many cases kill) the host. When you migrate legacy enterprise applications to serverless, the incremental and iterative approach of shifting functionality in small parts from the old application to a modern serverless stack is often compared with the lifestyle of a strangler fig.

The strangler fig pattern, introduced by Martin Fowler (*https://oreil.ly/kjMl7*) and inspired by the behavior of this plant, is the most reliable migration pattern to move workloads to serverless. Its benefits include:

- Lowering the risk involved in the migration process
- Providing visibility on the progress of the migration
- Allowing course correction without much disruption
- Reducing or even avoiding service disruptions and system downtime

Implementation Approaches

The most important aspect of applying this pattern is clearly knowing the end goal. In-depth knowledge of the system you are migrating and how the migrated system will take shape is essential to succeed.

When applying the strangler fig pattern, you can take inspiration from the set piece microservices development analogy discussed in Chapter 3. You take the *whole* system, and you identify the *parts* or *pieces* that you can gradually migrate toward your end target, ultimately "strangling" the source by moving all of its pieces to the target.

Most examples of the strangler fig pattern talk about the migration of APIs from the old to the new with some form of façade layer (as the strangler) to shift traffic or route requests. However, in enterprises, you will encounter varied use cases and varying implementations of this pattern. In addition, different areas of a given system may require different strangling approaches. You'll find that some parts can be migrated by applying the strangler pattern at a high level, and others at a lower level.

With a high-level strangler approach, you identify the frontend and backend services and APIs, data processing jobs, business report generation tasks, data analytics and insights, data stores, event flows, etc. At this level, your focus is on tactical migration, considering the dependencies, business criticalities, risks, regulatory compliances, complexities, etc. To apply the strangler pattern at a low level, you take each system part and implement the needed steps to progressively move it to the target serverless architecture.

Strangling Data Processing Flows

It is common in a functioning organization to have several data flows and data processing flows that span multiple domains, departments, and teams. Many of these flows are vital for the functioning of critical applications of the organization. Diverting these as you move from the existing legacy systems to serverless requires a well-planned, coordinated approach.

Figure 5-4 depicts a common data sharing approach with many legacy applications. Data files get placed in certain network file folders for consuming applications to fetch them at desired intervals using some form of file transfer protocol.

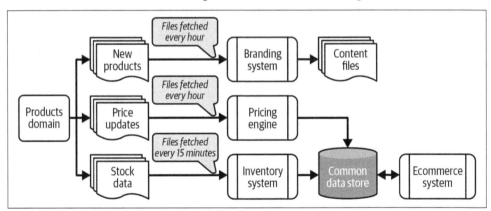

Figure 5-4. A legacy data sharing system that uses data files stored in folders and fetched by consuming applications at desired intervals

Before you embark on the serverless migration of such a system, you must create a vision of your end goal and what your migrated architecture will look like. It may not be perfect when you start, but it's important to at least sketch out a first draft that you can refine as you progress through the journey. The target architecture for this system is shown in Figure 5-5: it has newly implemented serverless microservices alongside in-house or external applications.

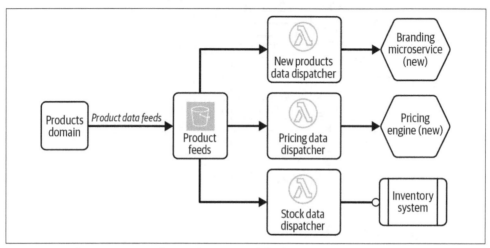

Figure 5-5. The target serverless architecture of the legacy data processing pipeline

You now have a vision, and your challenge is, as you learned in Chapter 3, to identify the set pieces and incrementally migrate those parts of the system by applying the strangler fig approach.

Figure 5-6 illustrates the initial evolution of the new data flow. Your goal is to gradually strangle the data feeds going into different network folders by directing all of them into a common place—an S3 product feeds bucket, in this case. Depending on the capabilities of your legacy system, you may have an intermediary phase before switching to a new backend. Figure 5-6 shows the rerouting of the new products data feed to the legacy branding system (assuming it has an API to receive data from the Lambda function). This will be followed by rerouting the price updates and stock data feeds. The new serverless pipeline improves efficiency by processing the feeds as soon as they arrive.

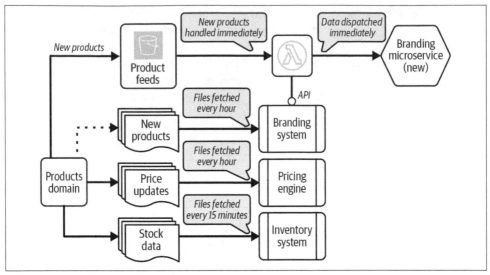

Figure 5-6. The first phase of the data pipeline migration: strangling a legacy data flow route

Strangling API Routes to Backend Services

The strategy to migrate API routes is similar to the data pipeline migration strategy you saw in the previous section: you take the existing legacy application, identify a piece of functionality—often a "low-hanging fruit" feature to start with—and build a newer replacement version in serverless. When it's ready, you gradually shift the traffic from the old endpoint to the new one. While doing so, you will run both the old and new endpoints in parallel, allowing you to observe and improve on the new service before strangling the old one. You then start with the next piece, and iterate until you have strangled everything from the legacy system.

 Often, when you migrate legacy monolithic applications to serverless, you will uncover opportunities to abandon synchronous endpoints and rebuild those parts as asynchronous services in the target serverless architecture. You may not need to build like-for-like endpoints.

While you're migrating your monolithic backend application to serverless microservices, you need a layer that acts as the "switchboard" to route incoming requests to the right backend endpoints. Two common implementation patterns that provide a façade layer to achieve this are the API gateway and BFF patterns, described in the following sections.

API gateway as the façade layer

Several API gateway products provide the capability to route requests to both the old and new endpoints. However, as you migrate your applications to serverless and operate them on the AWS cloud, Amazon API Gateway is the appropriate service. It offers several service integrations and can be used as a proxy to invoke HTTP endpoints.

Figure 5-7 shows the initial architecture, with a legacy API gateway acting as the façade layer. The target serverless architecture requires an improved solution.

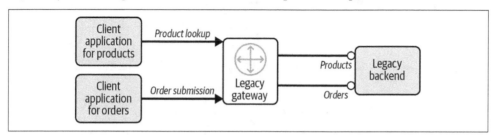

Figure 5-7. The original architecture, with a legacy gateway routing requests to backend application endpoints

Figure 5-8 shows the first phase of strangling the API route. While the new Amazon API Gateway becomes the target for one of the client applications, it in turn routes the requests to the legacy gateway while the new microservice is being developed. Note that introducing the new API gateway will require an update of the client application as well, as it will have a different hostname from the legacy gateway.

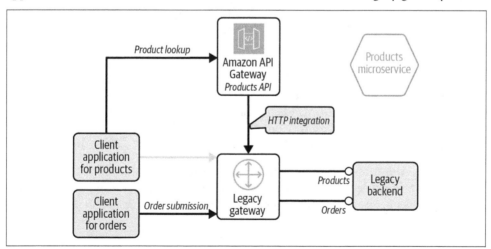

Figure 5-8. First phase of API strangling with the introduction of Amazon API Gateway as the target for an existing client application

When the new microservice—the products microservice, in this case—becomes available, you switch the routing and continue strangling the legacy system as you progress with the migration, as shown in Figure 5-9.

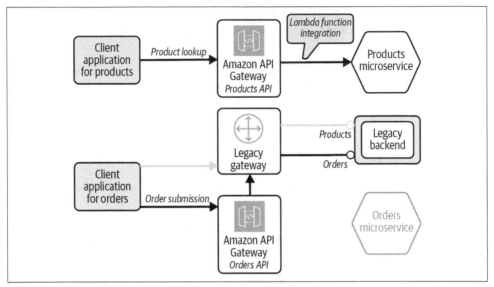

Figure 5-9. Switching from a legacy API gateway to Amazon API Gateway and migrating the legacy monolith to new serverless microservices

 When you route traffic from one API gateway to another during the legacy to serverless migration phase, the extra network route will add latency to the overall call. The added latency may be small, but it's still worth keeping in mind.

Backend for Frontend as the façade layer

The original intention of the BFF pattern was to have different backend services to serve the different types of frontend client applications, such as web browsers, mobile devices, tablets, etc. However, it is popular as a middle layer between the frontend applications and the backend microservices layer, as shown in Figure 5-10.

As with the API strangling approach, the BFF pattern offers the flexibility to shift from legacy to serverless services. It allows running both legacy and migrated applications in parallel before completely switching over to the new implementation.

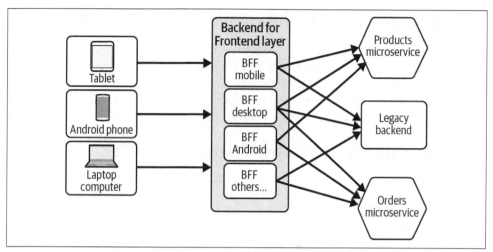

Figure 5-10. Typical Backend for Frontend architecture that enables managing routes to both legacy and serverless backend services

The Storage-First Pattern

The storage-first pattern is one of the newer patterns. According to Eric Johnson (*https://oreil.ly/CaB7z*), Principal Developer Advocate at AWS, who introduced the name, the main concept of this pattern is to store first and process after.

In an event-driven architecture, when you handle requests asynchronously by decoupling the receipt of a request from its processing, it is crucial that you don't lose the data. With the storage-first pattern, you first store the incoming data in an SQS queue, Kinesis stream, S3 bucket, or DynamoDB table, and then start the computation part.

Which service you use to store the data and for how long depends on the business case. For example, if there is a need to keep the data longer than a few days or weeks, you may consider DynamoDB or S3 over SQS and set the TTL or data retention policy to automatically remove the data after the desired period.

For business scenarios that handle sensitive data, there are restrictions regarding the details you can add to logs. In such situations, the storage-first pattern can also allow you to implement an audit log for the data.

The concept of the storage-first pattern is similar to that of the *inbox pattern*, but the implementation of that pattern mainly focuses on storing incoming messages in a database, whereas the storage-first pattern covers a variety of storage services. One of the key benefits of the storage-first and inbox patterns is the ability to enforce idempotency by checking the uniqueness of the incoming message against the storage to avoid duplication.

Resilient Architecture: The Circuit Breaker Pattern

The circuit breaker pattern is one of the most important and widely adopted architectural patterns in software engineering. Its part in a distributed services environment is crucial for resilient and highly available applications. The concept of *circuit breakers* comes from the electrical switches that are useful to open a circuit either manually or automatically to protect the electrical circuit from overload or outage.

Why Is the Circuit Breaker Pattern Relevant in Serverless?

It is common in a business environment to have heavily used and highly critical applications such as payment systems, order services, etc. A network issue that impacts the connection to such a system, a scheduled downtime, or an unexpected system outage can have severe consequences for applications that consume their services and impact millions of end users/customers.

During peak network traffic times, if one of your serverless microservices invokes an unresponsive remote application, you face the risk of:

- Cloud resources quickly reaching their allocated quotas or concurrency limits
- Lambda functions running longer, waiting for responses that cost more
- A delay in one service triggering a domino effect of application-wide gridlock

In addition, if yours is a user-facing service, your disgruntled users will likely send more requests while impatiently waiting for a response, adding to the chaos and exhausting your service resources.

In situations like these, you need a way to assess the unhealthy status of the service provider and fail fast rather than waiting—and implementing a circuit breaker pattern helps you limit the damage.

Core Concepts of Circuit Breaker Implementation

Understanding the core concepts of circuit breakers is important. They include:

A closed circuit
> Figure 5-11 shows a simple service that fetches customer order details from a SaaS platform, using a synchronous request/response invocation from the user's app to the third-party system and back. The diagram shows the connection between the Lambda function and the third-party system working as expected—it is a *closed circuit*.

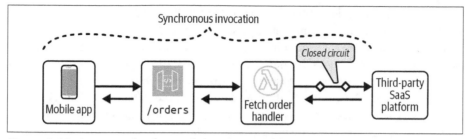

Figure 5-11. An example of a synchronous request/response communication pattern where the circuit is closed, indicating normal functioning

An open circuit

When a circuit is marked as *open*, the connection from one system to the other does not happen. In Figure 5-12, the Lambda function cannot successfully handle its requests if the third-party system is down or extremely slow to respond. In this situation, as the circuit is open, the function does not invoke the third-party SaaS platform but fails immediately and responds with an error.

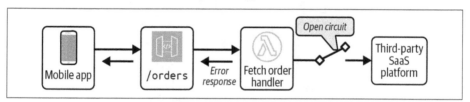

Figure 5-12. An example of a synchronous request/response communication pattern where the circuit is open, preventing a connection between two systems

The circuit breaker

The circuit breaker (or *manager*) is an object that wraps a protected function call and monitors for errors, using its defined logic to determine whether to declare a circuit (connection) as open or closed. This determination typically depends on threshold conditions: for example, five consecutive failures to reach the third party within two minutes could cause the circuit breaker to mark the circuit as open.

A half-open circuit

The circuit breaker needs a way to determine when it's safe to declare the circuit as closed again. As it has no way of knowing whether or not the external application has recovered, the typical approach is to wait for some duration and then let a few invocations through. Based on the success or failure of these calls and the circuit breaker logic, it then either marks the circuit as closed or keeps it open with a fresh timeout value to check again. This *half-open* circuit allows the circuit breaker to test the waters, as it were.

As of now, the Lambda service does not offer a built-in circuit breaking functionality. Hence, it is important to understand the pattern and its implementation. The exact implementation logic of a circuit breaker will depend on your use case. In general, you require a place to store the current status of the circuit as a bare minimum. In addition, you may want to store the threshold counter, timeout value, number of attempts, etc. Depending on the importance of the external system and its wider impact on the business, you may opt for a simple circuit status check mechanism or a dedicated service, as the following sections explain.

A simple status-checking function

If just one application is interacting with the third-party or external service, as in the example shown in Figure 5-12, you may use a Lambda function to check the status of the third party and store the status in a parameter in AWS Systems Manager (SSM) Parameter Store, as shown in Figure 5-13.

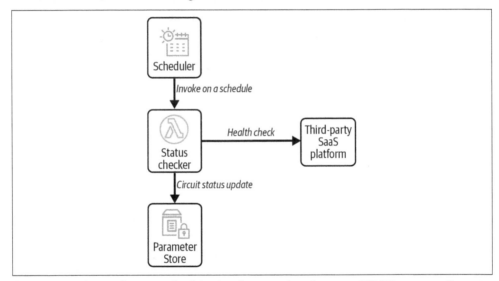

Figure 5-13. A simple status-checking implementation that uses SSM Parameter Store to store the circuit's current status

Now that you have a way to determine the status of the circuit, the order-fetching service can incorporate the status check before invoking the third-party system. This is shown in Figure 5-14.

The example shown here uses the SSM Parameter Store to store the current status of the circuit. You might also consider storing this information in DynamoDB, especially if your circuit breaker logic involves maintaining threshold counts, timestamps of the status changes, etc.

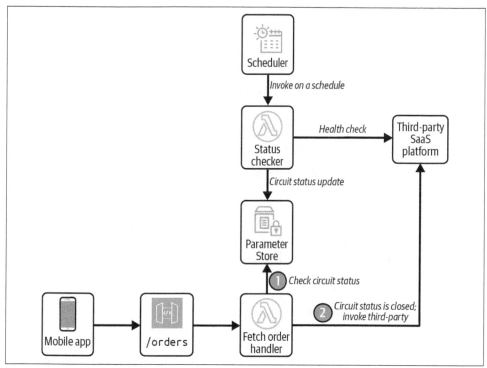

Figure 5-14. A Lambda function that checks the status of the circuit by reading a parameter value in the SSM Parameter Store before invoking an external system

This solution may be all you need for your use case. However, in an enterprise environment, you could have an application or service being consumed by several business units. In such situations, rather than having each consumer duplicate the status check, you might instead want to consider implementing a common service that every consumer can access to check the circuit's status. The next section discusses this approach.

A dedicated event-driven status-checking service

When you have a critical microservice or an external third-party application that serves several applications, you might want to implement a dedicated health check service, as shown in Figure 5-15.

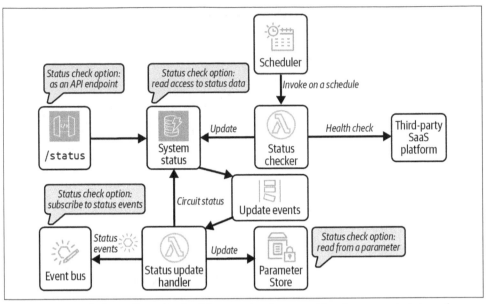

Figure 5-15. A dedicated status-checking service that provides the current status of a third-party system

As indicated in Figure 5-15, there are several implementation options for the status check functionality; you can choose whichever one is appropriate for your use cases and purpose. Here are a few thoughts on choosing the right one:

- If service consumers are in the same AWS account, the easy option is to store the current status in an SSM parameter to check before invoking the target service.

- A more sophisticated option is to provide status checking as a service via an API endpoint.

- Though not ideal, a simpler approach is to grant all consumers read access to the status item in a DynamoDB table.

- An event-driven approach benefits from the push notification of service status as an operational event. Example 5-1 shows what such an event might look like.

Example 5-1. An operational event that indicates the status of a third-party system

```
{
  "metadata": {
    "version": "1.0",
    "trace_id": "skdj834sd3-j3ns-cmass23",
    "created_at": "2023-12-30T10:15:03Z",
    "domain": "retail",
    "subdomain": "orders",
    "service": "status-checker",
```

```
      "category": "operational_event",
      "type": "status",
      "status": "down"
    },
    "data": {
      "system": "anytime-third-party",
      "current_status": "down",
      "previous_status": "up",
      "current_status_since": "2023-12-30T09:55:00Z",
      "last_checked_at": "2023-12-30T10:15:00Z"
    }
}
```

If an application does not provide a dedicated status-check end-point, invoking an endpoint to fetch some test data without causing any side effects is an alternative option.

If you decide to implement a dedicated status monitoring service, there are few considerations you need to be aware of:

Availability of a dedicated status-checking endpoint

The periodical status check of the third-party application relies on a dedicated health check API. Though most SaaS platforms offer this, you may find some legacy applications without this capability.

Potential benefits to your monitoring system

Having a dedicated service allows you to track the health of the external system on dashboards for monitoring purposes, providing continuous visibility. Plus, it enables you to raise alarms and send alerts to your on-call support engineers when necessary.

API quota and invocation limits

Make sure the status check calls do not eat into your API quota or overall invocation limit (depending on the cost model or the charging policy of the application provider).

Figure 5-15 illustrates the implementation of a dedicated service status check pattern where multiple applications that interact with the same external system can *query* the status via an endpoint. In a decentralized approach, rather than having a dedicated status-checking service, individual applications that experience connection issues with the external system can post status updates. The circuit manager can monitor these to determine the circuit status and send out updates when appropriate.

Failing Faster When the Circuit Is Open

Now that you understand the basics of the circuit breaker pattern, let's take a look at the most common use of the pattern: *failing fast*. As the name indicates, the goal here is that when an application or service that your application depends on in order to serve its clients cannot fulfill the requests within an expected time window, your application swiftly returns an error response. This has a few key benefits:

Increased end-user satisfaction
> Users of modern digital systems prefer fast responses from the apps they interact with. Dissatisfied customers leave and look elsewhere. In a highly competitive business world, that benefits your competitors.

Lower costs
> Computing resources cost money when in use. In a synchronous flow, when an external system takes a long time to respond to your Lambda function, it awaits a response up to its timeout. This adds to the Lambda cost. When you multiply that by thousands or millions of invocations, it can cause a substantial increase in your overall cloud costs.

Less risk of overburdening the already stressed system
> When users experience slowness in an application, the human instinct is to retry the request repeatedly. This behavior initiates more requests and overloads the already crippled service, with a high risk of resource exhaustion and hitting service quotas and concurrency limits.

Storing Requests When the Circuit Is Open and Replaying Them When Closed

Depending on the criticality of the application, another common use of the circuit breaker pattern that you might want to consider is storing requests when the circuit is open and replaying them when it's closed. Often, you can classify services as non-critical, critical, or highly critical. For example, a service that provides next week's weather forecast for a given location is probably not critical. In contrast, services that accept holiday reservations or take payments for orders, batch jobs that transfer money between accounts, and event notifications that inform you of the redemption of discount codes are critical. If such services are caught in an *open circuit* situation, you need a way to receive the requests, store them until the circuit closes, and then *replay* them eventually.

There are a variety of serverless services you can use for this purpose, depending on factors such as the volume of requests, the required speed/immediacy of replay, etc. The following sections describe some of the options.

Using a dedicated SQS queue for storage and replay

Storing requests in a queue and replaying them is probably the most popular option for ensuring the resiliency of an application. The concept is simple and straightforward:

- When the circuit is closed, the requests get processed as normal.
- When the circuit is open, the requests get pushed into a queue to be replayed later.
- When the circuit closes again, the requests from the queue are processed.

How you trigger the replay and reprocess the requests depends on your implementation logic. For example, you might:

- Retrieve the buffered requests into a processing queue that acts as the event source for a Lambda function.
- Start a scheduler when the circuit closes to periodically trigger a Lambda function to pull messages from the queue to process. During this operation, if the circuit becomes open, you must stop the process.

To choose the apt replay approach, you must know the capabilities of the target system. After all, you don't want to open the floodgate too soon and cause further degradation. You must also be mindful of existing rate limits and quotas as you replay requests.

Using DynamoDB to store the requests and fetch them to replay

It's a recommended practice in event-driven architecture for an application to store incoming requests or events before processing them (see "The Storage-First Pattern" on page 225). This ensures that, in the event of a service interruption or open circuit, you have the data to resubmit.

If you use DynamoDB to store requests, make sure you have devised the appropriate data query patterns and indexes for efficient data operation. A crucial attribute you should store for every data item in the table is `status`, indicating whether the request has been processed or requires resubmission. A sample list of values it can take includes:

RECEIVED
: Data has been received. Set as part of the storage-first implementation.

PROCESSING
: Data is being processed.

PROCESSED, RESPONDED, *or* SUCCESS
> Indicates the successful completion of the request.

ERROR
> Indicates a data processing error not related to the open circuit.

RETRY
> Indicates the request must be resubmitted. This is the status you set if the circuit is open.

> With DynamoDB, to capture the different stages of processing a request, you can consider keeping each stage separate rather than modifying the original data. You create appropriate partition key (PK) and sort key (SK) patterns to achieve this.
>
> Say you received an order with the ID 123-987-546-23. The order ID is your PK, but you may also keep SK values such as SOURCE, TRANSFORMED, SUBMITTED, etc. This allows a clear separation of data items and helps trace the data flow, among other benefits.

The main drawback of this approach is that when the circuit becomes closed, you will need to trigger a Lambda function or a Step Functions workflow to query the table for items to replay. In high-volume request flow use cases, due to DynamoDB's query result size limit of 1 MB, you might need to call this function repeatedly, and the clearing option can take a long time.

> To reduce costs and keep the table size optimal, set appropriate TTL values for the items in your DynamoDB table that have no business importance.

Using EventBridge's archive and replay feature

A relatively new approach to implementing the circuit breaker pattern is to use EventBridge's event archiving and replay capabilities. As you learned in Chapter 3, an event archive is a collection of events that satisfy a filter pattern. Events remain in the archive until they reach their expiry period or the archive is deleted. Figure 5-16 shows the high-level logic of this approach. When the circuit is in an open state, an event with a *retry* identity is created and sent to the custom event bus. A rule filters *retry* events and routes them to an EventBridge archive.

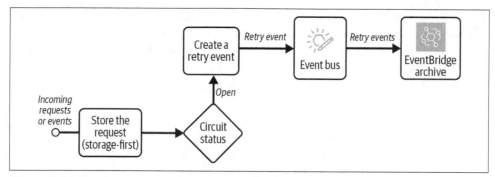

Figure 5-16. Routing retry events to an EventBridge event archive

When the circuit becomes closed again, you initiate the replay of events from the archive within a specified time frame (corresponding to the duration of the downtime). EventBridge will then put those events from the archive onto the bus. You set up a rule to filter these replayed events from the archive and process them for resubmission, as depicted in Figure 5-17.

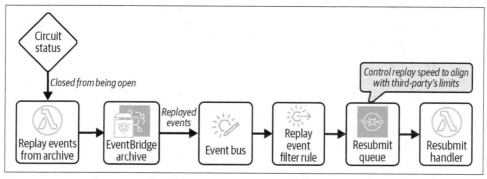

Figure 5-17. Replaying archived events

Using EventBridge archive and replay has its benefits. There is no limit on how many events you can store in an archive, making it possible to deal with lengthy downtimes and high-volume request flows. Also, as EventBridge replays the events within a requested time frame, it eliminates the need to implement extra logic for fetching events at frequent intervals.

 When it replays an event from the archive, EventBridge assigns it a new event id (refer to Example 3-3 in "How do you represent an event?" on page 142 for a refresher on what an EventBridge event looks like). If you have your idempotency check based on the event id, then you need a different way of identifying the event. One option is to use a trace_id that you add in the metadata section of your event, as shown in Example 3-5.

There are a few limitations that you must be aware of too. EventBridge does not guarantee the order of the events, and you cannot control the speed of events during replay. In addition, there is currently no option to delete the replayed events from the archive, so you need to maintain a journal of every replay time frame to avoid replaying events more than once.

 Another issue is that there may be a delay of several minutes between the time when an event is published to an event bus and the time at which it arrives in the archive and is available for replaying. In situations where the circuit breaker status fluctuates frequently within short time spans and you have a requirement to replay the requests immediately, EventBridge archive and replay may not be ideal.

The Outbox Pattern

"The Storage-First Pattern" on page 225 briefly mentioned the inbox pattern, which focuses on storing incoming messages in a database for later processing. The outbox pattern, on the other hand, is about an application persisting data in an "outbox" table so that another application can read and process the data or relay the data to a queue, for example.

In serverless, you often hear about the *transactional* outbox pattern. The common use case is when a Lambda function that handles the incoming data performs two actions: writing to a DynamoDB table and also emitting an event to the event bus or adding a message to a queue. Both actions must succeed to fulfill the functionality. To reduce the risk of this not happening, you can streamline the process by enabling streams in DynamoDB and having a Lambda function to handle the stream events and then send the data to downstream applications.

This is a common pattern that you will encounter frequently in serverless development. You may already be using this pattern in your applications without even realizing it.

The Functionless Integration Pattern

The terms *functionless*, *codeless*, *Lambda-less*, etc., express a common theme: reducing the use of Lambda functions in your serverless architecture. Though as an engineer you'll often hear the phrase "code is a liability," you know that you cannot build an application without code. As described in Chapter 1, in serverless, you compose your applications using managed cloud services. In this context, *functionless integration* means you no longer handcode your Lambda functions to connect or integrate two or more services; instead, you knit these services together using out-of-the-box features and IaC.

Figure 5-18 shows a simple architecture that receives data—say, product reviews—from customers via an API endpoint. It is an asynchronous operation, where the incoming reviews are pushed into a queue before downstream services process and publish them. Here, the engineer decided to use a Lambda function behind the API endpoint to *shift* the data from the API to the queue.

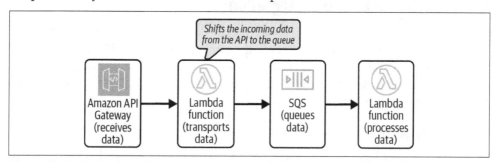

Figure 5-18. A simple architecture where a Lambda function transports the request data from the API to a queue

Figure 5-19 improves on this by applying functionless thinking. As the first Lambda function in Figure 5-18 performs data transport and has no business logic, you can eliminate it by using the native service integration feature of Amazon API Gateway, as shown here.

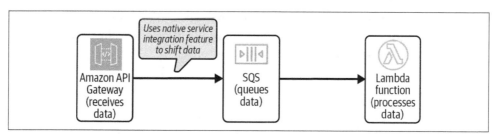

Figure 5-19. A serverless architecture that uses a native service integration between API Gateway and SQS

Though you can't eliminate the use of Lambda functions everywhere, the ambition of the functionless integration pattern is to apply this approach where it suits. Avoiding writing Lambda functions where possible has several benefits:

- You write, test, deploy, and operate less code.
- There are fewer points of failure and debugging hassles.
- You configure fewer IAM policies and permissions, meaning less security worry.

- You reduce the danger of exceeding your Lambda concurrent execution quota.
- You lower the monthly cost of your Lambda functions.

If you only have a handful of Lambda functions in your application you may not find the pattern appealing, but when you consider the potential benefits across your entire organization, it's easy to see that it can have quite a positive impact.

Use Cases for Functionless Integration

There are several parts of a serverless architecture where you have the possibility of reducing the Lambda footprint. However, the implementation details depend on your business domain and the types of AWS services you use for your workload. Let's take a look at some examples of how you can reduce the amount of custom code you need to write by using native service integrations.

Common AWS service integrations

Here are a few popular AWS services that aid in the reduction of the number of Lambda functions in a serverless application:

Amazon API Gateway
API Gateway supports over a hundred AWS services as the backend for an API endpoint. The part of the implementation that replaces the need for a Lambda function is a brief integration script written in Velocity Template Language (VTL) that provides the plumbing between API Gateway and the target service.

The following is a sample VTL script that takes the incoming API request payload, adds it as the EventBridge event payload body under the `Detail` section, and puts the event to the event bus `your-custom-bus`:

```
{
  "Entries": [
    {
      "DetailType": "customer-registered",
      "Source": "service-customers",
      "EventBusName": "your-custom-bus",
      "Detail": "$util.escapeJavaScript($input.json('$'))"
    }
  ]
}
```

AWS Step Functions
AWS Step Functions has direct integrations with services such as Amazon DynamoDB, SQS, SNS, EventBridge, etc. In addition, using the AWS SDK, you can integrate with hundreds of AWS services from your workflow without writing a Lambda function.

Here's a sample VTL script that takes the request payload body and provides it as input to a Step Functions workflow:

```
#set( $body = $util.escapeJavaScript($input.json('$')) )
{
  "input": "{\"body\": $body}",
  "name": "$context.requestId",
  "stateMachineArn": "<arn-of-your-step-function>"
}
```

AWS Step Functions supports two types of workflows: standard and express. While the standard workflows are asynchronous and can run for a year, the express workflows support both synchronous and asynchronous invocations and can run for up to five minutes. Due to their support for synchronous invocations, express workflows have become a popular option to integrate with API Gateway endpoints that provide a request/response-style invocation pattern—a key area for functionless integration.

Amazon EventBridge

As an event bus or a choreographer of microservices, EventBridge provides several ways to reduce the need to write function code. Several AWS services can send events directly to EventBridge, and several services can be targets to receive events directly from EventBridge. Though you may have scenarios where you need Lambda functions to perform some logic before putting an event onto EventBridge, the motivation with the functionless approach is to assess the possibility of integrating without a function—the functionless-first principle!

The sample Amazon States Language (ASL) script in Example 5-2, is for publishing an event from Step Functions to a custom event bus in EventBridge.

 ASL (*https://oreil.ly/AharQ*) is a JSON-based structured language used to define a state machine (a collection of states, tasks, state transitions, etc.).

Example 5-2. An ASL script to publish a custom event from Step Functions to EventBridge

```
{
  "Put SNS topic subscription event to event bus": {
    "Next": "Create EventBridge Rule",
    "Type": "Task",
    "ResultPath": null,
    "Resource": "arn:aws:states:::events:putEvents",
    "Parameters": {
      "Entries": [
```

```json
{
  "Detail": {
    "metadata": {
      "version": "1.0",
      "trace_id.$": "your_unique_event_id",
      "created_at": "2023-12-05T14:46:12.536Z",
      "domain": "YOUR-DOMAIN",
      "service": "your-service",
      "category": "internal",
      "type": "status",
      "name": "api-client-subscribed"
    },
    "data": {
      "client_name.$": "api-client",
      "topic_name.$": "client-sns-topic"
    }
  },
  "DetailType": "event",
  "EventBusName": "arn-of-your-event-bus",
  "Source": "create-subscription"
}
]
```

There are several other services and features that allow you to reduce the need for function code in your architecture. To give just a few examples, services such as Amazon DynamoDB and S3 offer automated data cleanup features via TTL values and lifecycle policies, respectively; AWS AppSync simplifies development with GraphQL; and Amazon SNS allows you to send notifications to millions of subscribers without having to write a Lambda function.

Sequence number generation using DynamoDB

Many traditional relational database systems provide sequence number generation as a feature that guarantees you a unique incremental number to use for several everyday use cases, such as order numbers, candidate roll numbers, visitor counts to a website, etc. You can set lower and upper limits for the number range and the increment, as shown in the following SQL script:

```
CREATE SEQUENCE ORDER_CATALOG
INCREMENT BY 1
MAXVALUE 900000000
MINVALUE 600000000
```

When you work with serverless services, especially with NoSQL data stores such as DynamoDB, you don't have an out-of-the-box solution that offers you such functionality. However, you can use the concept of *atomic counters* in DynamoDB for this purpose. The atomic counter is a number attribute that can be used to update a value atomically via the `UpdateItem` operation.

Once you know how to do this, it's just a matter of integrating with API Gateway to offer it as a service, as shown in Figure 5-20.

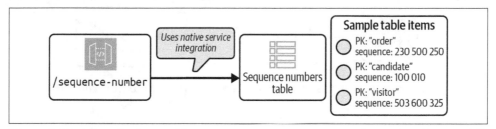

Figure 5-20. A functionless architecture to generate sequence numbers using DynamoDB and offer it as a service via API Gateway

The example shown here has a DynamoDB table that stores three different sequence values. The API will receive the type of the sequence number—order, `candidate`, or `visitor`—as a query parameter and return the respective incremented value.

An example VTL script that you could supply while configuring the API request mapping template is shown in Example 5-3.

Example 5-3. A VTL script to increment a value in a DynamoDB table

```
{
  "TableName": "sequence-numbers",
  "Key": {
    "id": {
      "S": "visitor"
    }
  },
  "ExpressionAttributeValues": {
    ":val": {
      "N": "1"
    }
  },
  "UpdateExpression": "ADD sequence :val",
  "ReturnValues": "UPDATED_NEW"
}
```

The `ExpressionAttributeValues` parameter specifies the increment; in this case, 1.

Invoking external HTTP APIs

Imagine you have a service that registers new customers to your business. As part of the registration, it requests the customer's consent to receive newsletters, promotional emails, updates on new product launches, etc., and records their preferences. Modern businesses might either store this data internally or use a dedicated external third-party application. Figure 5-21 is a high-level representation of the registration service communicating with a consent service provider.

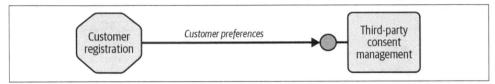

Figure 5-21. A customer microservice invokes a third-party API to store consent preferences

Storing a customer's preferences is a business requirement and happens at the end of every successful registration. As this is a decoupled event-driven activity, your initial architecture might look something like Figure 5-22.

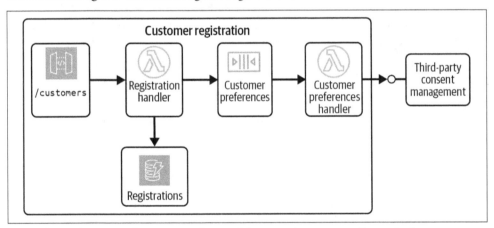

Figure 5-22. An event-driven serverless architecture that eventually sends data to an external application

This is a common serverless pattern where the synchronous API that receives the details is decoupled from the asynchronous backend that eventually sends the data to the external system. When you look at the customer preferences handler Lambda function, you likely expect it to be responsible for fetching one or more messages from the queue and invoking the third-party API. Now, consider the following additional tasks this function has to perform:

- Suppose the consent management platform uses OAuth to authenticate and authorize each request. The Lambda function must fetch the OAuth client credentials, request an access token by calling a different endpoint, store and reuse the access token until it expires, and fetch a new token when the current one expires.

- The SLA allows you to send only a certain number of requests per second. The Lambda function needs the logic to keep track of this and to adjust the message flow rate of the queue accordingly.

- If the third-party service is unavailable due to downtime or interruptions, the Lambda function should have the circuit breaker logic to buffer the requests and resubmit them once the service is healthy.

A simple Lambda function to send requests to an external HTTP endpoint has now become responsible for many critical operational tasks. In such scenarios, a proven pattern, service, or feature could become useful if it can abstract away the complexity to give you the needed development velocity. Amazon EventBridge offers an extremely powerful and highly secure feature that fits perfectly in these scenarios: API destinations!

API destinations (*https://oreil.ly/I-c89*) are HTTP endpoints that can be configured as targets for event routing rules on EventBridge. They help you natively integrate with applications using RESTful API calls, eliminating the need for Lambda functions.

Figure 5-23 shows the result if you rearchitect the solution in Figure 5-22 with an API destination.

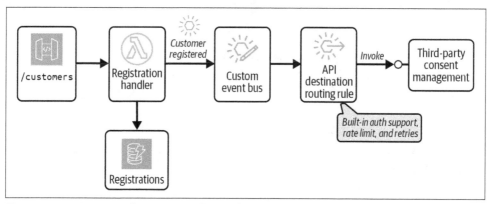

Figure 5-23. An event-driven serverless architecture that uses an API destination to invoke an external HTTP endpoint

With API destinations, you benefit from the following important features:

- The credentials you provide for the API connection are stored in AWS Secrets Manager. EventBridge handles the management and absorbs the cost, so you are not charged for using Secrets Manager.

- If the target endpoint uses OAuth for authorization, EventBridge manages the access token on your behalf.

- API destinations can retry sending the requests for a maximum of 24 hours or 185 times.

- You can attach a DLQ to catch the failed invocations.

- You can control the invocation rate, scaling it from 1 to 300 invocations per second.

There are, however, a few trade-offs you need to be aware of with API destinations:

- At the time of writing, there is no option to handle the responses from a target endpoint. API destinations do not publish the response payload onto the event bus.

- Calls to an API destination endpoint will time out after 5 seconds, and the request will be retried. Make sure the destination service has idempotency measures to handle duplicate requests.

Figure 5-24 shows the main components of an API destination, which you must configure when you create it. The connection manages the access permissions, and the endpoint defines the characteristics of the target endpoint.

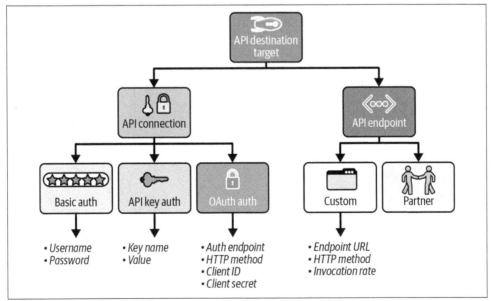

Figure 5-24. API destination components

EventBridge Pipes (*https://oreil.ly/gZTut*) is another feature that can eliminate the need for Lambda functions in many use cases. With EventBridge Pipes, you can create point-to-point integrations with optional event filtering, transformation, and enrichment, as Figure 5-25 depicts.

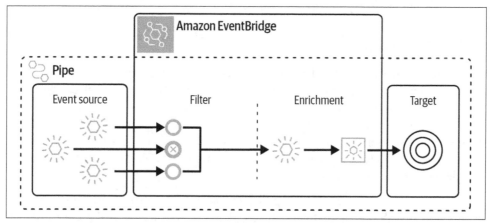

Figure 5-25. The main parts of an EventBridge Pipe to configure a point-to-point integration from a source service to a target (source: adapted from an image on the Amazon EventBridge Pipes web page [https://oreil.ly/v3ZvB])

Things to Be Aware of with Native Service Integrations

Just as microservices can have no APIs, you will come across microservices that do not require Lambda functions. While the functionless pattern has its advantages, there will be situations where you find it does not fit with your business and operational goals. Following are a few points to remember while designing your solutions:

A native service integration is like a black box with low visibility.
 You saw earlier how the VTL script sits at the integration request part of API Gateway. Though it works well, you do not get to see any logs or execution details of the integration code. Automated testing poses challenges, and you rely mainly on integration tests that can often add more complexity.

Debugging the integration code is nearly impossible.
 Investigating problems by debugging the integration code is practically impossible. Most AWS services publish execution logs to CloudWatch logs, but for services like EventBridge there is a need for better visibility.

EventBridge does not provide you with the response from the API destination's target.
 At the time of writing, when you provide native integrations via API destinations, you don't get the response payload from the target. In business cases where this is essential, you'll need to implement a polling mechanism to retrieve the details.

Apply the pattern only where appropriate.

As described earlier, you should apply the functionless pattern only in situations where it fits well with your architecture and business needs. For example, you may have critical business scenarios that demand detailed or censored log data, where you prefer having greater control.

The Event Triage Pattern

Alongside those finely crafted domain events that your microservices publish and consume, modern applications produce, capture, and process several categories of events, often in huge volumes. Data stream events from IoT devices, click events from websites, trajectory and altitude events from satellites and aircraft, email feedback events from mail servers, etc., are just a few examples. The Amazon Kinesis family of services, such as Kinesis Data Streams and Kinesis Data Firehose, efficiently ingest and deliver data to downstream consumers.

Think of a situation where your application acts as the processing hub for these events and distributes them to the appropriate targets in near real time to deliver business value. For example, the clickstream events of a user who is browsing products on an ecommerce website will be of interest to a product recommendation engine that can analyze the event data and recommend related products for that user. In another example, a service that ingests feedback events about emails dispatched from a domain might batch them and send them to different business units for insights.

Figure 5-26 shows a high-level view of clickstream event ingestion from a website via Amazon Kinesis Data Firehose, and distribution of those events.

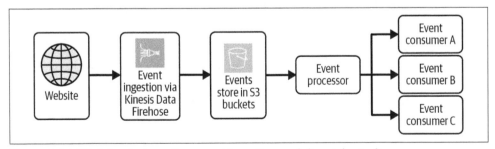

Figure 5-26. High-level view of an event ingestion and dispatch pipeline

What Is Event Triage?

In the software industry, the term *triage* is typically used to describe the process of categorizing and assigning priority levels to defects or bugs. In general, it refers to any process for classifying tasks or items and assigning them to the appropriate team or engineer for action. *Event triage* involves identifying each event by its type, grouping them by type, and dispatching them to interested targets. However, the processing application that triages the events need not have knowledge of all the consumers and how they receive these events (think single responsibility). So, it will just send the events to the respective dispatcher proxy for each consumer.

An event triage application should have the following capabilities:

- Drop events that are of no business interest.
- Know the types of events that are of interest to each consumer.
- Onboard new event consumers without disrupting the existing event flow.
- Remove existing event consumers.
- Adjust (add and remove) the types of events flowing to a target.

The functionality of the event processor in Figure 5-26 can be implemented as a Lambda function. This is shown in Figure 5-27.

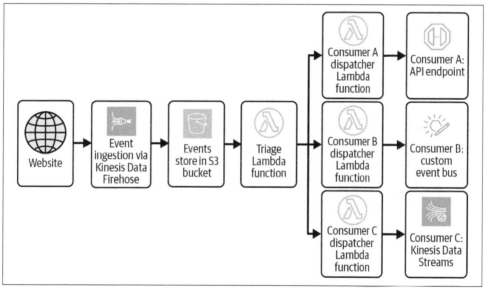

Figure 5-27. Events ingestion with an event triage function dispatching events to respective consumers

Implementation Details

Now that you have an overall understanding of the event ingestion pipeline shown in Figure 5-27, let's take a closer look at the characteristics of the triage function. This function is the main element of this pattern. It gets invoked when Firehose places a new event data file in the S3 bucket. Your Firehose data buffering parameters help optimize the function. For example, if your buffer size is 1 MB or an interval of 60 seconds, you can be certain that every file will be 1 MB or less. The triage function is responsible for:

Mapping event types to consumers via configuration

The logic to send the relevant event types to different consumers dynamically is the heart of the triage function. As not all event types will be of interest to every consumer, you need a simple but extendable mechanism to achieve this. A JSON data object, as shown in Example 5-4, that lists the name of the dispatcher function for every event type can be used here.

Example 5-4. JSON representation of the event type and consumer configuration

```
{
  "product_clicked_event": [
    "dispatcher-A-lambda-function",
    "dispatcher-B-lambda-function",
    "dispatcher-C-lambda-function"
  ],
  "page_loaded_event": [
    "dispatcher-B-lambda-function",
    "dispatcher-C-lambda-function"
  ],
  "item_added_event": [
    "dispatcher-B-lambda-function"
  ],
  "basket_updated_event": [
    "dispatcher-A-lambda-function"
  ],
  "payment_selected_event": [
    "dispatcher-A-lambda-function",
    "dispatcher-B-lambda-function",
    "dispatcher-C-lambda-function"
  ],
  "wishlist_updated_event": [
    "dispatcher-C-lambda-function"
  ]
}
```

You can store the configuration data in an SSM Parameter Store, and the triage function will be able to use this to dynamically triage events as needed.

Invoking the dispatcher functions

The data flow here is one way. The triage function is responsible for sending the relevant events to each dispatcher. What the dispatcher does with the events and how it delivers them to its consumer(s) is the dispatcher's responsibility. Because of this, the triage function can invoke each dispatcher asynchronously.

Controlling the event batch size

How the triage function processes the raw events depends on the business logic, and it can set the maximum batch size. Note that the asynchronous invocation of a Lambda function can accept a maximum payload size of 256 KB. As part of the configuration shown in Example 5-4, you can even specify the batching characteristics of each consumer.

Figure 5-28 expands the design with more event ingestion options to show the applicability of this pattern in different cases.

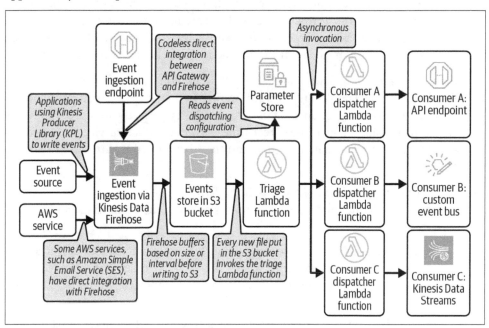

Figure 5-28. Event ingestion and triage pattern with important design aspects highlighted

 Using a Lambda function to transport data from one place to another is an antipattern in serverless development. In such scenarios, you would use services that provide data transport or support data streams rather than a Lambda function. However, in the event triage pattern, there is business logic and processing involved, and the function is not just shifting data from one service to the other.

Frequently Asked Questions

Here are a few questions that frequently come up with regard to the event triage pattern:

Isn't Amazon EventBridge apt for triage?

There are a few points to make here:

- The Amazon Kinesis family of services is purpose-built for high-volume event ingestion, whereas EventBridge is an event broker or bus for routing events to targets.

- The throughput of Kinesis Data Firehose can be hundreds of thousands of events per second, whereas it is tens of thousands for EventBridge.

- EventBridge does not offer event batching (at the time of writing), and its built-in event transformation capabilities are minimal. You often need to use an SQS queue as the target of an EventBridge rule and then have a Lambda function to read messages from the queue in batches and process them.

Can the triage function work without S3 being the data provider?

Yes, it can. The sample architecture shown in Figure 5-27 is a high-volume clickstream event ingestion pipeline where S3 fits perfectly to store the events before processing them in near real time. However, other services can also act as the event source or data provider, and the triage functionality can remain the same.

How does event triage differ from the fan-out pattern?

There are similarities and subtle differences between the event triage and fan-out patterns:

- The triage function has processing and business logic, which is not always the case in fan-out patterns where the goal is to send the data concurrently to many recipients of different types—Lambda functions, SQS queues, APIs, etc.

- A simplistic fan-out pattern often uses a single target Lambda function with concurrent executions, whereas with event triage there are various dispatcher functions.

- A popular use of the fan-out pattern is for ETL jobs. In ETL, due to the limited resources and execution time of a Lambda function, the main function splits the batch into smaller parts and concurrently invokes worker functions of the same type for each part. With the event triage pattern, each dispatcher has a specific purpose and is associated with a consumer.

- Fan-out patterns often include the corresponding fan-in implementation to consolidate the results, which is not the case with event triage.

In Chapter 2, you learned about the importance of domains and bounded contexts while developing serverless applications. When you share domain events, you require measures to ensure compliance, prevent data leaks, and so on. The gatekeeper event bus pattern discussed in the following section offers an extra layer of control when sharing events outside of your application boundary.

The Gatekeeper Event Bus Pattern

Every API you develop has a contract defining the request and response schemas, protocol, authentication and authorization methods, invocation quota and throttling limits, etc. But how do you apply these to your domain events as they flow into and out of your bounded context? As a start, you ensure that your domain events conform to an established schema, and you can secure events by encrypting them. But who controls which events from your bounded context can flow out of your application boundary into a different domain? As you learned in Chapter 3, your event-driven application architecture has one or more custom event buses that ingest and route all your custom events from and to the microservices within your domain —but who prevents the myriad internal and operational events from within your service boundary from being leaked?

Figure 5-29 shows some of the custom events within the user payments bounded context (introduced back in Figure 2-3, in "Domain-first" on page 40). Though the diagram shows a handful of events, in reality, there will be many more types produced and consumed by the microservices within this bounded context.

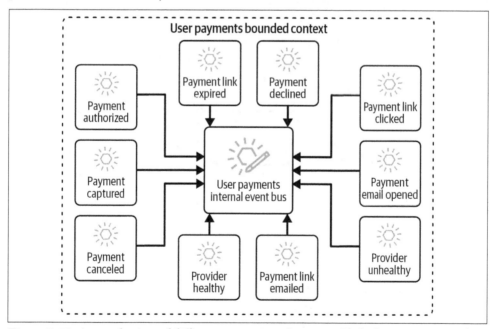

Figure 5-29. A sample view of different categories of events published onto an internal custom event bus within the user payments bounded context

The Need for a Gatekeeper Event Bus

Not all the events shown in Figure 5-29 are domain events useful to consumers outside of the user payments system. For example, whereas *payment authorized* is a domain event important to the checkout service to confirm a user's order and the *payment captured* event (which occurs at a later point, after authorization) is of significance to the finance domain, *provider healthy* is an internal operational event useful for circuit breaker implementation, discussed earlier in this chapter.

In environments with several categories and types of custom events and many event routing rules to send these events to multiple targets, you need fine-grained control and a streamlined approach to separate the concerns of onboarding external event consumers and producers, data encryption needs, and cross-account management. In such situations, rather than risking overloading the internal event bus, you can isolate these tasks to a dedicated event bus—a *gatekeeper* event bus for your bounded context. This is depicted in Figure 5-30.

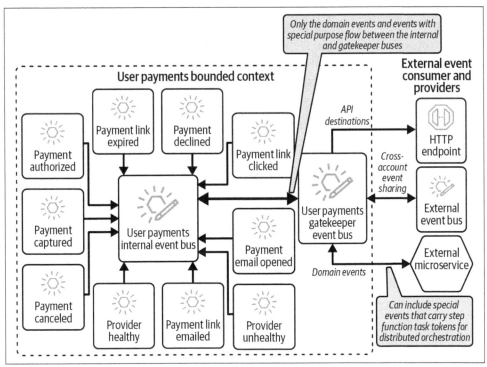

Figure 5-30. The user payments gatekeeper event bus interacts with the external systems to share and ingest domain events

The gatekeeper bus is a custom event bus that acts as the guarded event gate at your application boundary. While all the categories and types of events flow through the internal custom bus, only the domain events get to the gatekeeper event bus to be routed to consumers outside. Conversely, all events sent from other domains, applications, and third-party services to your applications flow through the gatekeeper bus, which routes only the required ones to the internal bus. In other words, it controls both the *outflow* and the *inflow* of events.

Implementation Approach

Along with established software practices such as separation of concerns, the "set piece" microservices architectural thinking you learned about in Chapter 3 suggests that it is beneficial to package the gatekeeper EventBridge custom bus and its related resources as an independent microservice. This helps isolate the event routing rules, cross-account event sharing configurations, event delivery failure DLQs, encryption, and other security measures from the internal event bus and the rest of the services, as shown in Figure 5-31.

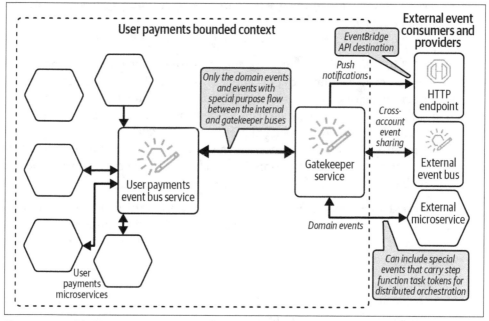

Figure 5-31. The microservices view of internal and gatekeeper custom event buses within the user payments bounded context

Use Cases for the Gatekeeper Event Bus Pattern

The gatekeeper event bus pattern works well in many situations and reduces the complexity of event-driven architecture. The following are just a few of several possible use cases:

Push notifications to API clients

As you saw in Figure 3-26 (in "Synchronous Communication" on page 112), push notifications are an efficient communication mechanism. As the name implies, with this approach your application sends (pushes) events to one or more client applications or service consumers to notify them when something relevant happens.

An important aspect of push notifications is that this is a one-way information flow where you notify a client by calling an API endpoint. The API destination feature of EventBridge is ideal for push notifications. Not all events go to every registered client, and you need strict rules to ensure this. In addition, the security and encryption requirements of each client can be different. Separating these concerns into a dedicated microservice that works with a gatekeeper event bus gives you better control.

Domain data sharing

Figure 2-3 in "Domain-first" on page 40 shows some of the domains and bounded contexts of an ecommerce application. With event-driven architecture, cross-domain event sharing becomes an essential part of the functioning of enterprise applications. When you share domain events from your application with other domains, you are likely to route the events from your custom event bus to the event buses in other domains, often in different AWS cloud accounts. You configure the cross-account permissions and related security measures before routing the specific events.

A dedicated gatekeeper event bus isolates the complexities and offers a clean way to perform necessary event transformations to comply with formats such as CloudEvents (*https://cloudevents.io*), AsyncAPI (*https://www.asyncapi.com*), etc., where required.

Cross-domain business orchestration

In "Service Orchestration" on page 259, you will see how events carry tokens and instructions to coordinate with multiple services to perform a business function. A gatekeeper bus can handle the task-request and task-response events between business domains efficiently.

Things to Be Aware of with the Gatekeeper Event Bus Pattern

Though this is a simple pattern to implement, there are a few essential points that you need to be mindful of. These include:

Breaking event schema changes
> Though this is not a problem that's specific to the gatekeeper event bus pattern, introducing breaking event schema changes will have severe consequences in event-driven architectures. As mentioned in Chapter 3, versioning your events is crucial to avoid impacting downstream systems.

Handling of sensitive data and PII
> When events leave your bounded context, you lose control and visibility of the downstream event flow and the destinations they reach. You need to have adequate measures in place to identify and protect PII and sensitive data. You cannot always remove such data from the events, as your consumers may require it. In such situations, employ the required event encryption measures to mitigate the risk.

Knowing the event payload limits of consumers
> The maximum accepted event payload size of Amazon EventBridge is 256 KB, at the time of writing. If a downstream consumer has a lower limit for data payloads, or if a microservice transforms or enriches events it receives in a way that makes them larger than this size, you need to find a way to handle this situation.

Handling duplicate events
> Many business domains are sensitive to duplicate events—financial account updates, online payments, etc., for example. In certain cases, the idempotency check gets pushed upstream to the event producer. Though duplicate events cannot be completely avoided due to the dependency on cloud services, networks, and factors that are beyond your control, the gatekeeper service can perform first-phase checks before sending events to consumers.

Microservices Choreography

Choreography is the process of creating sequences of movements. In dance, for example, the participants (dancers) learn a specific set of choreographed movements and perform them individually or as a group to the music. Importantly, no one person is instructing the troupe.

Event choreography is one of the most common and widely adopted event-driven patterns. You can relate the dancers to the various microservices, each with a specific contribution, that come together to complete a business process. There is no controller to instruct the services of their tasks; instead, services receive events and know how to react and what to do.

You've already seen several examples of service choreography in Chapter 3, but let's consider another one here. Figure 5-32 is a simple workflow of customers registering an electronic item that they've purchased.

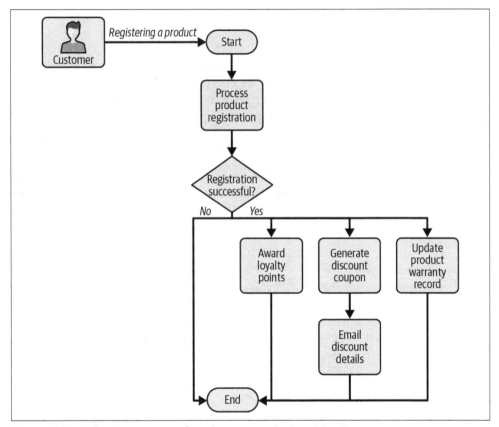

Figure 5-32. A business process flow for new product registration

As you can see, several applications take part in the product registration process. As the services belong to different domains of the organization, it would not be ideal to create unnecessary dependencies in a long and synchronous call chain. Instead, once a customer successfully registers a product, the product registration service emits an event that triggers several independent services to perform their actions. Figure 5-33 represents the solution as a choreographed event-driven pattern.

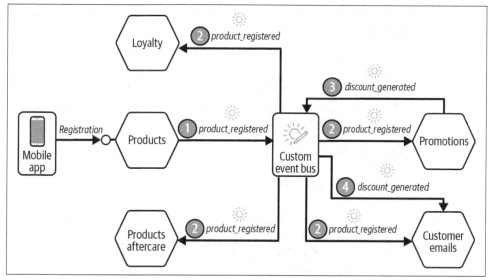

Figure 5-33. Several microservices participate in the choreography of a business process

Things to Be Aware of While Choreographing Services

Microservices choreography is a common pattern in serverless development, but there are various things you need to be aware of and consider during implementation. These include:

Loss of events
> In any networked system, there is a possibility of interruptions and data loss. Hence, it is essential that you incorporate measures to minimize their impact. EventBridge has a built-in capability to retry the delivery of events to a target for up to 24 hours. You can attach a DLQ to catch those events after their delivery attempts are exhausted.

Duplicate events
> As you learned in Chapter 3, handling duplicate events and implementing idempotency is the responsibility of every microservice. Failures in this area can cause serious issues in critical business processes.

Maintaining the sequence of actions
> Typical business processes in an enterprise comprise multiple steps, involve several applications, and can take a long time to complete—minutes, hours, days, or even months. There may be situations where you need to perform certain steps in a sequence. For example, in Figure 5-33, the service that emails the discount code to the customer may receive the product_registered event at the same time the promotions service receives it. However, it depends on the promotions service

to calculate the correct discount based on the product, value, market, etc., before emailing the customer.

In this case, the email service must wait until it receives another event—say, discount_generated—from the promotions service before acting. The promotions service will initially store the product_registered event details (the storage-first pattern) and will take action when the discount_generated event arrives.

Application resiliency is distributed

When you choreograph distributed microservices, there's no central controller keeping track of the success or failure of each service. Amazon EventBridge acts as the coordinator, but it is not an orchestrator like AWS Step Functions (discussed in the next section). Each microservice that is part of the business process choreography is expected to independently handle failures, third-party downtime, and retries and to implement circuit breakers (as discussed earlier in this chapter) to contribute to the overall resiliency.

Complexity increases with the increase in the number of services and events

Building microservices that are loosely coupled and self-contained is essential to a successful event-driven architecture. The structure and schemas of the events are also critical. In Chapter 3, you learned how to classify events and structure them with the necessary details. Adding the right classification levels to your events with the appropriate attributes and values allows you to configure suitable event filter patterns to target specific events.

The gatekeeper event bus pattern that you learned about earlier is a way of managing the influx of several types of events.

Visibility/traceability challenges

In a distributed event-driven microservices architecture, you must incorporate the required measures to enhance the end-to-end traceability of the overall application. A common approach is to use an immutable, unique event_id or trace_id attribute in every event.

There are tools and services, such as AWS X-Ray (*https://oreil.ly/HHIaj*), that can help improve the observability of your system.

Enterprises have several domains and functions that incorporate different business logic for different business use cases. Often, business processes require one or more services owned and operated by different teams. The microservices choreography pattern discussed in this section is one of the two most common patterns you will employ to implement the business processes. The other is service orchestration. As you will see in the next section, this is an important pattern that you will apply often in serverless development.

Service Orchestration

The flowchart (*https://oreil.ly/ABat-*) is arguably the oldest modeling tool in software engineering. Its simplicity, with a handful of symbols, makes it adaptable enough to illustrate the logic of the first program you wrote at school or a complex workflow at your organization. A workflow captures the different steps or processes involved in fulfilling a business functionality, often mixed with business processes. For example, onboarding a new employee in your organization is a process, and the workflow involves several steps, both manual and automated. The advantage of capturing a business process as a sequence of input, output, actions, tasks, decisions, etc., is that you can automate the entire process to improve efficiency.

Whether you use a workflow system or a business process management tool, there is an engine that has the knowledge of the overall workflow required to handle the input and output of each step, send commands to perform tasks, branch off to subflows based on certain decisions, collate results from multiple branches, and so on. This engine acts like a controller or conductor, instructing the different parts of the process to perform. Hence, this pattern is commonly referred to as *orchestration* of services, as in an orchestra where the conductor is the orchestrator.

AWS Step Functions is a serverless AWS service that offers orchestration capabilities.

What Do You Orchestrate?

Let's look at a simple example to illustrate business process orchestration. Imagine you are placing an order at a local take-out restaurant. You're at the point where you need to decide whether to collect the food you've ordered or get it delivered. Figure 5-34 shows a simple flowchart depicting the actions involved in each process behind the scenes.

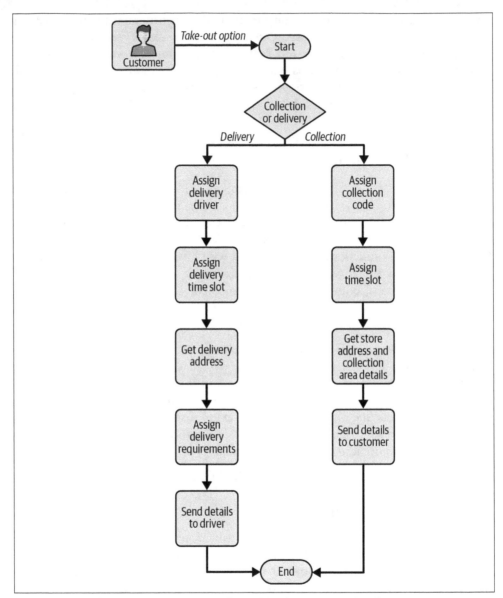

Figure 5-34. A flowchart depicting the flow of food delivery and collection activities

On the company's side, if you implement this logic with Lambda functions, you will have a function to receive the customer's choice and some if-else logic that branches off into collection and delivery paths and invokes other Lambda functions or external APIs. You may implement the main function as a monolith and create single-purpose functions for other tasks. Nevertheless, you must somehow chain these functions together to make the end-to-end flow work. Figure 5-35 shows the main Lambda function that acts as the controller of the logic.

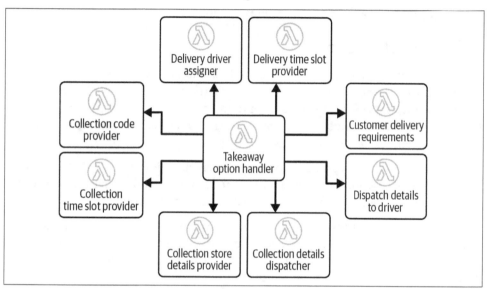

Figure 5-35. An unsustainable and unrecommended way of chaining Lambda functions to perform business logic

Creating hard dependencies between Lambda functions or making synchronous invocations between Lambda functions is not a best practice. In addition, as you learned earlier with the functionless integration pattern, there will be situations where you do not use Lambda functions to perform parts of your business logic. You need a way of capturing the business process as a whole and having a controller to coordinate with services that perform the different parts of the overall logic. Service orchestration is the architectural pattern that helps you achieve this.

In a distributed event-driven microservices architecture, you'll find three types of orchestration:

- In-service orchestration
- Cross-service orchestration
- Distributed orchestration

We'll dive into each of these in the sections that follow.

In-Service Orchestration

The most common and simplest form of orchestration is the one that happens within a microservice boundary. With in-service orchestration, all the AWS resources that are part of the orchestration logic belong to the microservice responsible for orchestration. This pattern avoids cross-resource usage from other microservices within or outside the same bounded context.

Figure 5-36 shows the workflow of a customer registration process that signs up a user to the business and issues them a unique identifier. Notice that it is part of the customer registration service within the customers bounded context.

The primary benefit of in-service orchestration is that it enables microservices to be self-contained. There is no dependency graph beyond the deployment boundaries of the microservice, with the possible exception of when events are published to the custom event bus within the bounded context.

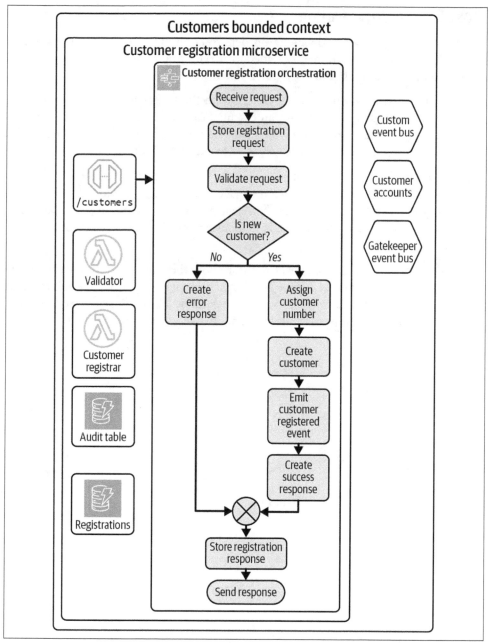

Figure 5-36. Customer registration orchestration as part of the customer registration microservice, which does not interact with outside resources

Cross-Service Orchestration

Cross-service orchestration opens up borders to communicate with services within or outside of the orchestrator's bounded context, which includes other domains, custom-built applications, and third-party systems.

The distributed orchestration model discussed in the following section is similar to cross-service orchestration, but with an essential difference. In cross-service orchestration, the external communication is mostly via synchronous API calls. Distributed orchestration, on the other hand, covers asynchronous interaction.

Let's say there is a dedicated team responsible for customer satisfaction, feedback, etc. As shown in Figure 5-36, this team engages with a customer to get feedback on the quality of the service soon after their registration. To enable this, the customer registration service passes some details to a customer feedback service, as illustrated in Figure 5-37.

As mentioned earlier, in cross-service orchestration, the communication between the orchestrator and the external service is via synchronous API calls. How the external service performs is not of interest to the orchestrator. With AWS Step Functions as the orchestrator, you can directly integrate and invoke external HTTPS endpoints.

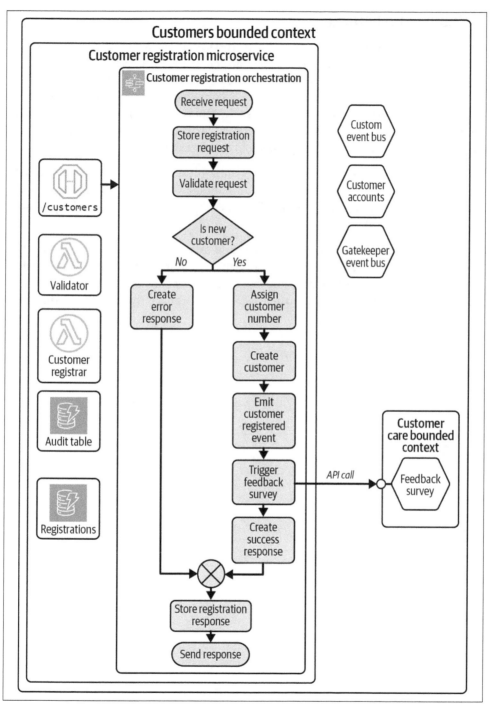

Figure 5-37. A customer registration business flow interacting with a service from a different bounded context to the orchestrating service

Distributed Orchestration

Avoiding hard dependencies between microservices allows you to build services that are modular and extendable. Hence, you are encouraged to use APIs or events as the mode of communication. APIs, however, have limitations with their underlying protocols and implementation, and most API connections last for only a brief period before timing out. If a service takes longer—minutes, hours, or even days—to complete and you depend on its outcome to proceed further in your workflow, you do not know how long to wait before progressing to the next step.

Imagine your business logic incorporates multiple long-running tasks offered by several microservices from different domains, as shown in Figure 5-37. How do you successfully accomplish this? The distributed orchestration pattern can help in such scenarios.

In Figure 5-38, the primary orchestrator inside microservice A requires the services of microservices B and C. Both of those services may have their own orchestrators to complete their tasks, but that is not the concern of microservice A. The respective steps in the primary orchestration will wait until B and C report completing their tasks.

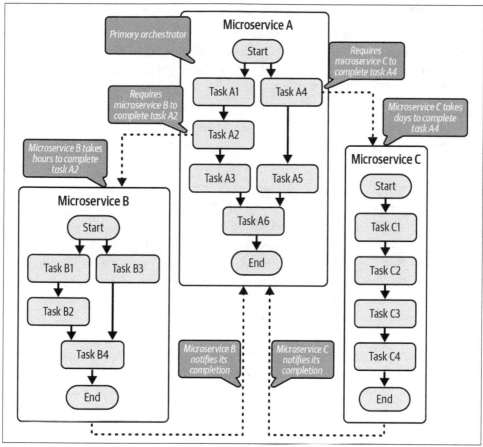

Figure 5-38. A primary orchestration flow asynchronously distributes tasks to other microservices

Coordinating the distribution with choreography

The primary orchestrator that distributes the tasks is agnostic of how the remote services complete those tasks. They could be implemented as simple Lambda functions or involve the orchestration of several services. Two important elements make distributed orchestration work seamlessly:

Events
> The communication mechanism to coordinate (choreograph) the microservices with Amazon EventBridge.

Task tokens
> Unique tokens (string values) that represent tasks. In a *callback task*, a service requester sends a task token to a service provider; the workflow is paused until the same token is returned by the service provider.

Let's go through a use case to explain the functioning of callbacks with task tokens. In the example shown in Figure 5-39, the customer accounts microservice is responsible for creating the customer's account details and requires the finance team's services to run a few checks on the customer. This is an asynchronous activity that takes minutes or hours, depending on the status of the external systems it interacts with.

Figure 5-39 shows how the distributed orchestration flow works. The numbered steps mark the end-to-end journey of one task token, where the *Get finance clearance* step emits a task token X and waits until the same token X is returned.

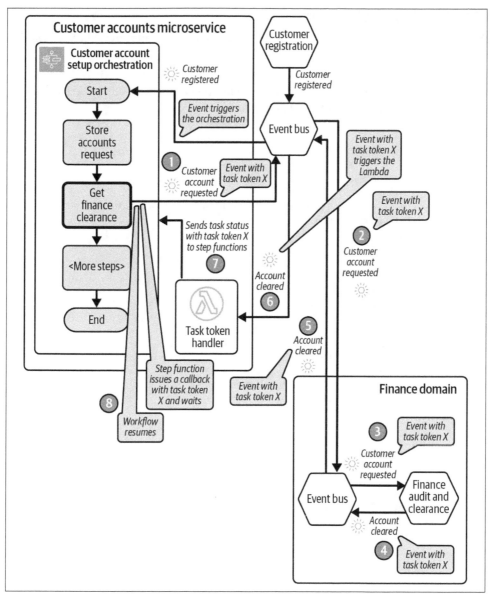

Figure 5-39. A primary orchestration workflow asynchronously requests another micro-service to perform a task and resumes on notification of completion

Generating and sending task tokens

You can easily generate a task token by writing a couple of lines of ASL. Example 5-5 shows an example script.

Example 5-5. Step Functions ASL script to publish an event onto a custom event bus that will wait for the callback with a task token

```
{
  "StartAt": "Get finance clearance",
  "States": {
    "Finance clearance": {
      "Type": "Task",
      "Resource": "arn:aws:states:::events:putEvents.waitForTaskToken",
      "HeartbeatSeconds": 6000,
      "Parameters": {
        "Entries": [
          {
            "Detail": {
              "metadata": {
                "version": "1.0",
                "trace_id": "djsf34hgsad8ndc2",
                "created_at": "2023-12-21T11:10:54.000Z",
                "customer_accounts_request_id.$": "$$.Task.Token",
                "domain": "Customers",
                "service": "customer-accounts",
                "category": "operational_event",
                "type": "task",
                "name": "account_requested"
              },
              "data": {
                "customer_id.$": "$.customer_id",
                "other": "details go here"
              }
            },
            "DetailType": "event",
            "EventBusName": "customers-event-bus",
            "Source": "customer-account-process"
          }
        ]
      },
      "Next": "Another Step"
    }
  }
}
```

The HeartbeatSeconds value in Example 5-5 indicates the timeout period for this task. The task will fail, timing out, once this value is met. You can, however, request a heartbeat extension to have Step Functions reset the timer.

The two important attributes in this script are `Resource` and `customer` `_accounts_request_id`. `waitForTaskToken` instructs the Step Functions workflow to wait at this step until the task token generated by `$$.Task.Token` is returned.

 You can attach the task token to any custom attribute of yours by assigning the token generated by `$$.Task.Token`. It's a good practice to use an attribute that is part of the custom event schema that the consuming service understands.

Things to be aware of while using callbacks with a task token

Here are a few important points you must be familiar with when working with callback task tokens in Step Functions:

Task token carriers need not be EventBridge events.
Example 5-5 uses a custom EventBridge event to carry the task token to the consuming application as it demonstrates event choreography between microservices, but this is not required. You can wrap the task token in an SQS message and have it handled by a Lambda function, for example.

Be flexible on the custom event category that contains the task token.
Depending on how you classify your events, the custom event that contains the task token can be a domain event, or you may use an operational event category for this purpose.

You can use multiple task tokens in a workflow.
For brevity, our example used a single task token. You can use multiple task tokens at different parts of your workflow to pause and resume the different arms of the flow. Step Functions manages the tasks and their tokens.

Task providers (token-consuming targets) have a responsibility.
Though event consumers are viewed as being agnostic of producers, in distributed orchestration, the consumers have an extra role to play. The primary orchestrator that sends the task token needs to know the consumers who fulfill each task. Only those consumers are expected to return the task tokens, and the primary orchestrator's service will have special event filters for this purpose.

Avoid task timeouts by extending the heartbeat interval.
Step Functions provides three options when resubmitting task tokens:

- `SendTaskSuccess` resumes the workflow from the paused step.
- `SendTaskFailure` fails the execution.
- `SendTaskHeartbeat` makes the workflow step wait longer.

When a task needs to wait longer, it's important that you extend the heartbeat interval to prevent it from timing out and making the workflow fail.

The code snippet in Example 5-6 demonstrates how you notify Step Functions of success.

Example 5-6. Sample code to send task success information along with the token to a Step Functions workflow

```
...
const taskToken = event.metadata.customer_accounts_request_id;
const output = JSON.stringify(event);

// Check the task completion status in the event data

const params = {
  output: output,
  taskToken: taskToken
};

const result = await sfn.sendTaskSuccess(params).promise()
...
```

The Saga Pattern

A saga is a long story recounting a series of events. In software, the term is used to refer to a business process or workflow comprising a series of steps. Each step can be a self-contained task known as a *transaction*. A local transaction can itself have multiple steps/operations, but as a whole, all of those steps/operations must succeed—the transaction is atomic.

Enterprise business processes can be complex, involving the services of several internal and external applications, and often human interactions as well. In most cases, if a step (i.e., a transaction) fails, the preceding steps can be reverted through a series of *compensating* transactions that bring them back to their initial state. If the saga and its steps are not time-critical, it may be possible to retry a step that fails, allowing it (and the saga as a whole) to succeed. The circuit breaker pattern discussed earlier in this chapter is common in those situations. An additional complication is that some critical business processes go through different stages and mark some of the steps or transactions as *pivot* transactions. In this case, successful completion of a pivot transaction might disallow reversal of the whole saga; once a certain point has been reached, there's no other option but to carry on until the entire saga is complete.

In distributed transaction scenarios, the saga pattern provides a useful way to maintain consistency across microservices. Both choreography and orchestration are popular implementation choices. As you learned in the previous sections, in choreography each step or transaction is performed by a microservice, and it emits an event that becomes the indicator for progressing, retrying, or rolling back the saga. With orchestration, the orchestrator (i.e., the Step Functions workflow) controls the series of steps and will have the necessary paths to handle the failures and retries.

Many business use cases of the saga pattern will use both approaches. While architecting, you must study the business requirements thoroughly to determine whether choreography, orchestration, or a combination of the two suits you better.

Summary

Evolutions in technology and the needs of modern systems are influencing engineers to develop new software patterns all the time. It's important that you be aware of these developments and use these new patterns where appropriate in your applications, regardless of where they're published. While textbooks like the ones mentioned earlier in this chapter can teach you the fundamentals and intricacies of many useful patterns, you must also be in a position to take your learnings and devise new ones as needed for your development.

The goal of this chapter was to inspire you by introducing a selection of patterns that cover some of the core areas of everyday serverless development. Be open to accepting new ideas from the people around you and engage in discussions to transform those ideas into adoptable patterns. The event triage, distributed orchestration, and gatekeeper event bus patterns, as well as some of the functionless pattern examples described in this chapter, all originated from simple conversations among engineers in serverless teams. There are also many other useful patterns that we didn't have room to discuss in this chapter, like conversational event-driven patterns and microservices data collector patterns. If you'd like to learn more, we recommend taking a look at Serverless Land (*https://oreil.ly/bIj-G*), an online portal full of patterns with various implementation-specific resources.

Your understanding of the various patterns described here will help you as you journey through the subsequent chapters, which provide guidance on solution design, implementation, testing, and operating your serverless applications in a sustainable way.

Interview with an Industry Expert

Jeremy Daly, CEO, Ampt, AWS Serverless Hero

Jeremy Daly (*https://oreil.ly/RRGpY*) is an AWS Serverless Hero who has been managing the development of complex web and mobile applications for over 25 years. He is currently the CEO of Ampt (*https://getampt.com*), a developer productivity platform reinventing how we build applications in the cloud with Infrastructure from Code

(IfC) (*https://oreil.ly/FQPQu*). Jeremy writes about serverless and shares thoughts about programming, product management, entrepreneurship, and productivity; he publishes the popular weekly serverless newsletter *Off-by-none* (*https://offbynone.io*) and hosts the Serverless Chats podcast (*https://oreil.ly/-W7lk*).

Q: Jeremy, for many years, you've inspired engineers and been an instrument to teams adopting serverless. Has convincing CTOs about serverless adoption become easier now?

Serverless has certainly become more mainstream as it's matured over the years, and as we've seen an abundance of success stories and case studies, it's become a less risky choice for organizations. Many of the services we consider "serverless" have already been widely adopted by organizations, even if only as part of their larger cloud technology stacks.

For start-ups and greenfield projects, I think a "serverless-first" approach has become the clear choice for most. However, there are a number of reasons why serverless still faces scrutiny from CTOs and other technology leaders, especially among established companies. There is a lot of technological inertia within organizations that have already begun their cloud journey. Containerization is still the standard, especially for larger organizations that have adopted Kubernetes as their platform of choice. We've recently seen a trend toward hybrid strategies that combine serverless and other more traditional approaches. While this is a step in the right direction, it often prevents companies from taking full advantage of the benefits of serverless architectures.

Serverless implementations let organizations focus on their core business rather than technology, but it's also very developer-centric, which requires both upskilling developers and cooperation with existing operations and security teams. So while I think the robust ecosystem, widening vendor support, cost optimizations, and reduced time to market make serverless a clear technology choice for CTOs, the skills gap and complexity of migration still create friction that can complicate the decision-making process.

Q: Patterns in software engineering have a long history and tradition, and many engineers have an emotional attachment to some of the foundational patterns. How much do you think the cloud and serverless adoption have disrupted the status quo of traditional patterns?

Most of the fundamental patterns we've been using for years are still highly relevant in today's cloud architectures. The main difference is that many of those patterns have become more explicit, requiring a deeper understanding of how they need to be implemented in distributed cloud systems. The vast majority of serverless primitives are rock solid and for the most part have removed the undifferentiated heavy lifting of managing their complexity. However, configuring the plumbing between these primitives (event mappings, IAM permissions, failover behavior, etc.) falls on the implementer, and with a plethora of options to choose from, this can dramatically affect the success of any given pattern.

We've also seen a major resurgence of event-driven applications thanks to serverless and the patterns it enables. I think this is a good thing, but most developers grew up in a synchronous world of request/response. Asynchronous events and eventual consistency are core to distributed workloads, which often adds more cognitive overhead to understanding how modern cloud patterns work.

Q: As the CEO of Ampt and promoter of IfC that offers a certain level of abstraction, how do you see the future need and awareness of patterns and their use in serverless?

Awareness of patterns will be just as important in the future as it is today, but the hope is that we can find the right level of abstraction to avoid reinventing the wheel every time we need to implement one. There are hundreds of published patterns and Cloud Development Kit (CDK) constructs available; however, choosing the right one isn't always straightforward. Even highly experienced architects need to experiment to find the combinations and configurations that best suit their workloads.

Also, off-the-shelf patterns may be easy to publish, but they're not always easy to manage and maintain. Patterns need to evolve as throughput increases, and different patterns have very real trade-offs when it comes to cost and performance. Static architectures produced by traditional IaC require manual optimizations, updates to business logic, and multistep migrations. This is inefficient, adds complexity, and introduces significant technical debt.

Abstractions have eliminated managing memory and setting up physical servers. It seems like removing the need to write low-level machine code for the cloud is the next logical step. IfC is a step toward autonomous software delivery and management that automatically selects, deploys, and upgrades productized patterns on the developer's behalf. This doesn't necessarily negate the need to be aware of the underlying patterns, but it does democratize them and dramatically reduces operational complexity.

Q: Managed cloud services from AWS and other cloud providers encapsulate many primitive patterns. AWS services such as API Gateway, SQS, SNS, EventBridge, etc., are good examples. What is your advice to a new serverless engineer wanting to learn and apply patterns?

There is a massive library of predefined patterns and CDK constructs available across the internet. Though some are better than others, they can be extremely helpful starting points that get you up and running very quickly. However, my advice is that before you blindly trust them with production workloads, you should take the time to learn what each pattern does, what primitives it interacts with, its security configurations, and what it will cost to run. This includes understanding the underlying managed services, their limitations, and their supported use cases.

Learning from others' work is great, but patterns generally need to be adapted to your specific situations. Run a lot of tests, ask for help when you need it, and gather the experience for yourself to successfully implement and operate your workloads.

Q: Your contribution to the serverless community is immeasurable. Your talks, blogs, Off-by-none serverless newsletter, Serverless Chats podcast, and creative and thought-provoking musical productions like LAMBDA and Goin' Serverless continue to inspire many. If there is one avenue that we are missing as part of serverless community engagement, what would that be?

Diversity of ideas, diversity of opinions, and diversity of perspective. One of the reasons why I started the *Off-by-none* newsletter was to amplify the voices of others, even if I didn't agree with them. Communities can quickly become echo chambers that too easily drown out differences of opinion that would otherwise lead to healthy debate and further innovation. The serverless community is one of the greatest I've had the privilege to be part of, and over the years I've seen it continue to grow and diversify. This only happened because dedicated people did the necessary work to reach out, educate, and inspire. More needs to be done, and I hope others will keep up the amazing work they are doing to create an inclusive environment for everyone.

CHAPTER 6

Implementing Serverless Applications

Don't try to create and analyze at the same time. They're different processes.
—Sister Corita Kent, "10 Rules for Students, Teachers, and Life"

The first five chapters of this book introduced serverless for the enterprise and explored architectural design, security, and implementation patterns. The next five chapters focus on how to develop, test, operate, budget, and sustain an enterprise-scale serverless workload on AWS.

This chapter discusses the aspects that make serverless software engineering unique and shows you how to approach developing and delivering a serverless application.

> This chapter is not a how-to guide for building serverless applications, nor does it make any recommendations for the tools or programming languages that you should use.

Although the code you write in your preferred programming language for serverless will likely be very similar to code you've contributed to websites, backends, and programs in the past, you'll need to adapt your development process to unlock the full potential of serverless.

Tread Lightly

I (Luke) introduced the concept of *treading lightly* back in early 2017 (*https://oreil.ly/Xws9b*), and it still holds true in 2023, at the time of writing. The idea is to accept change as a constant and optimize your application and development process accordingly: "Treading lightly describes an approach to product development whereby implementations are made on the smallest possible scale without over-commitment to a single technology or methodology in order to facilitate future enhancement."

Although serverless compute on AWS Lambda had been launched a few years before I wrote that article, in 2014, serverless in its current form (with myriad managed services and event-driven application integration options) didn't exist back then. Nowadays, however, it provides one of the best platforms for a constantly changing application.

Serverless engineers must optimize for change and experimentation: "For product innovation to thrive implementations must be kept basic and minimal. This doesn't translate to a lack of features, quite the opposite: by maintaining lightness progress becomes constant."

Software delivery is key to serverless. Serverless applications can be completely defined in code, deployed to any AWS account within minutes, and sit idle without costing a penny. Yet as teams adopt cloud native and by extension serverless technologies, they often bring their existing process and practices with them. This is understandable; ways of working and collective mindsets are naturally embedded in teams and cultures and are the hardest things to change.

But as teams migrate to serverless, they realize sooner or later that their sociotechnical habits must adapt in order for them to reap the maximum benefits of the shift. Put simply: there is no value in having an application that can constantly change if you cannot change it quickly and predictably.

The nascent practice of serverless software engineering has also begun to morph. AWS Lambda was the quintessential launchpad for serverless, and following its release engineering teams eagerly began packaging and deploying their business logic as functions that didn't run on servers they managed. At the time of writing, Lambda has evolved far beyond its original "function as a service" label to become a comprehensive event-driven programming platform. In recent years AWS has released new products like EventBridge and retrofitted classic services such as S3, SQS, and SNS with event-oriented features.

As the number of ways in which components in an application can be glued together has increased, the production code authored by engineers began to be viewed as a liability. Every line of code written and deployed is more real estate that must be tested, maintained, documented, and operated. There is a clear preference to delegate the undifferentiated heavy lifting to AWS and focus on solving domain-specific problems. This means serverless engineers find they begin to write far more infrastructure code than business logic as they define and configure the various managed services that comprise their applications.

When you first start designing and implementing a serverless application, it's important to keep in mind that the business logic of your application is at the core of a much wider set of components (see Figure 6-1). The pipeline to deliver code into production should be built on day 1 and run frequently after that. Cost and security concerns should be considered at every phase of software development. Application and infrastructure code should be automatically tested and optimized for sustainability. And the whole system must be operated primarily by the team of engineers who designed and implemented it.

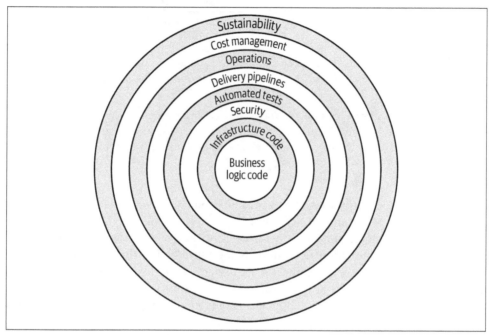

Figure 6-1. Concentric serverless objects

In this chapter we will explore the serverless computing model, defining infrastructure as code, and how to optimize software delivery. First, let's take a closer look at the most prominent serverless service on AWS: Lambda.

Serverless Compute with AWS Lambda

Serverless computing is based on the provision of machine resources, shared across many disparate clients, on demand. This shared resource model only works if the users of the servers are not allowed to greedily consume or hog the resources. Therefore, providers of serverless compute platforms must put usage constraints in place. As Figure 6-2 shows, in the case of AWS Lambda, the primary constraint is the number of concurrently executing functions (*https://oreil.ly/jtTt-*).

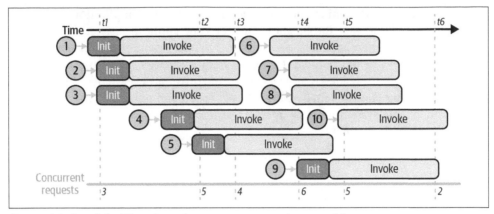

Figure 6-2. Lambda lifecycle and concurrent executions model

Be sure to read Julian Wood's article "Understanding AWS Lambda Scaling and Throughput" (*https://oreil.ly/NBhFh*) as you begin to leverage the Lambda service for your business-critical applications.

One of the most important lessons to instill in your team when getting started with serverless is that your unit of scale is concurrency. While memory consumption and execution duration are indicative metrics at the function level, the number of concurrent Lambda function executions is the ultimate metric to track when your application's compute needs begin to scale under exceptional traffic. If the number of concurrent function executions exceeds your account's limit, your functions will begin to be throttled. This essentially means requests to your Lambda functions will not be accepted.

Each AWS account has a default Lambda concurrency limit of 1,000 executions (*https://oreil.ly/VXuoH*) across all functions in a Region. This limit can be increased to tens of thousands by raising a support ticket to AWS with a valid use case. There is a different upper limit in each AWS Region.

Whenever you consider increasing the concurrency limit, keep in mind that throttling is a safety measure that AWS enforces to protect your resources from unexpected spikes in consumption—and therefore cost—and prevent any downstream resources from being overwhelmed. In this way, function throttling is, paradoxically, a crucial aspect of serverless autoscaling.

The astute serverless team always works within the constraints of the cloud. In Chapter 8, we'll dive into the subject of operating your serverless workload and how to understand the units of scale across various AWS services.

How to Write Lambda Functions

Although writing infrastructure code is becoming the prevalent model for developing serverless applications (as discussed in "Most of the Code You Write Will Be Infrastructure" on page 291), the now ubiquitous Lambda function is still an incredibly useful tool for executing isolated pieces of business logic, for example to process events, handle external API requests and responses, and authorize incoming API requests (see Chapter 4).

This section provides some guidelines to follow early in your team's adoption of serverless that can help contain the complexity of your codebase as your application scales.

> The AWS Lambda documentation includes an extensive set of best practices (*https://oreil.ly/u7Uu4*) to consider when developing and operating your functions.

Structure your codebase for serverless

If you are starting a brand-new serverless project, one of the first things you'll consider is how to structure your codebase and source control repositories. This is of course an age-old debate in the software industry, with many different opinions depending on developers' preferred languages, tools, and platforms. Ultimately, you should establish a folder structure and file naming convention that support your use case and feel right for your team.

In general, serverless applications with many microservices fit the monorepo model (*https://oreil.ly/iQt0h*). A monorepo (or single repository) allows you to standardize tooling for installing, building, linting, formatting, and testing your application's code across distinct services. This enables your engineers to easily work across multiple services without the need to switch repositories or manage different toolchains.

Another technique that will help your codebase scale is colocating your infrastructure stacks (see "Infrastructure as Code" on page 291) and Lambda function source code in the same top-level directory, rather than grouping your service infrastructure definitions together and keeping the business logic code separate (see Figure 6-3).

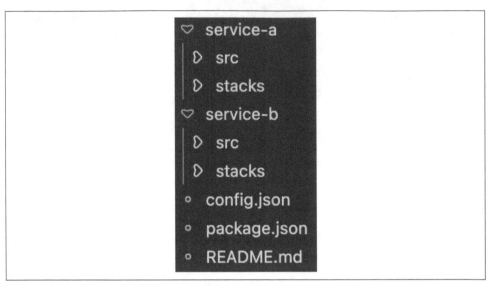

Figure 6-3. Serverless directory structure

If you ever begin to feel constrained by your folder structure, do not be afraid to evolve it where necessary. Your team must feel comfortable and productive when working with the codebase (see the final section in this chapter for the importance of productivity when it comes to continuous delivery).

Apply the single-responsibility principle

The single-responsibility principle (SRP) (*https://oreil.ly/EtYxg*) can be distilled to the following: do one thing and do it well. In the context of Lambda functions, this encourages you to keep your functions concise and performant. As you've seen, serverless compute is designed to be stateless and ephemeral and the constraints enforced in the Lambda environment force you to prioritize computational efficiency. Restricting the logic, network requests, and I/O in your functions to a single task will go a long way to ensuring you are operating a fleet of efficient functions. Single-responsibility Lambda functions also support your application of the principle of least privilege (covered in detail in Chapter 4), as each function can be given tightly scoped IAM permissions.

Strict adherence to the SRP inevitably leads to the tasks of a serverless microservice being split across many functions. In this situation, you may need to chain functions together. Jump to "Orchestrate complex business logic with workflows" on page 283 to explore the recommended approach to this challenge.

Stay in a single file

There are many reasons to abstract code into multiple files. You may feel it makes the code more readable and more organized, or less repetitive and more reusable. These are all valid reasons for code abstraction and often make sense when building a large, monolithic application where the logical and operational boundaries are much wider. But when it comes to Lambda functions, keeping the code in a single file can be an invaluable technique.

As illustrated in the previous recommendation to apply the SRP, Lambda functions should be as minimal as possible. Abstraction will still be necessary, but in an architectural sense rather than a code or file sense. Striving to keep your function code in a single file can be used as a measure of increasing complexity. If the file containing your function grows beyond a reasonable limit and you feel yourself considering abstraction to multiple files, this is the point at which to reevaluate your architecture. Ask yourself the following questions:

- Should this function now be split into multiple functions?
- Should the steps or tasks in this function be abstracted to a workflow?

 Code abstraction within your single file is still perfectly acceptable and indeed necessary when it comes to writing testable functions. See Chapter 7 for examples of abstraction for the purpose of testing.

Keeping function code in a single file will make your applications more testable, evolvable, observable, and resilient. Engineers responsible for understanding and maintaining the functions will be able to follow the control flow more easily, as they won't need to flick back and forth between files. In addition, the dependency tree of your functions will be linearized and obvious rather than spread across files and folders.

Orchestrate complex business logic with workflows

Workflow orchestration is an increasingly common pattern in serverless applications that allows you to chain multiple tasks across a single process or service (see Chapter 5 for a full overview of the concept of orchestration). Orchestration is often used to model complex business processes that involve multiple steps across many different AWS services.

As you apply the SRP and decompose your larger Lambda functions into separate pieces of business logic, AWS Step Functions can be used to execute tasks in a state machine–based workflow (*https://oreil.ly/vsUK0*), as shown in Figure 6-4.

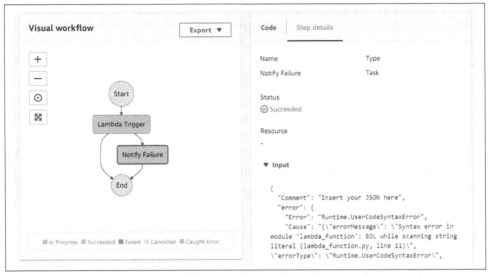

Figure 6-4. A Step Functions workflow can be used to orchestrate the tasks of a microservice, allowing you to decouple tasks across your single-responsibility Lambda functions

 Workflows offer a number of benefits: complex business process mapping, applying business rules and conditional processing, visualization of state machines via state charts, intrinsics (e.g., hashing, UUIDs, value interpolation, native application integration patterns, and SDK operations), waiting for events to complete (task callbacks, etc.), and fault tolerance.

As well as using workflow orchestration as a strategy for refactoring Lambda functions as requirements evolve, adopting an *orchestration-first* approach will help you to contain the complexity of the business logic in your application as it grows and scales (see Figure 6-5). An orchestration-first approach to your serverless architecture involves wrapping Lambda functions in Step Functions workflows (state machines) as a default. Rather than invoking the functions directly, your events will execute the parent workflow. Orchestration-first allows you to evolve your architecture beyond a single function to multiple functions, or even to replace parts of your function with direct service integrations and intrinsic functions, by simply iterating on the workflow without requiring any major rearchitecting.

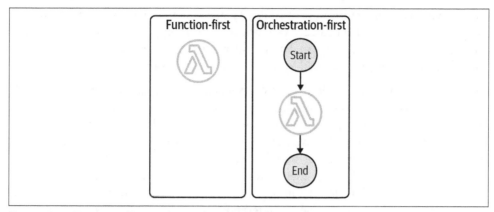

Figure 6-5. Function-first versus orchestration-first architecture

Leveraging workflow orchestration to react to the result of a Lambda function invocation is different from using Lambda destinations (*https://oreil.ly/CmOSe*). A destination will only receive an event in response to invocation failures, not failures in your logic. For example, if an invocation of your function was unable to correctly process its input and returned a 400 Bad Request response, this would trigger the success destination rather than the failure destination.

Use Lambda Powertools

The open source Lambda Powertools initiative (*https://oreil.ly/-tVPU*) provides an indispensable set of tools to use when developing Lambda functions. There are implementations (*https://oreil.ly/caP16*) in a variety of languages, including Python, Node.js/TypeScript, Java, and .NET.

The libraries are predominantly focused on observability and provide three core utilities: a logger, a tracer, and a custom metrics collector. However, more features are continually being added to the various libraries, such as tools to support idempotency (*https://oreil.ly/7SmFn*) and integration with parameter stores (*https://oreil.ly/Lfl7v*) like AWS SSM Parameter Store and AWS AppConfig.

Minimize deploy-time dependencies

As your serverless application grows, so will the number of microservices it is composed of. During this period of growth there will inevitably come a point where two or more services require access to a single resource. Without properly planning for the sharing of resources, you can inadvertently introduce tight coupling between resources and make it difficult to iterate on the connected components or introduce new connections.

In a serverless architecture it is common to have components such as S3 buckets, DynamoDB tables, or EventBridge event buses with multiple actors reading from or writing to these resources across distinct microservices. These can be referred to as shared resources, as they are used by more than one microservice.

The key to maintaining relationships between shared resources and the actors interacting with them is to avoid coupling them in delivery pipelines at deployment time. Interdependent resources should not be coupled between CloudFormation stacks that describe separate services. For example, let's say you have two microservices: Service A defines an EventBridge event bus that Service B consumes events from. Service B defines the EventBridge rule that matches event patterns and triggers a target. To attach the rule to the bus defined in Service A, Service B must make reference to the bus (e.g., via an ARN). For Service B's reference to Service A's bus to be resolvable to a resource deployed to AWS, Service A's CloudFormation stack must be deployed. This creates a deployment dependency in Service B on Service A.

Amazon Resource Names (ARNs) are unique identifiers for your AWS resources. They use a format similar to this: `arn:<partition>:<service>:<region>:<account-id>:<resource-type>/<resource-id>`. For example, the event bus `my-bus` in the Frankfurt region would have the ARN `arn:aws:events:eu-central-1:012345678901:event-bus/my-bus`. ARNs can be used to obtain references to your resources and used in CloudFormation templates.

Whenever a CloudFormation stack depends on a resource defined in another stack, you will need to consider how to discover and reference the resource. A common approach to service discovery is to broadcast the ARNs of shared resources via CloudFormation outputs (*https://oreil.ly/-FReQ*) or SSM parameters (*https://oreil.ly/jOZZ5*) so that they can be imported by any consuming stacks.

That single dependency may not seem too problematic, but as more services begin to depend on the central event bus in Service A it becomes harder and harder to maintain, evolve, or even decommission Service A. Deployment of Service B could also now be blocked unnecessarily by any issues with Service A (see Figure 6-6). The two services have now become tightly coupled and must be aware—and considerate—of each other.

Generally, it is advisable to keep shared resources to a minimum. When the need to share a resource across multiple microservices arises, a best practice is to place the shared resource in a separate stack; not a single stack for all shared resources but a stack per shared resource.

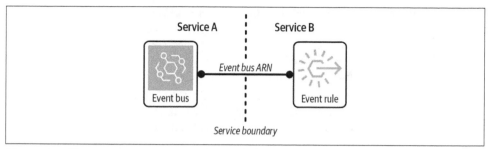

Figure 6-6. Sharing resources across decoupled microservices

Optimizing Lambda Functions

As a result of Lambda's computing model, functions that execute as fast as possible are always preferable. Following the preceding suggestions for writing Lambda code will get you a long way to building a fleet of efficient functions, but there are some additional things to be aware of when optimizing performance. This section presents some optimization tips.

Managing cold starts

A cold start (initially covered in Chapter 1) occurs when the Lambda service must initialize a function, which involves loading the function's code, booting the runtime, and running the function's init phase, described in the next section. Once initialized, the function's environment remains available to subsequent invocation requests for a short period of time after the first invocation is completed. These functions are sometimes referred to as "warm" and avoid the need for a cold start.

The impact of cold starts on your application will completely depend on your use case and business process. Ultra time-sensitive functions, for example, may not tolerate any cold starts at all, whereas a background process may be able to operate happily with unpredictable variance in execution times.

You should be able to observe your functions and measure the impact a cold start has on your application. Identify a performance threshold that you feel is acceptable and decide where to make the trade-off. We'll talk more about the importance of running your functions in production as soon as possible to understand behavior, including usage patterns and cold starts, later in this chapter.

It is vital that serverless engineers are aware of the fact that cold starts always decrease as traffic increases. This can seem counterintuitive at first, but it is a serverless truism: the more your application is used, the better it will perform.

AWS Lambda provides the *provisioned concurrency feature* (*https://oreil.ly/M5_fe*) as a strategy for mitigating cold starts. Generally, you will not need to configure provisioned concurrency for most serverless applications, but it is nonetheless important to be aware of it in case it suits a particular use case.

AWS also provides Lambda SnapStart (*https://oreil.ly/zZaKX*) to optimize your functions and reduce cold starts. Lambda SnapStart is only available for the Java runtime at the time of writing.

Optimizing function initialization

Each time a new Lambda execution environment is created (in other words, at each cold start), the function's static initialization code is run. This is part of what is known as the "init" phase in the execution environment's lifecycle, as shown in Figure 6-7. The init phase is run once per environment on start-up and is not run again if an invocation uses a warm execution environment.

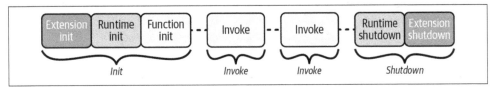

Figure 6-7. Lambda execution environment lifecycle (source: adapted from an image on the Amazon Lamba Execution Environment web page [https://oreil.ly/N5qDx])

You can think of the init phase as running the code outside of your handler and the invoke phase as running the code inside your handler:

```
// init phase
import { DynamoDBClient } from "@aws-sdk/client-dynamodb";

const dynamoDBClient = new DynamoDBClient();

export const handler = async () => {
  // invoke phase
};
```

You should keep the init code of your functions to an absolute minimum to optimize cold start times (*https://oreil.ly/TijBr*) as far as possible. That said, there are tasks that are more efficient to perform during the init phase than the invoke phase. Typically these are tasks that produce objects that can be reused over multiple function invocations in the same execution environment. This could include importing dependencies, opening database connections, initializing AWS clients, or instrumenting AWS SDK calls for X-Ray tracing, for example.

Optimizing compute performance

The compute performance of your functions can be optimized by making use of the AWS Graviton2 processor (*https://oreil.ly/Jp0PI*). Functions that use the Graviton2 processor will typically perform better and cost less. They will also consume up to 60% less energy (*https://oreil.ly/TS4JU*) compared to the alternative x86-based processors. For more on sustainability, see Chapter 10.

Analyzing performance

Lambda Insights (*https://oreil.ly/GBHZ8*) is a performance monitoring feature of Amazon CloudWatch. You can use Lambda Insights to understand the performance of your Lambda functions by analyzing key metrics such as maximum memory consumption, average execution duration, and average cost (see Figure 6-8).

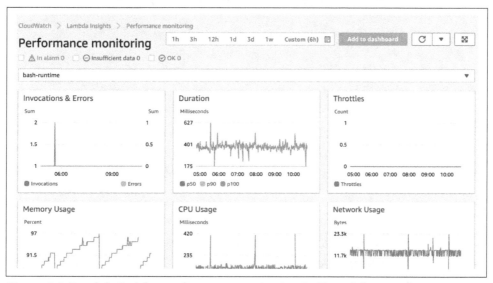

Figure 6-8. Lambda Insights performance monitoring dashboard for a single Lambda function (source: Amazon's Using Lambda Insights in Amazon CloudWatch web page [https://oreil.ly/quWGQ])

The Lambda Insights data can help you to decide on the best configuration (*https://oreil.ly/hui3o*) for your function. For example, if your function is allocated 512 MB of memory and routinely consumes 95% or more of this allocation, you may decide to increase it to avoid the possibility of exceeding the limit. Without surfacing the performance data via Lambda Insights, you might only discover this issue if it impacts your application's performance or your function fails at runtime.

There is no specific charge for the Lambda Insights service. Instead, when you enable Lambda Insights for your function, you will be charged for the metrics and logs sent to CloudWatch whenever your function is invoked. For more details on the costs associated with using Lambda Insights, see the CloudWatch pricing page (*https://oreil.ly/fOag9*).

In addition to the Lambda Insights service, you can use the open source tool AWS Lambda Power Tuning (*https://oreil.ly/JElQ3*). Power Tuning invokes your Lambda function with various memory configurations (from 128 MB to 10 GB) and suggests the optimum configuration to minimize cost and/or maximize performance, as shown in Figure 6-9.

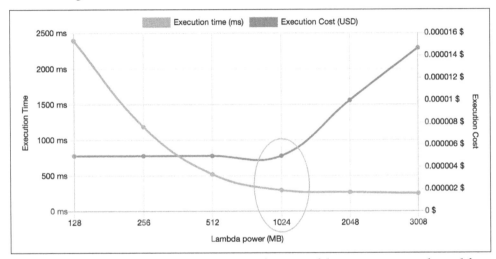

Figure 6-9. AWS Lambda Power Tuning visualization of the average cost and speed for each memory configuration (source: AWS Lambda Power Tuning GitHub repo [https:// oreil.ly/-9mQ1])

This chart demonstrates how the allocation of more memory can result in faster execution times at no additional cost. When the function is permitted to use a maximum of 128 MB of memory, it will take more than 2 seconds to execute. If the same function is allocated 1 GB of memory it will take substantially less time to execute, for the exact same cost.

You can use Power Tuning to obtain a baseline for the memory and timeout configuration for your function. However, as Power Tuning is typically executed in non-production environments or under test conditions, it should not be used as a substitute for analyzing the behavior of your functions under production usage levels. You should always go back and retroactively apply performance optimizations as you gain a greater understanding of production behavior.

Most of the Code You Write Will Be Infrastructure

Regardless of your team's domain and use case, it is likely your serverless architecture will consist of a variety of managed services interspersed with Lambda functions. Your business logic will reside in these Lambda functions. The functions will be triggered in response to events emitted by the managed services: an event is published to an EventBridge event bus, a record is written to a DynamoDB table, an object is added to an S3 bucket, and so on.

The configurations for the Lambda functions, the triggers, and the managed services can all be created and updated using the AWS console. However, any team operating at enterprise scale will quickly see the limitations of using the console for purposes beyond exploration and familiarization. Modern software engineering teams define their infrastructure *as code* and automate all aspects of software delivery and resource provisioning.

Infrastructure as Code

The core benefit of defining your infrastructure as code is automation. Automating the creation, modification, and deletion of your application allows you to deliver software safely and efficiently. The days of haphazardly deploying an application with various custom shell scripts over many perilous hours are gone.

Automation provides several advantages when running serverless applications in the cloud, such as:

Replication
> Infrastructure templates can be used to reliability and comprehensively replicate applications across AWS accounts and production and non-production environments. Replicas of an application can support automated testing pipelines, accurate sandbox environments for your consumers, and recovery from disasters such as accidental account or resource deletion.

Separation
> Infrastructure management of complex, distributed applications can be simplified by grouping and managing resources with logical separations, such as by microservice or resource characteristic (stateful and stateless, critical and non-critical, etc.).

Versioning
> Changes to infrastructure resources can be individually tracked and applications can be automatically rolled back to previous versions.

Defining your cloud infrastructure as code typically involves writing a set of declarative instructions that are translated to various AWS API calls. Next, we'll take a look at one of the IaC services available to you: AWS CloudFormation.

AWS CloudFormation

The primary tool for infrastructure management on AWS is AWS CloudFormation (*https://oreil.ly/gslGE*). With CloudFormation, you write your infrastructure in *templates* (*https://oreil.ly/AC-hW*) using JSON or YAML. You upload these templates to the CloudFormation service when deploying your microservices, and CloudFormation will then make API calls to the corresponding AWS services to create, modify, or delete the required resources.

Here's an example YAML template:

```yaml
AWSTemplateFormatVersion: 2010-09-09
Description: A custom event bus
Resources:
  SampleCustomEventBus:
    Type: AWS::Events::EventBus
    Properties:
      Name: "MyCustomEventBus"
```

There are many frameworks and tools available that support defining cloud infrastructure as code. These range from tools native to cloud providers—AWS has the AWS Cloud Development Kit (CDK) and the Serverless Application Model (SAM)—to vendor-agnostic, proprietary frameworks (such as the Serverless Framework, Terraform, and Pulumi).

As with any tooling choice, select the option that works best for your team. Infrastructure tooling is a highly active area and things are changing all the time; keep this in mind and *tread lightly* rather than going all-in on a single tool. Using multiple IaC tools is also an acceptable strategy, as long as you isolate the microservices and their infrastructure definitions during development and delivery.

The resources defined in a CloudFormation template are deployed and managed as a single unit, called a *stack*. Typically you will have a single CloudFormation stack per microservice in your application, but you might also choose to split the resources in a service across multiple stacks.

Robust cloud infrastructure

Incorrectly configuring your cloud infrastructure can lead to security vulnerabilities, application performance issues, and total service outages. Defining your infrastructure as code can help guard against these risks.

For your infrastructure to be resilient to change it must be verifiable (will it deploy successfully?), testable (does it behave as expected?), adaptable (can it be updated safely and quickly?), and portable (can it be deployed anywhere at any time?).

Infrastructure that has these attributes can also support several trends that can be observed in the serverless engineering community:

Writing less business logic

Every line of code you write can be considered a liability, and that can be extrapolated to the Lambda functions that encapsulate those lines of code. As the concept of application integration (*https://oreil.ly/NFaD0*) gains traction, Lambda functions are increasingly being used for transforming data, not transporting it. Entire functionless architectures (see Chapter 5 for details) are being deployed to production workloads. This code is being replaced by infrastructure code.

Rapid cloud development

Cloud providers (AWS CodeCatalyst [*https://oreil.ly/6VnEU*]) and start-ups (SST [*https://oreil.ly/INA_Q*], Wing [*https://oreil.ly/dGp51*]) are discovering new ways to improve the ergonomics of developing cloud native software. Engineers are demanding tighter feedback loops to understand whether their code is working correctly and want to work as close to the cloud as possible with zero emulation. Infrastructure as code is often at the core of these efforts, where deployment workflows are automated and patterns are shared between engineers via reusable collections of cloud components.

Infrastructure and configuration testing

Managed services shift the operational responsibility from engineering teams to AWS. Engineers are responsible for configuring those managed services and need a way to test the configurations without deploying and executing their applications. Defining the infrastructure configuration as code means it can be statically verified and tested just like any other piece of code in your application.

Principle of least privilege

The principle of least privilege is the gold standard for granting permissions in the cloud (see Chapter 4 for more on this topic). But the granularity and syntax of AWS IAM can often make applying it a tedious task. Modern IaC tools, like the AWS CDK, are able to automatically generate least privilege policies and per-resource execution roles in most scenarios. For example, if you define a Step Functions workflow that makes an AWS SDK request to DynamoDB, the workflow will be assigned a unique IAM execution role with a policy that has the least permissions required to perform this task.

Everything as code

The infrastructure as code movement has expanded to encompass defining many other operational aspects of software, including delivery pipelines, monitoring dashboards, alarms, synthetic canaries, and access control policies. Embracing the * *as code* paradigm will help you build your applications quickly and safely.

Environments and stages

The ephemeral, stateless nature of serverless resources and the pay-per-use pricing model allow for a strategy of treating instances of applications as disposable commodities. Instances of your application can be spun up and torn down effortlessly and cheaply.

Pets Versus Cattle

In the past, IT and operations teams were responsible for managing the entire lifecycle of a server, or fleet of servers, in a data center. These physical machines were known to the team and were dedicated to serving its applications; they were not shared with teams in another company or even another department in their organization. Given that the teams were very invested in the health and performance of individual servers, they were often anthropomorphized with names and personalities.

Way back in 2012, I (Luke) was working for a company with a server called Rodney. He was extremely temperamental and often needed a lot of encouragement to wake up in the mornings!

With the emergence of cloud computing, treating servers as "pets" began to be viewed as antiquated and inefficient. Businesses could now run their software on ephemeral virtual machines, and engineers were urged to treat these on-demand servers more like cattle (*https://oreil.ly/XG31e*), anonymously going about their business among a large homogeneous herd.

One of the superpowers infrastructure as code gives you is the ability to *template* your applications. In this way, IaC supports the disposable commodity model. Applications are transformed into cookie cutters that can be used to create an infinite number of replicas (see Figure 6-10). A common employment of this superpower is the provisioning of microservices in pre-production environments.

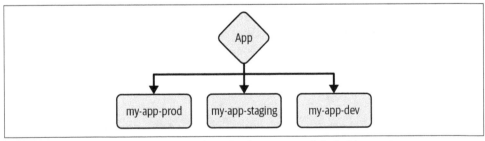

Figure 6-10. A single application with multiple instances labeled by environment or stage

The popular approach to distinguishing between these replicas is to use the construct of a *stage*. A stage usually maps to an environment, such as *production*, *staging*, or *performance*. This can be observed in CloudFormation stacks with names like `order-service-stack-staging` and Lambda functions called things like `process-order-function-prod`.

If this works for your team and helps engineers form a mental model of your application, then by all means adopt this practice. However, explicitly associating application instances with stages is usually a remnant of deploying monolithic applications to dedicated servers and becomes a constraint on velocity and adaptability at scale. You end up with a `STAGE` environment variable littered across your infrastructure and application code. This ties you into the existence of those named environments and makes your code harder to reason about.

The alternative to using a system of stage labels is to isolate environments by account (see Figure 6-11). This way, each account only ever contains a single version of your application. Accounts can still have names like Production, Development, and Luke.

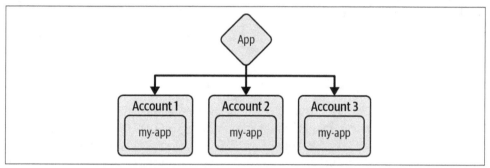

Figure 6-11. A single application with multiple instances deployed to separate AWS accounts

Direct Service Integrations and Delegating to the Experts

When AWS launched the Lambda service in November 2014 it was billed as a "zero-administration compute platform," integrated with three other AWS services: S3, DynamoDB, and Kinesis. Lambda functions could be triggered by objects created in S3 buckets, messages sent to Kinesis streams, and items updated in DynamoDB.

In the launch post for Lambda (*https://oreil.ly/tnvcW*), Jeff Barr (Chief Evangelist for AWS) teased the roadmap for Lambda: "We have a great roadmap for Lambda! While I won't spill all of the beans today, I will tell you that we expect to add support for additional AWS services." This roadmap proved to be the catalyst for what AWS calls *application integration* (*https://oreil.ly/ThiqG*)—"a suite of services that enable communication between decoupled components within microservices, distributed systems, and serverless applications"—and Lambda now integrates with around 30 services (*https://oreil.ly/cPrPd*). This explosion of integrations has turned Lambda from a FaaS into a complete event-driven programming platform.

Lambda played a pivotal role in popularizing the concept of fully managed services, where AWS takes care of the underlying operating system and runtime and manages resource scaling and fault tolerance. A key milestone in this journey was the Step Functions SDK integration release (*https://oreil.ly/41SVr*), which gave serverless engineers the ability to perform AWS SDK operations (such as getting an item from a DynamoDB table or putting a message onto an SQS queue) directly from a Step Functions workflow. These tasks would have previously needed to be performed in a Lambda function.

All of the aforementioned AWS service enhancements and feature releases have culminated in the evolution of serverless architectures from purely Lambda-based to a powerful mix of business logic and microservice integrations. Nowadays, the true power of serverless is the ability to blend compute on Lambda with AWS-native service integrations. You can delegate computing, storage, workflow orchestration, and event streaming to the experts and concentrate your energy on building the best application for your users.

Let's dive into how you can unlock the power of serverless through the use of managed services.

Benefits of managed services

A managed service (introduced in Chapter 1) encapsulates event consumption, event production, and metric emission (as illustrated in Figure 6-12). The internal logic of a managed service is exposed to you via an API. API requests can be made directly or via the various SDKs (*https://oreil.ly/4TMnl*). Managed services can also be triggered by events from other managed services.

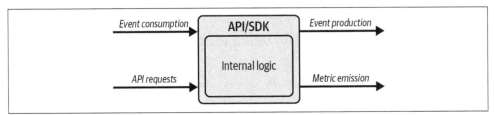

Figure 6-12. Anatomy of a managed service

Managed services provide the following key benefits:

Default metrics
> Every managed service continually emits metrics about usage and performance. These metrics can be used to build alerts and dashboards. Crucially, no additional configuration is required to activate these metrics beyond deployment of a particular resource. (For more about service metrics, see Chapter 8.)

Events

Managed services typically execute in response to an inbound event. Each managed service will also produce outbound events that are triggered by actions on resources. Most events will be consumable via EventBridge, allowing you to fully integrate managed services with the rest of your system.

Shared responsibility

The product and operations teams at AWS are responsible for designing, building, and operating the code that powers every managed service. The separation of responsibility between you and AWS reduces the undifferentiated heavy lifting you need to perform and impacts application security (see Chapter 4), testing (see Chapter 7), operations (see Chapter 8), and the total cost of ownership (see Chapter 9).

Functions calling functions

While the application integration options provided by managed services will usually be the glue between the components in your serverless application, it may be tempting, in certain cases, to call one Lambda function from another. Although this is technically possible, you should be aware that invoking a Lambda function from another function is generally considered an antipattern (*https://oreil.ly/LBii1*).

Calling functions from other functions tightly couples the execution of your business logic, which makes it difficult to handle failures and refactor at a later time. If the calling function must also wait for a response from the called function, this ultimately goes against the pay-per-use nature of serverless compute, as you will now effectively pay for this idle wait period. Functions waiting for other functions to respond will also unnecessarily count toward the maximum concurrent executions of Lambda functions in your account.

Function or functionless?

In addition to facilitating the integration between your Lambda functions, managed services can entirely replace a Lambda function in some scenarios. Indeed, as discussed in "The Functionless Integration Pattern" on page 236, a growing trend among serverless engineers is to only use Lambda functions to perform tasks when absolutely necessary and instead leverage various managed services to delegate work to AWS.

Writing and deploying a Lambda function comes with an obvious labor cost. The function's code must be tested, operated, and maintained for as long as it is in use. Of course, there will always be valid use cases for leveraging Lambda functions in your architecture, but it's important to consider whether a native service integration can be used instead.

Let's consider some common tasks and compare the utilization of Lambda functions and managed services:

Event data enrichment

As events flow through your system you will inevitably need to transform and enrich their payloads with additional fields. Managed services such as Step Functions (via input and output processing (*https://oreil.ly/1COeB*)) and EventBridge (via input transformation (*https://oreil.ly/_FtQ5*)) support static data operations using JSONPath (*https://oreil.ly/kprWy*). JSONPath operations can be considered static as they can only use the data provided as input and cannot generate new values, such as timestamps or calculated values. For dynamic data enrichment, you may be able to utilize Step Functions intrinsic functions (*https://oreil.ly/0OI1e*) or implement custom business logic in a Lambda function as part of your event processing pipeline.

Event communication and routing

Using Lambda functions to transport data is usually unnecessary. In the vast majority of cases you should rely on a managed service, such as Amazon Event-Bridge, SNS, Kinesis, or SQS, to transmit messages between producers and consumers and trigger activity in your serverless application. As Ajay Nair, General Manager for AWS Lambda, once said (*https://oreil.ly/PmqQ0*): "Use Lambda functions to transform, not transport."

Event batching

Many managed services support some form of batching or buffering, including Amazon Kinesis and SQS. Using a managed service should generally be preferred over implementing your own batch mechanism.

HTTP requests

When making network requests to third-party APIs, you can use the Step Functions HTTP task (*https://oreil.ly/o6iaK*) or EventBridge API destinations (as described in Chapter 5) if you do not need to handle the response.

Intensive compute

When you need to coordinate large-scale parallel data processing (*https://oreil.ly/1G0Ry*) you can use a Step Functions map (for up to 40 parallel executions) or distributed map (for up to 10,000 parallel executions) to invoke a single Lambda function concurrently, rather than managing the map in the function itself.

Production Is Just a Name

The concept of *environments* has long been ubiquitous in software engineering. Software is deployed to various pre-production environments, tested, and then promoted to production. However, this status quo is beginning to creak as teams push the limits of working in the cloud. Indeed, AWS knows nothing about your environments. Accounts are just accounts. There is nothing special about your production account, other than the fact that you choose to expose it to your users. Figure 6-13 shows a production and non-production account, both with identical applications deployed to them. As this demonstrates, environments are purely constructs with little meaning outside of your development workflow.

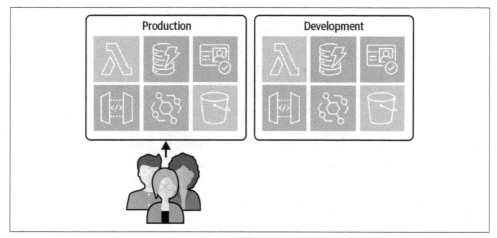

Figure 6-13. Spot the difference: production is just another version of your application!

To empower your serverless engineers to work creatively and collaboratively, it is important to remove the ceremony and fear traditionally associated with deploying code to production. Whether you choose to deploy on a Friday (*https://oreil.ly/NKnXv*) or not, identify hesitation and reluctance to deploy changes and decide how that can be addressed. The absence of habitual deployments can usually be traced back to a lack of confidence derived from tests, poor visibility into application behavior, historic failures, or even deeper cultural issues around incident postmortems.

Engineers must have their own sandbox accounts, or at least a shared "development" account. Engineers new to serverless and the cloud need to *feel* their code; they need to observe their code running in the cloud and have tangible evidence of the behavior and outcome of their applications. The best way to build serverless is to get something running in AWS and iterate on it.

Ship on Day 1, and Every Day After

Let's take a quick walkthrough of a greenfield scenario in order to illustrate the importance of prioritizing the delivery of your serverless application above anything else.

So, you've decided to build a brand-new serverless application. The first thing you should do is build an automated delivery pipeline. The first time it runs it will not deploy anything; it might even fail completely. Then, your next step can be to add a skeleton CloudFormation template and deploy that. Finally, begin layering in resources for functions, queues, buses, workflows, and tables. While you iterate on your business logic and infrastructure, your application will be continuously deploying. Delivery will become a habit that everyone in your team is comfortable with.

From Keyboard to Production

Software delivery is all about providing stable updates to the users of an application. Optimizing software delivery is all about removing barriers: helping engineers to move at a sustainable pace, feel productive, and be excited to get started on a code change, not daunted by the thought of getting something released.

According to the 2022 Accelerate State of DevOps Report (*https://oreil.ly/rUnkh*) by Google Cloud's DevOps Research and Assessment (DORA) team, it takes high-performing engineering teams between one day and one week to go from code committed to code successfully running in production.

Your software delivery lifecycle starts with an engineer's keyboard and finishes in production. The stability of your software depends on the optimization of the path from keyboard to production.

The case for continuous serverless delivery

It may seem counterintuitive to deploy an application or feature to your production and non-production accounts before any of it is built or even functioning. However, there is technically no simpler time to deliver something than before it exists; there are no potentially missing permissions, no tests to fail, no resources or environments to bootstrap.

Leaving pipelines and delivery to the end of your development cycles not only makes it more difficult to get the deployments working but also means you miss the opportunity to make software delivery a habit. To maximize the benefits of serverless, it is crucial to deliver your application continuously rather than at the end of large feature work.

One of the key differences with serverless applications is the use of managed services. With so many managed services, application integrations, and quotas in play, your serverless application is most definitely unique and cannot be easily compared to reference architectures or other applications in the wild. You need to deploy and operate your application before you can understand its behavior and begin to harden it.

 Continuous delivery mandates that every single change to your application, be it a new feature, a bug fix, or a dependency upgrade, is deployed individually. To understand the benefits of this approach, you can consider the introduction of a bug into your application, caught either by tests in your pipeline or by an alert in production.

In a continuous delivery pipeline it will be trivial to precisely associate the bug's genesis with a specific commit. In a pipeline that requires manual intervention or approval and where multiple changes can be batched into a single deployment, it can become an arduous task to track down the root cause of the issue among all of the disparate code changes. This can cause blockages in your pipeline as your team spends time diagnosing problems and will reduce your ability to integrate time-sensitive patch changes.

Adopting continuous serverless delivery

You can use the following set of guidelines to help your team adopt the practice of continuous serverless delivery:

Practice GitOps.
Put as much of your application, infrastructure, and configuration into your codebase as possible, and treat your Git repository as the single source of truth about the current version of the software deployed to production. Always trigger deployments to your cloud environments on code pushes to your trunk branch.

Optimize for experimentation.
Serverless allows you to decouple components in your application and iterate on them regularly. To ensure this platform for evolution is always available to you, optimize your development workflows for experimentation. The full requirements of your software are not usually known up front, and neither is exactly how the application will behave in production (e.g., managed services, traffic). Ship it and see!

Ship on day 1 and every day after that!

Always deliver as soon as possible after a code change is committed to your repository. Only delay in extreme circumstances. Remove the fear and ceremony around deploying to production—normalize it.

Go direct from keyboard to production.

Give your engineers an efficient, direct pipeline from their local machines to your remote cloud environments. Make deployment at every stage effortless, from local code changes (for example, via CDK hotswap) to integrating with other contributions and finally to production. Avoid emulation of the cloud on your local machines, as this will take you out of the direct-to-cloud feedback loop.

Automate everything.

Manual approvals in your pipelines indicate a lack of confidence in tests, fault tolerance, or observability. Manual intervention should be removed entirely from your pipelines and replaced with better tests, fault tolerance, and observability.

Deployment is not the same as release

When practicing continuous serverless delivery, the deployment and release of a code change should be considered separate phases. The deployment phase involves delivering the change to your AWS account, through the creation or modification of your infrastructure or business logic. The release phase involves delivering the change to your application's users and making that version of your application publicly available. In this way, many incremental deployments of individual changes could add up to a feature release.

It can be particularly useful to distinguish between deployment of code and the release of a feature to your users when facing doubts about continuously deploying a business-critical application, such as a payments platform. Adding manual approval processes and controls to the deployment of such applications is often suggested, but this actually runs counter to the intention of maintaining stability as it leads to queues of changes.

Instead, you can separate deployments from releases by adopting different release or versioning strategies based on the feature being introduced:

Dark releases

If your users are unaware of a new feature or cannot easily access it, code changes can be deployed to and tested in production without serving real traffic. This can be your default option for entirely new and isolated services, as it will allow you to release changes early and often, before the features are ready to be used.

Feature flags

Feature flags allow you to target groups of users with the release of new features. For example, you could activate a feature for users in a smaller market before rolling it out to larger markets. AWS AppConfig (*https://oreil.ly/jooC6*) can be used to manage and toggle feature flags in your environments.

Canaries

You can use a canary deployment strategy to achieve a gradual rollout of your code changes, rather than deploying them to all users at once. For example, you could choose to deploy a change to 10% of your users and then, if everything is scaling and working as expected, deploy it to the remaining 90% five minutes later. AWS CodeDeploy (*https://oreil.ly/ijlNv*) can be used to apply a blue/green deployment configuration to the release of Lambda functions. Failed deployments can also be automatically rolled back when using CodeDeploy.

Boring Delivery Pipelines—Safety, Speed, and Predictability

The highest barrier to adopting a practice of continuous delivery is typically a social one, rather than technological. Most engineers on your team will have worked in environments where releasing to production is someone else's responsibility and approached with maximum caution.

To foster a culture of accepting failure and turning delivery into a habit, it is vital to remove the ceremony and fear that go along with shipping to production. Automating all aspects of your pipelines, from execution to monitoring, is key to normalizing delivery into a safe, fast, and predictable activity.

Jidoka

Jidoka is one of the 12 pillars of the Toyota Production System, the now-famous lean manufacturing system that has been honed over many years to construct vehicles in the quickest and most efficient way and deliver them as fast as possible to customers.

Toyota describes *Jidoka* (*https://oreil.ly/CAnUF*) as "the principle of designing equipment to stop automatically and to detect and call attention to problems immediately whenever they occur.... It also liberates operators from controlling machines, leaving them free to concentrate on tasks that enable them to exercise skill and judgment instead of monitoring each machine continuously."

In simpler terms, *Jidoka* dictates that should a malfunction occur on the production line, operators have the power to cease production to resolve the issue.

The *Jidoka* principle can be translated to a software delivery pipeline: your pipelines should be observable, issues that prevent or degrade delivery of your application should trigger alerts, and these issues should be fixed as your highest priority. This

---

means that all feature work should be paused in favor of focusing your team on fixing the pipeline. This prioritization can also be extended to incorporating the fix in other pipelines if necessary. Figure 6-14 shows the continuous improvement lifecycle of the *Jidoka* principle.

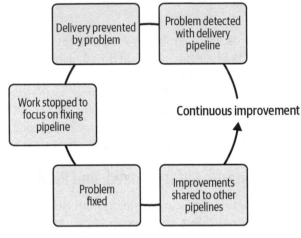

Figure 6-14. Continuous improvement of delivery pipelines

Continuous integration

Continuous integration (CI) is the practice of applying code changes to the releasable version of your application's source code on a regular basis. You can think of continuous delivery (as described in the previous section) as the overall aim for your software delivery lifecycle and continuous integration as the actual process of merging code changes with the deployed version of your codebase (see Figure 6-15).

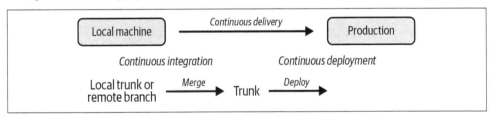

Figure 6-15. Continuous delivery, integration, and deployment

In a version control system such as Git, CI would typically involve merging feature branches via pull requests or committing local changes directly to your trunk branch (also known as trunk-based development [*https://oreil.ly/DXs0q*]). If you use a branching strategy like feature branching, branches should be short-lived and it should take no more than a day for pull requests to be reviewed and merged after they are opened.

 It is not necessary to be dogmatic when it comes to continuous integration and delivery. There is a lot of advice on best practice in this area, but the most important thing is to do what works for your team. Whether you choose to use feature branches and pull requests or trunk-based development and pair programming, the most vital aspect of software delivery is to mandate automation at every stage of your pipeline. Pipeline automation ensures that you can ship as often and as rapidly as possible while maintaining safety and stability.

Serverless architectures work well with CI, as loosely coupled microservices, infrastructure, and Lambda functions can be worked on in tiny increments and deployed in isolation. With a team of engineers constantly iterating on disparate parts of the same codebase, it is crucial to integrate code changes as often and as quickly as possible. CI will help you catch conflicts between multiple changes to the same file and any bugs that emerge from distinct updates.

CI is a vital part of your serverless engineering workflow. The more time you take to integrate changes, the longer you must wait to understand your users' experience of the features you ship.

Contrary to popular opinion and best practices often promoted in the serverless community, ephemeral environments provisioned to test code changes in feature branches can be considered the antithesis of continuous integration. In addition to non-production environments creating additional overhead for your team to manage, they promote a culture of slowing the progression of changes to production. After the introduction of pull request–based environments, teams become tempted to add more and more pre-production, whole-system tests. See Chapter 7 for more details about devising the optimum test strategy for your serverless application and how to balance testing with delivery to integrate as quickly and as regularly as possible.

The perfect pipeline

The optimal delivery pipeline is one that takes the most direct route from keyboard to production while providing full confidence to engineers about the validity and integrity of the changes being released.

When building your delivery pipelines, try to prioritize the following properties:

Atomic
> Give each service or stack in your application its own isolated delivery pipeline. Avoid batching changes to a service and deploy each change individually.

Automated
> Adopt a GitOps approach to delivery. This involves triggering atomic delivery pipelines based on changes to distinct directories in your codebase being merged to your trunk branch. Automate all steps, including tests and changelog generation and publication. Any manual intervention, such as final approvals, usually indicates a lack of confidence or fear of deployment.

Observable
> Any pipeline issues should trigger alerts to chat applications or ticket systems and be diagnosable.

Rapid
> You should define a maximum acceptable execution time for your pipelines, continuously monitor average durations, and optimize regularly to ensure pipelines are always as efficient as possible.

> Using a third-party continuous integration and deployment (CI/CD) platform to run delivery pipelines will typically involve storing AWS access credentials on the platform. If this is necessary, credentials should always be stored securely with encryption and should only be readable by the pipeline while it is running.
>
> Some CI/CD platforms, including GitHub Actions (*https://oreil.ly/ gDKp0*), support the use of OpenID Connect (OIDC). OIDC allows your pipelines to authenticate directly to AWS without the need to store long-lived access credentials outside of your account.

Now that you have an understanding of how to implement and deliver your serverless application, let's finally cover one of the less glamorous but equally important aspects of serverless implementation: documentation.

Documentation: Quality, Not Quantity

Although unlikely to be anybody's favorite task, generating clear, accurate, and relevant artifacts during the lifecycle of your software project or product is crucial to continued success, especially as contributors, requirements, and technologies change over time. There are many artifacts that will be useful to your team, but we'll focus here on technical documentation.

Given their distributed and decoupled nature, serverless, microservice-based, event-driven architectures are notoriously difficult to document. There are just so many components and interactions to describe; trying to document everything will rarely be a sustainable strategy. Instead, you should focus on documenting the most crucial aspects of your architecture—the parts you will need to understand when debugging production issues or making large-scale changes to the architecture.

It can be useful to treat documentation the same way you would a feature of your application, by prioritizing gaps according to demand and criticality. With this strategy, you wait until there is enough demand for a particular document before investing the time to create and maintain it. You may also find that half-written or outdated documentation is detrimental to efforts to understand the current state of the system, so don't hesitate to archive documents when they are no longer serving a purpose.

Serverless Solution Design

Being faced with researching, analyzing, and designing a solution to a set of business or user requirements can be daunting. A blank canvas is both exhilarating and terrifying!

Serverless solution design is no different. Structuring the solution design process around a common framework is crucial to ensuring you design robust, scalable features, services, and systems that are fit for purpose.

The discoveries, discussions, and decisions should be recorded throughout the entire process in a *solution design document*. A comprehensive solution design document should cover requirements gathering, data flows, architecture diagrams, data modeling, event design, threat modeling (covered in Chapter 4), reliability (see Chapter 8), cost estimation (see Chapter 9), and sustainability (see Chapter 10). You'll find a template to help you get started with solution design in Appendix C.

The solution design document and process will help you maintain the scope of a project and establish guardrails that direct efforts toward the best outcome. It can always be tempting to reach for the immediate and obvious answer to a problem statement, but through a thorough, collaborative approach you can surface and compare alternatives.

It is also important to treat your solution designs as *living documents*. This is the time to let ideas flow and encourage healthy discourse, so make sure you embrace the messiness within the structure! The formal documentation of a service can evolve from the solution design but should ultimately be distinct (the following section describes these artifacts in more detail).

For a deep dive into the solution design process, take a look at Sheen's two-part blog series (*https://oreil.ly/6gvwj*).

Here is a set of the most important pieces of documentation you can create for your application. Think of it as a place to start (the minimum viable documentation), rather than an exhaustive list:

Contributing guidelines

Establish clear guidelines for how to build, run, test, and deploy a service. Engineers should be able to get started on their first day. Make your contributing guidelines and onboarding process as succinct and simple as possible, and encourage engineers to incorporate changes based on their experience.

Solution designs

A pre-implementation design phase is crucial to the effectiveness of your application and can help you to understand how services will integrate in terms of data contracts and vendor quotas. See Appendix C for a solution design document template to help you get started. Solution designs can also include architectural decision records (ADRs) if you use those (see the Architecture Decision Log repository [*https://oreil.ly/Q4069*] for more information and a template).

Architecture diagrams

Architecture diagrams are a valuable resource for understanding your system's architecture and data flow. You can include key configuration details, such as SQS timeouts or batch size and EventBridge rule patterns. These diagrams are usually presented as part of a solution design or a microservice's *README* file.

API documentation

Any APIs, both synchronous (for example, API Gateway REST APIs) and asynchronous (such as EventBridge events) should be fully documented to facilitate frictionless and robust integration with your services. Human-readable docs can be automatically generated from standard schema specifications, such as JSON Schema, OpenAPI, and AsyncAPI. While useful for internal, inter-service APIs, API documentation is obviously crucial if you expose a public API to external consumers of your service.

State charts

The steps and transitions of a Step Functions workflow can be visualized as a state chart. These can be included as images in your solution designs and embedded in *README* files using Mermaid (*https://oreil.ly/Y1bLk*).

Event schemas

Every event in your system should be documented, including a description of the state change that the event captures and descriptions of each field in the event's payload, incorporating the field's semantics and syntax.

Summary

The adoption of serverless demands a novel approach to software engineering, and there are several layers that must be considered when implementing a serverless application. From cost optimization to security and testing to operations, enterprise teams must take a holistic approach. Rather than enforcing the traditional separation of concerns, these layers should be blended by considering them all at each phase of your software's lifecycle, particularly as you design, implement, and deliver your application.

As you design and implement with serverless, you will find that your work is focused on software delivery and infrastructure code as much as your business logic. You must understand this early and balance your team's education, planning, and practice across these key areas.

Serverless implementation is an exciting, collaborative, and creative process that you and your team will enjoy. But wait—before you put this book down and get building, make sure you establish your path to production first and build your delivery pipeline on day 1. You will be glad you did!

Interview with an Industry Expert

Sara Gerion, Senior Solutions Architect, Amazon Web Services

Sara helps companies follow architectural best practices by providing guidance and recommendations to develop cloud solutions that are resilient, cost effective, performant, secure, sustainable, and managed with operational excellence. As a Senior Solutions Architect at AWS, Sara works closely with companies to ensure their business ambitions are met. She is the former lead of the Powertools for AWS Lambda (TypeScript) team and author of the first Logger utility.

Q: Before becoming a Senior Solutions Architect at AWS you were a backend engineer at DAZN, one of the very early adopters of serverless. How has backend engineering evolved since the emergence of serverless and the move toward event-driven architectures?

I still remember vividly the first time I used an AWS Lambda function in production. It was 2018. Before then, I was already familiar with Amazon S3, but it was only when I learned about FaaS that I discovered the concept of serverless computing. At the time, AWS Lambda was nothing like what I had seen before and I was immediately intrigued by its simplicity and capabilities. That moment marked what I consider my first step into the serverless space. Shortly after, I intentionally joined a fast-paced company which was one of the early adopters of the serverless-first mindset, and learned firsthand how enterprises can leverage serverless in production to quickly deliver business value and differentiate themselves.

Anecdotally, I observed that by nature of its simplicity serverless made the entrance to the world of cloud more accessible to backend engineers who did not have much cloud experience beforehand. There is no need to learn how to manage servers at scale. Great, right?

Because of the monitoring solutions like logging or metrics provided out of the box by using serverless, I also observed that engineers got closer to the observability space and best practices. In my experience, backend engineers who ship code running on AWS Lambda functions tend to own and maintain not only the code of the business logic, but also the infrastructure as code codebase and the observability of the architecture and backend application. Taking ownership of the operational aspects contributes to a culture of shared responsibility, a "you build it, you run it" mindset, and a shift toward a wider adoption of DevOps practices. As a backend engineer, I remember I felt empowered to build anything: the sky is the limit.

A decade ago, designing and maintaining event-driven architectures that included, for example, a queuing system was a task mainly owned by system administrators. At a big scale, ownership of that task was not accessible to most backend engineers. Serverless made it easier to adopt and leverage event-driven architectures by removing the need to manage much of the underlying infrastructure.

I expect that the positive impact on the backend engineering community will continue with the introduction of new serverless services and integrations.

Q: You wrote a brilliant Twitter thread in December 2020 that included the statement "You'd want to get to a point when a production deployment is not a celebration, but a very boring, frequent occurrence." How can enterprise teams make their serverless releases as boring as possible?

The word "boring" can have a positive connotation when talking about software releases.

When serverless releases are rare, include many changes at once, have unpredictable outcomes, and are treated as extraordinary events, they are often followed by big celebrations or frustrations depending on the outcome of each release and may become a source of additional stress for the team.

Conversely, when serverless releases are frequent, uneventful, and predictable, teams responsible for those releases are empowered to deliver business value quickly and continuously.

Teams who want to make their serverless releases as boring as possible can do so by adopting certain strategies and best practices. I had the privilege of working in high-performing engineering teams in the past, and based on that experience I can say that this is a journey: changes do not happen from one day to another, but the results can be rewarding.

Enterprise teams need to pay particular attention to their feature release strategy and CI/CD pipelines. In each environment, the minimum viable product should include monitoring solutions that help teams understand the health of their workload at any time, without the need to guess or ship new code. Examples of such solutions are tracing, logging, together with a monitoring dashboard and alerts based on metrics.

Implementing automated tests as part of CI/CD pipelines will improve software quality, reduce manual effort, and accelerate the development lifecycle. Teams should of course implement the types of tests that make the most sense for their use case.

Planning a release strategy from the very beginning to make it incremental and with fast iterations will also accelerate the software development lifecycle. Additionally, when implementing a new code functionality, teams don't need to wait for it to be ready to get user traffic before deploying it in the production environment. Teams can already deploy it "turned off" and enable it when the time is right by using feature flags.

Resilience also plays an important role. Teams should design their MVP for fault tolerance and implement automated error handling by proactively asking themselves about the failure modes of their serverless architecture.

In general, automation is key to keep things boring.

From a more human perspective, I personally believe that empowering everyone in the engineering team to get used to deploying to production without fear will be beneficial to the whole team in the long term. To achieve this, each team member should learn what steps to do before, during, and after a deployment or release. Team members less used to deploying should be the ones who need to practice the most. Every person in the team should feel equally empowered.

Q: As a well-known member of the serverless community for a number of years, how important is the community when it comes to defining serverless best practices and how can teams tap into the power of the community to begin learning from other users and advocates?

I cannot stress enough how important the community is when it comes to defining serverless best practices. Serverless is a fast-paced, ever-evolving space and the community plays an important role in this ecosystem. Gaining insights about the perspectives of people from diverse backgrounds and roles had a huge positive impact on my own growth and skill development, and I am sure that applies to many others. People with different levels of proficiency in serverless technologies can equally contribute to this flourishing community by sharing their unique perspectives and experiences.

The community's strength can be harnessed in both digital and physical settings. The community is responsible for the creation of an incredible variety of tech content, such as blog posts and open source projects, together with different kinds of initiatives and resources, many of which are free. This makes learning about serverless accessible and inclusive of everyone.

Last but not least, attending in-person events organized by local community chapters and connecting with community members on social media platforms are both powerful ways to network, learn from each other, and find mentorship opportunities.

I am grateful to be a part of this community.

Q: You were a big influence in bringing the indispensable AWS Lambda Powertools developer toolkit to Node.js and TypeScript functions. What advice would you give to enterprise teams when it comes to writing and operating Lambda functions?

As a former member of the Powertools for AWS Lambda maintainers team, I had the privilege of working alongside incredible AWS employees and community members. During that time, I contributed to the library as the lead of the Powertools for AWS Lambda (TypeScript) maintainers team and author of its Logger utility, but I want to highlight the fact that the library and the impact it had on the community are the result of many brilliant and talented people who all worked together to make it happen.

Enterprise teams responsible for writing and operating AWS Lambda functions can adopt Powertools for AWS Lambda to implement serverless best practices without the need to write much custom code. The library, which includes utilities for logging, tracing, metrics, and idempotency together with many others, relieves the operational burden needed to implement these functionalities. This means that teams are free to focus on features that matter the most for their business. The library helps enterprises standardize their organizational best practices, but it's important to add that start-ups can also benefit from leveraging this library because its utilities are designed to be incrementally adoptable for companies of different sizes and at any stage of their serverless journey.

Q: Writing documentation is usually one thing engineers know they could do more of, but it can be a difficult task. How have the teams you've worked with approached creating and maintaining documentation about their serverless applications?

Writing documentation can sometimes be perceived as a chore and a task that is not as important compared to writing code. I myself used to think this way years ago. With time and experience, I learned how important documentation is and what value it can bring to a team.

Up-to-date, easy-to-understand documentation can accelerate the onboarding of a new team member, helping them quickly and efficiently familiarize themselves with a particular codebase in a self-service mode. It can also help retain knowledge within the team and clarify past decisions or design choices when a team member responsible for those decisions leaves.

Documentation does not only come in the form of text, but also of cloud architecture designs. A serverless architecture design is a living document owned by the team responsible for that architecture.

Engineering teams should consider creating an architecture design of their application before they start with the implementation. This can be an opportunity to brainstorm, validate the architecture against best practices, avoid painful rewrites, and seek feedback from other stakeholders in their organization.

CHAPTER 7

Testing Serverless Applications

You hear that Mr. Anderson? That is the sound of inevitability.
—Agent Smith, *The Matrix*

In this chapter, you will explore the attributes and failure modes of serverless applications that influence a novel approach to testing. You will learn how to devise a test strategy for your team, and how to apply this strategy to your tests. The result will be a vastly simpler approach to testing that doesn't fixate on test categorization or aim for maximum code coverage but instead meets the goals of rapid delivery, fault tolerance, and observability.

Efforts to promote software quality have traditionally been focused on identifying and eradicating bugs. The perceived quality of a piece of software was often measured by what went wrong with it. If bugs appeared in production, gaps in test suites were found and filled with more tests.

But software has evolved, and at the same time user demands have skyrocketed. Software must now be highly available, low-latency, and in a constant state of iteration. The way engineers build software has changed to meet these demands. Modern applications are cloud native, geographically and logically distributed, and a mixture of first-party, third-party, and open source code. To be able to build and operate software like this, while enforcing quality, engineering teams need to run tests that give maximum confidence in minimum time, deploy changes rapidly, understand application behavior instantly, and recover from failures automatically.

Bugs Are Inevitable

It's March 2016 in Seoul, South Korea. The greatest Go player of the past decade and winner of 18 world titles, Lee Sedol, sits down to play a new challenger. But there's one key difference to this opponent: it's a computer program. AlphaGo (*https://oreil.ly/YxMMb*) has been built and trained by its creator DeepMind with tree search algorithms, neural networks, and reinforcement learning.

Some 200 million people tuned in to watch AlphaGo defeat Lee Sedol 4–1; an emphatic, unexpected victory. This was a triumph for software engineering. But AlphaGo wasn't entirely void of performance blips, and at one point, midway through the match, it seemingly experienced a glitch. This prompted Andrew Jackson of the American Go Association to remark (*https://oreil.ly/mGFzS*) while commentating on the match: "If DeepMind has figured out how to write code that doesn't have bugs, that is a bigger news story than AlphaGo."

Even in the face of an incredible feat of artificial intelligence, the presence of bugs in software seems inevitable. Indeed, bugs are so synonymous with software that it can seem like a hopeless task to rid your applications of them entirely. Should you instead learn to live with, and even embrace, the bugs in your software?

In the pursuit of a development model that can support the required level of delivery, observability, resiliency, and scalability, software engineers have been on a constant quest to decouple components in their systems over the last decade. Several patterns and techniques have been devised to support decoupling, from domain-driven design to microservices, event-driven architecture to serverless itself. But approaches to testing software have not kept up. You can go to great lengths to decouple the development and operation of your software only to couple it again during testing (see Figure 7-1).

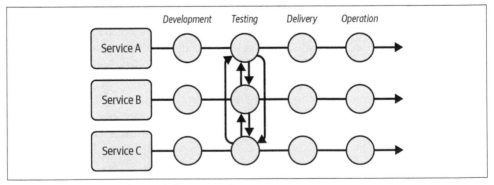

Figure 7-1. Coupling decoupled services during testing

Testing strategies are still rigid and heavily reliant on deploying applications in order to test them as whole systems. Once deployed, APIs are called, functions are invoked, database tables are written to and read from, events are produced, and messages are sent. Applications are tested from one end to another, and each step in the flow is asserted and verified. In reality, does a distributed, event-driven system even have two distinct ends?

In an event-driven serverless application, microservices (each a logical collection of resources scoped to a particular function of a domain) are decoupled by design. Serverless services can be iterated on independently from other services in the application's source code. Services are operated independently and can be scaled according to where demand is in the system. Crucially, services can also continue to operate normally even while other services are suffering from throttling or outages.

Ultimately, if your services are decoupled in development and at runtime, you must avoid coupling them in your tests. This chapter will help you to understand why serverless testing can be challenging and how to devise your own serverless testing strategy.

How Can Serverless Applications Be Tested?

Serverless is an entirely new software engineering paradigm. The low-cost, ephemeral nature of serverless technology provides benefits such as increased product delivery speed, abundant freedom to experiment and iterate, and bolstered confidence in the team's ability to ship scalable, resilient applications.

Of course, with these benefits come unique challenges—and testing serverless applications always takes the top spot when someone writes a list of "things that are hard about serverless."

Why Serverless Requires a Novel Approach to Testing

There are several attributes of typical serverless applications that make them difficult to test and force us to devise a different approach:

Latency
> Requests to microservices and APIs can vary in latency, with high or unpredictable latency common in services that consist of multistep workflows or require the use of third-party webhooks to complete processing (see "Understanding the performance measures of distributed serverless applications" on page 48). Tests with highly variable execution times can often time out unexpectedly and can be difficult to comprehend and debug.

Event-driven communication

Aside from request/response API endpoints, the majority of components in a serverless application will be logically decoupled and triggered into action by events from other components. These could include asynchronous APIs, which implement mechanisms that only return an acknowledgment to the consumer rather than a full response. Event-driven architectures can be notoriously difficult to test when applying strategies not fit for purpose.

Managed services

Managed services are the defining feature of serverless applications deployed to AWS. The code that powers these services is developed and operated by AWS. This makes them opaque boxes dotted around your architecture; components you do not own, control, or fully understand. The key question here is what parts of these managed services you should be testing, if any.

Distribution

Whole applications and even distinct microservices can be distributed across networked computers, cloud resources, regions, and accounts. Backups, replicas, shards, and eventually consistent database tables can make systems under test moving targets.

Cloud native

At its core, serverless is a modern evolution of cloud native technology. Serverless was born in the cloud and designed to fully leverage the benefits of the cloud. This is incredibly powerful when operating your workloads in production but has presented challenges to engineering teams that are used to running and testing their code locally before pushing it to a production, or production-like, environment. Numerous tools and techniques exist to make emulating AWS resources on your machine possible. But the fact remains: it is inordinately difficult to run traditional integration and functional tests without deploying resources to the cloud. This results in a longer feedback loop and development cycle and can severely slow test execution.

A distributed, event-driven, serverless application with all of these attributes becomes very difficult to build, test, deploy, and operate as a whole—treating a serverless application as a single application simply does not scale as the codebase grows.

You should instead view your serverless system as a collection of distinct applications. And, by extension, you can only ensure the quality of the whole system by applying quality controls to its components. Each component is intentionally decoupled and operates with minimal interfacing with or dependencies on other components. If you attempt to control the quality of the system as a whole you will negate many of the benefits of serverless and, ultimately, fail to properly or efficiently enforce quality.

You will most likely be able to see this already in the your engineering practices: you may have begun to split services into directories so they can be worked on independently, you may deploy these services in isolation via their own dedicated delivery pipelines and CloudFormation stacks, and you may have pinpointed service-level metrics to trigger alerts rather than generic application or API-level ones.

The Serverless Square of Balance: The Trade-off Between Delivery and Stability

It is time to introduce the *serverless square of balance* (Figure 7-2). The square of balance illustrates the four key activities that must be undertaken to achieve a resilient, high-quality serverless application: *test*, *deliver*, *observe*, and *recover*. Crucially, it is not enough to simply conduct these activities; they must be designed and undertaken in the most efficient way possible. In addition, they must all be balanced against one another, without overly relying on one or two techniques. Achieving this balance of focus in your microservices is the key to serverless harmony.

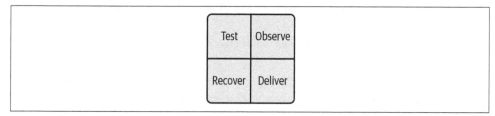

Figure 7-2. The serverless square of balance

The authors of Google's book *Site Reliability Engineering* (O'Reilly) assert that software can be *too stable*, to the point that stability can be detrimental to quality: "maximizing stability limits how fast new features can be developed and how quickly products can be delivered to users, and dramatically increases their cost, which in turn reduces the number of features a team can afford to offer." They encourage you to take calculated risks when verifying your software before shipping it: "Our goal is to explicitly align the risk taken by a given service with the risk the business is willing to bear. We strive to make a service reliable enough, but no more reliable than it needs to be."

The risks you take to increase delivery speed by reducing test coverage must always be counteracted with useful alerts, automated recovery from failure, and effective debugging of root causes.

Move fast and make things

Chapter 6 discussed the importance of establishing and maintaining a rapid development and delivery workflow, as well as preparing for everything to fail by making operations tolerant of faults and able to recover automatically.

The quality of a serverless application relies on delivery speed and application stability. In most cases, speed should always be preferred to stability. Stability is a product of speed; without speed there is no stability.

Optimizing for speed is often seen as a decision to sacrifice quality. Take the old Facebook engineering adage: "move fast and break things." This implies your applications must be broken if you are to develop them quickly. Research by DORA (*https://oreil.ly/S429w*) found the opposite to be true among high-performing software product teams. First published in the book *Accelerate*, by Nicole Forsgren, Jez Humble, and Gene Kim (IT Revolution), the Google Cloud team's research found that high-performing teams delivered code into production (from commit to deployment) 440 times faster than low-performing teams while having a change failure rate 5 times lower.

In serverless applications, maintaining the quickest possible delivery speed underpins your entire strategy for promoting quality and a great user experience. It's no use budgeting for errors and fine-tuning your alerts to identify bugs as soon as possible if you cannot remove the bugs from your production environment rapidly.

Balancing test coverage with observability and recovery

As your serverless application grows, exponentially adding tests for new features and regressions will prove to be the biggest drag on delivery speed. Excessive test suites will drastically slow down your engineers and your pipelines. Instead, you need to find a way to balance between pre-deployment testing and observability and resiliency in production.

As Cindy Sridharan says in her seminal post "Testing Microservices, the Sane Way" (*https://oreil.ly/YMl1P*): "When it comes to testing...microservices, most organizations seem to be quite attached to an antediluvian model of testing all components in unison. Elaborate testing pipeline infrastructures are considered mandatory to enable this form of end-to-end testing where the test suite of every service is executed to confirm there aren't any regressions or breaking changes being introduced." She goes on to suggest: "to be able to craft a holistic strategy for understanding how our services function and gain confidence in their correctness, it becomes salient to be able to pick and choose the right subset of testing techniques given the availability, reliability and correctness requirements of the service."

By far the most effective strategy to improve delivery speed is to reduce pre-deployment test coverage. This may seem counterintuitive to preserving quality at first, but only when this action is assessed in isolation. Reducing test coverage without introducing any other quality assurance (QA) methods is never going to be a good idea.

Any perceived drop in pre-deployment test coverage made to preserve delivery speed should be balanced with other forms of QA, including alerting of degraded performance of critical user experiences and the ability to recover from any bugs that may be introduced. You can read more about the emergent practice of observability in Chapter 8 and more about fault tolerance in Chapter 6.

The key to a scalable, effective set of tests is defining a clear test strategy to help engineers understand what to test and when to test it. Without this strategy, test suites and staging environments can quickly balloon out of control and grind development and delivery to a halt.

Serverless Failure Modes and Effects Analysis

To decide on an appropriate test strategy for your serverless application you first need to understand what can go wrong. Given the extensive use of managed services in serverless applications, it is also important to understand the division of responsibility between you and AWS.

 This chapter primarily covers the aspects of software testing that are unique to serverless and how your mindset needs to shift. However, it's important to note that your fundamental approach to testing will largely remain the same, and the majority of the tests you usually write will still need to be written and executed. This is particularly true for the business logic you implement in your language of choice and run in Lambda functions. You should use unit tests to maintain the quality of this code in the exact same way as when you ran it on servers.

What can go wrong?

Failure modes will largely depend on the architecture and logic of the application. When designing or implementing a new serverless application or feature, you should analyze the architecture and explore the things that could fail in production.

To help frame your analysis, let's review some common serverless failures:

- Insufficient IAM permissions is a very common issue. It typically manifests in "unauthorized operation" or "access denied" errors when a resource attempts to perform an operation not permitted by its IAM role. Wherever possible, IAM policies should be automated with an IaC tool (see Chapter 6 for more information).

- Requests to API Gateway endpoints can fail due to misconfigured integrations with Lambda function handlers or responses that exceed the maximum timeout (*https://oreil.ly/nvUzR*), which at the time of writing is 30 seconds for HTTP APIs and 29 seconds for REST APIs.

- Lambda function invocations can time out or exceed their memory allocations. Function invocations can also be throttled if the maximum number of account-wide concurrent executions is exceeded.

- DynamoDB operations made via the AWS SDK could fail due to incorrect syntax or document paths. Read and write operations could also be throttled if the associated capacity units are exceeded during spikes in traffic.

- EventBridge rule invocations could fail if the target is incorrectly configured. An event bus could also fail to ingest an event if the maximum payload size of 256 KB (at the time of writing) is exceeded. Such a failure can easily occur at runtime if you have a property with a potentially large value.

- A Step Functions workflow may not execute to completion if a step with a direct service integration fails. A workflow could also fail to execute if the maximum input size of 256 KB (at the time of writing) is exceeded. Again, such a failure can easily occur at runtime if you have a property with a potentially large value.

- SQS queues with dead letter queues and automatic redrive policies are susceptible to "poison-pill" messages that will continue to fail whenever delivery is retried. If these build up, it can disrupt the queue and any downstream consumers.

- Kinesis streams can fail if delivery targets are misconfigured.

Failure Modes and Effects Analysis worksheet

The Failure Modes and Effects Analysis (FMEA) worksheet in Appendix C can be used to determine and categorize potential failure modes for the services in your application. As you analyze the types of failures that could occur when operating your application in a production environment, use the FMEA worksheet to guide your analysis, recording the details of possible failures along with their causes and effects.

For each failure, you should rate the probability of it occurring, the severity of the failure's effects if it does occur, and the likelihood of the fault being detected by a test suite before deployment to production (for example, using a five-point scale). Each failure can then be assigned a risk level by multiplying the probability by the severity and adding the detection rating. The risk levels can be used to prioritize test coverage or work on observability and fault tolerance.

Designing a Serverless Test Strategy

The test-driven development (TDD) movement that was popularized in the early 2000s made testing a primary concern for software engineers and championed automation over human toil. Automated testing has since become the status quo. Manual testing still has a role to play, but it should only be applied in appropriate scenarios, never as the default. Predictability is of course a key feature of automated tests, and this will be explored later in this chapter.

Beyond the sociotechnical behaviors TDD encourages, the core practice of TDD involves first writing tests that will fail based on a feature's requirements and then implementing that feature until the tests pass. In reality, with cloud native serverless applications you will find you rarely run tests locally, aside perhaps from directly before committing the code changes to source control. This is mainly due to the difficulties associated with emulation.

With web applications or monolithic backends, it is trivial to spin up local instances and continually run full end-to-end test suites in response to every code change you make in your IDE. Testing *can* be a part of the development cycle. Testing cloud native software involves a different approach in order to integrate it into a rapid development feedback loop; this has forced engineering teams to rethink the role testing plays in developer workflows.

 When you're getting started with serverless, it can seem like a disadvantage to not be able to trivially run your code locally. However, if you can find an ergonomic, *quick-enough* workflow that suits you (see Chapter 6 for more on this topic), exclusively running and testing your code in the cloud will provide the most accurate (if not the fastest) feedback. You certainly won't have any "it works on my machine" debates anymore.

Serverless engineers work best when contributing tightly scoped changes and frequently integrating these changes with the rest of the codebase. The changes can be deployed in isolation to the cloud and tested in full. The difference is that the feedback an engineer receives is obtained remotely, in a delivery pipeline running on a continuous integration platform, rather than locally in a terminal on their machine.

Any serverless test strategy must be designed with the unique attributes of serverless applications in mind and optimized to support the serverless engineering workflow, as described in Chapter 6. Devising a test strategy as early as possible in the lifetime of your application is absolutely crucial to the scalability of its development and its stability. Applying an ill-conceived or organically evolving test strategy will eventually catch up with you and drastically slow down delivery, which in turn will impact stability and quality.

Identifying the Critical Paths

A critical path is typically a user experience that is critical to the operation of your business. Examples of user requests that follow critical paths include ordering a taco, making a payment for your child's Christmas present, donating to a charitable cause, or tracking a parcel. If these requests go wrong or don't work as expected, it can be considered detrimental to the service your business offers to its consumers.

Identifying the critical paths in your application can help you decide how to apply the serverless square of balance and focus your engineering resources.

Critical paths

Your users are usually *present* at some stage of a request's journey along a critical path. These requests are typically time-sensitive and expect a synchronous response. When it comes to critical paths, recovery from failure (or fault tolerance) is a less viable strategy for supporting the quality of your application. Retrying requests could increase latency to an unacceptable level, and your ability to retry these operations will be diminished when the user is no longer present or available to give explicit permission.

The operational quality of critical paths should be primarily supported through extensive test coverage and alerting. You must ship as few bugs as possible to these microservices.

The topic of load testing may seem redundant when it comes to serverless workloads. After all, you have chosen serverless for scalability. Yet, while your APIs and Lambda functions will usually surprise you with their effortless ability to scale to your spikiest traffic, it is still very worthwhile to conduct a series of tests that put your application under various load profiles. Load testing your critical paths in particular is essential before any user events of significant scale.

You should analyze your predicted traffic and usage patterns and design performance test scenarios based on these predictions and historical data. Pay particular attention to integration points between different AWS managed services where usage volume quotas apply (see Chapter 8) and any connections between your application and third-party APIs or internal downstream systems that may not be capable of the same scalability as your application.

Noncritical paths

The noncritical paths in your application will usually be background processes. These will not be time-sensitive and will be fully recoverable in the event of performance degradation or outages resulting from transient bugs or persistent errors, or following a code fix or rollback.

The operational quality of noncritical paths should be primarily supported through alerting and fault tolerance. You can afford to ship a higher percentage of bugs that disrupt these paths, within your error budgets (see Chapter 8 for more information about error budgets).

Is it a critical path?

Here are some questions you can pose about your microservices to understand whether they include critical paths:

- Is someone or something relying on the request being served in a timely manner; either near-immediate (synchronous responses) or as-soon-as-possible (asynchronous responses)?
- Can the request be idempotently retried at a later date?
- Does handling the request involve storing or updating application or business-critical data?

Just Enough and Just-in-Time Testing

As you have seen so far in this chapter, with serverless your test coverage should be kept to a minimum and be focused on your critical user experiences. You should test just enough of your application to provide the confidence required to release a change into production—serverless testing is not about catching all possible bugs, it's about catching the bugs that will wreak the most havoc on the user experience.

Per the serverless square of balance, testing cannot restrict your ability to deliver. If you have more than "just enough" tests and they take too long to execute (or even worse, are flaky and require multiple runs to pass), this will harm engineering productivity. In some cases, an inefficient test strategy can deter engineers from making frequent releases due to the burden and frustration associated with deploying changes.

Just enough testing

Adopting a test strategy of "test everything all the time" simply does not scale. As your application's codebase grows and becomes increasingly fragmented across microservices and infrastructure stacks, this all-encompassing test strategy will require you to continually add more tests, spreading those tests across more service boundaries. No matter how much you optimize the performance and parallelization of these tests, they will inevitably take longer and longer to run and become more complex to orchestrate.

Test coverage can be limited to the minimum level by adapting it according to production stability and risk of bugs: reduce tests for highly stable user experiences and temporarily increase coverage for unstable ones until they stabilize. Remove tests that rarely or never fail, as they are probably not testing anything that is likely to break in production. Also remove flaky tests that often fail initially and pass when retried. Flaky tests will promote a culture of easily ignoring test results and quickly erode confidence in your test strategy, similar to an alert that is always ignored.

 While removing tests that provide little or no value is a sensible strategy for achieving an efficient balance between delivery and stability, this approach should always be used with caution. You must fully understand the purpose of a test and be sure of its lack of value before removing it. You can also consider running the test less frequently before removing it altogether.

Mutation testing (*https://oreil.ly/nqjKy*) is a technique that involves deliberately introducing bugs and seeing which tests catch them. As your application matures and grows, you can use mutation testing as a method for identifying useless tests.

Your test suites can also be limited by the types of tests that you write and execute. A sound strategy to apply to serverless applications is to prefer *static* testing as far as possible. Static testing does not require deployment of microservices to the cloud and can be implemented via unit tests and static analysis. These static tests can be further limited by primarily focusing them on your critical paths.

Just-in-time testing

To efficiently test and deliver your serverless applications, it is not enough to limit your test coverage; you must also limit the number of times those tests are run.

Serverless and infrastructure as code make it possible and inexpensive to replicate your production environment. However, if a test passes in one non-production environment, it is likely to pass in any others. What really matters is that the code runs as expected in production. This means it is crucial to deliver that code as quickly as possible to your production environment and leverage observability to learn about your application's behavior under real traffic.

The practice of continuous integration encourages teams to integrate code changes as regularly as possible and is a prerequisite for continuous delivery. The Minimum Viable CD manifesto (*https://oreil.ly/yUmcQ*) recommends that "work integrates to the trunk at a minimum daily."

 For a deep dive into continuous integration, be sure to read Martin Fowler's canonical article from 2006 (*https://oreil.ly/YO-Nk*).

Prior to releasing your code, the most important thing is iteration speed and integration. The closer you test your code to production, the more valuable the results of these tests will be. You need to *shift right* on testing and make it later in your software's delivery lifecycle. In general, you should perform the bulk of testing *just* before deploying to production; this is when it matters most as the code is closest to being released to your users.

The best time to catch a bug is before it has the chance to impact a large percentage of your users—just in time. This could be in a pre-production staging environment or in production itself, through post-deployment tests like synthetic canaries or efficient, finely tuned alerts.

Environments

The traditional approach to software testing involves the use of multiple pre-production, or *staging*, environments. A snapshot of the application is deployed to the first environment in the chain and then promoted to the next environment as soon as all the tests pass, until this version of the application finally reaches production.

The common perception here is that testing the application multiple times provides a greater guarantee of quality. While this may be true for monolithic applications, the opposite is true for distributed, serverless applications. Simulating the variables and emergent complexity of your serverless application's production environment is impossible. You should instead run tests in as few environments as you are comfortable with; ideally no more than one or two. The further away a code change is from production, the less confidence (and therefore value) a test can provide.

One of the conundrums of serverless is the proliferation of non-production environments. The ability to provision and replicate applications across AWS accounts with speed and integrity is definitely a major benefit of serverless. However, this has been misused in an attempt to provide temporary environments to run automated tests for every single pull request. This is ultimately the antithesis of continuous integration. Many serverless teams that have adopted this practice have seen their pull request integration times exponentially increase as their codebases grow.

These ephemeral pull request environments can still be useful, but they should be used sparingly for specific scenarios. In general, you should use pull request environments with caution and only run tests against deployed resources when you absolutely need to. Instead, you should leverage *instant* environments if you need to run integration tests on deployed resources. Instant environments are provisioned just for tests and are isolated to the system under test, which is usually two or three integrated components.

Upholding Standards with a Definition of Done

You may have encountered different forms of a "definition of done" or seen various implementations of such a document. The Scrum.org Scrum Glossary (*https://oreil.ly/ bvvIu*) defines this as:

> A formal description of the state of the Increment when it meets the quality measures required for the product. The moment a Product Backlog item meets the Definition of Done, an Increment is born. The Definition of Done creates transparency by providing everyone a shared understanding of what work was completed as part of the Increment. If a Product Backlog item does not meet the Definition of Done, it cannot be released.

The core intent of a definition of done is simple: if a change "meets the quality measures," it can be released. A definition of done can be used to provide a very simple indicator of whether a change to your application can be shipped to your users. That moment of merging a change to the trunk and triggering an automated deployment can be tense and fraught. To counteract these feelings, it can be useful to remind yourself of what "done" really means.

Defining Done

Nothing is ever truly done. Software is never perfect. Bugs are inevitable.

The Cult of Done Manifesto (*https://oreil.ly/urUhZ*) is a motivational resource for getting things done, whatever your task may be. Point 12 rings particularly true for serverless software engineering: "If you have an idea and publish it on the internet, that counts as a ghost of done." This can be interpreted as defining "done" as getting something in front of your users. It doesn't matter if that thing is complete and polished; what matters most is that it is now gathering usage data that can be used to inform improvements.

Shipping imperfect features should never be confused with promoting unilateral, careless engineering. Software engineering should always be a social activity and the needs of your users held in the highest regard. But the best software is always software that is being used.

If you don't ship your software you will never know if it really works in production, under real traffic and with all the other code and variables out there in the wild. A definition of done checklist will give you the right confidence to ship: not so much in whether your change will work but in that you'll know if it isn't working.

Go forth and release the ghosts of done!

Answering the following questions will allow you to pragmatically decide whether a change can be released or not. Document them somewhere accessible to your engineers and attach this document to any artifacts associated with the work being undertaken, such as pull requests or task tickets:

How will the quality of this code be measured?
> This will be down to your team to decide. You could link quality to service level objectives (explored in Chapter 8), application performance metrics, or business metrics.

How will this code be released to production users?
> It might be released immediately upon deployment, rolled out with a blue/green strategy, or constitute a dark release where it is available in production but not publicized to users.

How will you know if this code is broken before production?
> What pre-deployment tests are in place, and what aspects or failure modes of the code do they cover?

How will you know if this code is broken in production?
> What alerts are in place, and under what conditions will these alerts be triggered?

How will you be able to debug this code if it breaks in production?
> Is distributed tracing enabled for this component? What logs are available? Is there a runbook for triaging potential or known failures?

How will this code recover from failure in production?
> How is this code tolerant of faults, either its own or others? What recovery mechanisms are in place (for example, dead letter queues and retries)?

Hands-on Serverless Testing

From the previous sections of this chapter, you should have started to form a mental model of how to approach testing a serverless application. Now it's time to look at applying this model to an example architecture.

Before testing any application, it is important to understand exactly *what* you are testing. As you've seen in this chapter, serverless applications will most likely be substantially different from other types of applications you and your team have tested in the past, such as monolithic server-based backends or client-centric web applications. The two attributes of serverless that most impact testing are the extensive use of managed services and the event-driven interaction between these services as data flows through the system.

Event-Driven Testing

If you look beyond the purpose of your software product and the myriad AWS services available to you and instead scrutinize the patterns and actors in a serverless application, you will notice a group of recurring elements (see Figure 7-3). When dissected, an event-driven serverless application consists purely of business logic, managed services, and the integration points between them. Effective testing relies on a clear delineation of the responsibilities between you and AWS. You are responsible for testing the business logic and integration configuration that you own. Take care not to test the managed services, events, integrations, and APIs that AWS owns.

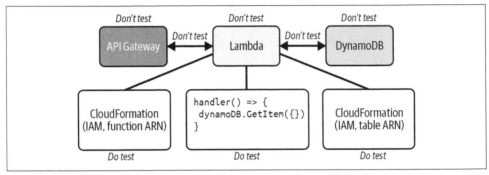

Figure 7-3. What to test and what not to test in a serverless application

Let's take a closer look at where you should focus your testing efforts.

Business logic, integration points, and data contracts

These are the three fundamental building blocks to event-driven, serverless applications that are crucial to understand in order to test such applications:

Business logic

The code that you write and deploy to AWS for execution is the business logic of your application; the parts of your software that encode the functional requirements and business rules of the application's domain. The business logic is the internal mechanics of your system that you own. You are responsible for authoring, maintaining, deploying, and operating this code. You are also responsible for testing this code.

Integration points

The distributed components of a serverless application operate in isolation and communicate their independent activity to each other through asynchronous events or synchronous requests. Architecturally speaking, these events and requests reside in a zone between the source and target that can be referred to as an *integration point*. The integration point between two components represents the method of communication and the format and structure of the messages passed between them. The integration points in your system will almost exclusively be owned and operated by AWS, but you will be responsible for configuring these integration points and defining the rules that govern the communication.

Data contracts

A data contract is an encoded ruleset to facilitate communication between logically decoupled services. These contracts are applied between two components in your system, at their point of integration, and enforce the target's expectations of a source. As well as facilitating verifiable communication at runtime, data contracts are crucial to enabling a scalable and efficient test strategy.

Figure 7-4 shows how these elements map to a simple serverless architecture: the EventBridge managed service is used alongside business logic in a Lambda function, and you can see two integration points and the types of data contracts that can exist between the components. The following sections introduce the types of tests that can be used to test this architecture.

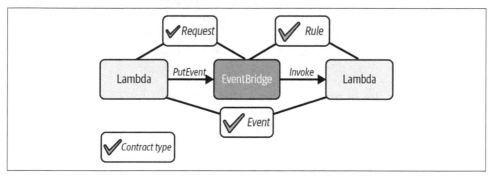

Figure 7-4. Reference architecture of a simple event-driven flow showing a common serverless pattern

Integration points testing checklist

For each integration point you should capture the failure modes for the categories listed in Table 7-1 and decide whether to cover them with tests.

Table 7-1. Integration points testing checklist

Failure category	Description	Recommended tests
Configuration	You are responsible for configuring the integration points between managed services, such as event buses and rules. You should verify that the integration exists and is configured according to AWS rules and your business requirements.	Infrastructure tests, unit tests
Permissions	You are responsible for granting the necessary permissions for integrated components to interact with each other. You should verify that the source component has permission to publish events or messages and the target has permission to consume them.	Infrastructure tests

Failure category	Description	Recommended tests
Payloads	The communication channel and message payload used by integrated components should be verified to ensure that an event producer is sending messages according to the contract and the consumer is handling input according to the contract.	Unit tests, contract tests, static analysis

 Remember not to couple decoupled components in your tests. Whenever possible, test the source and target of an integration point separately.

Unit Testing Business Logic in Lambda Functions

The business logic of a serverless application is written and executed in Lambda functions. The bulk of business logic testing can thus be achieved through unit tests that assert the various operations of a Lambda function. You will usually test the individual operations of a Lambda function in isolation rather than testing the function as a whole, by calling the handler method, for instance.

Making your Lambda functions testable will usually involve abstracting and isolating your business logic and sharing the methods with test files. In this simple example of a testable Node.js Lambda function, the `greeting` method can easily be called and verified:

```
export const greeting = (name) => {
  return `hello ${name}`;
}

export const handler = async (event) => {
  return greeting(event.name)
};
```

The corresponding unit test can import the abstracted method and verify it in isolation:

```
import { greeting } from "./";

test("Should say hello world", () => {
  const actual = greeting("world");
  const expected = "hello world";
  expect(actual).toEqual(expected);
});
```

Mocking

Unit tests should be predictable. In other words, a unit test should produce the same result every time it is executed with the same input.

Take the `addNumbers` method shown here:

```
export const addNumbers = (numbers) => {
  return numbers.reduce((a, b) => {
    return a + b;
  });
};

export const handler = async (event) => {
  return addNumbers(event.numbers);
};
```

This method can be unit tested, as any assertions will always produce the same results:

```
import { addNumbers } from "./";

test("Should calculate 1+2+3+4=10", () => {
  const actual = addNumbers([1, 2, 3, 4]);
  const expected = 10;
  expect(actual).toEqual(expected);
});
```

Any nontrivial Lambda function will usually contain side effects, such as network requests to third-party vendors or AWS SDK calls. These side effects are inherently unpredictable—a side effect could rely on a network connection to the public internet, for example. The computed result of a side effect may also depend upon a third-party implementation that is subject to change.

To keep unit tests predictable (and fast), side effects must be mocked.

A popular criticism of mocking (or "stubbing") parts of a system under test is that it is not a true test of the system. This is certainly a valid criticism, but only if your aim is to properly replicate the whole system in order to verify its quality and adherence to its requirements.

You have already begun to see why testing a serverless system as a whole may not be the optimum strategy. Identifying the parts of your Lambda functions to mock is usually a byproduct of drawing the boundaries of responsibility between you and your vendors. It is a sensible strategy to mock any code that you are not responsible for testing or fixing.

Mocking is an essential tool when testing serverless microservices, but it is not without its pitfalls. The problem with mocking comes at scale. Your tests will scale with a lot less friction if you isolate mocks to individual tests and units under test rather than mocking once on a global level.

The following example uses the JavaScript AWS SDK to put an event on an Event-Bridge event bus:

```
import { EventBridgeClient, PutEventsCommand } from
    "@aws-sdk/client-eventbridge";

export const eventbridgeClient = new EventBridgeClient();

export const handler = async () => {
  const putEventsCommand = new PutEventsCommand({
    Entries: [
      {
        Detail: JSON.stringify({ "order": "1234" }),
        DetailType: "OrderCreated",
        EventBusName: "order-bus",
        Source: "service.order",
      },
    ],
  });

  await eventbridgeClient.send(putEventsCommand);

  return;
};
```

The send method on the EventBridge client can be mocked in the unit test. When the Lambda function handler is called, the SDK request won't be made. Instead, a *spy* can be attached to the mock, allowing you to assert that the SDK request will be made with specific parameters:

```
test("Should put event", async () => {
  const putEventsCommandSpy = jest
    .spyOn(eventbridgeClient, "send")
    .mockImplementation(() => {});

  await handler();

  expect(putEventsCommandSpy).toHaveBeenCalledTimes(1);

  expect(putEventsCommandSpy).toHaveBeenCalledWith(
    expect.objectContaining({
      input: {
        Entries: [
          {
```

```
                Detail: '{"orderId":"1234"}',
                DetailType: "OrderCreated",
                Source: "service.order",
            },
        ],
    },
    })
  );
});
```

Static analysis

If you are using a language and runtime that support static typing, you can leverage static analysis as a method to verify the requests sent to a third party and your handling of their responses.

 Static analysis is the process of verifying software without executing it.

Third parties will often provide official type definitions in various programming languages. These type definitions should be applied to operations in your Lambda functions that involve sending API requests and handling responses. Provided the type definitions are correct and synchronized with the version of the API you are using, you can assume that the request you send will be accepted and produce the expected result:

```
import { PaymentRequest, PaymentResponse } from "@payment/api"

const handler = async () => {
  const response: PaymentResponse = await fetch("https://pay.co/api/payment", {
    body: JSON.stringify({ "amount": 100 } as PaymentRequest),
      method: "POST",
  });

  return response.paymentId;
};
```

Aside from some specific scenarios, there is usually no need to make the API request to verify your integration with a third party. The type definitions represent your data contract with the third-party vendor. Figure 7-5 shows how this might look as a conversation.

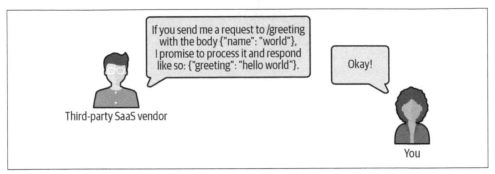

Figure 7-5. Contracts can be established between you and your third-party providers through request and response schemas and enforced in your codebase with type definitions and static analysis

Contract Testing Integration Points

The typical approach to testing the integration between two or more components (or microservices) in a system involves deploying the components, making a request to an entry point, such as an API endpoint, to trigger the integrated process, and asserting on the intermediate and ultimate state of the components.

This integration testing strategy usually requires the creation and maintenance of a complex delivery pipeline and produces brittle test suites that couple the decoupled components under test. While there may be scenarios where this approach makes sense, it will probably generate far too much overhead to be valuable.

Testing of the Cloud

One additional consideration for serverless applications is the role of managed services. The business logic components in your application will most likely be integrated with a managed service. Where integration points involve managed services, it becomes necessary to consider the remit of your operational and, by extension, your testing responsibility. You should only be testing the code you are responsible for and make sure you are not testing AWS. It can be useful to keep in mind the mantra, "If you can't fix it you shouldn't test it."

The shared responsibility model (covered in Chapter 4) for cloud security can be extended to provide guidance on where to draw the boundaries of application testing. The responsibility of AWS can broadly be described as *testing of the cloud*. Take the example of an EventBridge rule. It is your responsibility to configure the custom event bus that will receive events (unless you're using the default event bus), the event pattern to match against incoming events, and the target to trigger when matching events are received by the bus. AWS will operate the event bus, accept incoming events, analyze events for matching patterns, and trigger the corresponding targets.

You are responsible for the configuration of managed services and AWS is responsible for their operation. To preserve this boundary in your tests, you should be able to test this configuration without the need to invoke the underlying services.

Instead of testing integration points by deploying and invoking the integrated microservices and managed services, you can use data contracts to verify the correctness of integrations.

 You may have encountered contract testing before. The prevalent approach to contract testing involves the use of the Pact framework (*https://pact.io*). While you may choose to use such a framework, it is important to distinguish between the principle of contract testing (statically testing requests and responses against agreed data types) and the implementation of contract testing via frameworks such as Pact.

This chapter explores contract testing as a form of unit testing, without the use of any additional frameworks beyond standard primitives like JSON Schema.

In the context of a serverless application on AWS, a data contract can exist between any distinct resources that are connected by an asynchronous (e.g., event or message) or synchronous (e.g., API request) communication. A data contract could be enforced to verify the correctness of an integration for SQS messages, API Gateway integrations, Step Functions inputs, DynamoDB operation payloads, and so on.

As highlighted earlier in this section, for each integration point there are usually three elements to test: permissions, payloads, and configuration. Let's look at an example for each of these elements based on the reference architecture described in Figure 7-4.

Testing integration configuration

In our example architecture, you are responsible for the configuration of the custom EventBridge event bus and the EventBridge rule, which includes the event pattern and the target.

Using an IaC framework such as the AWS Cloud Development Kit allows you to make assertions about the resources in the underlying CloudFormation template.

This example demonstrates a strategy for testing EventBridge event patterns to ensure the rule will match events as expected:

```
import { Capture, Template } from "aws-cdk-lib/assertions";
import { EventBridgeClient, TestEventPatternCommand } from
    "@aws-sdk/client-eventbridge";
import OrderCreated from "./schema/service.order@OrderCreated-v1.json";
```

```
const eventbridge = new EventBridgeClient({});

test("OrderCreated rule event pattern matches OrderCreated events", async () => {
  const eventPatternCapture = new Capture();

  template.hasResourceProperties("AWS::Events::Rule", {
    EventPattern: eventPatternCapture,
  });

  const testOrderCreatedPatternCommand = new TestEventPatternCommand({
    Event: JSON.stringify({
      account: stack.account,
      "detail-type": OrderCreated["x-amazon-events-detail-type"],
      source: OrderCreated["x-amazon-events-source"],
      time: new Date(),
      region: stack.region,
    }),
    EventPattern: JSON.stringify(eventPatternCapture.asObject()),
  });

  const testOrderCreatedPattern = await eventbridge.send(
    testOrderCreatedPatternCommand
  );

  expect(testOrderCreatedPattern.Result).toEqual(true);
});
```

Testing integration permissions

In the example architecture, you are responsible for applying the necessary permissions for the event producer function to put events on the event bus and the rule to invoke the target function:

```
test("EventProducer function has permission to put events on OrdersBus", () => {
  template.hasResourceProperties("AWS::IAM::Policy", {
    PolicyDocument: {
      Statement: [
        {
          Action: "events:PutEvents",
          Effect: "Allow",
          Resource: {
            "Fn::GetAtt": [getLogicalId(stack, stack.eventBus), "Arn"],
          },
        },
      ],
      Version: "2012-10-17",
    },
    Roles: [
      {
        Ref: getLogicalId(stack, stack.eventProducer.role),
      },
    ],
```

```
    });
  });

  test("OrderCreated rule has permission to invoke EventConsumer function", () => {
    template.hasResourceProperties("AWS::Lambda::Permission", {
      Action: "lambda:InvokeFunction",
      FunctionName: {
        "Fn::GetAtt": [getLogicalId(stack, stack.eventConsumer), "Arn"],
      },
      SourceArn: {
        "Fn::GetAtt": [getLogicalId(stack, stack.orderCreatedRule), "Arn"],
      },
    });
  });
```

Testing integration payloads

In the example architecture, you can test the payload sent to EventBridge by the event producer Lambda function by verifying it against a schema definition of the event.

In JavaScript, you could use a JSON schema validation library, such as Ajv (*https://oreil.ly/RAxG5*):

```
import Ajv from "ajv";
import { generateOrder } from "./producer";
import OrderCreated from "../schema/service.order@OrderCreated-v1.json";

test("Should generate valid order", () => {
  const actual = generateOrder();
  const ajv = new Ajv();
  const validate = ajv.compile(OrderCreated);
  expect(validate(actual)).toEqual(true);
});
```

Summary

Testing serverless applications is generally considered a difficult task, but this is often because it's being viewed from the perspective of a traditional approach to testing. The reality is that there are attributes of a serverless application that can make certain testing strategies difficult to practice. So, you must reassess the way you test, as well as reconsidering your overall aims for testing and quality assurance.

Rather than battling with your serverless system under test, use its unique properties, such as its event-driven architecture and integration with managed services, to design a tailored testing strategy. Serverless testing provides maximum confidence with minimum coverage and should always be balanced with the needs of delivery, observation, and recovery. Understand what can go wrong with serverless, but recognize that bugs are inevitable. Focus on critical paths and use static unit tests and type analysis as far as possible.

Your first step should be to use the serverless square of balance to guide the process of defining your serverless test strategy. The earlier you do this in your project the better. Once you have identified your critical paths and agreed upon the components and integrations you need to cover with tests, you can begin to get an idea of how it feels to write and run these tests and gauge the confidence they give you to deliver code into production at speed.

You must be brave enough to learn about your application's behavior and layer in tests over time to account for emerging quirks and failures. As the serverless square of balance shows us, the key to a reliable application is leveraging observability and recovery alongside testing to maintain stability and speed. Armed with this understanding, it's time for you to explore serverless software operations!

Interview with an Industry Expert

Sarah Hamilton, AWS Community Builder and Senior Software Engineer

Sarah Hamilton is a Senior Software Engineer and an AWS Community Builder. During her career she's been a huge supporter of serverless technology, and she takes great pride in contributing to the entire development cycle, from designing architectures to the hands-on process of building and deploying solutions. Sarah enjoys sharing her knowledge by speaking at conferences and writing blog posts.

Q: Serverless has matured as a technology in the last couple of years, and best practices continue to evolve. However, testing still seems to be something teams find difficult to get right with serverless. How do you see the current state and best practice of serverless testing?

Undoubtedly, the testing of serverless applications is frequently overlooked or seen as an afterthought. Whilst I believe that our overall understanding of testing serverless applications is improving, there is still a lot of work to do. There are a few reasons why I believe we haven't progressed at a faster rate.

Firstly, whilst testing strategies for frontend applications are generally well understood and well documented, with unit tests for business logic and end-to-end browser tests, there is a lack of understanding over exactly what to test in the backend. A lot of my testing knowledge comes from speaking to others in the community and asking what they do. I will outline my current strategy toward testing:

1. Write unit tests for business logic before writing the logic itself. This is in line with traditional test-driven development. However, I find it to be far more important in serverless development as it speeds up your development feedback loop. You can simply develop while running your tests rather than deploying to test that your business logic works.

2. End-to-end tests are crucial, and the real infrastructure should be tested upon. When we build tests, we want to ensure that the testing environment mimics the production environment, and the best way to do this is to test on a deployed copy of the production environment. One caveat is that end-to-end tests tend to require more development time and creativity, and take longer to run in your CI/CD pipeline. That is why I would advocate choosing business-critical flows to test and investing in those. As an example, take a payment system comprising a few different services. An end-to-end test may simply be "Given an order is placed, then the orders table is updated." Whilst many different processes may have taken place in the services in between, the end-to-end test is capturing that a particular input produces a particular output. This is a useful test, as it indicates the overall health of the system. If the test fails, then we can assert that something is wrong. But how do we diagnose the exact service that is broken?

3. Integration tests! To have a better view of the system and diagnose a fault, it is important to have integration tests that test a narrower part of the system. You may have several integration tests which break down the overall end-to-end test. The following would be examples of integration tests:

   a. "Given an order is placed, then an `orderCreated` event arrives on the event bus."

   b. "Given an event arrives on the event bus, then the orders table is updated."

   You can see that the end-to-end test has been broken into two. If *a* fails and *b* passes, then we can assume there is a fault at the beginning of the flow—but the end-to-end test does not give you that level of detail.

Another issue that arises for developers writing tests is how to deal with the asynchronous nature of serverless applications. When testing on real infrastructure, you must handle the time taken to complete a process—after all, you designed your architecture to be decoupled and asynchronous. Unfortunately, there is no particularly smart way of handling this at the time of writing. I would opt for implementing retries on the assertions you are making and, after a reasonable amount of time, failing the test if your expected result doesn't come back. Of course, these timings and the number of retries can be tweaked as you get to know how your system performs.

In addition to this, some serverless services cannot be inspected easily with the cloud SDK you are using. Storage services can often be easily asserted, as you can usually get the object with the SDK and check the result you are expecting. Other tests can be trickier. Recently, I wanted to test that "Given an object is placed in storage, then the output of the subsequent function is X." I soon realized that I had no way of inspecting the output of the actual function using the SDK. I found myself writing unwieldy tests to inspect the logs to find the output which had been logged in the function. The test required many retries of various SDK calls. In the end, the test worked, but I decided to abandon it because it was not robust and would be confusing to any other developer who came across it. I decided that the end-to-end test would suffice. The lesson I learned from this is that integration testing is sometimes difficult and overcomplicated, but invaluable when done properly.

Q: As a serverless consultant you worked with many start-ups building diverse serverless applications. How did the test strategies differ between these teams and projects?

Given the context of collaborating with start-ups aiming to swiftly deliver applications to customers, a strategic decision must be made regarding the extent to which testing should be undertaken, with the ultimate goal of achieving a high-quality application.

During my time as a consultant, it was clear that some stakeholders, possessing a background in development, understood the significance of writing tests and upholding quality. Conversely, other stakeholders, with a background in business, emphasized speed over quality to meet deadlines. Consequently, the scope of testing could vary somewhat between projects.

With the passage of time, my perspective has evolved, highlighting the necessity of personally advocating for quality assurance. I now ensure that I withhold the label of "completion" until a satisfactory level of testing accompanies the code being deployed. That's not to say that you shouldn't have some flexibility, because "satisfactory" really does vary depending on the scale of the application being developed.

My definition of "satisfactory" (in terms of testing) for a start-up looking to quickly deliver to market would look something like the following:

1. Unit testing is done to a high standard—which means that there is high coverage. Any business logic should be well tested. Whether this is a start-up or a larger enterprise, this is nonnegotiable. It's a quick win and delivers a lot of confidence in your code and business logic. They also have a low overhead—unit tests tend to run extremely quickly, and therefore don't take up a large amount of time and resources in your CI/CD pipeline. In addition to this, artificial intelligence pair programmers are very effective at writing unit tests for code, making them extremely quick to produce (of course, these should be used with caution and should only be used as a guide). Code changes should not be merged without unit tests accompanying business logic.

2. An end-to-end/integration testing strategy is put together for business-critical paths. End-to-end/integration testing can be somewhat time-consuming, so it's understandable that a vast amount of time spent on this may not be welcomed by stakeholders pushing to get a product out. This is where it's about compromise. Identify your business-critical paths—the paths that must work for the application to be functional. For an ecommerce website, this may be the "modifying cart" flow and the "payments" flow. Once you have identified these, think of a

testing strategy that will be effective, but also efficient. Usually, a simple end-to-end test will be a good fit, testing that an input produces a certain output. This will give you the confidence that your overall system is working as expected.

Q: As well as working with start-ups on greenfield projects, you have also seen how mature, enterprise-scale workloads operate in production. How do the enterprise teams you've worked with approach testing event-driven serverless systems, and what role do quality assurance engineers play?

At the enterprise level, the impact associated with defects on an application can be very high (in terms of revenue loss, brand reputation, etc.). Consequently, as companies expand and evolve, more money is invested in upholding quality standards.

Whilst application engineers continue to write their own unit tests and integration tests where they see fit, QA engineers are designing and implementing clever end-to-end tests, regression testing, and ensuring quality is upheld within teams. Of course, application engineers would likely have the skill set to do this; however, many of the more complex tests and overall upkeep of the test suite can be very time-consuming and distract from features those engineers are building. In my view, a notable distinction between start-ups and larger enterprises concerning testing lies in the pronounced emphasis on test coverage, balanced with the efficiency of the CI/CD pipeline to maintain productivity.

One challenge in enterprises is the mindset shift from manual QA work to writing effective automated tests for serverless applications. Since writing tests for serverless applications will likely require the use of an SDK to interrogate cloud resources, it can be a steep learning curve. It is important that this learning curve is taken, as I believe that automated testing is the only way a business can scale with confidence in the increased number of deployments. I believe that QA engineers can get more job satisfaction by owning and maintaining a comprehensive test suite. I have also found that this shift in mindset helps QA engineers and application engineers work more closely together and thus achieve higher-quality products.

Q: You are an outstanding member of the AWS and serverless community, notably as an AWS Community Builder, speaker, podcast guest, and open source contributor. What role can the community play in improving the state of affairs when it comes to serverless testing?

I've spoken to many developers about their thoughts on how to test serverless applications, and it is clear to me that there is currently no "golden path" regarded by serverless engineers. I think that the best way to develop best practices for testing serverless applications is to share our knowledge with each other. Therefore, I think it is very much the community that can drive innovation in our approach to testing serverless applications. Approaches can be very opinionated, and therefore it is beneficial that we have increasing content so that developers can form their own opinions on how best to test their applications.

Back in 2021, I wrote a blog article about an integration testing strategy for EventBridge-based serverless architectures. I didn't anticipate a wide readership, but I believed it was worthwhile to share the strategy my colleagues and I had devised. I consider the blog post a success as it continues to attract a substantial readership even today. However, I believe a contributing factor to its sustained reader interest is the relatively limited amount of content available on this subject—there is a clear need for more opinions on this topic!

I think many people are worried about putting the "wrong" opinion out there for all to see. However, we can all only speak from our own experiences, and those experiences are not "right" or "wrong." Personally, I'd love to see more blog posts delving into the challenges and setbacks developers have encountered. At times I think of something to try out, only to discover a lack of related content. Yet, after investing time working on it, I realize it doesn't work in the way I'd like. It's possible that many others have tried the same thing as me, but chose not to share their unsuccessful experiences, as we generally refrain from publicizing our failed attempts. However, I firmly believe that expanding our collective knowledge base empowers us all.

Q: What advice would you give to enterprise software teams starting out with serverless testing?

First and foremost, ensure that you have good coverage on your unit tests and end-to-end tests written for your business-critical paths—those are the basics. Once you have those covered, you can begin to think about integration testing, which can help developers to diagnose issues more efficiently.

During this Q&A I've purposefully avoided discussing mocking and so-called "offline testing." As a rule of thumb, I'd always opt for testing on the real infrastructure (for integration and end-to-end testing). However, that isn't to say there isn't a place for mocking. Mocking third parties can be especially useful. Your tests should test the code that you can control, not the third-party code. Third parties go down often, which will cause tests to fail. When the tests are integrated into the CI/CD pipeline, the engineers will be blocked from pushing code into production. However, this shouldn't be the case if the fault isn't due to the codebase you can control. Therefore, large enterprises may want to think about a strategy to mock third parties—if you do this and your test fails, then you know that it's down to something under your control and not a third-party error. If you do choose to mock your third parties, then the response should be identical to what you would expect from the third party so that it mimics what should happen.

Therefore, if you have the basics covered and are looking to improve your integration/end-to-end tests, I'd suggest setting up a way of mocking the third parties that you use. I advise this for enterprises, as the initial investment is worth it when you have many engineers working on a codebase that could be blocked by the unnecessary failure of the tests.

CHAPTER 8

Operating Serverless

Revolution is not a one time event.
—Audre Lorde

In the previous two chapters you explored how to develop, test, and deploy a serverless application. In this chapter you will learn how to operate your serverless application in production. The fundamentals of operating serverless are similar to those of non-serverless software: ensuring the application is performing as expected, receiving alerts when performance degrades, recovering from incidents, and using logs and traces to debug issues. However, the key characteristics of serverless require some adjustments to the traditional approach to operations.

Perhaps the most important aspect of serverless when it comes to operations is scalability. Serverless technology and managed services offer automatic scaling of compute, storage, and communication from zero to your spikiest peaks. This is obviously a huge advantage to an engineering team with a business or product that experiences regular spikes in demand, such as an ecommerce website with seasonal and promotional sales events. But it is crucial that serverless engineers know their units of scale and understand the impact of scale on their pay-per-use billing. When you deploy a serverless application on AWS, you are entering into a cloud contract: AWS provides the autoscaling and high availability, but you must operate within service limits and make informed decisions about scale when designing your architecture. Even if the underlying services scale, your application may not.

Chapter 6 discussed the importance of deploying your application to production from day 1 and every day after so that you are immediately and continuously analyzing its behavior. This has well-documented benefits for building a product that meets business and user needs, but it is also crucial for optimizing your architecture for serverless scale. Once your application is deployed, the practice of observability becomes your most valuable tool for understanding how your system is performing.

There Is No Substitute for Production

Moments after he saw his Manchester United team beat Bayern Munich 2–1 in the Champions League final in Barcelona in 1999, Sir Alex Ferguson was asked for his reaction in a touchline interview. In a state of shock and disbelief, he simply said (*https://oreil.ly/92g6B*): "Football. Bloody hell."

With the full 90 minutes of the game played, 3 additional minutes were added on to account for pauses in play. United went on to score in the first and third minutes to win the cup. No wonder Sir Alex was shocked. Union of European Football Associations (UEFA) President Lennart Johansson also later said: "I can't believe it. The winners are crying and the losers are dancing."

Football (or soccer, if you prefer) teams train regularly and plan meticulously, but the 1999 final shows that the environment of a stadium on match day cannot be replicated and the outcome of a crucial game can rarely be accurately predicted. The thousands of fans in the stands, the weather, the lighting, the grass; there are so many variables. Every game of football is played within the same rules and constraints, but the outcome is always different and difficult to guess.

Manchester United and Bayern Munich could have played that game 100 times and produced a different result each time. It is certain that neither team could have planned for or predicted the two late goals that won the game.

Believe it or not, the same unpredictability applies to serverless! The lesson here is to continuously deploy to production (see Chapter 6) and continuously observe behavior to understand your application. There is no substitute for operating your serverless application in production. You cannot replicate all of the variables and you cannot account for every eventuality.

Using serverless managed services all but eliminates the need for infrastructure monitoring, allowing you to focus on monitoring the application itself. Of course, you still need to monitor your usage of the managed services, but not the underlying servers, hardware, or network. Fully leveraging the serverless approach to operating your application results in only worrying about system health when you are alerted to a critical issue. Serverless engineers should not be watching dashboards, trawling through logs, or searching for the alerting needle in a haystack.

In Chapter 7 you made peace with a serverless software fact: bugs are inevitable. As the CTO of Amazon, Dr. Werner Vogels, famously said, "everything fails all the time." In a distributed system some parts will always be functioning unexpectedly. To compound this fact, most bugs often appear over time as components interact in unexpected ways through the combination of their isolated iterations, as they morph further and further away from initial implementations, with additional edge case solutions and adjustments. This is known as *emergent complexity*.

A key serverless trend is the shift from business logic to application integration; away from custom code executed in Lambda functions to connecting services, like SQS and EventBridge, and workflow orchestration with Step Functions (see Chapter 6). With this shift, bugs move from code to operations. You should keep trying to catch functional bugs pre-production (as shown in Chapter 7), but you've got to *ship and run* to catch operational problems, such as service request throttling, poison-pill messages, and exceeding service limits. We'll begin this chapter by exploring the importance of understanding AWS service limits to ensure your application operates smoothly at scale.

Identifying the Units of Scale

Most of the serverless managed services you will use in your architecture will provide automatic scaling and pay-per-use billing. This means you will be able to scale your application to respond to any level of demand while only paying for the resources you use, when you use them. For example, if one of your Lambda functions is invoked once in an hour, you will only pay for that single invocation. Likewise, if the function is not invoked at all during the month it will not appear on your bill at all. Conversely, if that function suddenly becomes very popular and is invoked thousands of times in a day, you will not have to change the configuration or code and will be billed accordingly.

Non-serverless scaling involves monitoring the CPU and bandwidth utilization of resources or the remaining disk space available and adding additional servers or clusters to cope with demand. While these concerns are alleviated by serverless, there are still units of scale in an autoscaling application; they are simply different units. With serverless, the units of scale will depend on the type of resource (e.g., compute, storage, application integration) and the quota stipulated by the managed service. For example, Lambda scales in terms of function execution concurrency (see Chapter 6 for more information), Kinesis streams have input and delivery buffer limits, DynamoDB restricts read and write capacity, and API Gateway tracks response latency.

Each AWS managed service enforces an implicit contract of usage: the service provides features and performance guarantees in line with acceptable usage within documented quotas. These constraints force you to be creative with your architectural decisions and designs and can, in many cases, promote sensible and optimal use of managed services.

You should become very familiar with the quota pages in the documentation for the managed services you are using—for example, the Step Functions quota page (*https://oreil.ly/3yO_t*)—and pay particular attention to whether a limit is soft or hard (i.e., whether it can be increased or not). Understanding service limits should be a part of your solution design process and cost estimation (see Chapter 9). Architecture diagrams can be annotated with expected usage and limits to be mindful of. Analysis of bills or production incidents must include inspection of related service limits and pricing, and any consequent optimizations can be driven by quotas.

Promoting Serverless Observability

The primary goal of observability is to provide engineers with maximum visibility of their software. Observability is all about optimizing your software engineering practice with a view toward building observable systems—that is, systems that can be inspected and analyzed to understand their behavior, performance, and health.

 For a deep dive into observability, we highly recommend the book *Observability Engineering* by Charity Majors, Liz Fong-Jones, and George Miranda (O'Reilly). One resource that can be helpful when getting started with observability is the Observability Maturity Model (OMM) introduced in Chapter 21 of that book. The OMM should give you an idea of where you are now and how you can improve your general observability practice.

Observability is more a sociotechnical concept than a matter of deploying a particular tool or using only open source standards. It's about ensuring the data is there when you need to answer questions about your application's behavior. Whereas monitoring can be seen as an active pursuit that involves engineers watching dashboards and trying to spot anomalies, observability is very much a passive process. After releasing a feature to users, your engineers should get back to building the next feature and improving the product, rather than worrying about supporting issues or analyzing performance. You should have confidence in your alarms to alert you to potential problems and in your metrics, logs, and traces to support efficient debugging when required.

With serverless, monitoring of infrastructure (such as network and hardware performance and failures) is delegated to the cloud vendor. Application monitoring becomes your sole focus. However, the application is now a highly distributed, ephemeral, event-driven mix of your business logic and the vendor's managed services. This can make failure modes difficult to predict and comprehend. In turn, this means it is more important than ever to be able to view and understand your application's behavior in production. The issue here is that traditional monitoring and alerting tools and strategies are inadequate for the task.

Adopting a culture and practice of observability in your team is crucial to the smooth operation of your serverless application. As you saw in Chapter 7, the distributed, asynchronous, decoupled, and event-driven nature of serverless applications raises special challenges with regard to testing. These same properties make serverless systems and microservices inherently difficult to monitor using traditional methods, such as "monitor all the things," dashboards, and logs. You are no longer monitoring a single process running on a few machines, and operational status can no longer be understood via a few key metrics on a dashboard.

Observability cannot be a post-deployment afterthought or the responsibility of operations teams. Effective observability relies on the data and information about the system under observation being readily available. This means you cannot simply observe a system; you must first build a system that is capable of being observed. You must make observability a concern at every stage in your software delivery lifecycle, from design and development to operation and monitoring.

Observing the Health of Critical Paths

Monitoring the performance of a distributed, serverless application at a given point in time can be challenging. The sheer number of parts operating independently across services, stacks, regions, and accounts can be overwhelming. Rather than trying to monitor everything, focus on the most critical parts of your application; the parts that must be working at all times. Dig into anomalies on noncritical paths over time (refer to Chapter 7 for guidance on identifying your critical and noncritical paths).

Be mindful that a complex software system is never completely healthy. Distributed systems are unpredictable and prone to partial failures. That is the trade-off you make for the benefits. Sometimes this can even be viewed as a positive aspect. After all, you will always prefer part of your system to fail than all of it!

The documentation for each AWS service will usually have a monitoring section that will include hints about the key health metrics to track. The following is an overview of some core serverless services and their key metrics of scale and performance:

Lambda

The total count of account-level concurrent function executions is the key to determining whether your Lambda usage is scaling to meet your application's traffic (see Chapter 6 for more details on account-level concurrency). Other function-level invocation metrics, like the counts of errors or throttles, are useful to understand your application's behavior and the possibility of bugs. You should also monitor memory usage and duration to understand the performance of your functions (see Chapter 6 for information about how the Lambda Insights service can help you to analyze this data). For more information, see the Lambda documentation (*https://oreil.ly/gd1lI*).

API Gateway

The core metrics for your APIs are the total count of requests received by your API and the total number of 400- and 500-series errors returned. Always use a percentage of 400 and 500 errors when configuring alarm thresholds to ensure you account for spikes in API requests. You should also monitor whether latency levels are remaining within the integration response limits. By default metrics are emitted per API stage, but they can be emitted per API method if you enable the detailed metrics setting. For more information, see the API Gateway documentation (*https://oreil.ly/DAF-1*).

Step Functions

You can use the `ExecutionsStarted` and `ExecutionsSucceeded` metrics to monitor the expected behavior of your workflows and the `ExecutionAborted`, `ExecutionFailed`, `ExecutionThrottled`, and `ExecutionTimedOut` metrics to detect issues with workflow execution. The `ExecutionTime` metric can be used to monitor the overall latency of your workflows. For more information, see the Step Functions documentation (*https://oreil.ly/Pay2S*).

DynamoDB

You should consider setting alarms based on the `ConsumedReadCapacityUnits`, `ConsumedWriteCapacityUnits`, and `ThrottledRequests` metrics to be alerted to issues at scale. The `UserErrors` metric is also useful for indicating bugs with

DynamoDB SDK client requests, such as invalid parameters. For more information, see the DynamoDB documentation (*https://oreil.ly/U-Cc-*).

SQS

One of the key SQS metrics is `ApproximateAgeOfOldestMessage`. You should consider configuring an alarm for this metric with a threshold that allows you to take action before the message exceeds the maximum retention period of the queue. For more information, see the SQS documentation (*https://oreil.ly/4Ygd_*).

Kinesis Firehose

You can monitor the expected volume of data being processed by a stream using the `IncomingBytes` and `IncomingRecords` metrics. To ensure data is moving through your stream efficiently, you should monitor the `DataFreshness` and `Success` metrics. Stream processing errors can be monitored using the `ThrottledRecords` metric. For more information, see the Kinesis Firehose documentation (*https://oreil.ly/Ixrg2*).

EventBridge

EventBridge emits various metrics (*https://oreil.ly/Cnc_k*) that can be used to determine the performance of your rules and the delivery of events to targets. For example, you can keep track of the `TriggeredRules` metric to understand whether your rules are being triggered to expected levels based on the volume of upstream requests in your application. And the `DeadLetterInvocations` and `FailedInvocations` metrics can be used to understand whether your targets are failing to receive events.

Synthetic Monitoring for Low-Traffic Critical Paths

Synthetic monitoring involves sending artificial traffic to your application in a production environment. It is a form of what is known as *testing in production*, where the functionality of the system under test is verified post-deployment, under production conditions and against production services and databases. Synthetic monitoring can be used to implement a simple "heartbeat" check or to simulate full user journeys. Scripts are usually executed periodically. For example, a synthetic monitor might make an HTTP request to an API endpoint every 15 minutes to check if a 200 response is received.

The predominant use case for synthetic monitoring is low-traffic critical paths. For example, you may have an API resource that is only used between certain times or irregularly throughout the day that you want to ensure is operating correctly when it is eventually required. Or perhaps you have a daily or nightly batch process, such as an Amazon Macie pipeline or data lake export job, that you cannot afford to have fail when the time comes.

Typically, you would not use a synthetic monitor to track the health of your high-traffic critical paths as it is unlikely the synthetic traffic would surface any problems that real user traffic would not.

If you have a good use case for synthetic monitoring you should consider implementing and executing your test scripts with Amazon CloudWatch Synthetics (*https://oreil.ly/LkKbs*), a fully managed synthetic monitoring solution.

Metrics, Alarms, and Alerts

Metrics are the data that provides insights into the performance and health of your system. The metrics emitted by managed services give you a window into your utilization of the provided resources. You can also emit custom metrics from your Lambda functions (see Chapter 6 for information on using the open source Lambda Powertools toolkit for custom metrics). In AWS, all native and custom metrics are sent to CloudWatch. These metrics can then be forwarded to other AWS services or third parties for further analysis and aggregation.

An alarm is a combination of a metric and a threshold. If the metric breaches a certain threshold, the alarm will be triggered. For example, you could configure an alarm to trigger if the number of 400 errors returned by your API exceeded 27% of the total number of requests in the last 5 minutes (see Figure 8-1).

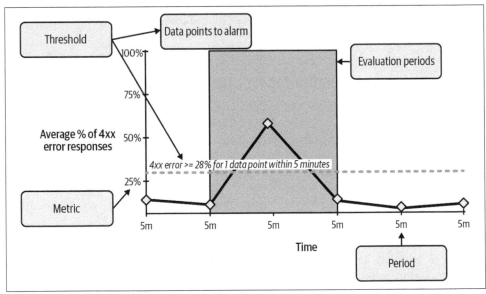

Figure 8-1. Anatomy of a CloudWatch alarm

Alerts are the actions performed when an alarm is triggered, such as sending a message to your team's chat channel or creating a bug report in your ticketing platform (see Figure 8-2). Alert configuration is important—after all, if an alarm sounds but nothing is listening, will it be heard? That said, you should keep in mind that not all alarms need to trigger an alert. Alarms can be used in operational dashboards to indicate potential issues for delayed investigation or even in retrospective analysis of historical patterns.

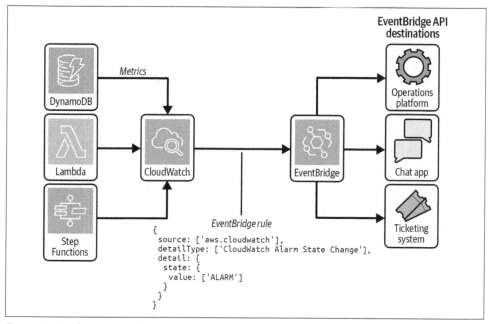

Figure 8-2. Alerting pipeline

Combining metrics, alarms, and alerts is key to surfacing issues with your serverless application. If you don't make use of these tools, your users are going to be the first to find out about problems and will be your main source of bug reporting. However, without a structured approach, alert noise can quickly overwhelm your team. Alarms that are too granular or sensitive will fast become dismissable and contribute to overall distrust of your alerting pipeline. It can become impossible to filter the signal from the noise. Alerts should be used sparingly and only for the aspects of your application's performance that are absolutely critical to your users and business.

A useful alert has the following properties:

Obvious
    The impact on the user experience or critical path should be clear.

Actionable
    The alert should be associated with a clear action.

Singular
The alert should be unique. Problems shouldn't be reflected by multiple triggers of the same alarm. You should receive one alert per distinct issue.

 Refer to Google's *Site Reliability Engineering* book for more information about the desired attributes of an alert.

Later in this section you will be introduced to the concept of service level objectives and capability alerting, which can help you to decide on the metrics and indicators to use for your alarms and keep noise to a minimum.

Critical Health Dashboard

Just as you saw with testing in Chapter 7, operations can benefit from a focus on your critical paths. But even your critical paths will have aspects that are more important than others when it comes to assessing operational health and performance at scale.

You can apply the RED method (*https://oreil.ly/o6WFN*) to ascertain the critical health of your system and services:

Rate
The rate of requests being received

Errors
The number of requests that are failing

Duration
The time taken to respond to requests

When launching a new feature, service, or product, it can be useful to create a critical health dashboard with charts showing the rates, errors, and durations for your core components (see Figure 8-3). This dashboard should collect all of the key metrics across your application or microservice to provide a single view of system health. At a glance, you can then immediately answer the question, "Is everything working?" Of course, in a distributed serverless application there will always be plenty of nuance and hidden elements to overall health, but this can at least provide a place to start your assessment of critical health.

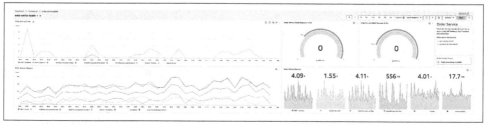

Figure 8-3. A critical health dashboard

After releasing a code change into production, you can use your dashboards to monitor the impact of the change and spot any immediate bugs—but you should rely on your alerts to catch emerging bugs and transient faults over time, rather than constantly watching your dashboards.

Use your critical health dashboard to spot potential anomalous performance. Look for spikes and curves in the charts, alarms that are being triggered, and status reports from third parties.

A critical health dashboard can also include information about the services in use, the key metrics being monitored, and links (or even dynamic data if there is a suitable API provided) to third-party status pages. Building out a comprehensive dashboard in this way will enable a wide pool of people in your organization to use it to make assessments, without needing deep working knowledge or experience of the system being observed.

Although a critical health dashboard can provide instant reassurance in certain high-pressure scenarios, like product launches and sales events, you should keep in mind that it is more useful (and accurate) to operate and observe your serverless application as a set of distinct applications.

If you follow the guidance provided throughout this book, you will take the utmost care to decouple your serverless microservices. This deliberate isolation should continue into operation, and you should resist trying to monitor decoupled services as one whole system.

Capability Alerting

Take a moment to imagine the following scenario. The day has finally arrived: you have spent weeks designing and building your beautiful serverless architecture, and now it is time to release it to your expectant users. But you recognize that a diligent serverless engineer never operates an application in production without alerts. How else will you know if your users are seeing errors without them telling you? You take a step back and look at all the components in your system: an API Gateway REST API, multiple microservices consisting of Lambda functions and Step Functions workflows, a DynamoDB table to store application state, and several EventBridge rules connecting all the services together. You wonder which metrics are important and when you should trigger alarms. Which parts do you need to know are broken, and when? You select the obvious, key parts: API 5xx errors, Lambda function errors, DynamoDB write throttles, and EventBridge delivery failures.

What follows is an all-too-common experience. With a large set of alarms for very specific metrics and thresholds, your engineers will quickly become overwhelmed by a barrage of alerts, many of which will be false positives (the threshold was too low or the selected metric was incorrect) or deemed acceptable ("this usually fails") or expected ("that's a known error").

While this is a perfectly acceptable start to introducing alerting to your observability practice (and is much better than having no alerts at all), you should be aware of an alternative approach. *Capability-based alerting* involves assessing the overall health of a critical component or service in your system. Let's say one of the critical capabilities of your system is to generate a PDF and store it in S3. In this instance, you would combine metrics across the components in this workflow to form an overall idea of the health of this service and establish a baseline of acceptable performance in a CloudWatch composite alarm (*https://oreil.ly/5Yabc*). You would then receive an alert when this threshold was breached and would know the performance of this capability had degraded enough to warrant your immediate attention. Without capability-based alerting, you would have instead received multiple alerts tied to specific resource metrics, which would have created a lot of noise and been ineffective at pinpointing the area on which to focus your initial debugging efforts.

Ideally, you want to receive alerts based on the health of your system's capabilities (see Figure 8-4). Monitoring the health of your entire system is far too broad to provide actionable insights, while monitoring the health of your system's components is much too granular to give any useful indications.

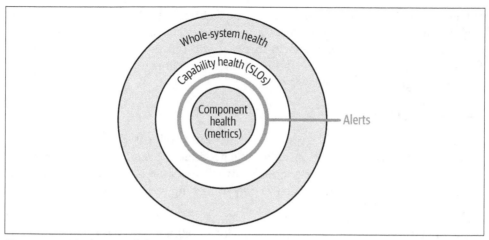

Figure 8-4. The layers of alerting

Service level objectives can also be used to answer the question "How will the quality of this code be measured?" from "Upholding Standards with a Definition of Done" on page 328.

Service level objectives

Service level objectives (SLOs) are targets for performance that provide an indication of how often your service can fail before the experience of your users is significantly degraded. SLOs are based on the realization that you cannot operate your product at 100% success all the time, and at some point, your users will encounter issues. The goal is to determine the amount of unreliability they will tolerate and, rather than striving for the impossible goal of perfection, to ensure the service operates at least at that level at all times.

SLOs are informed by service level indicators (SLIs). An SLI is essentially a binary measure of whether your service is performing well or not. For example, you could establish an SLI for your API's response time of 6 seconds. All requests that are responded to within 6 seconds are considered "good" and any outside this limit are "bad." You could then set an SLO of 99.98%, meaning that your objective is to respond to 99.98% of API requests within 6 seconds.

For a comprehensive guide to SLOs, we recommend Alex Hidalgo's book *Implementing Service Level Objectives* (O'Reilly).

When establishing an SLO for a service or feature, you should set the threshold slightly lower than the level at which a user may begin to experience unacceptable levels of frustration or discontent. In this way, you can normalize a certain level of failure (among users and engineers alike) without reaching a point where confidence or trust is negatively impacted.

Decoupling what from why

In *Observability Engineering*, the authors state: "Decoupling 'what' from 'why' is one of the most important distinctions in writing good monitoring with maximum signal and minimum noise." Your alerts should only tell you *what* is wrong. After receiving an alert, it is then up to you to discover *why* something went wrong, using your logs, traces, metrics, and dashboards.

If you attempt to use your alerts to tell you why something went wrong, you are likely to end up with a barrage of meaningless, unactionable alerts. This is usually the case when using system-level metrics and thresholds to trigger alarms.

Consider one of the metrics used to indicate the health of a Kinesis Firehose stream with an S3 target: `DeliveryToS3.Success` (the percentage of the total number of put requests to S3 that succeeded). An alarm based on this metric could indicate that something is wrong with data delivery to S3 from the Firehose stream. This could be due to issues with the target S3 bucket, the stream's permissions, the S3 or Kinesis services themselves, and so on. However, it could also be an external issue, such as excessive demand on the stream. It also doesn't tell you if there is an unintended drop in the number of records being put on the stream.

SLOs can be used to configure alarms and determine when you should receive an alert instead of specific, system-level metrics. An SLO-based alert will simply tell you that the critical service or capability being monitored is not working as expected. You can then utilize the core analysis loop (described later in this chapter) to debug from first principles and form a holistic view of the potential root causes.

Event-Driven Logging

Application logs, combined with traces (see the next section), are essential for debugging and troubleshooting issues, either in real time or retrospectively. However, logs are easily overused and overly relied upon in serverless applications. This can result in an exponential increase in the time and knowledge it takes to debug an issue, as well as high costs (see Chapter 9) and security concerns (see Chapter 4), such as leaking sensitive data and secrets.

In an event-driven system, a log should ideally be a record of the occurrence of an event and its payload. These logs are very useful and can be used as an accessible, short-lived mirror of your application's event store, allowing you to see the events that have occurred for a particular user journey or transaction. If you are also using a standard event envelope, like CloudEvents, this ensures log data is consistent and queryable. Here's an example of an event payload that adheres to the CloudEvents specification:

```
{
  "data": {
    "countryCode": "DK",
    "orderNumber": "1234"
  },
  "datacontenttype": "application/json",
  "id": "5x6y7z8",
  "source": "/myapp/public",
  "specversion": "1.0",
  "subject": "Order.Created",
  "time": "2020-07-28T12:04:00Z",
  "type": "com.myapp.order.created"
}
```

Efficiently aggregating and analyzing vast amounts of logs across multiple service contexts and Lambda functions requires consistency in the format and properties of a log. You can use Lambda Powertools (see Chapter 6) to enforce standard log metadata and can consider providing type definitions to engineers to restrict the attributes that can be included in log data.

Beyond these event-based logs, you should only use logging as a last resort in your observability stack. Whenever you feel the need to add a log to record activity or state, consider whether the same information can be captured in a custom metric or a trace. Generally, tracing is a much more powerful and useful method for understanding the behavior of your system.

Using Distributed Tracing to Understand the Whole System

The most common challenge with understanding the health of a serverless system is the inherent distribution of compute across microservices and managed services. This is also true when that health is diminished and the system is experiencing an issue that requires debugging and remediation. The traditional means of determining the root cause of an issue is to analyze application logs. In non-serverless applications, logs are typically emitted from a single process and tell a linear, chronological story of a transaction in one stream, without needing to be augmented by any other information to provide an understanding of the complete picture.

In contrast, logs from disparate services can be difficult to correlate and order chronologically. Logs are also only as useful as the data they contain, and missing or incomplete logs may mean you only see part of the problem. In a serverless application, there are logs that you control—primarily from Lambda functions—and logs from managed services. Some managed services allow you to customize the logs they emit (such as API Gateway access logs [*https://oreil.ly/QagUx*]) but most do not.

Prefer traces to logs

A robust tracing setup will always tell the full story across entire distributed systems, through owned and managed services. Logs can tell you what went wrong, but you first have to know where to look. Traces can tell you *where* something went wrong, and then you can dig deeper.

To achieve an effective level of serverless observability, you must move from a reactive approach to monitoring that relies on logs and dashboards to a proactive approach that fully leverages traces.

> You should be aware that your application's observability can be impacted by your architectural decisions. For example, you cannot initialize traces when using API Gateway HTTP APIs.

AWS X-Ray

X-Ray is the native AWS solution for distributed tracing. It is a key component in the AWS observability stack and is fully integrated with the Amazon CloudWatch console. X-Ray provides tools to configure your application to collect trace data across owned and managed services. You can use the X-Ray console (*https://oreil.ly/XZD4_*) to analyze your traces and comprehensively understand the behavior and performance of your distributed services and system as a whole. You can also use the CloudWatch ServiceLens dashboard to get an overview of your trace data and the services that have been traced through (see Figure 8-5).

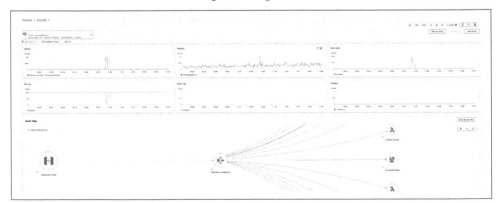

Figure 8-5. The Amazon CloudWatch ServiceLens dashboard

The ServiceLens dashboard is often a good place to start when trying to pinpoint performance issues before diving deeper into an individual trace or group of traces to identify patterns that point to a root cause (later, we'll talk more about using the core analysis loop to debug issues).

 It's important to note that trace data is only retained for a maximum of 30 days. Traces can also only be retrieved via the X-Ray console for periods of up to 6 hours. This means that if you need to analyze traces over, say, a 12-hour period, you'll need to perform two searches and aggregate the results yourself. Traces are therefore primarily useful for debugging immediate and recent production issues. Metrics, logs, and other application data should be used to build up a retrospective picture of your system's behavior beyond 30 days in the past or across longer continuous periods of time.

The following is a list of the high-level components of a trace:

Segments

A trace is a collection of segments that are generated by a single request, such as calling an API Gateway REST endpoint or invoking a Lambda function. The trace data in a segment will include details such as the request URL and method and the HTTP response code, as well as the total duration of the request (see Figure 8-6).

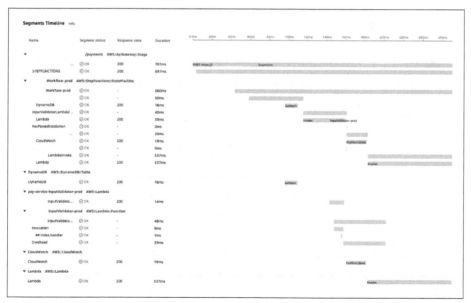

Figure 8-6. X-Ray segments timeline

Subsegments

The work performed during a segment is split into subsegments. For example, for a segment generated by a Step Functions state machine execution, each step or task would be represented by a subsegment. The same information is available as for a segment, just at a more granular level.

Annotations

Annotations are key/value pairs that can be added to your traces to augment the default data that is included by the X-Ray SDK. Annotations are indexed by X-Ray, allowing you to filter and group traces based on the annotation data. You can add up to 50 annotations per trace. For more information about annotations, see "Annotation" on page 365.

Metadata

Metadata can be attached to your traces to provide additional context when analyzing trace data. Use metadata to record data you want to store in the trace but don't need to use for searching traces.

Exceptions

An exception is recorded in a trace if an error occurs during an instrumented request. In this case, the trace will include details about the exception, including the error message and stack trace if available.

To begin collecting traces of transactions across your serverless application, you must focus on two things: instrumentation and annotation. We'll dive into these building blocks in the following sections.

Usage of the X-Ray service is priced based on the number of traces recorded and retrieved (via the AWS Console, CLI, or SDK). The Free Tier (*https://oreil.ly/BS87S*) includes 100,000 traces and 1,000,000 retrievals for free, at the time of writing (see Chapter 9 for more details on the AWS Free Tier).

If you are generating and analyzing a greater volume of traces than this, you should set a sampling rate (*https://oreil.ly/ZXp_g*) based on the cost you are willing to incur. X-Ray uses your sampling rate to decide what percentage of requests to record. For example, you might consider a sampling rate of 100% when launching a new service to capture as much data as possible. This rate can then be reduced over time as you begin to fully understand the service's behavior and can better anticipate its failure modes.

Instrumentation

Instrumentation is the process of configuring the microservices and managed services in your system to emit trace data when making API calls and performing tasks. For managed services, API calls are instrumented via the configuration of the resources you create. For example, to enable tracing for a Step Functions workflow you would include this configuration in your CloudFormation template (see Chapter 6 for more information about CloudFormation):

```json
{
  "Type": "AWS::StepFunctions::StateMachine",
  "Properties": {
    "TracingConfiguration": {
      "Enabled": true
    }
  }
}
```

You will also need to attach an IAM policy to the role used by the resource to allow it to write to X-Ray. This is generally the same policy regardless of the managed service or resource. For example:

```json
{
  "Version": "2012-10-17",
  "Statement": [
    {
      "Effect": "Allow",
      "Action": [
        "xray:PutTraceSegments",
        "xray:PutTelemetryRecords",
        "xray:GetSamplingRules",
        "xray:GetSamplingTargets"
      ],
      "Resource": [
        "*"
      ]
    }
  ]
}
```

Instrumenting your serverless microservices will typically involve using the X-Ray SDK from your Lambda functions. The AWS Powertools toolkits are the best way to do this (see Chapter 6 for full details). By instrumenting your Lambda functions, you can collect trace data about operations such as AWS SDK calls and third-party HTTP requests.

Annotation

Annotations are the key to building an effective collection of traces that can be used for rapid debugging of production issues. The X-Ray SDK will collect core data about the requests and responses your application makes, such as the name of the service or managed resource and the duration of the request, but annotations allow you to augment the default trace data with application state and transaction-specific information.

Annotations can be added to the segments and subsegments of your traces as your application code is executed. All annotations are indexed by X-Ray and can then be used to filter your traces (*https://oreil.ly/ztdfE*) when trying to understand how your application is currently behaving. See Figure 8-7 for an example.

Distinct traces can be correlated across services, including across first- and third-party systems, by using a common *correlation ID*. You can use a dedicated correlation ID, but the primary identifier of transactions in your application will typically suffice, as this is likely to be present in most of the events that occur. For example, in an order management service this might be the order ID.

Your correlation ID should be added to the annotations of every segment of your trace to ensure it can be used to accurately group and filter traces across your system.

Segment details: ## index.handler

Overview	Resources	Annotations	Metadata	Exceptions	SQL

clientId
☐ Sample789

countryCode
☐ US

ColdStart
☐ false

paymentReference
☐ Sample1234

paymentMethod
☐ credit-card

Service
☐ payments-service

Figure 8-7. X-Ray segment with annotations

You can create *trace groups* (*https://oreil.ly/ZIhWD*) to store a common set of queries your team may need to run to filter traces. You can create up to 25 trace groups per account.

In the event of a critical error occurring in your production workload, you can combine the default trace data and your custom annotations to filter traces that point to the root cause via the X-Ray console. Figure 8-8 shows an example of how this can be achieved.

Figure 8-8. Using the X-Ray console to filter traces with erroneous HTTP response codes on a specific node

Figure 8-9 shows how exceptions can then be surfaced from trace data to facilitate rapid debugging and accurately pinpoint the root cause of a production issue.

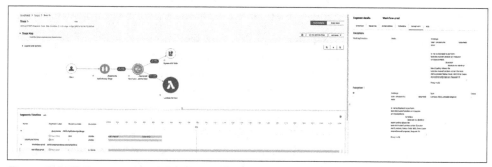

Figure 8-9. X-Ray segments timeline with exception

Next, let's look into what happens when an error occurs in your application and how you can write code that is tolerant of faults.

When Things Go Wrong

The sheer volume of variables and emergent complexity in the operation of a production serverless workload mean things will go wrong. This does not mean you should be complacent and resist trying to minimize the number of things that could go wrong, of course. You should optimize your development practices, testing strategy, delivery pipelines, and observability culture to ensure you eliminate bugs before they reach production if possible, but can catch and fix them rapidly if they do.

Alongside testing, delivery, and observability, the fourth quadrant of the serverless square of balance (first presented in Chapter 7) is recovery. Recovering from failures in production involves making your services and workflows fault tolerant. Fortunately, fault tolerance is usually a key feature of serverless managed services on AWS—and it's one that you must leverage to get the most from serverless.

Accepting Failure and Budgeting for Errors

You were introduced to the application of service level objectives for targeting alerts previously in this chapter. The other aspect of SLOs is the concept of an *error budget*. Error budgets specify a threshold for the volume of errors that are permitted to occur in a particular feature, service, or product. For example, a service exposed to users via an API endpoint could have an error budget of 5% for a month. If the percentage of 5xx errors returned exceeds 5% of all responses from that API endpoint, then the error budget will be completely used up.

Error budgets can be used to give your engineering team the permission to release bugs into production. As you've seen in Chapters 6 and 7, the balance between stability and delivery speed is crucial to sustaining a resilient and useful application in the long term. Your engineers must have the ability to deliver code safely without being slowed down by excessive test suites. In this way, error budgets are a limiting force and can be used to establish reasonable thresholds for shipping bugs to users.

A surplus in your error budget gives you the confidence to go ahead and deliver new features or improvements to your users rather than trying to squash bugs. Conversely, if you are regularly exceeding your error budget this provides a clear indication that you need to shift your efforts to improving stability and performance.

Everything Fails All the Time: Fault Tolerance and Recovery

As you design your serverless architecture and build your functions, workflows, and microservices, you should always code for failure. Coding for failure requires you keep in mind the mechanisms and strategies available to you for recovering from failures. This ranges from a try/catch in a Lambda function to retry and replication configuration in your infrastructure code. By coding for failure, you ensure that the execution and operation of your code in a production environment will be tolerant of bugs.

Coding for failure involves writing clear, maintainable, and debuggable code. In serverless, this includes careful separation of concerns between your business logic and AWS managed services, keeping Lambda functions and Step Functions workflows simple, and leveraging service integrations. For advice on how to write better Lambda functions and infrastructure code, see Chapter 6.

There are two broad categories of failures:

Transient faults
> These faults can be automatically retried and usually succeed in time. Examples include third-party service downtime and network connection issues.

Permanent faults
> A transient fault becomes a permanent fault after the retries are exhausted. These faults are routed to dead letter queues for manual inspection or to trigger automated reprocessing at a later time or after a known issue is resolved. Permanent faults can also include processes and requests that cannot be retried, such as synchronous processes like customer payments once the customer is no longer actively sending a request. Lastly, permanent faults also incorporate data loss or destruction of cloud resources where recovery is possible through a restoration process, using a backup or replica.

Most AWS managed services and SDK libraries offer built-in mechanisms to help your application recover from failures. The following list gives you some examples:

AWS SDK
> You can configure the maximum number of retries to attempt (*https://oreil.ly/ HskdF*) and the backoff rate for each AWS SDK client your application uses. See Mark Brooker's AWS blog post (*https://oreil.ly/5GirX*) for more details about exponential backoff and jitter.

Step Functions
> When using direct integrations with managed services, retries and backoff can be configured in the same way as when using the AWS SDK in your application code. See the Step Functions documentation (*https://oreil.ly/ww_bB*) for details.

EventBridge
> Each EventBridge rule should be configured with an SQS dead letter queue to store undeliverable events for automated or manual retry at a later time. You should also consider attaching an event archive to allow for replaying events across a certain period of time. Events can also be sent across Regions, from sources in one AWS Region to destinations in another, to help synchronize data in cross-Region data stores. See "Multi-Account, Multi-Region: Is It Worth It?" on page 373 for more details on when to consider adopting multi-Region architectures.

DynamoDB
> Tables can be replicated across AWS Regions using global tables (*https://oreil.ly/ BjRTW*), and point-in-time recovery (*https://oreil.ly/GvbBv*) can be used to restore tables after accidental operations are performed. Enabling the deletion

protection setting (*https://oreil.ly/rZnc9*) will prevent inadvertent deletion of a table via the AWS Console or CloudFormation.

No matter how fault tolerant your application is, persistent errors will always occur with any application of significant complexity and business criticality. If you cannot prevent these errors with testing or recovery, you must rely on your ability to observe your system and to effectively identify (and remediate) the root cause. Next, you will be introduced to a useful strategy for debugging production issues.

Debugging with the Core Analysis Loop

When you receive a notification, either from an alert or directly from a user, that something in your application is not working correctly, you know that something is wrong but you do not know why.

Following the *core analysis loop*, as introduced in the book *Observability Engineering*, allows you to use telemetry "to form hypotheses and to validate or invalidate them with data, and thereby systematically arrive at the answer to a complex problem" (see Figure 8-10).

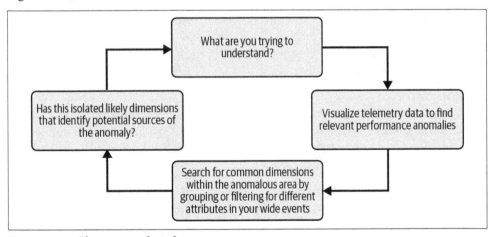

Figure 8-10. The core analysis loop

Start by verifying the problem that has been reported to you by analyzing the health of the surrounding systems and services. Use your critical health dashboard to spot curves, spikes, or dips in metric graphs. Find the outlying data points or events causing this deviation from stable performance and identify patterns that could point to a root cause. Next, go back to the wider observability data (traces, logs, metrics) and filter by the pattern to validate your hypothesis. If you are confident the root cause has been found, you can attempt to remedy it. Otherwise, if the problem remains undiagnosed, start the analysis loop again to refocus your investigation.

Always try to resist reactionary conclusions like "That's always breaking," "You can't rely on third party X," "We've seen this before," and "It's probably due to Y." This can result in missing root causes and general apathy toward operational tasks. The core analysis loop helps your engineers to debug from first principles.

Disaster Recovery

Architecting and operating your serverless application to be tolerant of faults cannot guard against all types of failures. You will have parts of your system that represent a single point of failure (*https://oreil.ly/bxtl2*) that could cause entire critical paths to break in the event of a fault. The uptime of your application is also subject to the status of the third-party software services you depend on, including AWS.

Avoiding Single Points of Failure

Single points of failure can occur at integration points in your system, such as your public API and authorization layer, workflows that depend on a third-party API, or centralized resources like event buses and databases.

While certain single points of failure are very difficult to avoid, your aim should always be to eliminate single points of failure over time. Any potential failure of these components can also be mitigated through various strategies, including replication and backups.

Any single point of failure should be developed, deployed, and operated in isolation from the other parts of your architecture. For instance, you should define your Cognito user pools or application state data stores in separate stacks from the microservices that interact with them. This separation allows you to deploy these resources only when they change, which is typically not often, and not when dependent components change. Chapter 6 provides more details on separating and sharing resources across decoupled services.

 Cognito user pools cannot natively be replicated or backed up. This makes them very susceptible to catastrophic faults. Use synthetic monitoring and metric alarms to ensure you are alerted to any issues with authorizing API requests against your user pool. Define your Cognito user pool, app clients, and scopes and any supporting infrastructure, like Route 53 custom domains, using an infrastructure-as-code tool. Deploy the infrastructure via an isolated, direct pipeline. This will allow you to rapidly iterate or re-create your Cognito resources in the event of failure.

Understanding AWS Availability

At a high level, the global cloud infrastructure of AWS consists of two primary concepts: Regions and Availability Zones (*https://oreil.ly/MeFpE*). A Region is a geographical area, such as North Virginia (*us-east-1*), London (*eu-west-2*), or Tokyo (*ap-northeast-1*). Each Region consists of at least three Availability Zones (see Figure 8-11).

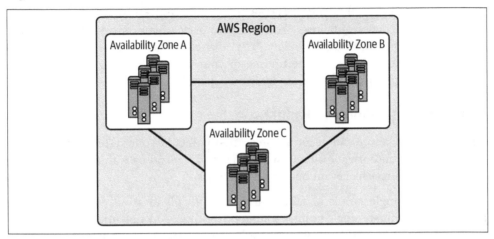

Figure 8-11. AWS Regions and Availability Zones

An Availability Zone (AZ) is a physically isolated section of an AWS Region with one or more data centers. Each AZ is designed to operate and fail independently. They are physically separated by up to 100 km (60 miles) and connected by high-bandwidth, low-latency networking that allows for synchronous replication between AZs. Practically, this isolation protects your applications against issues such as power outages and natural disasters.

It is this global infrastructure of Regions and AZs that enables you, as an AWS customer, to build highly available, fault-tolerant, and scalable applications.

 At the time of writing, there are 32 Regions and 102 Availability Zones, with 15 more AZs and 5 more Regions planned in Canada, Germany, Malaysia, New Zealand, and Thailand.

Choosing a Region to deploy your application to will usually depend on where the majority of your users are located, as well as where your organization is legally permitted to operate and process and store user data. However, many AWS services also provide features that allow you to operate your workload across multiple AWS Regions and AWS accounts.

Multi-Account, Multi-Region: Is It Worth It?

The effort involved in designing, developing, and operating a cloud native application across multiple AWS accounts or Regions is substantial. You will need an in-depth understanding of all the implementation details. This means the answer to the question of whether it's worth adopting a multi-account, multi-Region strategy to disaster prevention and recovery has to be: it depends. It will depend on your use case, your team's ability to build and support this architecture, and, to a lesser extent, the geographical location of your business and users.

In assessing this approach, you should consider the likelihood of a disaster, the time to recover, and the potential impact on your business and users during this time. These aspects must then be traded off against the overhead of operating across cloud accounts and physical Regions.

 The AWS Post-Event Summaries page (*https://oreil.ly/MxyD4*) states that when a service outage incident "has broad and significant customer impact that results in the failure of a significant percentage of control plane API calls, impacts a significant percentage of a service's infrastructure, resources or APIs or is the result of total power failure or significant network failure, AWS is committed to providing a public Post-Event Summary (PES) following the closure of the issue."

You can also view the previous 12 months of service and Region health data via the AWS Health Dashboard (*https://oreil.ly/Kyz4i*).

Perhaps in the future cross-account and cross-Region application development and operation will become abstracted away from engineers. But until then, this strategy will always be a trade-off with the overhead involved.

Summary

In this chapter, you have learned about your role in operating your serverless application at scale in production. While AWS is responsible for the availability and resiliency of the managed services in your architecture, you are responsible for the configuration and usage of these services. It is crucial that you are aware of the service limits in place and how to monitor that your usage stays within these limits.

You have also seen how the observability of your system is key to understanding its behavior, especially considering the distributed nature of serverless, event-driven architectures. Just like your testing strategy, your observability strategy must be concentrated around your critical paths. You should adopt critical health dashboards and capability-based alerts to enable your team to immediately detect issues with your serverless application, and tracing should be preferred to logs to support your team's debugging efforts when errors occur.

Finally, you saw that fault tolerance is a key attribute of serverless and how you can begin to leverage AWS to introduce automated recovery from failure to your microservices.

Interview with an Industry Expert

Yan Cui, AWS Serverless Hero

Yan is an experienced engineer who has run production workloads at scale on AWS since 2010. He has been an architect and principal engineer in a variety of industries, ranging from banking, ecommerce, and sports streaming to mobile gaming. He has worked extensively with AWS Lambda in production since 2015. Nowadays, Yan splits his time between advancing the state of serverless observability as a Developer Advocate at Lumigo and helping companies around the world adopt serverless as an independent consultant.

Yan is also an AWS Serverless Hero and a regular speaker at user groups and conferences internationally. He is the author of *Production-Ready Serverless* (*https://oreil.ly/iV0S5*) and coauthor of *Serverless Architectures on AWS*, 2nd edition (Manning). Yan keeps an active blog at The Burning Monk (*https://oreil.ly/Hgdow*) and hosts the popular Real-World Serverless podcast (*https://oreil.ly/HW-xL*).

Q: You've been running production workloads on AWS since 2010 and were one of the first AWS Heroes for Serverless in 2018. How does operating serverless software differ from traditional ops?

For starters, there is a lot less for you to do, so it frees you up to focus on things that actually differentiate your business. I used to spend ~70% of my time on configuring, maintaining, patching, and troubleshooting the infrastructure that runs my code—the EC2 instances, load balancers, VPCs, security groups, you name it. There is a lot to do, and there is a lot of toil on a small team. It was tough to do all that and still deliver the features the customers were demanding. On a personal level, it was very stressful and it often meant sacrificing myself and working long hours.

With serverless, there's far less demand on you as the engineer because most of the operational concerns are taken care of by the cloud provider. That means you can focus more of your time on the things that matter, not the infrastructure beneath them. On the personal level it means less stress, less things that can go wrong, and in general a much happier and more productive team. For the business, it also means you get more out of your engineers. There are fewer problems, so you have a more stable product, which means happier customers. It also means, for a start-up, you can defer the point at which you need to hire full-time specialists to help you manage your infrastructure and ease the operational burden on the application teams.

Q: The practice of observability has become integral to modern engineering teams, as they operate software that is increasingly distributed and event-driven. How would you define observability in a nutshell and why is it a good fit for serverless?

My favorite definition for observability is that it's a measure of how well you're able to infer the internal state of a system just from its external outputs. Put it another way: do you know what's going on inside your system without attaching a debugger and stepping through every line of code, one at a time? In a live system, it's just not feasible. So you have to be able to go by the breadcrumbs and clues that your system leaves behind.

Observability is not so much a good fit for serverless, but a mandatory requirement for operating any system in the real world, serverless or otherwise. If you don't know what the system is doing then you have no business running it in production.

Q: You have worked on lots of serverless and event-driven architectures through your consultancy work and helped tell the stories of many serverless teams on your Real-World Serverless podcast. What are some of the common issues that teams encounter when operating serverless applications in production?

Some common issues include:

- They don't know how to effectively test their application, so they only discover problems in production.
- Cold starts still affect many teams. Maybe they have a Lambdalith and need to load too many dependencies, or maybe they're using JVM or .NET and don't know how to optimize cold start performance for JVM and .NET functions.
- They run into throughput limits because they're working with services they're unfamiliar with and didn't know what limits would affect them.
- They don't have good observability into the system, so they can't troubleshoot problems easily.
- They have a poorly designed system, such as a "ball-of-mud" event-driven architecture, or the system boundaries are wrong or not clearly defined. Or maybe they just chose the wrong service to use, for example.

Q: Over the last few years, you have established The Burning Monk as one of the most prominent serverless blogs. In August 2020, you wrote an indispensable article about choreography and orchestration in serverless. How can engineers optimize these architectures for resiliency and recovery from failure?

If resiliency is your main concern and you're happy to pay extra to get that resiliency, then Step Functions is the way to go. Moving the retries and the exponential backoff out of your Lambda functions and into the state machine alleviates the tension between 1) having a good security posture and have short timeouts so you're less vulnerable to denial of wallet attacks, and 2) having a long timeout so you allow sufficient time for retrying failures and exponential backoff and jitters (to avoid retry storms).

It's one reason why you often see Step Functions in order and payment processing systems—because these are business-critical workflows, and most people would be happy to pay a premium to make them more robust and resilient. So the extra cost of Step Functions is more than justified. And it's much easier to troubleshoot failed Step Functions executions because of the built-in visualization and audit history!

Q: Through your dedication to contributing a treasure trove of content to the community, you have helped so many engineers and teams get started with serverless. What advice would you give to enterprise teams on their way to operating their first serverless workload in production?

It depends on where your team is coming from, if they're already familiar with building and running microservices and the challenges that come with that, and their level of AWS experience. But for most enterprises, I would recommend having a platform team—not as gatekeepers to decide what gets deployed to production, but as a team of enablers to ease the burden on the feature teams.

Most enterprises have a myriad of organization-specific requirements, maybe for compliance reasons or maybe down to legacy reasons. Instead of every team needing to find a solution to meet these compliance requirements, it's much better to invest in a common set of tools, libraries, and approaches that everyone can follow; a golden path, if you will. That's where the platform team comes in, to create and maintain a thin layer of organization-specific guardrails. For example, this platform can include account templates so every AWS account comes with CloudTrail enabled and all of its CloudTrail logs are centralized in an audit account. And it can include service control policies (SCPs) that prevent any tampering with CloudTrail settings and logs. And this platform might include organization-specific CLI tools that can automate many of the day-to-day tasks, such as onboarding a new developer, or initiating a break-glass request to acquire write permissions in production.

It's important to also make sure that the platform team does not build in a silo. They should be treated as partners and equals to the application teams they support. In fact, they should work with the application teams to identify cross-cutting requirements and challenges and provide the extra bandwidth and expertise to tackle them.

CHAPTER 9

Cost of Serverless Operation

We are prone to overestimate how much we understand about the world and to underestimate the role of chance in events.

—Daniel Kahneman, *Thinking, Fast and Slow*

One of the key innovations that serverless has brought to software operations in the cloud is the pay-as-you-go pricing model. In this chapter, you will explore the pay-per-use model that is characteristic of the predominant serverless services, including AWS Lambda, Amazon DynamoDB, and AWS Step Functions. You will learn about the intrinsic link between your monthly bill and the efficiency of your serverless architecture and how to estimate the cost of your architecture before implementing and releasing it. You will also be equipped with a comprehensive set of best practices when it comes to monitoring and reducing the cost of your serverless application over time.

In Chapter 8, you saw the importance of designing and operating a serverless application with service quotas and pricing in mind. Next, you will see how to use these quotas and prices to effectively estimate production costs to ensure your bill does not spike disproportionately to your traffic. Of course, with the pay-per-use model, you should expect costs to rise and fall with the volume of requests sent to your application. However, there have been plenty of instances of architectural inefficiencies causing teams to experience unexpectedly high costs.

This is why the serverless pay-per-use model should be approached with caution as well as optimism. Running serverless at scale can mean inefficient usage is penalized with huge bills.

Understanding Serverless Cost Models

When evaluating your options for hosting and operating your software, cost is usually a key consideration. In recent years, serverless has emerged as a sound choice for teams and organizations looking for simplicity and cost-efficiency. With the combination of managed services and a pay-per-use pricing model, there is huge potential for serverless to allow you to focus on building software to meet your business and user needs without breaking the bank.

Serverless allows teams to scale usage of their applications from zero, paying very little or nothing at all, to peak demand, with rising costs (see Figure 9-1).

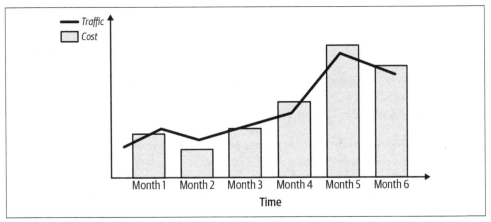

Figure 9-1. On-demand usage versus cost

There are three core contributing factors (*https://oreil.ly/szT5C*) to the cost of running a workload on AWS:

Compute
> The cost of compute will depend on the managed service you choose, but the crucial aspect of serverless compute is that you will only pay for what you use. We'll take a closer look at the pricing models for AWS Lambda and AWS Step Functions in "Compute Costs" on page 383.

Storage
> The cost of storing data is based on the amount of data written to and read from your chosen data store. You will also be charged for storing the data over time. Additional charges may be incurred for encryption and replication, depending on your architecture. Keeping storage costs low is all about optimizing your data model and access patterns, using compression strategies to reduce the space your data consumes, and efficient usage of caches. Keep in mind that you will likely store both application state and operational data, such as traces, logs, and

metrics. You will see examples of the pricing models for two popular storage options, Amazon S3 and Amazon DynamoDB, in "Storage Costs" on page 385.

Outbound data transfer
> The cost of outbound data transfer is mostly associated with sending data outside of containers or managed services running on the EC2 service to the public internet. For serverless applications, outbound data transfer costs could include sending CloudWatch metrics to a third-party application monitoring platform, leveraging S3 object replication, or using DynamoDB global tables. For more information and examples see the AWS blog post "Overview of Data Transfer Costs for Common Architectures" (*https://oreil.ly/RAhFm*).

While you will incur costs for outbound data transfer, for a serverless application, your costs will mostly concentrate around compute and storage. We'll look at the pricing models for the primary serverless compute and storage services shortly, but first, let's go beyond the monthly bill for a moment and take a broader look at cost.

Total Cost of Ownership in the Cloud

Your monthly bill shows you the obvious, regular cost of running your serverless application in the cloud. There is, however, another cost: the cost of ownership.

Total cost of ownership (TCO) is an established concept that helps organizations understand the cost of software over time, not just at the point of acquisition or creation. TCO can be significantly diminished when using serverless technology, primarily through leveraging managed services with a pay-per-use pricing model. But there are still key costs beyond your monthly bill that should be incorporated into your estimates and budgets.

When assessing your serverless TCO, you should consider the following costs:

Engineering
> The cost of the humans who design, build, and operate the application. This will in all likelihood be your most significant cost. Optimize your tools, process, and delivery to ensure your team spends time working on the things that generate value (see Chapter 6 for tips on optimizing your implementation, Chapter 7 for testing, and Chapter 8 for delivery and operations).

Delivery
> The cost of delivering code iterations to your users. The longer delivery pipelines run, the more they cost. The longer your fixes take to deploy, the longer your bugs live in production and potentially adversely affect your business.

Operations
> This is the cost you'll see on your monthly bill. Every piece of code you deploy will have an operational cost: storage, compute, data transfer, and so on. This

cost will scale with your traffic due to the serverless pay-per-use model, but there will be other constant costs, such as monitoring (see "Avoiding Serverless Cost Gotchas" on page 388) and security.

Maintenance

The cost of maintaining the application over time. The amount of hours dedicated to maintenance, as opposed to new feature development, will depend on factors such as complexity of the codebase, collective knowledge of the codebase among the team, and stability of the application. Software is maintained for much longer than the time it takes to create it.

Ownership of software is essentially ownership of the lines of code that have been contributed to the source code. It is commonplace in the software industry to view lines of code and the number of contributions to a codebase as measures of success and productivity. Many think the more code, the better. In fact, running software in production for a long period of time has proven the opposite to be true: code is a liability.

As you have seen, TCO can attribute a cost to every line of code in your codebase: the cost of creating it, deploying it, operating it, and maintaining it. Reducing your total cost of ownership is all about reducing the amount of code you own and simplifying what is left. As the authors of *The Value Flywheel Effect* put it (*https://oreil.ly/42R46*): "not unlike poetry, extraordinary code is elegant and precise."

There will be broadly three types of code in your software inventory:

Production code

Code that runs in production. This is the code you want to own and keep as simple as possible. This code delivers features to your users and generates value for your organization.

Non-production code

Code that does not run in production. If code is not being executed by the actions of your users it is not generating value. This code should be kept to an absolute minimum and be purely dedicated to ensuring the stability of your application.

Third-party code

Code that runs in production but is written by someone outside your organization. This is also code that you want to minimize (see "Think before you install" on page 186). Integrating this code, especially after major or minor updates to the library, can often demand a high investment of time and energy. Bugs introduced by third-party code can also be fiendishly difficult to isolate and usually depend on someone else to fix and release.

Now that you've taken a zoomed-out look at your total costs, let's focus on the two pillars of serverless cost on AWS: compute and storage.

Compute Costs

Serverless compute using AWS Lambda will typically be widespread in your serverless architecture. It is one of the most important cost models to understand when you are getting started, as it probably differs the most from what you are familiar with.

Compute Will Cost Less Than You Expect

What may surprise you if you have not yet operated a serverless workload in production is that Lambda is rarely the most expensive line in your monthly bill. If you have previously operated containerized applications, on Amazon EC2 or AWS Fargate for example, the cost of compute on your servers will have been a primary concern and high on your bill. But compute costs do not translate from containers to functions and cannot be compared like-for-like.

As you design and implement your serverless architecture, you will begin to spread your business logic and compute across many distinct managed services, including Step Functions, EventBridge, and SQS in addition to Lambda. You may not even have a single Lambda function in your application (see "The Functionless Integration Pattern" on page 236).

So, your serverless compute bill may be less than you expect, but it will also be spread across various services and not just concentrated around your Lambda functions. The following sections discuss the cost implications of using other serverless services as well as operational tools, such as CloudWatch. As you'll see, these costs can actually be much higher than your compute bill.

AWS Lambda pricing

AWS Lambda has always been the serverless trailblazer, and its pricing model is no exception. Lambda pioneered the serverless pay-per-use model when it launched in 2014, with teams quickly realizing the immense potential of only paying for compute that your application actually uses. No more paying for servers while they sat idle!

Lambda pricing is split into two areas: requests and duration. You are charged for each request made to the Lambda service to invoke a function and for the time it takes to complete each invocation.

The invocation duration is calculated from the time your code begins executing until it returns, throws an error, or exceeds the amount of time allocated to it. (Refer to Chapter 6 for tips on optimizing the request duration of your Lambda functions by fine-tuning the memory allocation and timeout configuration.)

There are various tiers of duration billing, depending on the memory allocated to the function. For more information, see the AWS Lambda pricing page (*https://oreil.ly/gzdbc*).

The cheapest Lambda function is one that is never invoked! You can use the request validation feature (*https://oreil.ly/OzxRM*) of API Gateway to prevent Lambda function invocations when invalid API requests are received.

The AWS Free Tier (covered later in this chapter) allocates 1 million requests per month for free. After that initial 1 million, you are charged $0.20 per 1 million requests (or $0.0000002 per request).

Free tier allocations are offered per AWS account.

Here's an example: if you make 3 million function invocation requests to Lambda per month, you will incur a cost of $0.40. If each of those function requests was allocated 1,024 MB of memory, the cost would be $0.0000000167 per 1 ms. So, if each invocation took 4 seconds to execute, the total duration bill would be $0.0000668. The combined request and duration bill would be $0.4000668.

AWS Step Functions pricing

In addition to AWS Lambda, you may use AWS Step Functions to execute your business logic code. Step Functions also uses a pay-per-use pricing model, so you only pay for the resources you consume.

There are two types of Step Functions workflows: standard and express. Standard and express workflows differ in several ways, including billing. For more details on the differences between the two types of workflows, see the Step Functions documentation (*https://oreil.ly/2iS1l*).

For standard workflows, you are charged based on the number of state transitions. The AWS Free Tier offers 4,000 free state transitions per month. Beyond this, you are charged $0.025 per 1,000 state transitions (or $0.000025 per state transition).

If your workflow includes a retry mechanism for handling step errors, such as AWS SDK requests, each retry will be charged as an additional state transition.

For express workflows, you are charged based on the number of requests for your workflow (at a rate of $1.00 per 1 million requests, or $0.000001 per request) and its duration. Workflow duration is calculated from the time it starts executing until it completes successfully or is terminated. The price per 100 ms for the duration of your workflow depends on the amount of memory consumed during execution. See the Step Functions pricing page (*https://oreil.ly/8gZ2G*) for full details of the various pricing tiers for express workflows.

> The memory consumption of an express workflow execution is based on various attributes: the size of the workflow's definition, the use of map or parallel states, and the size of the initial payload provided as input to each execution.

Storage Costs

In the previous section, you learned that serverless compute costs can be significantly lower than you might expect. Conversely, the cost of storing operational data and application state will most likely be similar to the non-serverless applications you have operated in the past.

Let's take a look at the pricing models of the common storage services found in serverless architectures: S3 and DynamoDB.

Amazon S3 pricing

There are two primary costs to be aware of when using Amazon S3: storage and requests. You are charged for the amount of data stored in a bucket, based on the size of the objects, how long the objects have been stored during the month, and the storage class.

> You can apply a compression algorithm to your data before storing it in S3 to save on storage costs. If you are using Kinesis Firehose to stream data into an S3 bucket, you can use the built-in support for file compression.

S3 provides a number of storage classes, each optimized to store specific categories of data under different use cases. See the AWS documentation (*https://oreil.ly/BlA8o*) for a full list of the storage classes. Table 9-1 shows a comparison of storage costs between storage classes.

Table 9-1. Comparison of pricing across S3 storage classes

Storage class	Storage pricing (per GB)
Standard	First 50 TB/month: $0.023 Next 450 TB/month: $0.022 Over 500 TB/month: $0.021
Standard-IA	$0.0125
One Zone-IA	$0.01
Glacier Instant Retrieval	$0.004
Glacier Flexible Retrieval	$0.0036
Glacier Deep Archive	$0.00099

A very useful feature of S3 is the ability to move objects across storage classes in the same bucket. For example, an object could be initially stored in the Standard class while it is frequently accessed by your application's processes, then moved to an archival storage class—such as Standard-IA (Infrequent Access) or Glacier Instant Retrieval—once it will only need to be retrieved as part of an ad hoc process, such as an audit.

Objects can also be automatically expired (*https://oreil.ly/6eCAN*) and removed from a bucket once they are no longer required by your application. You can use the S3 storage analytics tool (*https://oreil.ly/ephO8*) to analyze data access patterns and help you decide on your object lifecycle policy (see Figure 9-2).

 When determining your lifecycle policy, you should be aware of the minimum duration charges when expiring or transitioning objects in certain storage classes. Refer to the S3 documentation (*https://oreil.ly/VQIhk*) for details.

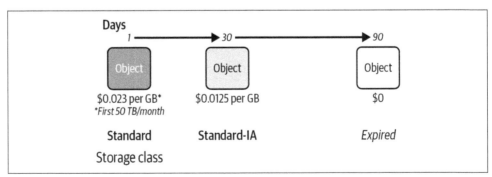

Figure 9-2. Object lifecycle policy

In addition to the storage of objects in your buckets, you will also incur costs when making requests to S3 buckets and objects, for example to store and encrypt new objects, or to retrieve and decrypt existing objects.

> If you are encrypting (and decrypting) S3 objects with AWS KMS, you should use bucket keys (*https://oreil.ly/RdYnf*). Bucket keys are reused over a limited period of time to reduce the requests from S3 to KMS. This can result in a cost reduction of up to 99%.

Amazon DynamoDB pricing

Your DynamoDB tables will be charged based on the number of read and write requests to the table and the amount of data stored in the table. Storage is billed per GB per month.

Read and write requests can be handled with two billing modes (*https://oreil.ly/pI5Cs*): provisioned or on-demand. With the on-demand capacity mode (*https://oreil.ly/4eDbY*) you pay per read and write request to the table. With the provisioned capacity mode (*https://oreil.ly/LsvuD*) you specify the projected number of read and write requests that your application requires and pay based on the amount of capacity that you provision, whether you use it or not.

The capacity mode that is most cost-effective for a table will depend on the expected usage. In general, on-demand mode is suited to tables with unknown, unpredictable, or bursty traffic that scales rapidly. Provisioned mode is ideal for consistent or predictable traffic that scales gradually.

> Consider the cost implications of your DynamoDB tables when designing your data models and analyzing access patterns. Alex DeBrie provides a lot of great content in *The DynamoDB Book* and his blog post on estimating DynamoDB costs (*https://oreil.ly/9mGZC*).

Similar to S3, you have different storage class options (*https://oreil.ly/h4DHt*) for your DynamoDB tables: Standard and Standard-IA. The Standard-IA table class is ideal for long-term storage of data that is accessed infrequently and can reduce storage costs by up to 60% (*https://oreil.ly/T9ihq*). If storage is your dominant cost factor, then you should use the Standard-IA table class; otherwise, you should go with Standard.

> You can use the Time to Live (TTL) attribute in your table to automatically remove expired data. See the DynamoDB documentation (*https://oreil.ly/8zUdW*) for more details.

Read and write requests can be reduced by enabling DynamoDB's in-memory cache, DynamoDB Accelerator (DAX) (*https://oreil.ly/D5WNg*). DAX can reduce the operational cost of DynamoDB, particularly if your table is read-intensive or is subject to sporadic bursts of read requests. DAX is charged per hour based on the size of the cache, so make sure you will achieve enough of a cost saving to make it worthwhile.

 You will incur additional charges related to storage and read and write requests if you enable any extra features, including backups, replication via global tables, and change data capture via streams.

Avoiding Serverless Cost Gotchas

In the next section, we'll explore the tools and techniques available for estimating serverless costs. However, the cost of a serverless application that is distributed across many managed services, interacting constantly as traffic flows into and through your system, can be difficult to predict.

These more obscure costs can be seen as secondary costs of an application. Primary costs are incurred by usage of services that are core to your application, such as Lambda function invocations or DynamoDB storage. Secondary costs are typically incurred by service integrations. For example, services may perform API requests to facilitate integration with other services, such as retrieving KMS encryption keys to encrypt or decrypt data at rest or in transit, or operational tasks, such as sending logs to CloudWatch.

In Chapter 6, we recommended that you deploy to production as soon as possible to truly understand the behavior of your application. The same applies for monitoring costs, covered in the last section of this chapter—cost estimation will only get you so far, and for an accurate picture you'll need to run your application in production. But not everything needs to be learned the hard way with billing surprises!

The following list describes some of the most common billing gotchas to be aware of when designing and operating your serverless application:

CloudWatch costs
> CloudWatch is usually at or near the top of any serverless bill. You will be charged per GB of data ingested by CloudWatch Logs and per GB of data stored. Keep logging to a minimum (see Chapter 4 for how this can also improve security and reduce the risk of logging sensitive data) and prefer tracing with X-Ray where viable (see Chapter 8 for more information about tracing). Always set a retention period (*https://oreil.ly/ut-A7*) for your log groups (logs are kept indefinitely by default) and only retain log data for as long as it is useful.

Consider moving log data to a cheaper alternative, such as S3 Glacier (*https://oreil.ly/1Ccvx*), if you require a long-term archive. CloudWatch alarms can also become expensive, as you are charged per metric listed in the alarm for every hour that the alarm is active during the month. Per the advice in Chapter 8, any alarms without a clear purpose should be removed.

Transfer-out costs

A common operations strategy is to transfer logs and metrics from CloudWatch to other systems for aggregation and analysis. If you do this for logs, you will be charged per GB of data transferred out from AWS to the internet. When transferring metrics out of CloudWatch, you should understand your options. Be aware of third parties that use the CloudWatch API to poll for metrics, as this will incur a high cost at scale. Prefer to use metric streams (*https://oreil.ly/ay_ka*) where possible.

Expensive caching

Caching is often viewed as a cost-saving technique: less requests means less compute and less cost. However, this may not always be true with serverless compute on Lambda, and you should always estimate costs based on volume with and without a cache. For example, in some high-volume scenarios applying API Gateway caching in front of your Lambda functions can get very expensive, as you are billed per GB of cache size per hour (*https://oreil.ly/gTYEw*). Consider applying a caching strategy in future iterations once you have validated the need for it in production and confirmed it will reduce costs. In addition to API Gateway caching, you should also evaluate the other caching options available for your architecture, including Amazon Elastic File System (EFS) (*https://oreil.ly/c3IP3*), Amazon ElastiCache (*https://oreil.ly/6YvpQ*), Amazon ElastiCache Serverless (*https://oreil.ly/crSyt*), and Amazon CloudFront (*https://oreil.ly/0zVFc*).

Services calling other services

Many AWS services make use of other services. The associated costs of these underlying operations can always be found in the pricing page for a service, but they're not always obvious when making architectural choices, especially without applying the context of volume to your estimates. For example, Amazon Athena can be a very inexpensive service for medium-volume SQL queries when taken at face value ($5.00 per 1 TB of data scanned, at the time of writing [*https://oreil.ly/e1uP_*]). However, Athena will incur costs for other services, such as when making requests to the Amazon S3 API to query data, using the AWS Glue Data Catalog to model data, and retrieving encryption keys from AWS KMS if the source data in S3 is encrypted. Be careful with estimates and always monitor costs in production when releasing new pieces of infrastructure.

Infinite Lambda loops

It is possible to create an infinite loop of Lambda function invocations when the function outputs to the same service that triggered it. For example, a function may be recursively executed if it puts a message on the SQS queue that invoked it. You can use Lambda's recursive loop detection feature (*https://oreil.ly/THrD6*) to automatically detect and break recursive invocations.

Non-production costs

Be careful of pay-per-use in non-production environments. If you have services that are continually called, for example via scheduled jobs, continuous integration pipelines, or third-party webhooks, the costs could add up. As recommended in Chapter 6, keep pre-production environments to an absolute minimum. Reducing non-production costs is also closely associated with the first point in this list: CloudWatch costs. CloudWatch alarms will usually only be useful in your production environment, and you can also reduce the amount of log data ingested through the use of logging levels depending on your needs in non-production environments.

Serverless Cost Estimation

Now that you know how much some of the popular serverless services cost, it's time to figure out how to estimate costs for your own operations. Cost estimation can be a very useful exercise, especially when designing new serverless applications or microservices and evaluating architectural options. However, it can be difficult to accurately predict operational costs for an application that is distributed across myriad managed services, all with pay-per-use pricing models.

Before attempting to estimate the total cost of your application, you need to understand the parts of your architecture—the integrations, operations, and resources—that will generate cost. Figure 9-3 shows an example architecture, consisting of an API Gateway API integrated with a Step Functions state machine that makes a read request to DynamoDB and puts events onto an EventBridge event bus. CloudWatch is used to collect logs and metrics across all the services and maintain alarms based on the metrics. Each point that will generate cost is shown with a $.

Precise cost estimates also rely on fairly accurate knowledge of expected traffic. You should encourage estimation within your team, but keep in mind that your estimates are just estimates. For this reason, estimation should always be balanced with cost monitoring and continuous optimization, which we'll discuss in the next section.

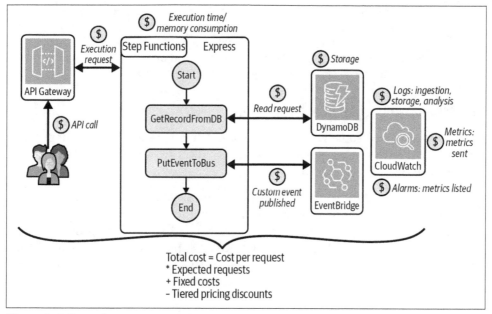

Figure 9-3. Serverless cost generation

If you are improving an existing service running in production, historic cost analysis (*https://oreil.ly/hqVQD*) can also help inform future cost estimation.

How to Estimate Costs

You can follow these steps to get started with serverless cost estimation:

1. Gather data on the expected volume of requests to your application, including normal levels and peak periods.

2. Identify the areas of your architecture that will generate cost (see Figure 9-3).

3. Extract the relevant costs from the pricing pages of the AWS services in your architecture.

4. Use your preferred tool to capture cost estimates based on pricing and expected volume. This could be a spreadsheet, a FinOps platform, or the AWS Pricing Calculator (*https://calculator.aws*).

Your organization may have an AWS support team consisting of one or more solution architects. You should always consult these experts when designing your architecture and estimating the cost of new features and applications, as they can offer valuable insights into managed service pricing models and functionality.

The More You Use, the Less You Spend

Earlier we discussed some gotchas to avoid, but there are also several more direct ways to save costs. Tiered pricing is one such strategy, where the cost of certain resources becomes cheaper as your consumption increases.

There are various AWS pricing models that include tiered pricing. Your usage of a managed service or particular resource will determine the pricing tier your application is subject to. As your consumption increases and you move up tiers, the cost per resource will decrease. For example, CloudWatch metrics (*https://oreil.ly/PU04Q*) and S3 Standard storage class buckets (*https://oreil.ly/dy3Cl*) both have tiered pricing. Tables 9-2 and 9-3 show the pricing schedules at the time of writing.

Table 9-2. CloudWatch metrics tiered pricing

Tiers	Cost (metric/month)
First 10,000 metrics	$0.30
Next 240,000 metrics	$0.10
Next 750,000 metrics	$0.05
Over 1,000,000 metrics	$0.02

Table 9-3. S3 Standard tiered pricing

Tiers	Cost (metric/month)
First 50 TB/month	$0.0245 per GB
Next 450 TB/month	$0.0235 per GB
Over 500 TB/month	$0.0225 per GB

It is important to be aware of tiered pricing when estimating costs and making architectural decisions.

How Much Can Be Done with the AWS Free Tier?

The AWS Free Tier (*https://oreil.ly/EHMId*) is an indispensable tool to be aware of when planning and calculating your serverless operation costs. The free tier is primarily aimed at teams who are just starting out with deploying new applications to the cloud and allows for exploration without a monetary commitment. It's great for teams that are finding their feet with serverless or want to evaluate particular services before fully committing to an architecture.

 Whenever you try things out, remember to clean up. Not only is this good practice from a security perspective (see Chapter 4), but it will help you avoid unexpected costs from non-pay-per-use resources, such as secrets in AWS Secrets Manager, notebooks in Amazon Neptune, or Amazon Managed Streaming for Apache Kafka (MSK) clusters.

There are three categories of offers in the free tier:

Free trials

Short-term trial periods for individual AWS services, such as free usage for the first two months of Amazon SageMaker or 30 days of Amazon Macie. Free trials are great for experimenting with a new service or running prototypes.

12 months free

Free usage of services activated when you create an AWS account; expires after a year.

Always free

A free allocation of resource consumption that never expires. This free pricing tier is excellent for low-scale applications and for reducing costs during low traffic periods. Offers include 1 million free Lambda requests per month and 25 GB of free storage in DynamoDB per month.

Most AWS services provide offers in one or more of the free tier categories, giving you the opportunity to experiment with new features or apply cost-saving strategies based on your traffic.

Serverless Cost Monitoring Best Practices

In this section you will learn how to monitor the cost of your serverless application and how to reduce that cost over time as your application evolves. Like serverless security, discussed in Chapter 4, optimizing serverless cost is not a one-time, preproduction activity. Cost optimization must be a continuous process that is part of the fabric of your team.

Creating Cost Awareness in a Serverless Team

The foundation for continuously optimizing cost over the lifetime of your serverless application is to make operational costs a primary concern of the team responsible for building and operating it. Cost should be discussed and considered at every stage of your application's delivery lifecycle, from the design of its components to operation in production and retrospective analysis of billing (see Figure 9-4).

Figure 9-4. Serverless cost lifecycle

Cost-driven design

Cost estimates should be included in your solution designs (see the solution design template in Appendix C) when designing new features and applications. The engineers in your team should be aware of the pricing models of the services they use and the cost implications of their architectural decisions and trade-offs.

The architecture diagrams you draw as part of your solution design can be annotated with information pertaining to a cost estimate of the solution. This could include the configuration of a Lambda function or SQS queue and the prices of AWS API requests or resources. You can also include service quotas and resource limits that will support your operations (see Chapter 8). Figure 9-5 shows an example architecture diagram with cost and operations annotations.

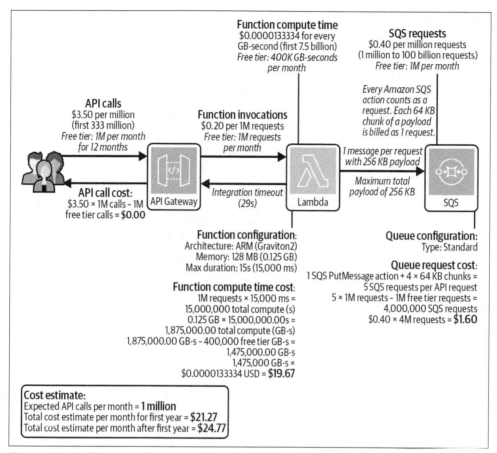

Figure 9-5. Architecture diagram with cost estimates, pricing, and quotas

You build it, you pay for it

The DevOps movement was neatly captured in a phrase coined by Amazon CTO Dr. Werner Vogels in 2006 (*https://oreil.ly/_UOnk*): "You build it, you run it." The same approach is now being applied to the financial operations related to software engineering. The emergent practice of FinOps (*https://oreil.ly/bInk_*) is crucial to continued operational and cost efficiency. The cost of operating your application should be monitored in the same way as its performance and health.

Conducting regular AWS Well-Architected Framework reviews as a team, with a focus on the Cost Optimization pillar (*https://oreil.ly/kPsn8*), can be an effective way of establishing cost awareness in your serverless team.

Billing analysis

To create cost awareness in your team, it is absolutely essential to provide access to your AWS bills. The AWS Billing console (*https://oreil.ly/D0M4K*) and Cost Explorer (*https://oreil.ly/5571W*) are both integral tools for analyzing the cost of your serverless application and should be made available to all engineers in each of your AWS accounts, including production.

You should establish a monthly billing analysis process in your team to identify consistently high costs. Start by using the Cost Explorer to group costs by service, as shown in the screenshot in Figure 9-6.

Billing analysis should happen immediately if a critical billing alert is triggered. Your monthly analysis should cover expectedly high costs, whereas your alerts should catch unexpected and sudden increases in costs.

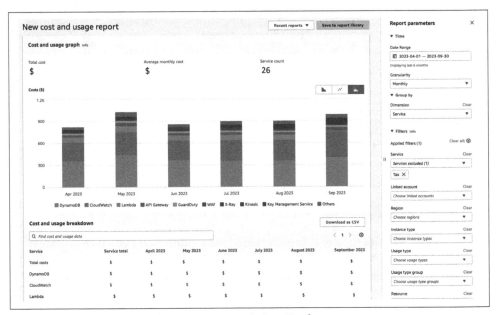

Figure 9-6. Grouping costs by service in AWS Cost Explorer

Identify the three services with the highest costs and ask each other whether the cost of each seems reasonable, or if it has significantly increased since the previous month.

If something doesn't look right and needs further exploration, you can then drill down into the individual line items in your monthly bill via the Billing console, as shown in the screenshot in Figure 9-7.

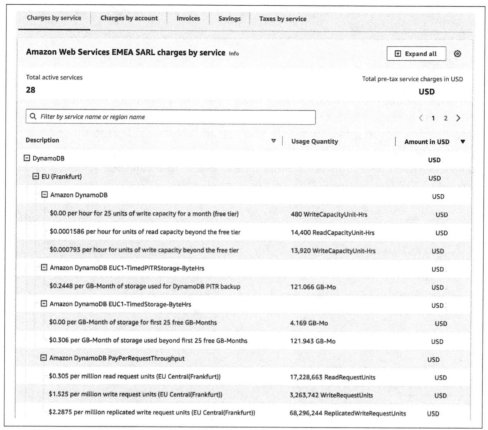

Description	Usage Quantity	Amount in USD

Charges by service | Charges by account | Invoices | Savings | Taxes by service

Amazon Web Services EMEA SARL charges by service Info

Total active services
28

Total pre-tax service charges in USD
USD

Q Filter by service name or region name

‹ 1 2 ›

Description	Usage Quantity	Amount in USD
⊟ DynamoDB		USD
⊟ EU (Frankfurt)		USD
⊟ Amazon DynamoDB		USD
$0.00 per hour for 25 units of write capacity for a month (free tier)	480 WriteCapacityUnit-Hrs	USD
$0.0001586 per hour for units of read capacity beyond the free tier	14,400 ReadCapacityUnit-Hrs	USD
$0.000793 per hour for units of write capacity beyond the free tier	13,920 WriteCapacityUnit-Hrs	USD
⊟ Amazon DynamoDB EUC1-TimedPITRStorage-ByteHrs		USD
$0.2448 per GB-Month of storage used for DynamoDB PITR backup	121.066 GB-Mo	USD
⊟ Amazon DynamoDB EUC1-TimedStorage-ByteHrs		USD
$0.00 per GB-Month of storage for first 25 free GB-Months	4.169 GB-Mo	USD
$0.306 per GB-Month of storage used beyond first 25 free GB-Months	121.943 GB-Mo	USD
⊟ Amazon DynamoDB PayPerRequestThroughput		USD
$0.305 per million read request units (EU Central(Frankfurt))	17,228,663 ReadRequestUnits	USD
$1.525 per million write request units (EU Central(Frankfurt))	3,263,742 WriteRequestUnits	USD
$2.2875 per million replicated write request units (EU Central(Frankfurt))	68,296,244 ReplicatedWriteRequestUnits	USD

Figure 9-7. Inspecting lines in a bill in the AWS Billing console

Compare the costs to the previous month, discuss the possible reasons for any cost increases (such as recent code changes or increased traffic), and finally decide on the potential cost-reduction options to explore.

Monitoring Costs with Budget Alerts

You can use AWS Budgets (*https://oreil.ly/PdafR*) to proactively monitor your monthly expenditure, setting budgets for your application and receiving alerts when those budgets are exceeded.

Monitoring costs is all about being proactive. You don't want to be alerted to spiraling costs after they have been accrued; you want to detect a monthly bill that is increasing at a faster rate than usual so you can take action immediately.

You can set budgets to alert against either actual values or forecasted values.

A sensible strategy for setting budget alerts is to first establish a baseline by calculating your average bill over the past few months. If your expected traffic can be unpredictable or susceptible to bursts, you can add a reasonable amount of buffer to this baseline. For example, if your average bill is $1,100, you might want to set your budget as $1,500 to account for fluctuations in traffic. You can then set alerts at 80%, 90%, and 100% (see Figure 9-8).

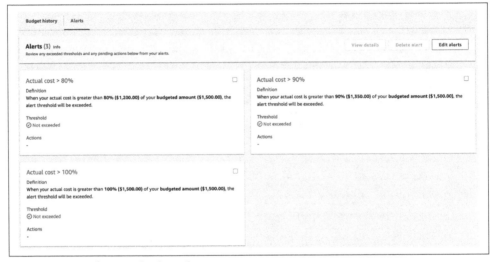

Figure 9-8. Configuring budget alerts

The AWS Cost Management console includes a cost anomaly detection feature (*https://oreil.ly/AdLsP*) that uses machine learning models to alert you to anomalies in your spending.

Reducing the Operational Cost of Serverless

Due to the use of multiple interconnected managed services in a serverless application, cost is intrinsically linked to architecture. Excessive and expensive usage of a service or direct integration usually indicates architectural inefficiencies. If you're doing something expensive, there is probably a better way to do it!

A drive toward cost reduction can also provide data-driven motivation for paying off technical debt. Rather than refactoring for the sake of refactoring, you can target your refactoring to specific areas of your architecture and business logic (see Chapter 11 for information about continuous refactoring). The impact of these refactors can also be accurately measured by the change in cost.

The following is a high-level list of strategies for reducing the cost of your application during its lifetime:

Continually monitor application costs.
As mentioned previously, look for anomalies in your bill over time in order to identify potential optimizations.

Architect for cost.
Make architectural decisions informed by the pricing of the managed services in your infrastructure. This includes the recommendations made earlier in this chapter, such as using S3 object lifecycle management, choosing on-demand mode for your DynamoDB tables, and preferring express Step Functions workflows.

Minimize Lambda functions.
Understand the alternatives to running your code in a Lambda function, such as direct integrations (*https://oreil.ly/6LWkA*) (refer to "The Functionless Integration Pattern" on page 236 for more details), and apply them as much as possible to reduce operational and ownership costs. Functions should not be minimized by combining business logic or tasks into single, monolithic functions, though (see Chapter 6 for details about applying the single-responsibility principle to your functions).

Batch events and requests.
Consider batching events and data processing activity in your system to reduce costs. A lot of managed service pricing models are linked to AWS API requests, and batching can be an effective strategy for reducing the number of requests and, in turn, cost. For example, if you are encrypting objects in an S3 bucket, each `PutObject` request would have an associated `Encrypt` request to KMS. Instead of putting each object into S3 individually, you could batch objects using Kinesis Firehose and make the request to KMS per batch rather than per object.

Use caching.
Utilize the caching functionality (*https://oreil.ly/4KZLj*) of managed services such as Amazon API Gateway, CloudFront, and DynamoDB, where viable and cost-efficient. An efficient cache can significantly decrease your API request handling and storage retrieval costs.

Only deploy operational resources where needed.
> Only deploy operational resources, such as CloudTrail events and CloudWatch alarms, in public environments (i.e., in production, and potentially a public sandbox environment if applicable).

Architect sustainably.
> Many of the patterns and recommendations presented in the Well-Architected Framework's Sustainability pillar (*https://oreil.ly/q5Hmd*) correlate to resource consumption and, therefore, cost efficiency. Refer to Chapter 10 for serverless sustainability best practices.

Consider savings plans.
> If you can predict your application will use a consistent amount of compute over a one- or three-year term, a compute savings plan could save you up to 17% (*https://oreil.ly/i3Onw*) on your AWS Lambda bill.

Summary

The potential to reduce the costs of developing and running your software is likely to be one of the primary reasons you are considering, or actively adopting, serverless. There is obvious appeal in only paying for the resources your application consumes— no more servers costing you money while sitting idle—and this is definitely a good reason to go serverless.

However, you shouldn't stop there. Your ability to take full advantage of the cost efficiency that serverless offers depends on cultivating a cost-aware team. While it is true that you will not incur any costs if your application is not in use, the opposite is also true: if your application begins to receive a significant amount of traffic your costs will increase at the same rate. In this way, the pay-per-use cost model can be both a huge benefit and a significant risk.

In this chapter, you have learned that cost should be a primary concern for your team as you design, build, and operate your serverless application. Cost estimation should always be conducted as you design your architecture. Depending on the complexity of your architecture and predictability of your traffic, it can be difficult to precisely estimate costs, so it is also crucial to balance this with billing alerts and monitoring in production. One of your first tasks should be to establish budget alerts to avoid sudden, unexpected spikes in costs.

Interview with an Industry Expert

Ben Ellerby, Founder, aleios, AWS Serverless Hero

Ben Ellerby is the founder of aleios and a dedicated member of the serverless community. In 2020 AWS named him a Serverless Hero (*https://oreil.ly/yiWQl*), recognizing his outstanding work and innovation in cloud and serverless. He is the editor of *Serverless Transformation*: a blog (*https://oreil.ly/N4fpr*), newsletter (*https://oreil.ly/euIDa*), and podcast (*https://oreil.ly/wyRz-*) that share tools, techniques, and use cases for all things serverless. He co-organizes the Serverless User Group in London, is part of the ServerlessDays London organizing team, and regularly speaks about serverless around the world. At aleios, Ben helps start-ups disrupt and large organizations remain competitive by building with serverless.

Q: As an AWS Serverless Hero and the head of aleios, you have been involved with several serverless implementations. How has serverless changed the way teams pay to deliver and operate their software?

Serverless provides an optimal total cost of ownership by removing complexity and providing a unique pay-per-use billing model that allows us to match cost with demand, all while enabling high levels of scalability. Done correctly, this lowers the cost of delivering and operating software, reducing the cost of building, running, and maintaining it. However, there is a shift from CapEx (fixed assets) to OpEx (ongoing) and the potential for surprises in costs.

Teams need to work to develop their FinOps maturity to ensure they maintain low costs while creating predictability. This is not just a change for the technology team, but a change in budget ownership and in the interaction mode between finance and technology.

Q: You've been a great thought leader in the serverless community, delivering talks, publishing the Serverless Transformation newsletter, and sharing innovative ideas through your blog posts. Are we getting the most out of serverless, or could teams still generate more business value and reduce costs even further?

Serverless is a good step, but it's always part of a larger vision. Whether that vision is reducing time to value or creating an optimal TCO, teams need to be driven by their North Star and leverage serverless to reach it. Serverless can remove complexity, yet when done in a naive way it can create additional cost and get in the way of business value. Serverless is a technology that works well when combined with event-driven and domain-driven design patterns, and when an organization moves to think in a "serverless-first" way.

Q: You have worked on diverse projects with many enterprises over the last few years. How have you estimated the total cost of ownership with serverless, and how effective has that process been?

TCO is typically the core driver for enterprises in their adoption of serverless, be that from a cost perspective or as an enabler for reduced time to value. TCO covers the infrastructure cost (the charge for resources consumed), development cost (the up-front cost to build), and of course the maintenance cost (operational running of the application).

Several organizations have publicly referenceable figures on their achieved TCO results with variation based on the use case, industry, and method of measuring.

When working with enterprises on their adoption of serverless we use our Serverless Staircase framework to structure the modernization program. The first stage, Vision, works to set a North Star Metric as well as lagging and leading indicators. The IDC 2018 study (*https://oreil.ly/ZpExT*) is a useful reference in baselining targets during this phase.

It's difficult to compare TCO results between different organizations and even different divisions of a large enterprise, but it is possible to demonstrate reduction and tie this down to an ROI figure. In practice this means finding a way to baseline your current TCO and finding relevant data points to reality-check your target.

Q: The combination of a pay-per-use billing model and highly scalable serverless operation can result in surprises and unpleasant bills. From your experience, which are the potential billing mistakes teams should watch out for?

Indeed, serverless can scale to large levels, and the pay-per-use model can lead to less predictability. Firstly, service limits/quotas should be raised to levels that enable your application to function well, but they should not be raised blindly—they are a protection. Secondly, analysis should be made of your application architecture, and coupled with load testing, this allows you to model expected costs. Costs should be monitored, and alarms and alerts configured to spot issues early. Some cost spikes will come from natural traffic, others from application errors or from malicious actors. Security should be at the core of your application design to prevent denial of wallet attacks, and protections against common antipatterns like recursive Lambda functions should be in place.

Finally, the ability for serverless to scale, especially in reaction to downstream errors, makes the design of integrations with third parties a key element to get correct. For instance, leveraging a circuit breaker pattern (see "Resilient Architecture: The Circuit Breaker Pattern" on page 226) between your application and a third party not only protects both applications, but also protects against generating large amounts of expensive calls to a paid API.

Q: Through your consultancy work with aleios and Theodo, you have firsthand experience witnessing organizations benefit from migrating their workloads to serverless. What advice would you give to enterprise teams on cost awareness as they design, implement, and operate their first serverless applications?

The key is to recognize that the model of IT procurement has changed. It's no longer provisioning large resources with a predictable and forecasted approach, but instead is a completely dynamic cost, embodied in the move from CapEx to OpEx. This is not just a change in accounting but a change in how costs are managed and evolve.

While the engineering team needs to design and manage costs, it should work closely with finance as a joint team, sharing responsibility. The FinOps movement is a good example of this and can be put into practice with shared cost dashboards, FinOps retros (involving both the engineering and finance teams), and a holistic cost strategy that is able to measure TCO, enabling the right short-term and long-term cost trade-offs to be made.

CHAPTER 10

Sustainability in Serverless

Let everything you do be done as if it makes a difference.
—William James

Before you start reading this chapter, think about or write down three things related to your understanding of sustainability.

While speaking at a serverless conference in Europe, I (Sheen) asked the audience what sustainability meant to them. Their answers were:

- Having a green environment
- Reducing carbon footprint to ensure a sustainable future for our planet
- Using natural resources sensibly so that they can be replenished

A university researcher was traveling to developing countries to collect data for her work, which required visiting remote villages and interacting with various people from local communities. Here is what some of them said to her about their understanding of sustainability:

- Fetching drinking water from afar is a daily struggle. Every day will be good if there is a sustainable way to bring water close to our dwellings.
- Access to hospitals and medical facilities to lead a healthy life for human families and livestock.
- We need support to run our local school, so our children and future generations have better life choices.

A news reporter was making a documentary on how the COVID-19 pandemic had affected people's family lives and what sustainability measures they thought were necessary. Their responses were varied. For example:

- A mother of three young children said the pandemic lockdown taught her to consider financial sustainability for her children's education, holidays, and future.
- A teenager completing her high school education said she wanted people to adopt a healthy lifestyle with respect to food, commuting, recycling, and activities.
- A young software engineer who worked from home for almost three years during the pandemic said he would like to reduce the number of days he drives to work. He thought it would help him lower his carbon emissions, be financially better off, live a healthier life, and be more environmentally responsible.

Compare your thoughts on sustainability with those of these fellow humans—are they aligned, or different?

One theme you might have noticed is that although many of us relate sustainability to the environment we live in—the green energy initiatives and other similar measures—when you get closer to people from different socioeconomic backgrounds, the answers vary.

All answers are correct and related to each person's lived experience. Chapter 1 discussed how the Earth's surface can be considered as a series of connected ecosystems. We are all interconnected in one way or another on our planet, and our ideas about sustainability, however varied they may be, have a common goal.

This chapter looks at sustainability from the serverless technology point of view. It examines how sustainability connects with the serverless ecosystem and its impact on how we build serverless applications and operate them in the cloud.

So, What Is Sustainability?

Let's start with a generic definition of sustainability, not associated with any particular context:

> The ability to keep something going for a prolonged period by nurturing it with a continuous provision of nourishment to ensure its growth and existence.

It gets specialized definitions and meanings when associated with our planet, society, economics, industrial processes, technology, transportation systems, and so on.

The Three Pillars of Sustainability

In 1983, the Brundtland Commission (*https://oreil.ly/L4Cur*) was formed to unite countries on sustainable development. In 1987, it published its report, "Our Common Future," and gave a standard and easily relatable definition of sustainable development:

> Sustainable development is the development that meets the needs of the present without compromising the ability of future generations to meet their own needs.

The commission also identified three pillars or dimensions of sustainable development, as shown in Figure 10-1: social equality, environmental protection, and economic growth.

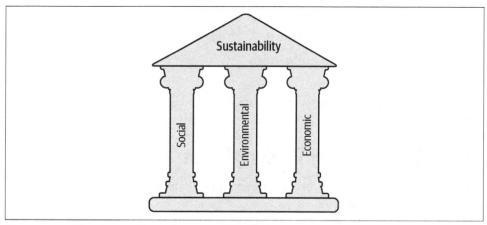

Figure 10-1. The three pillars of sustainable development

Though they are shown here as distinct components, they overlap with dependencies between them—environmental limits, for example, are the primary constraint for social and economic growth.

 The Brundtland Commission was previously known as the World Commission on Environment and Development, a suborganization of the United Nations. It was named after its chairperson, Gro Harlem Brundtland, the former Prime Minister of Norway and a champion of public health.

The UN Sustainable Development Goals

In 2015, the United Nations General Assembly (UNGA) formulated its set of 17 Sustainable Development Goals (SDGs) (*https://sdgs.un.org*) as "A shared blueprint for peace and prosperity for people and the planet, now and into the future." These goals are interlinked and touch every aspect of human life and the environment on this planet. For each one, 8 to 12 targets were identified and up to 4 indicators were defined to measure the progress of reaching each target.

The 17 SDGs are:

1. No poverty
2. Zero hunger
3. Good health and well-being
4. Quality education
5. Gender equality
6. Clean water and sanitation
7. Affordable and clean energy
8. Decent work and economic growth
9. Industry, innovation, and infrastructure
10. Reduced inequalities
11. Sustainable cities and communities
12. Responsible consumption and production
13. Climate action
14. Life below water
15. Life on land
16. Peace, justice, and strong institutions
17. Partnerships for the goals

That's a rather big-picture view of sustainability. So how does serverless fit in? Let's take a look.

Why Is Sustainability Thinking Necessary in Serverless?

The scale of cloud operation is beyond most of our imagination. When consuming cloud services, as an end user or value-added reseller, you only see the face of those services: APIs, functionality, service limits, etc. Most of us never get to take a deeper look at their operation.

Take, for instance, the hugely popular, highly successful, and exceptionally efficient Amazon DynamoDB—the NoSQL data store as a service from AWS. In any given Region, thousands of organizations and software engineers work with millions of DynamoDB tables to store anywhere from a single data item to trillions of items. You may work with its APIs to create, read, update, and delete items in a table—the popular CRUD operations. Beyond that, you may configure its various options for scaling, data retention, streams, replication, etc. But have you ever stopped to imagine the sheer scale of computer resources that must be available to continuously provide such a mammoth service?

Now, multiply that by the number of AWS Regions around the world (at the time of writing, there are 32, with 102 Availability Zones). Add to that other data store services available from AWS—S3, Redshift, Aurora, RDS, etc. Then, add the resources that are in operation to support the functionality of all the other services from AWS across all of those Regions—Lambda functions, message queues, event streams, machine learning, AI, logs, reporting, and so on.

And that's just AWS. Now picture the same for every other cloud provider and the hundreds of services each one operates. That gives you a glimpse of the scale of the cloud operation that supports and influences our daily lives in so many ways. Because it's so vast, to understand its impact on the environment and equip you to think sustainably in serverless, we'll start by breaking it down into its three main components.

The Three Elements of the Cloud

Chapter 1 briefly mentioned the three main elements of the cloud:

Compute resources
> The computing power behind the machines that execute the program instructions

Storage resources
> The myriad data stores and different storage media types where near-infinite volumes of data are stored as bits

Network resources
> The cables that wrap the Earth to take those bits, transport them, and deliver them to your fingertips

When you look at an AWS cloud data center, located in a specific Region and Availability Zone, the racks of equipment spread across acres of enclosed buildings primarily provide these three elements. We consume their interplay as cloud services, including managed services for our serverless applications.

A key element of the sustainability of the cloud is that the cloud infrastructure is securely shared across users, which enables the cloud providers to make very efficient use of it in a way that individual users or organizations cannot. Nevertheless, it takes energy to move data across the network, store data on and retrieve it from disks, or get your Lambda function to perform what it's programmed to do. Every action requires electric power. If you stop to think about this, you can begin to understand why environmental sustainability is hugely significant to cloud operation, and thus to serverless.

The Serverless Sustainability Triangle

As is always the case with software development, building applications using serverless technologies goes through certain phases, such as the inception of an idea, analysis, design, implementation, and operation in the cloud. The techniques you apply and the processes you follow in each phase may be different in serverless, but the underlying ideas are the same.

In a similar way to how we broke down the three main elements of the cloud, if you partition serverless development, you have the *products* you build, the *processes* you follow during the development lifecycle, and the *cloud* where you deploy and operate your applications. When you place sustainability at the center of your serverless development, you can relate its meaning to all of these. Figure 10-2 depicts these three areas as a sustainability triangle. It shows how sustainability adoption is central to serverless solution development.

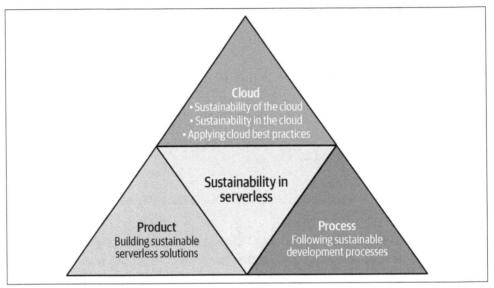

Figure 10-2. The serverless sustainability triangle

In the sustainability triangle:

- Sustainable products (serverless applications) are long-lived, garnering maximum benefits over a long period.

- Sustainable processes are the principles and practices that guide you in developing sustainable products.

- The cloud (the operating platform where your application runs) implements environmental sustainability measures.

The subsequent sections expand on the parts of the serverless sustainability triangle with guidelines and best practices to equip you for your sustainability journey in serverless.

Building Sustainable Serverless Applications

In this section we'll explore what it means to build a sustainable serverless application. The first point to make is that a distinction can be drawn between *maintaining* and *sustaining* an application. Maintaining an application as what you do when it's nearing the end of its life, and you're just making the essential fixes and patches needed to keep the lights on (KTLO). This corresponds roughly to what legacy applications of the past went through with the waterfall development process, as shown in Figure 10-3: products would get released after being in development for months or years, and once released, most of their development activities would cease. Often, a dedicated team would then be responsible for basic KTLO maintenance tasks.

Figure 10-3. The different phases in the waterfall software development lifecycle

With the modern agile, incremental, and iterative development model of serverless applications, you do not spend months developing the product's first iteration. Instead, a stream-aligned engineering team quickly delivers a minimum viable product to customers, then iterates fast to add more features. The same team carries out any necessary fixes while adding new functionality. Rather than KTLO, the team's motivation is to nourish the product to sustain it to last longer, as illustrated in Figure 10-4—the longevity of the application is the ultimate goal.

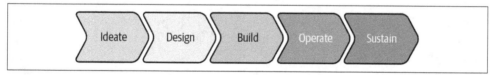

Figure 10-4. The modern agile and incremental way of developing serverless applications

Sustainability in the context of serverless applications refers to building the application in such a way that it has a long lifespan and is continuously nourished with new features to cater to unique and evolving customer needs and business demands. This maximizes the value of the resources used, and avoids wasting resources on obsolete products.

How Do You Identify Unsustainable Serverless Applications?

There is no simple, single measure to easily categorize an application as sustainable or not. Growth-oriented organizations are constantly changing, adopting new technologies, development patterns, and practices; launching new products; and reaching new markets. The pace of technical advancements in cloud and serverless computing, APIs, machine learning, and other fields disrupts the status quo of many enterprises. Keeping up requires a radical rethinking of business domains, boundaries, team structures, and application ownership.

When a team of engineers become the new custodians of an application and begin to understand its architecture and implementation, if you witness any of the emotions shown in Figure 10-5, you know it is a challenging product to sustain.

Figure 10-5. Emotions when engineers analyze or start working with an unsustainable application

Unsustainable applications are not always characterized by the use of legacy technologies. In most cases, it is about *how* the technology has been used to architect and develop the applications.

The following terms are common in the industry when describing unsustainable software:

Big ball of mud (BBoM)
> This is a system that lacks any coherent, understandable architecture; growth is unregulated, dependencies abound, and there is no clear separation of concerns. Many legacy monolithic applications fall into this category, due to years of negligence and a large number of accumulated fixes and hacks.

Lasagne architecture
> As briefly mentioned in Chapter 3, this is an antipattern of layered architecture where there are too many layers, each depending on the one beneath it in the stack.

Spaghetti code
> Spaghetti code refers to unstructured and tangled code with a high degree of hardwired dependencies, making it difficult to modify or extend the software.

Ball of serverless mud (BoSM)
> The BoSM is proof that even using modern technology, you can still build unsustainable applications, as shown back in Figure 2-2 (see "Serverless is not a silver bullet" on page 39).

Characteristics of a Sustainable Application

Once, someone asked Dr. Werner Vogels, CTO of Amazon.com, how we should think differently about software development. He replied, "Your software needs to be operated for decades longer than it took you to write it. Keep that in mind."

As you have learned in this book, a serverless application has many characteristics—security, scalability, and high availability, among other things. But the three most important aspects of a *sustainable* serverless application are:

- Modularity
- Extensibility
- Observability

These characteristics are vital to the architecture, design, development, and operation of serverless applications, as described in the following sections.

Modularity

The concept of modularity in software is not new. Engineers have been thinking in modules for decades, grouping program code as packages, modules, and libraries in a way that promotes code sharing and building layered applications. Chapter 3 discussed how to bring modularity into serverless applications and build microservices as *set pieces*.

To build modular serverless applications, you must think in terms of:

- Domains, subdomains, and bounded contexts, as explained in Chapter 2
- Independent and loosely coupled smaller microservices, as you saw in Chapter 3

The rewards system shown in Figure 3-34 (see "Applying set piece thinking in serverless development" on page 121) is an example of a modular event-driven application.

Extensibility

As highlighted in Chapter 1, incremental and iterative development is a winning way of building modern applications, where teams start small with the minimum viable product and evolve it into a maximum value product. To evolve a product, you need to extend it from its current state into a feature-enriched future state. Extensibility is thus a vital characteristic of a sustainable serverless application.

Chapter 3 demonstrated how asynchronous communication and event-driven computing enable microservices to remain loosely coupled and thus make a serverless application extendable; Figure 3-35 depicts an extended version of the modular application architecture shown in Figure 3-34.

Observability

You should start thinking about observability measures during the architecture and design phases and continue into development and operation. If you cannot observe your application, you do not know how to nourish it to enhance its longevity (i.e., make it sustainable).

As detailed in Chapter 8, the three main ingredients of an observable application (often referred to as the three pillars of observability) are:

- Structured logs
- Distributed traces
- Measurable metrics

Now that you're familiar with the main characteristics of a sustainable serverless application, you can apply the principles and practices described in Chapters 2, 3, 6, and 8 in your serverless development. When you build serverless applications, think of the engineers who will inherit your applications and nourish them in the future to add more business value. It is your responsibility to make them sustainable.

Development Processes and Practices That Promote Sustainability

When developing a sustainable serverless application, you must pay attention to the following three key elements:

People
    Both the producers and consumers of a product

Processes
    The principles and practices that enable you to build the product

Products
   The cloud services you consume to build your product

Discussion of processes always creates some apprehension among engineers, due to the fear of learning new things or disrupting existing practices. Engineers will also need to shift their mindset to think about and accommodate new nonfunctional requirements and consider sustainability measures.

Follow Lean Development Principles and Reduce Resource Waste

Value stream mapping is a popular lean exercise that allows software development teams to optimize their delivery processes by identifying waste in the product lifecycle. A value-stream map visually represents the critical steps in a process, showing the time taken at and between each stage and the outcome. Figure 10-6 shows a simple value-stream map of the journey of a feature from the point of code commit to release in production.

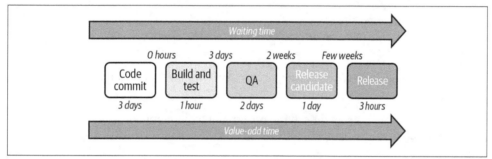

Figure 10-6. Value-stream map of a software change from development to release in the production system

In this figure, the *value-add time* is the duration of each activity. For example, it took three days for an engineer to make the code changes and commit them to the repository. The *waiting time* is the duration between the phases. For example, the release candidate was not created until two weeks after QA was completed. This two-week period is wasted time for the business.

From a sustainability point of view, the waiting time between the phases is a concern. Generally, the resources used for each phase (compute, storage, network) are kept active until the pipeline moves to the next phase. This means the resources used for QA will remain active for two weeks longer than necessary, while waiting for the release candidate to be created. During this time, they will be consuming energy and adding to the overall carbon footprint.

Start from a Simple Set of Requirements and Scale Fast

We've talked a fair bit about the benefits of the incremental development approach in serverless. It's a low-risk, "fail fast, learn faster" approach where you start simple and make decisions late, allowing you to assess and improve in every iteration (Figure 10-7).

Incremental development and delivery is a good fit with serverless because many of the managed services you consume to compose your application are pay-per-use and provisioned on-demand. You don't need to make up-front resource commitments beyond what is necessary for your application at each iteration. This is cost-effective and benefits cloud sustainability due to optimal resource and energy consumption.

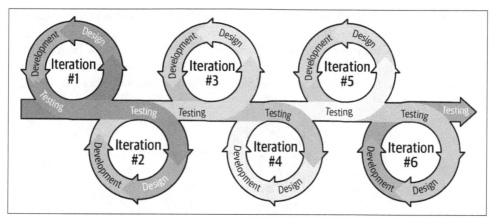

Figure 10-7. The Agile methodology of incremental, iterative development (source: adapted from an image by Pacific Research [https://oreil.ly/6hUeX])

Automate Everything Possible

Automate everything you can, from testing to code deployment pipelines, observing your application, and remediating issues. Automation is the core of serverless development and operation (DevOps). In addition to improving development velocity, reducing resource waste is another crucial benefit of automation. Tasks that rely on manual intervention add slack to the overall duration of your deployment pipeline, as shown in Figure 10-6. Adding automation to your development process can help improve the value stream by reducing waiting time.

Automation can also be used for provisioning the right-sized cloud resources at the time of need and decommissioning them soon after they have served their purpose—tasks like deleting stale data, cleaning up logs, and removing unneeded data stores (even if they don't cost you anything) all have sustainability benefits.

Rethink the Throwaway Prototypes of the Past

Every software engineer builds prototypes during their career. It's a great way to experiment with your ideas and prove the concept before making it real. In the past, prototypes and proofs of concept (PoCs) tended to be quick and hacky, minimalistic implementations intended just to showcase the suitability of technology or ideas. They were used to get buy-in from stakeholders, then typically abandoned or deleted, as they held no value beyond that unnecessarily specific purpose.

You can develop a different mindset when working with cloud and serverless technologies. As shown in Figure 10-8, the cloud resources you consume are the same across your different environments or stages: dev, test, QA, UAT, sandbox, performance, prod, etc., are simply logical separations. You work with the same cloud services in your development account that serve customers in your production account.

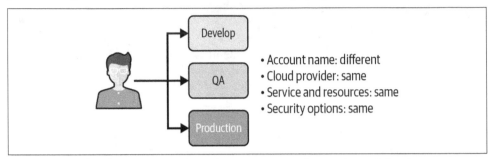

Figure 10-8. Cloud accounts are logical separations and groupings of cloud resources with the same physical characteristics

With some up-front thinking and planning (and depending on the nature of the prototype), you can build your prototypes in a way that enables you to evolve them from minimum viable products to maximum value products. This is known as *evolutionary prototyping*. With a throwaway prototype, you waste engineering hours and increase the amount of service churn by repeatedly provisioning and removing cloud resources. Evolutionary prototyping maximizes the efficiency of your resource use.

Nurture Your Serverless Engineers

To effectively implement sustainable serverless applications by following sustainability-enabling processes, you need a pool of talented engineers who understand your enterprise's goals and have the right attitude to accomplish them. In Chapter 2, we discussed how to nurture serverless engineers with the necessary support and encouragement.

Establishing a sustainable team of serverless engineers in your organization takes time, requires much effort, and is a long-term investment. How quickly you can grow serverless engineers and establish expert teams depends on your organizational structure and culture. However, it's well worth it, as by doing so you cultivate and sustain talents that share your sustainability goals.

Sustainability and the AWS Cloud

Chapter 2 stressed the importance of considering your cloud provider as a partner and working together with them to optimize your consumption of their cloud services for the betterment of your business. AWS provides numerous services, tools, and best practice guides that you can use to achieve your desired goals. It even offers direct assistance in some areas, such as event management and architecture review. However, in most cases it's up to you to use these resources appropriately. Cloud and serverless security is a good example: when you develop serverless applications, you must use the provided services correctly and apply the required security measures in your application. The responsibility here is shared between AWS and you. (Chapter 4 discussed this topic in detail.)

Like security, achieving your sustainability targets for the cloud is a shared responsibility between AWS and you. As a sustainability-conscious cloud consumer, your goal is enabling your organization to fulfill its sustainability promises by reaching its sustainability targets. As a sustainable cloud provider, AWS aims to equip you with the tools you need to reach this goal.

While working for AWS, Adrian Cockroft, technology strategy advisor and a pioneer in sustainability measures, proposed the shared sustainability responsibility model (*https://oreil.ly/CkCKG*), depicted in Figure 10-9:

- AWS is responsible for the sustainability *of* the cloud.

- You are responsible for the sustainability *in* the cloud.

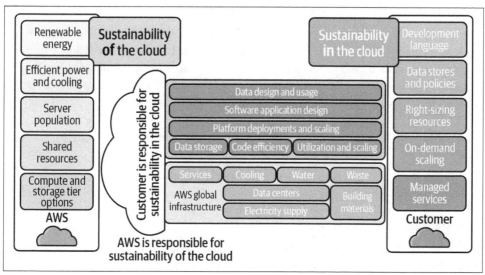

Figure 10-9. The shared sustainability responsibility model recommended by AWS

Depending on the nature of the business domain and the types of serverless applications you develop and operate, there are various patterns and best practices covering different areas that you can use as guides. For example, if your application processes a high volume of data, sustainability patterns and practices specific to handling and storing data will be significant to you. The following section presents implementation patterns for different areas of the serverless development cycle.

Implementation Patterns and Best Practices for Sustainability

In terms of patterns and practices, there are four distinct areas you can focus on for sustainability as part of your daily consumption of cloud services:

1. User behavior
2. Software architecture
3. Data and storage
4. Development and deployment

The following sections discuss each of these in detail.

User Behavior

When you release a new feature, you assess how your consumers use it so that you can identify issues and make enhancements quickly. With sustainability thinking, you must add measures to align with your sustainability goals as well.

For example, suppose your customers use the application during regular office hours in a particular region. In that case, you do not need to run all the cloud resources during out-of-office hours. You plan to be efficient in resource consumption, which, in turn, enables energy efficiency. This section presents you with best practices based on the usage of your applications and the consumers' behavior.

 Serverless-first thinking is the first and foremost user behavior pattern for sustainability in the cloud.

Understanding consumer demand

Observability is a key characteristic of a sustainable serverless application. The survival of your application and the value it brings to your business depend on how visible its functioning is. Knowledge of the usage of your application is a key factor that forms the basis of your contribution to sustainability in the cloud. Here are some best practices surrounding consumer demand:

Use the minimum resources necessary to meet the demand.
The managed cloud services have built-in elasticity to scale on demand. You do not need to overprovision resources as the platform will scale up and down depending on the demand.

Remove expired customer content promptly.
In several situations, your application uses data for operational purposes and it is not needed in the long term. To reduce your storage consumption, you should remove any customer content that you're storing when it is no longer needed for business purposes.

"Data and Storage" on page 426 explains the sustainability best practices for handling data in detail.

Scale as per the service level agreement, and not over.
Chapter 1 briefly mentioned optimizing your application for sustainability. Traditionally, scaling and optimization techniques have focused on the cost and performance of an application. With sustainability as the third element, you need to balance the trade-offs between them carefully.

The general rule of thumb is that if you optimize for cost, you will likely favor sustainability as your application will consume fewer resources. However, if you scale to target the highest performance factor, you will likely consume more resources than you need to meet your application's SLA.

Planning for high-traffic events

A key area in which you will benefit from working with AWS as partners is in preparing to face business-significant occasions such as high-sales events (like Black Friday), new product launches, the opening of ticket sales for a popular event, the release of a much-awaited movie trailer, and so on. Some events happen globally, and others are regional. Either way, there is a huge amount riding on your organization's ability to handle these crucial events well—the implications are not only financial, but extend to brand value and customer trust.

AWS Infrastructure Event Management (IEM) (*https://oreil.ly/ uDq9B*) is a support option included with the Enterprise Support plan and available as an extra to Business Support customers. IEM "offers architecture and scaling guidance and operational support during the preparation and execution of planned events, such as shopping holidays, product launches, and migrations…. [It] will help you assess operational readiness, identify and mitigate risks, and execute your event confidently with AWS experts by your side."

While the focus is primarily on the business, you must also consider the sustainability impact of such high-impact events. You can share your organization's sustainability ambitions and goals during event preparations with your AWS technical account manager (TAM) to get advice and actionable steps. Here are a few key points to keep in mind:

Collect and study historical metrics.

For many enterprises, special events are a recurring thing. You may have a monthly new product launch event, or seasonal sales. As you and your team gain experience, you'll be able to prepare for many of these events yourselves without needing the support of AWS. A practice that builds confidence and equips you to do so is the creation of a record of metric data from previous and historical events. You can quickly extrapolate to identify new measures based on past data and current business ambitions.

If your organization has multiple domains and teams, event planning may happen within specific domains or product areas. As there will be several teams and AWS accounts working separately, it becomes the task of a platform or enabling team to coordinate with everyone to collect the relevant details and identify representatives as necessary.

Provision extra resources just for the events.

A primary benefit of infrastructure event management is identifying the critical applications and services that will bear the brunt of the event traffic. This in turn enables you to identify the relevant cloud services and resources that require attention.

For instance, the global pre-launch of a new product by an online retailer exclusively for account holders would require the customer account microservice to handle a very high volume of user sign-in activity. If API Gateway, Lambda, and Cognito are the primary AWS services used by that microservice, you can plan for provisioning the resources where necessary. To meet the goal of sustainability, you should aim to provide extra resources for the duration of the event but avoid keeping them in a ready or running state for longer than necessary.

Taking services closer to the customers

As explained earlier, networking is a crucial element of the cloud, along with computing and storage. As data moves from one application to another, one account to another, or one region to another, all three main elements of the cloud must work together. As you know, network resources consume energy and have a potential environmental impact. Hence, the recommendation is to limit data movement where possible as you serve your customers. Here are a few best practices to keep in mind:

Deploy services close to customers to avoid network round trips.
The advice here is simple, but as you can imagine, the implementation of it is more complex than it may sound. Analyzing and identifying the requests for data that you receive and the types of data you can move closer to your users is vital.

Some of the challenges you may face include:

- There is a legal requirement to keep your customer or account data in one Region. However, you have neutral content, such as product details, that has no restrictions and is ideal for keeping closer to the customers, in their Regions.

- You want to store customer data in a Region close to your customers, but not all of the cloud services you use may be available in that Region.

Data ingestion and processing is an area that causes sustainability concerns due to the sheer volume of data moving across the network. The best approach is to process the data close to where you collect it so you can run data analytics and capture business insights before transferring the results to your main account after discarding the unneeded data.

Cache frequently accessed content at the edge.
Caching frequently accessed and static content, such as videos, images, reports, etc., at edge locations worldwide to bring it closer to users is a common and popular pattern.

AWS services such as CloudFront, ElastiCache, and Lambda@Edge suit this purpose. You can also employ API response caching and database caching, such as DynamoDB Accelerator.

> While working to reduce the environmental impact of your operations in the cloud, it's important to also assess the cost implications to your business. Some of the caching options are expensive in comparison to others. For example, Amazon API Gateway caching is charged by the hour, and for heavily used and data-intensive API endpoints that require a large capacity, the cost can be higher.

Operate your workloads in AWS Regions that run on green energy.
AWS has set a goal to power all its Regions with 100% renewable energy by 2025. At the time of writing, several AWS Regions, including many in the US and Europe, already operate on 100% renewable energy (*https://oreil.ly/mrvtn*).

While choosing a green AWS Region to operate your workloads sounds like the right thing to do to promote a sustainable environment, other factors can influence your decision. Depending on the types of applications you operate,

---

the customer base you serve, and the location of your business, you may have government and industry regulatory compliance measures to consider that affect your choice of Region. For example, you may have a regulatory requirement to keep customer data within a particular country or continent, and this may preclude choosing a Region that runs on green energy.

Another factor is the availability of the AWS services and features you require to develop your serverless applications and operate them in the Region of your choice.

 You can follow Amazon's latest sustainability developments on its dedicated sustainability site (*https://oreil.ly/sHz7K*).

Software Architecture

You've already learned a great deal about serverless architectures, patterns, development, and operating practices in this book. In this section, we'll explore how they are relevant to promoting sustainability in the cloud by looking at some best practices.

 A decoupled event-driven serverless application composed of managed cloud services is a step closer to being environmentally friendly.

Prefer reactive and event-driven microservices

Chapters 3 and 5 discussed the microservices architecture and several implementation patterns to consider while developing serverless applications. By using event-driven architecture and push event notifications, you can design your system for eventual consistency and avoid scheduled polling of services, reducing traffic and optimizing the consumption of cloud resources.

 Imagine an online shopping site that takes up to 10 seconds to process your payment and successfully place your order. The front-end application repeatedly polls the backend every second to find the status. An example architecture depicting this scenario was shown in Figure 3-25, in "Synchronous Communication" on page 112. Every time it polls the API, the application makes a network round trip call. You can eliminate this non-sustainability-friendly operation with an event from the backend to notify the application when it has the final status of the order.

Optimize data queries to fetch just the required data

There are various forms of data, and data stores cater to these diverse needs. Consequently, the data storage and access patterns differ. A common mistake many serverless engineers make is not spending enough time understanding the data access requirements and patterns of their applications. If you optimize your data operations and prevent over-fetching of data, you will save on computing and network costs.

Use queues to buffer requests and smooth workloads

If your application experiences unpredictable traffic spikes, planning and provisioning the required extra resources can be challenging. For example, if you set the Lambda provisioned concurrency level too high, you'll end up wasting resources and incurring unnecessary costs. In such situations, you must identify and separate synchronous and asynchronous operations.

To deal with a spike in an asynchronous operation, you can buffer the extra requests into an SQS queue or Kinesis data stream and process them with the resources already provisioned without demanding more from AWS. As AWS optimizes the use of resources in a sustainable way, you are making your workload promote the sustainability of the cloud.

Employ throttling with usage quotas to control traffic flow

In a synchronous request flow scenario, you can control the handling of unexpected spikes by configuring the request quota and throttling limits to maintain a steady rate of request flow.

With Amazon API Gateway, you can configure usage plans and quotas for each API consumer. In addition to the sustainability benefits, this protects your application from DoS attacks.

 Before you set a throttling limit on an API, ensure the API clients can resubmit the throttled requests to prevent losing critical data. Alternatively, you can buffer the API requests into a queue and process them steadily.

Delete unused services and resources

There are two main reasons why neglect of unused resources is common. First, as many managed services are pay-per-use and cost you nothing when idle, you do not see them impacting your monthly cloud bill. The second reason is the speed of high-performing teams. As teams keep delivering new features, they don't set aside time to audit their serverless stack and cloud resources and weed out resources that are no longer needed.

You may have more abandoned resources in your non-production environment than in your production environment. Say you have a DynamoDB table created for a PoC. As the table contains no data and is unused, it costs you nothing. However, the DynamoDB service still maintains the details of your table and the disk space. Multiply that by millions of such abandoned tables across different AWS Regions, and you can gauge the scale and sustainability impact.

The use of serverless services such as Lambda functions makes your non-production environments more sustainable when compared to running containers. These environments are mostly active only during the engineers' working hours.

Run batch jobs during a low energy consumption period

Nightly batch jobs that perform data consolidation, engineering analysis, business analytics, payment settlements, and other tasks are common in many organizations. Working with AWS, identify the quieter periods in your cloud Region and schedule your batch jobs during those hours. Batch jobs usually have a predictable load and are ideal for provisioning resources in an efficient way.

Data and Storage

Data drives our lives in the modern digital world. *Data-driven* has become a common term in boardrooms—data-driven decisions, data-driven marketing, data-driven design, data-driven culture, data-driven thinking, data-driven mindset, etc., are some of the many variants you may hear.

Every time you share data, you initiate countless data operations via the digital equipment you hold. Capturing, storing, and processing data requires cloud computing, storage, and network capabilities, and these resources consume energy. As data travels through the vastness of the cloud, it leaves a carbon footprint in our environment. Hence, for a sustainable serverless application, it's essential to think about and care for your data.

In many organizations and teams, data is commonly overlooked and forgotten once it has served its purpose. Unless the storage services are expensive enough to make a dent in your monthly cloud bill, engineers become casual with data.

If the data you consume is not valuable or you do not need a piece of data, don't store it.

Propagating data retention requests

When you work with a distributed event-driven microservices architecture where data ownership is isolated to individual microservices, aligning data lifetime across the application is challenging. If you hold on to the data longer than is necessary, it violates sustainability principles. If you delete it too soon, failures are likely when the services coordinate to perform a distributed task. Word of mouth, email, chat messages, and design documents are common approaches teams adopt to propagate data retention dependencies. In an event-driven architecture, you can use events to carry such information. When you emit a domain event, if the event has data significance, you can add data retention indicator attributes to reflect these details, as shown in Example 10-1. The applications that subscribe and react to these events can use these indicators to align their data retention policies. (Make sure the recommended data retention value aligns with legal and regulatory requirements!)

Example 10-1. A sample event that contains attributes to specify the data retention mandate

```
{
  "detail": {
    "metadata": {
      "version": "1.0",
      "domain": "PAYMENTS",
      "service": "payment-authorization",
      "category": "domain-event",
      "type": "data",
      "retention_period": 28,
      "retention_unit": "day"
    },
    "data": {
      // payment authorization data
    }
  }
}
```

Data lifecycle

The sheer volume data we produce and consume in the modern digital world is beyond what our brains can imagine. Just imagine the working of the famous flight tracking service Flightradar24 (*https://oreil.ly/P0Y-o*). It maps every operating flight across the globe, as shown in Figure 10-10, at any point in time and shows each one's movement at frequent intervals. To provide such a unique experience, it collects and processes data from multiple satellites, radars, airlines, airports, etc.

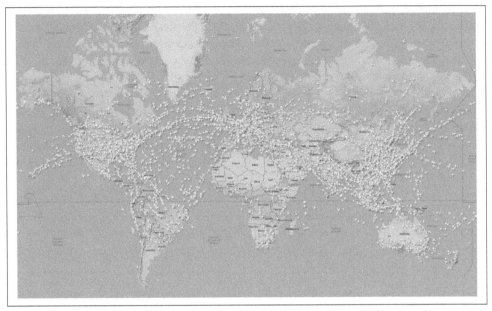

Figure 10-10. A map of all aircraft in operation globally at a particular time (source: Flightradar24 [https://oreil.ly/sNoob])

As your applications are swamped by more than they can digest, you need policies and adequate processes as part of the data lifecycle, as shown in Figure 10-11. You often hear businesses equate digital data to gold. The key difference between the data gold and the real gold is that not all digital data remains gold forever. Once the data has been processed and the insights extracted, much of it turns into data dust that is useless to anyone. If you neglect it and don't deal with it in time, the dust settles and slowly forms data-waste dunes that offer no value—but they do have a cost to the business, and crucially, they pose a hazard to a sustainable environment.

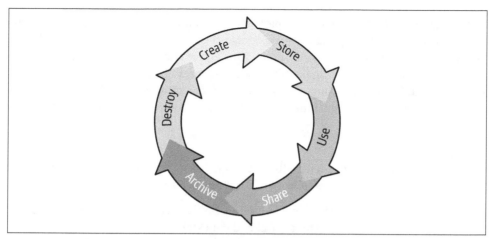

Figure 10-11. A typical data lifecycle, from creation to destruction (source: adapted from an image on the Blancco website [https://www.blancco.com])

Sustainability patterns for data and storage

As data goes through its lifecycle, you can apply patterns and practices at every phase to aid sustainability in the cloud. The following sections provide some tips.

Select a suitable data store for your data and access patterns. As mentioned in Chapter 1, there are many types of databases available (object storage, key/value, relational, document, graph, etc.). Each type has its purpose, and choosing the right one based on its fitness for your purposes is key. By offering various data storage services, AWS has already optimized operations on several factors, including sustainability. It is your responsibility to choose the right one and avoid getting into a "square peg in a round hole" situation.

 Amazon S3 is a high-performing object store. It is not designed to operate efficiently with structured data and perform the data operations you normally do in a relational database.

Classification of data and tagging. As part of the solution design for your serverless application, it is a good practice to recognize the data classifications and designate appropriate tags. You can classify data in your enterprise in several ways, depending on the context—sensitivity, shareability, secrecy, durability, etc. If you classify data based on durability, for example, you can assign a retention period specific to each category instead of keeping all the data for the same duration. Possible classifications include:

Temporary cache data
> Temporary data might include the ephemeral data associated with Lambda functions, API caching, caches in front of databases, ElastiCache, etc.
>
> *Example*: A news website could serve a popular article from a cache to avoid excessive operational load on its backend data store.

Short-term operational data
> You may classify the data you store while handling an API request or when reacting to a domain event in a microservice as short-term data. This data need not be retained beyond a certain period—typically after the request processing is completed. Most of the data you store when implementing the storage-first pattern introduced in Chapter 5 is short-term.
>
> *Example*: The browsing details of a customer who signs into their account to purchase a product can be retained within the user session.

Long-term and active business data
> This is data that is part of a business operation and holds significant value. Loss of such data could have severe consequences, such as customer dissatisfaction, legal problems, regulatory violations, etc.
>
> *Active* data does not mean the data is constantly accessed and updated, but rather that it is kept in a state that enables immediate access should a need arise.
>
> *Example*: If a retail store allows the return of purchased items for a refund for up to 60 days, the system must keep the order and payment details active for at least 60 days.

Archivable data
> As the name implies, archivable data does not require immediate accessibility, but it carries business and legal importance and warrants you to retain it for a long period. The transition of a piece of data from its current state to archived may happen rapidly or after a period of weeks, months, or even years, depending on your business requirements. The duration for which the data should remain archived can also vary.
>
> *Example*: The land registry details of a property must be maintained indefinitely.

Organizations that ingest data from many parts of their business into a data lake or big data platform and make it available to consumers at the corporate level often operate with different data *layers*, such as *bronze*, *silver*, and *gold*. The bronze layer is where all the data-producing product teams send their data. The silver layer represents the first level of filtered data from the bronze layer for consumers, and the gold layer is the further purified data from the silver layer for select consumers. Such classifications allow enterprises to apply the necessary data protection and compliance and retention policies.

Removal of unwanted data. Deleting unwanted data is the fundamental activity you can do as a best practice to aid with sustainable cloud operation—both *of* the cloud and *in* the cloud. Following are some of the common ways to remove data in serverless applications:

Simple TTL
  The simplest way to remove unwanted data is by setting the data expiry period and letting your managed services do the rest. For example:

  - In DynamoDB, you can enable TTL capability on a table and add an expiry time value to every item.
  - You can configure a lifecycle policy on an S3 bucket to automatically expire the data object.
  - When you set up a log group in CloudWatch, you can specify the retention period.
  - You can configure cache expiry at the optimal level for services such as API Gateway.

  While the main focus is on the primary data stores, you must also consider the lifetime of messages in SQS queues (including DLQs), Kinesis streams, EventBridge archives, etc.

TTL with data transition
  When a piece of data is accessed frequently, it is considered *warm*. As the access frequency drops over a period, it becomes *cold*. Eventually, it becomes archivable data that you can transition to an infrequently accessed low-cost storage. For example:

  - When DynamoDB deletes an item via the TTL expiry, you can transition the data to a long-term data store such as S3 or Redshift, or to an infrequent access (IA) table class in DynamoDB.
  - You can use S3 lifecycle policies to transition data to infrequent access sections or archives.

Scheduled data cleanup

When data stores do not offer automated data removal or cannot be utilized for some reason, scheduled data cleanup activities become helpful. You can use EventBridge Scheduler to configure one-time or recurring data removal tasks by invoking a Lambda function or a Step Functions state machine that initiates, respectively, a single or a sequence of cleanup actions.

Data transition policies and use of apt storage.   As described in the previous section (under "TTL with data transition"), the transitioning of cold data to less accessed and low-cost storage types is essential from a sustainability and cost point of view. For example, an ecommerce application may transition retired product data to cold storage after a certain period. The data classifications mentioned earlier form the basis for most data transition actions.

S3 storage lifecycle policies are simple to configure and efficient in operation.

Reducing high-volume data movements.   Data transfer, whether between different applications, services, business domains, or regions or across other boundaries, happens constantly; no application or business operates without moving data from one place to another. However, there are ways you can limit expensive data movements to aid sustainability in the cloud. For example:

- You may not require replicating data from your DynamoDB tables to other AWS Regions as a global policy. Identify the tables that benefit from being global, and enable this option only for those tables.

- Check if the DynamoDB tables on which you have replication (the global table option) enabled are update-heavy tables. If so, always use the correct data patterns to limit updates to large datasets.

- Frequently review your data replication policy and audit your data stores (S3, DynamoDB, etc.).

Development and Deployment

As you've seen, in addition to cost and performance, sustainability is an important optimization factor for serverless applications. The following guidelines offer best practices for sustainability in the area of development and deployment:

Automate every possible development and deployment task.
>Automation is a core part of modern software development, especially in cloud and serverless development. It enables optimal use of cloud resources, automatically provisioning them when needed and deleting them once they're no longer required.

Take advantage of new and improved features and services.
>AWS frequently introduces new services and improves existing services with new features and performance updates. Make sure you have processes to evaluate new features and services and establish their sustainability advantages quickly. One such process is continuous refactoring, which you will learn more about in the next chapter.

Vary resource allocation per need and optimization per resource.
>You do not provision the same amount of RAM for all Lambda functions. Instead, you watch the metrics on memory use and configure the resources accordingly. Likewise, you should examine the tables, queues, streams, logs, etc., in each microservice and optimize for sustainability.

Introducing Sustainability in Your Engineering Teams

Corporate sustainability efforts typically start by defining a sustainability promise (to the organization itself or its customers), setting targets, and devising strategies to achieve those targets.

Adrian Cockroft (this chapter's industry expert) classifies organizations into two categories: those that operate primarily online—for example, banks and SaaS providers—and those that operate mainly in the physical world, with warehouse operations, office space, and large numbers of commuting employees. The former mainly move electrons around, and have a relatively low carbon footprint. The latter move atoms around, and their carbon footprint is comparatively high.

When they start thinking about sustainability, it's common for these organizations to concentrate their focus on the workplace, procurement, transportation, suppliers, manufacturing, etc. Their IT departments often take a backseat. But with the scale of digital operations in modern enterprises, it is of the utmost importance that you bring sustainability measures to the digital teams. The two essential steps in this process are:

Awareness
>Creating sustainability awareness among the technology teams

Action
>Identifying and implementing action items for teams to follow

The following sections present some ideas about how to approach both of these.

Sustainability in Technology: Awareness Day

Depending on the working pattern and the spread of your team, you can organize an in-person or remote workshop and dedicate a few hours or an entire day to bringing sustainability awareness to the engineers.

In the workshop, you divide your time into four parts, as follows:

1. Introducing sustainability to the team
2. Sustainability in technology, the cloud, and serverless
3. Sustainability responsibilities in social life
4. Sustainability day outcomes, actions, and wrap

The outcomes of your sustainability awareness day might include:

- Identifying blockers to adopting sustainability measures in your team
- Identifying opportunities for your team to engage with sustainability measures in development
- Setting up a support system so engineers have a place where they can raise their ideas and concerns
- Developing a sustainability community to engage the team, provide them with information, and share achievements

After the initial awareness day, it is beneficial to conduct regular sessions for the team to assess its progress and address blockers. Such meetings are ideal opportunities to discuss carbon footprint reports, as shown in Figure 10-12, and related sustainability measures.

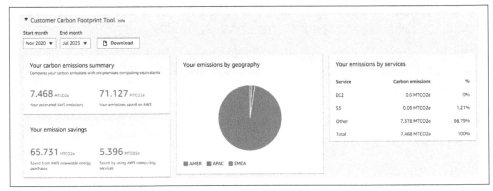

Figure 10-12. The AWS Customer Carbon Footprint Tool (https://oreil.ly/50b2c) summarizes the carbon emissions generated by your use of AWS services

Include a section in your solution design document recording all your thoughts and recommendations about sustainability. This will help ensure appropriate sustainability patterns and practices are adopted during implementation.

Refer to Chapter 6 for more on the importance of solution design and Appendix C for a solution design document template.

Sustainability Focus Areas for Your Team

Determining where a team should focus its sustainability efforts for maximum impact will be dependent on its domain, type of workload, application specialty, etc. You may be able to identify specific cloud services where you will be able to apply sustainability practices.

For instance, suppose you work in a data processing domain where your services handle petabytes of data flowing through several AWS services and data stores. Here, your main sustainability focus will be adopting sustainability patterns for data and storage. Your efforts will likely be concentrated on optimizing your usage of DynamoDB, S3, and so on.

Alternatively, you might be part of a high-velocity team that performs multiple daily releases to production. In such an environment several automated pull request, integration, test, and deployment pipelines will be in progress. One focus area for this team might be the optimal (and sustainable) use of build and cloud resources in development, testing/QA, staging, etc.

Sustainability Audit Checklist

Chapter 1 discussed the AWS Well-Architected Framework, which includes sustainability as one of its pillars. To apply the Framework's principles to serverless applications, AWS has a Serverless Application Lens (*https://oreil.ly/4xVds*) that covers the details that are specific to serverless development. Many teams building serverless applications compile a checklist based on the best practice recommendations from the Serverless Application Lens and use it as an audit step as part of new service development.

You can create a similar sustainability-focused checklist based on the patterns and practices described in this chapter. It will guide engineers to familiarize themselves with and apply sustainability thinking as they design and build serverless applications.

Summary

Sustainability is one of your responsibilities in modern software development. This responsibility starts with understanding and acknowledging the need for sustainability thinking and stays with you as you build serverless solutions and operate them in the cloud. It requires both awareness and action.

We began this chapter by exploring different views and interpretations of sustainability, which as you saw are heavily influenced by context. While the sustainable operation of the cloud has immediate relevance to our planet's environment and future, you also learned the importance of building sustainable serverless applications that can evolve and exist for longer.

This chapter presented several sustainability patterns and practices that you can apply at your enterprise. Remember, these are guidelines for you and your team to consider, and they will need to be adapted to your specific circumstances. Many organizations—big and small—do not consider sustainability principles in software development as a priority. You can certainly make a difference here. Often, it is the small things that you do that bring recognizable changes in your workplace.

Interview with an Industry Expert

Adrian Cockcroft, Partner, OrionX

Adrian Cockcroft is best known as the cloud architect for Netflix during its trailblazing migration to AWS. He was a very early practitioner and advocate of DevOps, microservices, and chaos engineering, helping bring these concepts to the wider audience they have today. Before retiring from Amazon in the summer of 2022, Adrian spent a few years as a VP at the company, deeply immersed in the dual challenges of helping Amazon itself—one of the largest companies in the world—and its enterprise and public sector customers (via AWS, one of the largest technology suppliers in the world) become more sustainable. He currently works via *OrionX.net* as an advisor, consultant, and analyst.

Q: Adrian, you had an illustrious career spanning many decades, contributing to groundbreaking initiatives. At what point did sustainability awareness happen in your career, and what was the trigger?

I have a degree in applied physics and electronics, and I've been tracking the science of the climate crisis in detail since around 2006, when the Stern Report on the potential economic impact of climate change was released. I wanted to help push back on the orchestrated denial that is documented in the book *The Merchants of Doubt*, by Naomi Oreskes and Erik Conway (Bloomsbury Press), and became active on social media. We also wanted to lead by example; we added solar panels to our house in 2009 and got our first electric car in 2011.

Q: Though many in the software industry are committed to having a sustainable world, there is often a gap in adopting sustainability principles and practices as part of the development process. Why do you think the progress is slow, and what measures do we need to improve sustainability thinking among software teams?

Sustainability is one of those nonfunctional requirements that people tend to ignore until it becomes an issue. Secure development practices become a priority after a cyberattack, and sustainable practices are becoming a priority now that people are breathing the smoke and fleeing the fires and hurricanes. Disclosure regulations are spreading around the world, so that large companies will soon have to account for their carbon and the risk to their business from the climate crisis. The end-to-end supply chain carbon footprint of both hardware and software needs to be managed and instrumented. There is a lot of advice out there for software teams to consider. I contributed to the AWS Well-Architected Guide for Sustainability, and the Green Software Foundation has published guidance and is developing useful standards like the Software Carbon Intensity specification.

Q: You have been very vocal about better visibility of the cloud vendor's carbon footprint and proposed a real-time carbon footprint calculation standard. What new measures would you like to see from AWS and other leading cloud providers?

All the cloud providers are doing an excellent job decarbonizing their energy supply and supply chain. It's one of the most forward-looking industries in the world, and they have commissioned tens of gigawatts of renewable energy for their private use. However, AWS is far behind in transparency, provides lower-resolution information than other cloud providers, and still needs to disclose Scope 3 emissions and data center power usage efficiency, which Azure shared in 2021. All the cloud providers currently provide monthly data, several months in arrears, that is only useful for audit reports. I made a proposal in March 2023 that led to a Green Software Foundation project to develop a real-time standard that would be accurate enough to support development of carbon monitoring and optimization tooling.

Q: The adoption of serverless and the use of managed services certainly promote the sustainability of the cloud. Due to this, there is a misunderstanding in the industry that achieving sustainability in cloud operations is solely the cloud provider's responsibility. In this regard, what would be your advice to organizations adopting serverless?

We're already used to sharing responsibility for security, and the same is true for sustainability. Cloud providers are responsible for the sustainability of the cloud, and customers are responsible for using the cloud in a sustainable manner. Serverless moves the maximum amount of responsibility to the cloud provider and dependent services, but it's still important to build and operate applications efficiently. Much of the cost in serverless applications ends up in database backends and logging, so using good archiving processes and compression to reduce long-term storage capacity can be helpful.

Q: AWS is on target to power all its Regions with 100% renewable energy by 2025 and reach net-zero carbon emissions by 2040. In your opinion, what must be the next big focus areas for AWS on its sustainability journey?

There are three aspects to sustainability. The first is to measure and reduce your direct emissions and migrate to renewable energy sources, reporting on progress as you go. AWS is doing well at this aspect. It released an update in mid-2023 that included a long list of Regions that are now 100% renewable, meaning that AWS generates and buys as much renewable energy as it uses. This is averaged over the year using the "market method," which is also used by Azure. It would also be useful to report based on the 24/7 hourly "location method" that Google has adopted. Both methods are needed.

The second aspect is all about supply chains, understanding how sustainable your purchases are, putting pressure on suppliers to clean up their products, and disclosing information to your customers. AWS is doing well at working with its suppliers, but it doesn't provide the information that its customers need to correctly attribute and allocate the carbon footprint of their use of AWS to individual products and their own customers in turn. AWS is several years behind Azure and Google in providing the level of detail required and needs to focus on catching up. Legislation that mandates supply chain disclosures is in place in the European Union, and it's spreading to other countries.

The third aspect is climate risk measurement and reporting. This includes physical risk to buildings and communications infrastructure from sea level rise, fire, extreme weather, and impacted employees. It also includes market risk as high-carbon products are replaced by sustainable products and stranded assets where insurance is denied due to the risk. This is a big area that is going to need focus in the future and has its own legislated reporting rules on the way. For example, AWS states that it carefully makes sure that Zones in a Region are separated by enough distance that they wouldn't fail at the same time. But if a Region has Zones in a high-risk flood plain or in a "tornado alley," that is a risk that some customers might need to understand as they model their own risks. None of the cloud providers have any climate risk information at present (late 2023), and I think this area is going to need attention over the next few years.

CHAPTER 11

Preparing for the Future with Serverless

We are just getting started with serverless. It has decades of life in front of it.
—Jeff Barr

Cattle farmers go through calving season every year, when they welcome many newborn calves. When a calf is born, it gets exposed to an entirely new ecosystem, outside the comfort of its mother's womb. Its new home is a vast, complex, crowded, and confusing world. It needs a good cleanup (by its mother) before its eyes can sense the new environment.

When you are new to serverless, your experience can be similar to that of a newborn calf. Technology looks complex; you hear opinionated statements; people argue on the definition of serverless; you see everything distributed; many things are managed for you; you get caught in asynchrony, and the world around you becomes event-driven. You feel like you are drowning in serverless. Chapter 1 of this book was an attempt to help you open your eyes and see this technology from a clearer perspective.

Soon, the calf starts seeing things—notably its friends and family members standing on four legs. Its desire to get up and struggle to stand on its own hooves begins. To overcome the challenge and accomplish this tiring act, it must rewire its brain and shift its thinking to see the world around it differently from the stillness of the womb.

The early chapters of the book enriched you with details needed to enable the shift to a serverless mindset, helping you to see technology differently from legacy ways of building software applications. From being a programmer siloed in a team churning out code all day, you become a multiskilled engineer able to compose serverless microservices using managed services. You learn how to build modular and extendable serverless applications that live longer.

As the calf stumbles to get up and take its first steps, it learns a crucial life lesson—make sure you can stand steadily before attempting to walk. Amidst its relentless trials, it comes to understand that standing steady is more daunting than standing up.

Your initial understanding of serverless often creates a false sense of confidence; you want to immediately start building everything serverless. To safeguard you from such mistakes, in Chapter 2, you learned the vital principles of how to structure your teams and draw service boundaries.

The mother cow is pleased to see its newborn can walk to places to find food and drink. The calf observes and learns its daily routine. Within days, it becomes autonomous and operates all by itself.

The foundational ideas around microservices, serverless patterns, and event-driven architectures you learned in this book will guide you as you start developing, testing, and operating applications in the cloud. As you build and operate serverless services, your processes get refined, your optimization strategies become balanced, your cost awareness gains clarity, and your sustainability thinking sees purpose.

Like the calf comfortably navigating its earthly surroundings, you have developed the expertise to utilize the serverless technology ecosystem to bring value to your business faster than before. Alongside this, you now have teams of engineers who bring new possibilities to your organization with the help of serverless and modern cloud services. Everyone is thrilled that you are now successfully running serverless!

The crucial question is, for how long and how far?

What do you do if you get tired? How do you recover from exhaustion? How do you keep up with the evolution of serverless technology? And how do you plan to play the long game for sustainable growth in your organization?

You will find answers to all these questions and more in this chapter.

Emerging Trends in Serverless

Technology is always evolving, with ceaseless efforts to develop new capabilities to meet the changing needs of everyone and everything. Chapter 1 gave you the history of how we got to serverless. But where is it heading? This section examines a few potential future trends.

The Low-Code and Functionless Promise

The phrase "less is more" can confuse those new to the English language, but its meaning is beautifully captured in this definition from Writing Explained (*https://oreil.ly/wqVwy*):

> Simplicity is better than elaborate embellishment; Sometimes, something simple is better than something advanced or complicated.

We all strive to make things simple. The entire serverless ecosystem is based on that ethos—leave the undifferentiated heavy lifting of server management to the cloud provider so you have a simplified approach to making sophisticated modern applications.

During his keynote at the AWS re:Invent conference in 2017, Dr. Werner Vogels made a bold claim: "All the code you will ever write is business logic." This statement baffled many pundits at the time, when serverless was still in its infancy. A few years later, if you look at the developments in serverless technology, you will appreciate his foresight.

The principle of enabling managed cloud services to work seamlessly with minimal or no custom function code is becoming part of the cloud offering. Unlike in the early days of serverless, you don't need Lambda functions to act as glue code between various services, as native integrations between these services fill the gap.

You learned about this in Chapter 5, which discussed the functionless integration pattern. With AWS adding ever more capabilities to its managed services to encourage native integrations, the trend of using less function code, or the *functionless promise* of serverless, will influence the way you architect and build distributed serverless applications.

The Renaissance of Event-Driven Architecture

If you've read through the chapters on serverless architectures, patterns, and development practices, you should understand the significance of event-driven architecture. As mentioned in Chapter 3, the event-driven concept is not new. The success of the GUIs in the early versions of macOS and Microsoft Windows can be attributed to the concept of event-driven computing and reacting to messages. The Java Swing API (*https://oreil.ly/QY-7Q*) for building user interfaces is also based on event-driven architecture.

So, event-driven computing and event-driven architecture have been with us for decades. Perhaps their full potential was somewhat masked by how we built legacy monolithic applications, or the past architectural ecosystems didn't pay enough attention to event-driven concepts. Regardless of what happened in the past, the promise of event-driven architecture is central to serverless development. Its presence will be stronger in the future, for the reasons described next.

The role of event-driven architecture in the data economy

Along with the wealth of data handled by modern applications, policies and regulations have become stricter, with severe penalties for noncompliance and data breaches. Chapters 2 and 3 taught you how in serverless, smaller, autonomous teams own services and data within domain boundaries and develop smaller, loosely coupled microservices. Modern enterprises favor federated data ownership with self-service data publishing and consumption. Domain events therefore play a crucial role in sharing data across the domains in your organization.

As you publish events onto your event buses or enterprise-wide event broker platform, you can set checkpoints to audit your data and governance roles and responsibilities:

- What data elements get added to an event?
- Who can consume and have visibility of the data?
- What data requires encryption, and what is the level of encryption?
- Do you need encryption at rest, in transit, or both?
- Based on sensitivity, do you classify events as red, amber, or green?
- Do you classify data as bronze, silver, or gold based on value?
- Do you tag PII and sensitive data attributes?

The acceptance of eventual consistency in modern systems

As you migrate from monolithic systems or develop new applications, the use of smaller, distributed, loosely coupled microservices enables you to discover asynchronous flows where it is acceptable to maintain eventual consistency. You identify real-time versus near-real-time scenarios and strong versus eventually consistent data operations. For many engineers and architects, it's a paradigm shift from the legacy ways of conceptualizing an application.

As you have seen in this book, the benefits of event-driven systems are aplenty—from well-defined service boundaries, separation of concerns, modularity, and extensibility to a reduced problem blast radius and many more. Though it may take time for event-driven architecture to make inroads into some of the legacy engineering mindsets, adopting serverless and modern developmental processes is transitioning everyone's thinking.

Event-driven architecture fuels functionless and low-code integrations

Several event-driven service integrations now follow a functionless or low-code pattern—for example, EventBridge API destinations, EventBridge Pipes, and the SDK integration for Step Functions. This is a great motivation as it lets you focus more on business logic than writing integration code. You saw the application of these concepts in previous chapters (especially Chapter 5, which showcases some of the advanced implementation patterns in serverless).

Connecting diverse systems and technology stacks

Event-driven communication is a common thread that can enable the collaboration of many modern applications operating on multiple technology stacks. Emerging standards such as CloudEvents (*https://cloudevents.io*) and AsyncAPI (*https://www.asyncapi.com*) help make communication seamless across varied tech stacks.

Multicloud Orchestration

The operational needs of an enterprise depend on several software systems—legacy and modern, on-premises and cloud, internal and external. In such a varied technological landscape, you cannot always expect everything to align perfectly with the offerings of one cloud provider. There are various reasons that might compel you to operate in a multicloud environment. For example:

- The migration of applications from one cloud to another may be unfeasible.

- You might want to leverage the best available cloud services from different providers to meet your business requirements.

- Your business processes may require the coordination of services from public, private, and gov clouds.

In such cases, the best approach is to have one primary provider orchestrate services from others as necessary. This won't be simple: you will face challenges when orchestrating your business processes and relying on custom APIs for cross-cloud interactions. At the time of writing, there are no common standards or open specifications to seamlessly integrate with services of the same nature from different providers; however, we will likely see new initiatives in the future that aim to ease these hurdles.

Leveraging the best services from multiple cloud providers is typically a better option than attempting to develop portable and cloud-agnostic solutions. While cloud agnosticism sounds great as a concept, the complexities and high developmental and operational costs can be detrimental to an enterprise. Similarly, operating the same workloads on different cloud providers is not recommended without a strong business case. This can hamper business velocity and requires a specialized skill set.

Infrastructure from Code

Infrastructure from code (IfC) is an abstraction of cloud and serverless development where your IfC framework selects, creates, configures, deploys, and manages the cloud resources for your application. To enable this, you avoid explicitly referencing any specific cloud resources in your business logic code, and the tool makes the decision behind the scenes about which services to use. For example, your code specifies the need to store customer data, and the IfC framework decides which data storage service to use for this purpose.

IfC providers such as Ampt (*https://getampt.com*), Nitric (*https://nitric.io*), Encore (*https://encore.dev*), Wing (*https://www.winglang.io*), and Darklang (*https://darklang.com*) use three main approaches:

- Embedding special IfC annotations in the code
- A programming language with special constructs specific to IfC
- An IfC SDK to use with code

The industry is divided on whether or not this is a useful approach, and as yet it has not gained wide adoption.

Motivations to use IfC

The advantages highlighted by the IfC providers include speed of development, cloud-agnostic deployment without the need to change the code, and code colocation. Due to the heavy abstraction, the cognitive load on engineers to learn and understand the different cloud services is also low.

One area where IfC may be beneficial is when experimenting or prototyping a complex system, as it allows you to focus on the outcome of your experiment rather than learning the intricacies of cloud services.

In addition, in many organizations, the enabling teams or supporting domains provide utility services such as service status information, static data, etc., for others to consume. In most cases, the selection of infrastructure for such services is not as critical as for those in your core business domain. IfC may be an option to bring up the services quickly.

Drawbacks of IfC

Some of the benefits of IfC often turn into drawbacks. For example, the high degree of abstraction and the lack of in-depth understanding of cloud services can make investigating problems in a production environment much more complex.

As you have seen throughout this book, when you architect and develop a serverless application, your choices with regard to cloud services—which managed services and resources to use, how you configure permissions and policies, etc.—are driven by the business requirements and logic. In this sense, you cannot isolate and hand over the infrastructure choices to a tool. This is the basis for one of the strongest criticisms of IfC.

As enterprises adopt cloud and serverless technologies, they invest in aligning their enterprise architecture strategy with their chosen cloud provider, such as AWS.

Teams across business domains interact and share information via APIs, events, and so on. Consider just the data operations of your enterprise—data ingestion, classification, tagging, storage, access, analytics, etc., are massive and complex operations. Due to legislation and industry regulations, you cannot give away the responsibility to an IfC tool that abstracts the related infrastructure from you.

Finally, while the reduction of the cognitive load on engineers may be seen as an advantage of IfC due to its abstraction, the counterargument could be the lack of transferable cloud skills. With limited or no exposure to the underlying cloud infrastructure, engineers face a steep learning curve when they change roles or organizations and are required to work with infrastructure as code.

Observability as code (OaC) is another new initiative, in the observability space. The motivation behind OaC is often attributed to the complexity of modern distributed and loosely coupled applications. With OaC, your application's tracing and monitoring capabilities are considered during development and incorporated as part of the implementation. Alerts are defined in code and embedded as best practices alongside other code that is reviewed and tracked, rather than in dashboards (as code for these can get very complex and often needs to change often as services/metrics evolve).

Baselime (*https://baselime.io*) is an observability tool in the serverless space that supports defining alerts, dashboards, and log queries as code.

The Evolution and Influence of Generative AI

It's fascinating to read about advancements in technology. Chapter 1 briefly walked through the history of how we got to serverless, and you saw how certain tech milestones influenced and accelerated further growth. The network protocols that served as building blocks for the internet and virtualization leading to the cloud are great examples.

The field of artificial intelligence is going through a tremendous amount of transformation. In fact, it is a neural network architecture called the *Transformer* (*https://oreil.ly/WyStx*), introduced in 2017, that has fueled this growth and made generative AI a possibility.

Generative AI

Generative AI (GenAI) refers to AI models that are able to create entirely new content (text, images, code, music, etc.), learning in a self-supervised way. It's an evolution in the field of artificial intelligence. While AI and traditional machine learning (ML) models have existed for many years, they typically performed a single task, such as classifying images or predicting the next word in a sentence. The explosion of data in modern systems brings different flavors of information from many sources. This in turn has enabled the creation of advanced foundation models (FMs) that can be adapted to a wide range of tasks. Organizations can use these FMs as base models together with GenAI to create all sorts of specialized applications, training them with their own data. This is much more efficient than the traditional process of building models from the ground up, and opens up numerous exciting possibilities.

Here are a few GenAPI applications and services that you should be familiar with:

- ChatGPT (*https://oreil.ly/REYIV*), short for Generative Pre-trained Transformer, is a chatbot from OpenAI (*https://openai.com*) based on a large language model. As of early 2023, ChatGPT was the fastest-growing consumer application in history. It accepts prompts (instructions or questions) in natural language and replies in a conversational style, almost instantaneously generating novel content ranging from whimsical poems and bedtime stories to working Lambda function code.
- DALL-E and DALL-E 2 (*https://oreil.ly/c5Tem*), also from OpenAI, generate digital images from text descriptions. The text-to-image model uses deep learning to generate high-quality realistic images based on the descriptive details in the prompt.
- Amazon Bedrock (*https://oreil.ly/kzG0k*) is a fully managed service that helps you build and scale generative AI applications with foundation models from Amazon and other model providers.

Generative AI is certain to disrupt and revolutionize our lives. Enterprises are already preparing to capitalize on the possibilities it enables. In the early days of serverless, the use cases that attracted engineers were relatively simple (e.g., image upload, transformation, and storage). Now, we have a much more mature ecosystem with much more power and functionality to draw upon. If the initial goal of serverless adoption was to move away from the undifferentiated heavy lifting of hardware and infrastructure provisioning to allow teams to focus on the business logic and guide organizations on a fast track of development and growth, imagine what the combination of serverless and generative API can achieve!

You will soon start to see organizations with a modern serverless/tech stack moving even faster, extending their lead as they combine these resources with GenAI to conceptualize, build, and monetize new ideas. As a serverless engineer, GenAI holds the promise of relieving you of the burden of mundane and repetitive work and freeing you up to focus on innovating for the next iteration of features and functionality.

Keeping Up with the Evolution of Serverless

As you have seen in this book, adopting serverless brings about a technology transformation that fuels engineering and business efficiency. However, one of the biggest differences between serverless and legacy technologies is that serverless is not a technology that can be left unattended once successfully adopted in your organization. Your motivation to adopt serverless should never be to migrate a system or build a new application, put it into production, and not take care of or sustain it. If you were to approach serverless with that mindset, because of the speed of changes and improvements in modern technology, you would quickly run into trouble.

This section looks at some challenges faced by enterprise teams that adopt serverless and approaches you can take to remain up-to-date on your serverless journey.

Challenges Facing Enterprise Teams

When an enterprise accelerates its serverless adoption, it faces two common types of challenges:

- Organizational/cultural challenges (how to manage the growth of teams and maintain technical consistency across the teams)
- Technology challenges (how to keep up with the evolutionary changes in the serverless technology ecosystem)

Both require adequate measures to be put in place before they become a hindrance to the business. Here we'll focus on some of the cultural challenges, and shortly we'll discuss an approach called *continuous refactoring* that addresses the technology challenges.

The adoption of serverless in an organization can transform it in different ways. Many expect the process, the transformation it brings about, and the growth to be organized and organic. However, if you approach serverless adoption without sufficient forethought and care, the transition from a happy environment to a chaotic one can be rapid. What's more, some issues won't be visible from the outside; you'll need to get into the engine room and observe how the different teams operate to understand how to fix them.

The following are some common concerns enterprises face as they grow and expand their serverless teams:

Siloed serverless teams
> As you learned in Chapter 1, serverless promotes diverse teams with varied skills to develop and operate its applications. However, as adoption accelerates and the organization grows, teams may become busy chasing their individual goals, objectives and key results (OKRs), targets, deadlines, etc. In such a fast-track

environment, they find no time for cross-team collaboration and become siloed within their service boundaries or bounded contexts.

Disparity in serverless skills across teams

When you're part of a small start-up, there is a high degree of interaction, knowledge sharing, and togetherness that fuels high morale and levels up skills. As the organization grows, new teams are established and more engineers are brought into existing teams. With the speed of recruitment, you may lose uniformity in the recruitment process, with each team onboarding engineers with different levels of serverless skills.

Differences in development practices and design principles

One peril of fast growth is the dilution of established principles and practices. Teams lose their shared understanding of best practices, well-architected principles, and serverless development practices in general. Each team develops its own rulebook, causing further divisions and silos.

Team autonomy without guardrails

Autonomy comes with responsibilities. But if teams become irresponsible and deviate from common principles and guardrails, it causes friction, and product quality suffers. For example, a team that decides to skip the solution design phase and jump straight into implementation can end up building unsustainable applications.

Though you can expect to have a certain level of difference between teams, it's vital that they have a shared awareness and understanding of the recommended best practices, architectural principles, and design patterns. Chapter 2 discussed the role of "serverless enablers" in an organization. A person in this role can be the common thread that connects the teams and guides them through the early stages of a project with regular check-ins to maintain consistency.

Sustaining a Serverless Knowledge Pool

Finding and retaining skillful engineers is one of an organization's biggest challenges when venturing into cloud and serverless technologies. While the initial success of serverless adoption increases business opportunities and thereby accelerates the growth of teams, it makes it even more difficult to onboard new talent and keep meeting stakeholders' expectations. As serverless itself is relatively new, you won't find a large pool of experienced serverless engineers to hire from. Most engineers are still new to serverless and its technology ecosystem. They'll require adequate support and guidance to advance their learning and keep their enthusiasm high. There are several strategies you can apply for this, depending on your organizational structure and corporate policies.

Chapter 1 mentioned that becoming a successful serverless engineer often requires developing a whole new set of skills. For this, you must provide sufficient training and learning opportunities. Getting engineers involved in AWS community activities is a good way to engage them in serverless activities inside and outside of the organization. Later in this chapter, you will learn about serverless evangelism and the ways to take part, and also the importance of a serverless guild or center of excellence.

There is no one specific way to form a talented pool of serverless engineers; it relies on a combination of different factors, both technical and nontechnical.

Embracing Continuous Refactoring

Engineers have been refactoring code for decades. The practice is often related to the painful ordeal of updating and improving legacy monolithic applications in a way that avoids altering their functionality, and thus is not looked upon fondly. However, it can be viewed in a more positive light, as a process of *continuous improvement* or *continuous renewal* of your applications.

Continuous refactoring allows you to offer the best services to your customers, now and in the future. Offering the best services requires building the best solutions, and building the best solutions requires the best technologies—such as serverless. However, technologies tend to mature over time, with increasing levels of stability and feature richness. Continuous refactoring allows you to always be sure you're getting the best out of the technologies you use by constantly improving your solutions.

Why is serverless refactoring different?

It's been more than two decades since the initial publication of Martin Fowler's book *Refactoring: Improving the Design of Existing Code* (Addison-Wesley Professional), which discusses refactoring as a process of simplifying object-oriented code and making it easier to maintain. Over that time, the influence of object-oriented principles and programming languages has waned, and the meaning of refactoring in the software industry has changed.

Serverless development, for example, is not just about writing functions in a particular language. As you compose your serverless applications using various managed services, serverless refactoring also involves *rewiring* services. One of the advantages of refactoring in serverless is that you can refactor several parts of the ecosystem at granular levels. Examples include:

- Refactoring the code of Lambda functions
- Refactoring infrastructure code to upgrade or adopt new IaC tools
- Refactoring to improve the overall performance of an application
- Refactoring to lower the costs associated with an application

- Refactoring to improve the sustainability of the application
- Refactoring to consume new features and managed services
- Refactoring to introduce well-architected principles

As you gain experience developing serverless applications, you may argue that everything is still code—Lambda function code, infrastructure code, integration code, deployment pipeline code, and so on. However, the distinction between these code constructs becomes increasingly blurry in serverless. For example, say you are refactoring a Lambda function to increase its timeout due to a change in business logic. Would you attribute the timeout change to the function or the infrastructure?

 When you approach refactoring in serverless, you must have the necessary automated integration tests and the confidence to test in production, as you learned in Chapter 7.

Introducing serverless refactoring in your organization

High-performing serverless teams often face unrealistic expectations from business stakeholders. As you follow an incremental and iterative development process, the delivery cycles become shorter and bring continuous visibility of outcomes as the team progresses toward its goal. If stakeholders become greedy and demand more, your team will become a *feature factory* with no time for any refactoring work. This can demoralize teams and cause a negative impact on productivity. Organizations with a good rapport between engineering teams, product teams, and stakeholders successfully balance new feature development and reduction of technical debt.

You can make refactoring a justifiable activity in a few ways:

Turn your technical needs into business goals.
Chapter 2 highlighted the significance of domain-driven design and the importance of speaking a common (ubiquitous) language inside a domain to align everyone's interpretation. Similarly, you must translate the technological side of your refactoring needs into business goals that are understandable to everyone, especially stakeholders.

After completing your refactoring tasks, remember to share the improvement metrics with the stakeholders. Here's an example. For a very long time, the maximum number of messages a Lambda function could poll from an SQS queue was 10. AWS then increased the limit to 10,000 messages. Sensing that a few queues in your application would benefit from this, you decided to do some refactoring to take advantage of the higher limit. You can justify this work to the business by saying your application will be able to handle double or triple the number of customer queries or orders, resulting in improved performance.

As another example, say you've been thinking of changing your APIs to improve latency by a couple of hundred milliseconds. You can justify this by explaining that the performance gain will improve customer satisfaction and your organization's Net Promoter Score (NPS).

Make refactoring a recurring part of your development process.
As you likely know, agile teams perform retrospectives to reflect on team motivations and challenges. Every team must pause regularly to dedicate time to engineering activities such as refactoring, experimenting with new concepts, etc. Taking inspiration from nature and how it renews with the change of seasons, allocate time every quarter for your team's refactoring needs. You might want to maintain a team idea board or backlog where you capture refactoring needs to discuss and prioritize.

Perform refactoring as a technology motivator for the team.
Frequent refactoring exercises clear tech debt regularly and avoid the trap of it piling up into a mountain. Engineers prefer a cleaner codebase, and it lowers their cognitive load. For many engineers, the chance to use new cloud services or architectural patterns is a good motivator for performing refactoring. For example, the distributed orchestration pattern you learned about in Chapter 5 was made possible by the introduction of the callback task token feature in AWS Step Functions. Such enhancements inspire engineers to discover better capabilities in the services they own.

As with life, technology never stands still. The more you iterate and innovate, the better your services become. Today's top technologies may be obsolete next year. As the serverless ecosystem changes, you must keep up to prevent falling behind. In that respect, continuous refactoring is essential to your serverless development cycle.

Playing the Long Game

An August 2023 survey by Datadog (*https://oreil.ly/4JYwx*), a leader in the observability space, showed that more than half of the companies that have moved to the cloud have adopted serverless. The rate of adoption will almost certainly increase as more enterprises benefit from serverless technology and others see that it enables them to deliver new features faster than before, bringing better value to the business. However, to sustain this momentum, adequate measures need to be taken to ensure success. This section explores some of the practices organizations and team members can explore to support the transition to serverless and keep everyone aligned on the mission.

Establishing a Serverless Guild and Center of Excellence

As described in Chapter 2, people are the most valuable resource in an organization. When its people come together for a common purpose and feel valued and supported, it makes the organization stronger. In addition, when there are common themes across the teams in your organization, it is beneficial to have uniformity in the way those themes are put into practice or implemented. The use of cloud and serverless technologies, development of APIs, implementation of security, and integration of external software systems are some examples of themes you might find across an organization, or a division or department.

A center of excellence (CoE) is a group of people dedicated to establishing best practices, guidelines, and policies and providing the required support and advice. When enterprises move their workloads to the cloud and focus their new development efforts there, they aim to gain the benefits of the cloud, such as increased agility and velocity. Forming a cloud center of excellence (CCoE) is a great way to steer the organization as a whole and the individual teams in the right direction, helping everyone get up to speed quickly and maintain a high quality of cloud operation.

A serverless center of excellence (SCoE), or serverless guild, works similarly to a CCoE. It's a small team of four or five people with a collective skill set comprising, for example:

- Good understanding of the serverless technology ecosystem
- Familiarity with the AWS Well-Architected Framework and Serverless Lens
- Knowledge of observability principles, including structured logs
- Proficiency with the IaC framework or tools in use—CloudFormation, CDK, Serverless Framework, etc.
- Ability to guide teams on microservices principles, API guidelines, and data legislation
- Awareness of AWS and serverless resources

These are just a few common areas, and they will vary depending on the serverless operation of your organization.

One of the primary objectives of the SCoE is to address some of the issues mentioned in the earlier section on the challenges facing enterprise teams. The SCoE should work closely with the leadership teams to become enablers of the serverless teams and help improve the developer experience and the quality of product outcomes. Inconsistencies across the teams cause confusion and reduce efficiency.

The SCoE must play a careful balancing act. On one side, it establishes the guardrails, principles, standards, etc., for serverless teams to adopt. On the other side, it shouldn't become an impediment where teams and engineers must wait to receive a go-ahead for everything. One of the primary objectives of the SCoE is empowering engineers and teams by providing direction.

Becoming a Serverless Evangelist

In our highly networked universe, we are fortunate to have several avenues by which to share the threads of our different knowledge streams. You don't need to be an expert in everything, but if you possess one or more of the following skills, someone will always benefit from your experience:

- You are a programming expert in the language runtimes supported by AWS Lambda.
- You have experience in and knowledge of architecting serverless applications.
- You have set up and grown serverless teams with great success.
- You deeply understand domain-driven design and have the know-how to apply it.
- You have broken down monoliths and built serverless microservices.
- You have a wealth of knowledge about event-driven architecture.
- You know how to implement observability for serverless applications.
- You have hands-on experience with IaC tools and frameworks.
- You have guided organizations to use serverless services on their data journeys.
- You are a great teacher, reaching many via your blogs, vlogs, and other content.
- You work with cutting-edge technologies such as GenAI, large language models (LLMs), and the like, combining them with serverless for futuristic innovations.

As a serverless enthusiast, you may have something new to add to that list based on your unique experience. Chances are you have something to offer, and there are many ways for you to become a serverless evangelist in the tech world. Sharing is caring!

Joining a Serverless Community

Many of us are fortunate to have vibrant AWS and serverless communities within reach—but our collective challenge is to take the benefits of serverless to the remote corners of the tech world and grow serverless communities everywhere. Chapter 1 introduced the various AWS developer community support options. There are several avenues you can explore to share your experience with a wider audience:

Become an AWS Community Builder.
    At the time of writing, the application period to become an AWS Community Builder opens every year, and there is a category for serverless. You can register

your name (*https://oreil.ly/ykVsy*) to get notified when the application window opens.

As an AWS Community Builder, you can interact with hundreds of other builders and AWS members and participate in AWS product briefings and early-release showcases. These are opportunities to share your experiences and feed your ideas into the evolution of AWS services.

Get invited to be an AWS Hero.
Unlike the AWS Community Builder program, becoming an AWS Hero is by invitation only. Again, there are several categories, including serverless. AWS never reveals the selection criteria, but it is quite evident from the profiles of the people who have become AWS Heroes that community contribution is a major factor.

As an AWS Hero, you become part of an elite community with greater access to the AWS products roadmap, ideation process, beta programs, etc., as well as opportunities to participate and speak at conferences such as AWS re:Invent.

Publish a serverless newsletter.
Serverless newsletters are a great way to connect communities, providing a medium for articles about serverless to reach a wider readership.

Some popular serverless newsletters circulating at the time of writing include *Off-by-none* (*https://oreil.ly/1Vchc*), *Ready, Set, Cloud!* (*https://oreil.ly/hJMYF*), and *The Serverless Terminal* (*https://oreil.ly/7-7VE*).

Share insights via podcasts.
Podcasts are a gateway to bring serverless expertise to everyone's ears. As a host, you can invite guests with practical knowledge and share varied case studies from different industry sectors and business domains.

Serverless podcasts by AWS Serverless Heroes include the *Real-World Serverless* podcast (*https://oreil.ly/y-dU1*) by Yan Cui, the *Ready, Set, Cloud!* podcast (*https://oreil.ly/4DakB*) by Allen Helton, and *Serverless Chats* (*https://oreil.ly/lGpZ9*) by Jeremy Daly.

Organize local serverless meetups and conferences.
Serverless meetups are a great way to unite tech communities and share knowledge. The serverless journey of one of the authors of this book (Sheen) began when he started attending serverless meetups in London.

ServerlessDays conferences (*https://oreil.ly/RgY_R*) are another way of bringing a larger audience together in one place. As an organizer of a serverless event, you are more likely to become visible and a contender for the AWS Community Heroes program.

Contribute to open source projects.

Open source contribution is a great way to share your engine room experience with the wider community. Serverless Land (*https://oreil.ly/IJxlP*) is one place to share utilities, patterns, code constructs, framework extensions, etc. Lambda Powertools (*https://oreil.ly/OvA9h*) is another with community backing.

In addition to these opportunities, you can collaborate with publications to write technical content, publish bite-sized videos on YouTube, author training courses, and more. Every little contribution you make to the serverless community can go a long way in shaping the future of engineers, teams, and organizations around the world.

Summary

It's been an amazing experience sharing everything we've learned over the years about serverless, including our experiences with the technology, its adoption at enterprises, architecting and building solutions, guiding engineers and teams, learning from AWS and tech community experts, and interacting with many of you. Thank you for accompanying us on this journey.

A central theme of this book has been that technology evolution is happening all the time, along various streams. While some streams are independent, others influence each other and are interdependent. Needless to say, the evolution of serverless depends on and is influenced by the cloud.

As technology evolves all around you, your aim is to identify the technological path that will provide you with the easiest, fastest, and most straightforward way to reach your destination. At the end of the day, your responsibility is to help your organization grow: grow faster, grow better, grow in feature richness, grow its customer base, grow in wealth, grow in reputation and trust, and above all, grow its people.

With your newfound understanding of the serverless technology ecosystem, you now have clarity on your technology choices. As you learned in Chapter 2, serverless fits well in most cases, but it's not your only option. You will face situations where a different technology choice may be a better way to reach your goal. Adopt serverless-first thinking, but always assess the business needs and follow the first principles of serverless. Choose the apt technology for the problem at hand to help your organization offer the best to its customers.

Finally, take care of the technology you love. Help it evolve, spread, help others reach new shores.

You are now part of the serverless ecosystem. Go forth and prosper!

Interview with an Industry Expert

Farrah Campbell, Head of Modern Compute Community, AWS

Farrah operates with a team-first mentality. Her passions are technology and connecting with people, and she personifies the openness and welcoming attitude of the community. Farrah considers championing others and working with diverse teams critical for success in an organization and with the teams she works with cross-organizationally. She always tries to be thoughtful about how she impacts the big picture and how the interconnected parts of the organization work together to benefit everyone.

Q: During your career in the tech industry, you have traveled to several events and interacted with many tech enthusiasts. Compared to previous decades, we are well connected and informed, thanks to modern technology. Still, we strive to bring everyone in tech worldwide closer via AWS and serverless communities. What significance do communities have in the current tech world?

Community holds immense importance in my life. Without the support and connections I've found through various communities, I wouldn't be writing this, wouldn't have my job at AWS, and wouldn't have the privilege of calling people from all corners of the globe friends. The significance of communities, particularly in domains such as AWS and serverless technologies, has grown significantly. Modern technology enables access to extensive information and communication, but the value of personal interaction and the collective knowledge provided by communities remains invaluable and cannot be substituted.

Communities are like vibrant hubs of knowledge where a multitude of experiences converge. In AWS communities, individuals with varying levels of expertise can collaborate to exchange knowledge, push boundaries, and learn from their collective experiences. They engage in a wide range of discussions, covering everything from basic problem solving to sophisticated architectural techniques. The accumulation of knowledge in a shared and accessible space expedites the acquisition of new information and fosters innovation. While working in Berlin, a developer might encounter a serverless architecture issue that has already been successfully resolved by a fellow community member in Tokyo a few months back. Through active participation in the community, these answers are readily shared, eliminating the need for redundant efforts.

Communities foster a sense of belonging and collective identity. Through active participation in the AWS or serverless communities, users can forge connections with individuals who possess similar interests and encounter similar challenges, creating a strong sense of camaraderie. The feeling of belonging can serve as a powerful incentive and morale enhancer. For instance, local AWS meetups, Slack groups, and

Community Days offer social and professional support networks where participants can seek guidance, encouragement, and recognition.

Furthermore, communities provide a space for individuals to express their creativity and work together. They foster the sharing of ideas that may not emerge in solitude. In the serverless community, I often witness people coming together to contribute their own unique approaches to improving the efficiency of Lambda functions, or sharing insights on optimizing serverless architecture costs or maintaining a GitHub repository with a collection of useful AWS Lambda function templates. This not only inspires others to expand upon these concepts, but also results in novel and sometimes counterintuitive answers to problems. People with varying experience and education levels and from diverse backgrounds and cultures collaborate to raise the bar for everyone involved.

Communities also play a crucial role in advocating for and shaping services, features, and upgrades that prioritize the needs of users. The valuable input from the community often drives organizations like AWS to make necessary adjustments or develop innovative services that better cater to the needs of users. For instance, the AWS community voiced a shared need for more precise control over cloud resources, leading to the development of specific features in AWS Lambda. And luckily, this is something I get to work on internally every day.

Online communities have a vital role in ensuring that knowledge is accessible to all individuals. They remove barriers of distance and income, offering cutting-edge information and resources to anyone with internet access. Regardless of their location, anyone with a laptop and internet [connection] can tap into a wealth of communal resources, attend webinars, and seek expert advice, just like professionals in Silicon Valley and other technology industry hubs. Communities in the tech industry are vital ecosystems that drive the exchange of knowledge, foster innovation, and cultivate a strong sense of unity. They elevate individual voices and democratize learning, making it more likely that technical advances are inclusive and complete, going well beyond just technological improvement to include human collaboration and advancement.

Q: Farrah, you are currently head of the Modern Compute Community at AWS. What challenges do you face in this role that you would like to share with readers to make them aware and motivate them to become part of the global AWS community?

I would like to think that I have more benefits than challenges in my line of work. I get to work with so many people globally, helping to amplify their work, whether it be internally or externally. I get to connect them with others who may be facing the same challenges, and I get to learn so much about the world and how different cultures/regions operate.

Leading and overseeing a diverse team of individuals can be quite challenging. Coordinating schedules across different time zones can often hinder group work and lead to team members feeling disconnected. Individuals who frequently have to adjust their schedules may experience feelings of being overlooked and discouraged by this disparity.

In a world where individuals come from diverse backgrounds, there may be a reluctance to express oneself openly due to concerns about being misunderstood or facing criticism. This reluctance inhibits the unrestricted exchange of ideas and stifles the creativity of the team as a whole. Various cultural perspectives and practices add to the intricacies. It's important to recognize that what may be considered normal in one place might be unfamiliar or even offensive in another, which can lead to a lack of understanding and respect. Some people may have reservations about adjusting their communication style for others, seeing it as an unfair demand or a compromise of their identity. That, however, is not the case. It is essential to embrace the diversity of viewpoints and motivations while remaining genuine to your own personal style. For instance, some individuals favor the use of tabs, whereas others favor the use of spaces. Both viewpoints are correct, given that they originate from distinct experiences and motivations.

In some environments, competition is encouraged over collaboration, making it difficult to prioritize community well-being over individual success. When individuals perceive their involvement as a competition, it diverts attention away from the collective objectives toward their personal interests. Finding a middle ground between personal goals and the greater good can be quite demanding, especially when both seem equally significant.

To successfully navigate these challenges, I prioritize accomplishing the following: I am committed to prioritizing everyone's schedules and requirements to the best of my ability and building a warm and inclusive atmosphere that recognizes and values each individual, promoting a strong spirit of collaboration. I work to build a community where every individual's voice is highly valued and their contributions are respected, and I believe that by encouraging a spirit of teamwork and togetherness among community members, I can help create a path toward the advancement and success of our community as a whole. I also attempt to offer many opportunities for engagement, which I hope enhances the overall experience for all individuals involved.

At AWS, we sincerely welcome and celebrate a wide range of perspectives, fostering an atmosphere where individuals can openly express their thoughts and ideas. I find great value in genuinely engaging with individuals from diverse backgrounds and immersing myself in their communities. Through active listening and embracing their life stories, I aim to cultivate a profound sense of understanding and challenge any preconceived notions that might be present.

Q: You regularly speak at conferences on the importance of being inclusive, considerate, sharing, and welcoming. Often, we avoid addressing these values but focus too much on the technology itself. How can we instrument the shift in our thinking to make community and human values a bigger part of tech journals, books, conferences, etc.?

I love this question, and I am glad that you asked it. We can start by doing just what you did by asking me to contribute to a chapter in your book.

We must diligently change our collective perspective in order to bring community and human values into the domains of technological journals, books, and conferences. First, we need to widen our viewpoint when it comes to technology. Throughout history, the foundation of technological discourse has been built upon the technical and functional aspects of invention—the "how" and "what." The "why" and "for whom" need to be ingrained in these conversations and in marketing if we are to shift in the direction of a more human-centric narrative. I personally would love to see more talks at events or authored content that included this topic.

Facilitating a more inclusive discussion at conferences by inviting leaders and speakers from around the world and from different backgrounds on panels is a good first step. By incorporating diverse perspectives and fostering a broader dialogue, advancements in technology become more relevant and easily accessible to a wider audience. Technology-related content, such as blogs, whitepapers, and tutorials, could benefit from focusing on the human element, which would benefit readers on both the professional and personal fronts.

Context and delivery are important. Using language that is inclusive and easy for nontechnical individuals to understand can make tech ideas more relevant and less intimidating. Storytelling is a highly successful strategy for humanizing and making content relatable. It takes complicated ideas and converts them into engaging stories that appeal to a wider audience.

Finally, it is important to emphasize the importance of fostering a conversational style that recognizes, appreciates, and honors the unique qualities and values of each individual. We should highlight and make space for content that highlights the significance of individuals in the development process and encourages a progressive mindset. This is a complex problem that will need time, persistence, and patience to solve.

Appendices

Appendix A: PostNL's Serverless Journey

The content of this online-exclusive appendix can be downloaded by readers at *https://oreil.ly/riwzp*.

Appendix B: Taco Bell's Serverless Journey

The content of this online-exclusive appendix can be downloaded by readers at *https://oreil.ly/R325t*.

Appendix C: Templates and Worksheets

The content of this online-exclusive appendix can be downloaded by readers at *https://oreil.ly/Nw9fs*.

Index

Transport Layer Security (TLS), 200, 203
treading lightly concept, 277, 292
triage, defined, 246
trunk-based development, 304
trust, 63, 74, 186
TTL (Time to Live) value, 16, 54, 145, 206, 387, 431
202 Accepted, HTTP status code, 114
two-tier client/server architecture, 96
type definitions, 335
TypeScript, 134

U

UN Sustainable Development Goals, 407
"unauthorized operation" errors, 321
UNGA (United Nations General Assembly), 407
uniformity, 145, 152
uninstalling unused packages, 187
unit testing, 331-335
United Nations General Assembly (UNGA), 407
unpredictability, 348, 352
unused services and resources, deleting, 425
usage plans, 195
usage quotas, 425
user behavior, 420-424
user pools, 191, 371
UX (user experience) designers, 80

V

value stream mapping, 415
value-add time, 415
vaults, storing encryption keys and secrets in, 202
Velocity Template Language (VTL), 238
vendor lock-in, 60-63

versioning, 152, 255, 291
video processing, 115
virtual private clouds (VPCs), 6, 9
virtualization, origin and development of, 4
visibility, 258
VPCs (virtual private clouds), 6, 9
VTL (Velocity Template Language), 238
vulnerability scanning, 187, 203, 204

W

WAF (Web Application Firewall), 196
waiting time, 415
warm data, 431
warm function containers, 12
waterfall software development lifecycle, 411
Web Application Firewall (WAF), 196
webhooks, 116, 197
Well-Architected Framework, 26-27, 435
wildcards (*), 177, 203
Wing Cloud, 444
workflow orchestration, 283-284
workload assessment, 47-52
World Commission on Environment and Development, 407

X

X-Ray, 362-364

Y

Yip, Nicole, 207-211
"You build it, you pay for it" approach, 395

Z

zero trust security, 173-174, 192, 197
.zip archive, 66

About the Authors

Sheen Brisals is an AWS Serverless Hero and guides enterprise teams in architecting and building serverless solutions. He has held several positions at leading software organizations over his long career. He is very passionate about serverless and loves sharing knowledge with the community. His writings and thoughts on serverless adoption have successfully helped several engineers and organizations on their serverless journey. Sheen is an international speaker who talks about serverless at conferences around the world.

Luke Hedger is a seasoned software engineer and AWS Community Builder. He has worked at all layers of the software stack, building backend applications and state-of-the-art React apps, blockchain networks and viral marketing websites, open source tools and a pineapple delivery system. Luke has been leading serverless engineering teams since 2019 and believes we are only just beginning to unlock the full potential of serverless technology.

Colophon

The animal on the cover of *Serverless Development on AWS* is the South African ostrich (*Struthio camelus australis*), or southern ostrich, a subspecies of the common ostrich (*Struthio camelus*).

Ostriches can reach up to 9 feet in height and weigh over 300 pounds, though most individuals are smaller, and South African ostriches typically weigh less than 200 pounds. They are sexually dimorphic, with males and females of the species exhibiting differences in size or appearance. As depicted on the cover of this book, female ostriches (left) are grayish-brown and white, whereas males (right) are mostly black.

Despite being the largest living birds, ostriches have a reputation for hiding their heads in the sand when threatened. Indeed, in the face of threat, ostriches typically flee—reaching speeds of up to 40 miles per hour!—or hide by lying flat against the ground, though they can deliver a powerful, even fatal, kick when cornered.

Ostriches are heavily farmed for eggs, meat, and feathers. In the wild, their greatest threat is habitat loss, but they remain fairly abundant throughout their range and, as such, have been listed by the IUCN as being a species of least concern. Many of the animals on O'Reilly covers are endangered; all of them are important to the world.

The cover illustration is by Karen Montgomery, based on an antique line engraving from *The Pictorial Museum of Animated Nature*. The series design is by Edie Freedman, Ellie Volckhausen, and Karen Montgomery. The cover fonts are Gilroy Semibold and Guardian Sans. The text font is Adobe Minion Pro; the heading font is Adobe Myriad Condensed; and the code font is Dalton Maag's Ubuntu Mono.

O'REILLY®

Learn from experts.
Become one yourself.

Books | Live online courses
Instant answers | Virtual events
Videos | Interactive learning

Get started at oreilly.com.

9 781098 141936